Mussolini's Shadow

Mussolini's Shadow

The Double Life of Count Galeazzo Ciano

Ray Moseley

Yale University Press
New Haven and London

Set in Goudy by Print Line, New Delhi
Printed in Great Britain by Biddles Ltd, Guildford and Kings Lynn

Library of Congress Cataloging-in-Publication Data

Moseley, Ray, 1932–
Mussolini's Shadow: the double life of Count Galeazzo Ciano / Ray Moseley.
Includes bibliographical references and index.
ISBN 0–300–07917–6 (cloth: alk. paper)
1. Ciano, Galeazzo, conte, 1903–1944. 2. Italy—History—1922–1945.
3. Fascism—Italy—History. 4. Statesmen—Italy—Biography.
5. Fascists—Italy—Biography. I. Title.
DG575.C52M58   1999
945.091'092—dc21
99–34242
CIP

A catalogue record for this book is available from the British Library

2 4 6 8 10 9 7 5 3 1

Contents

Acknowledgements

Robert Baldock at Yale University Press in London has provided firm support for this book and helped immeasurably to improve it, as has his fellow editor Candida Brazil. My friend Catherine Henry is owed special thanks for having steered me to Yale University Press.

Don Larrimore, a close friend from the days we both lived in Rome more than thirty years ago, gave me much of the initial encouragement to undertake the book, supplied most of the research material from American sources, corrected mistakes in the text and was helpful in countless other respects. My daughter Ann also helped dig out some vital American source material. Bill and Beverly Landrey, Jim and Mel Barden and John McLaren read the text and offered many useful suggestions for improvements.

Particular thanks goes to those friends and associates of the Cianos in Rome, charming and delightful people all, who were generous with their time and shared their recollections with me. Although some may not be happy with my conclusions about Ciano, none set any condition on their cooperation and for that I am truly grateful. I am especially indebted to Princess Cyprienne Charles-Roux del Drago, who generously made available the unpublished memoirs of her late husband, Prince Marcello del Drago. Others whose help I wish to acknowledge are Romano Mussolini, Countess Marozia Borromeo d'Adda, Fey von Hassell, former Ambassador Mario Mondello, Ambassador Bruno Bottai, Count Bartolomeo Attolico and Lady Maria Carmela Hambleden. Giordano Bruno Guerri, Ciano's excellent Italian biographer, gave helpful suggestions, and Leonora Dodsworth assisted with Italian research and contacts. Michele Sarfatti of the Fondazione Centro di Documentazione Ebraica Contemporanea in Milan supplied information concerning Ciano and the Jews. I would also like to acknowledge the valuable contributions of several persons in Italy who declined to be identified.

Others whose assistance in various ways I remember with thanks are Jon Randal, Professor Dermot Keogh of University College, Cork, John Cooney, Chris Ogden, Bill Tuohy, Janet Stobard, Thom Shanker, Jay Shanker, John Tagliabue, Paula Butturini, Elan Steinberg of the World Jewish Congress, John McCarthy Jr., Bill Fowler, John Taylor and

Kenneth Schlessinger of the U.S. National Archives, Owen Chadwick, Harold Tittman III and Ray Zwick, librarian at the *Cincinnati Enquirer*.

Almost last, but always first in my appreciation, my wife Jennifer endured with remarkable patience and good humor the hours stolen from her by my devotion to Ciano, and repaid my inattention with constant encouragement. To her this book is lovingly dedicated.

Finally, a word about the late William Shirer, historian of the Third Reich and a *Chicago Tribune* correspondent long before I became one. His *Rise and Fall of the Third Reich* introduced me to Galeazzo Ciano thirty years ago, and fired me with the determination to write about him, which I quite belatedly did. Without him, this book most definitely would not have been written.

Illustrations

Photographic credits: AKG, Berlin: 9, 11, 12, 15, 18, 25; Associated Press: 14; Author's collection: 23, 24, 26; Hulton Getty: 4, 5, 7, 13; Ullstein, Berlin: 1, 2, 3, 6, 8, 10, 16, 17, 19, 20, 21, 22.

Prologue

On Saturday, January 8, 1944, a peasant woman and two men check into the little Hotel Madonnina in Viggiu, Italy, a village nestling between Lake Como and Lake Lugano in the foothills of the Alps. The woman, who appears to be heavily pregnant, registers under the false name Emilie Santos, and gives her address as Rome. The men also use assumed names: this is wartime, these are hunted people and they can take no chances. But the woman cannot disguise an appearance made haggard by exhaustion and worry. Under the strain of a nervous breakdown, she is barely able to keep going.

Far to the south, the war is gradually moving up the boot of the Italian peninsula as German and Fascist forces fight desperately to hold in check the steady advance of the Allies. The war still has more than a year to run, but the twenty-one-year dictatorship of Benito Mussolini is over. The Duce, overthrown six months earlier, clings to the illusion of power in a little villa on the shores of Lake Garda, but he is merely a puppet of the Germans now, a sad and broken man.

Across northern Italy, Gestapo agents have fanned out in a search for the woman in Viggiu, under orders to prevent her at all costs from crossing the frontier into Switzerland. Adolf Hitler has taken a personal interest in her capture, and Mussolini is also anxious to make sure she does not get away. But no one in Viggiu knows that. The woman and two men dine in the hotel restaurant, and retire early.

On Sunday morning, the snow-covered mountains cast their reflection on the nearby lakes. Viggiu is at peace and villagers wrapped in their overcoats go off to Mass as usual. At about 1.30 p.m., the peasant woman and one of the men, a tall, thin individual with a military bearing, leave the hotel after an early lunch and make their way out of the village on foot. The woman carries a revolver concealed in a coat pocket. It is to be used on Nazi or Fascist guards if necessary to facilitate her escape, or on herself if she is captured. The couple's movements are determinedly casual as they head in the direction of the nearby border. At about 5.30 p.m., as darkness closes in on the village, the man returns to Viggiu alone. Shortly afterward, he and his male companion drive away, tired but exhilarated. The woman is safely in Switzerland.

On that same day, in Verona, the city of Romeo and Juliet, a man goes on trial for his life in a Fascist court. The charge is treason. Five other men stand in the dock beside him, in an old fortress converted into a courtroom which is jammed with Fascists.

The woman who has made her escape is Countess Edda Mussolini Ciano, the Duce's favorite daughter. Under the voluminous peasant dress designed for her by her lover, the Marquis Emilio Pucci, who accompanied her to the frontier, is a set of documents that the Nazis and Fascists are determined should not fall into Allied hands. The documents are strapped around Edda's waist inside the sleeve of a pajama shirt to make her appear pregnant.

The man on trial in Verona is Count Galeazzo Ciano, Edda's husband and formerly Mussolini's Foreign Minister. He is the author of the documents she carries, which offer the only possibility of saving his life. Written in five Red Cross notebooks, they are the diaries he has kept during his last four years in office. These are potentially explosive documents. If published, they would reveal to the world the shabby and disdainful way in which the Nazis have treated their Italian ally, the weakness of Mussolini and his contempt for the Italian people, and the perfidy of Hitler, Ribbentrop and the other Nazi leaders. Mussolini and the Nazis will face an ultimatum from Edda: free Ciano, or she will hand over the diaries to the Allies.

In Switzerland, although she does not know it yet, Edda has an appointment with America's most celebrated spy: Allen W. Dulles, who will head the Central Intelligence Agency after the war. Soon he will be on the trail of the documents she carries as she stumbles across the frontier, into the arms of waiting Swiss border guards, and announces her real identity.

Chapter One

Galeazzo and Edda

The drama that culminated in Edda Mussolini Ciano's flight to Switzerland in 1944 began in more banal circumstances fourteen years earlier. Edda was nineteen and Count Galeazzo Ciano,* an Italian diplomat newly returned from a tour of duty in China, was eight years older. They had met at a party and, after just seventeen days, had fallen in love. On the afternoon of February 13, 1930, as they sat together in a darkened Roman movie theater, Ciano leaned toward her and whispered, "You must know, Edda, that I am in love with you. Will you marry me?" Edda hesitated only for a moment. "Why not?" she said with characteristic nonchalance. When the film was over, she ran home to break the news to her father as he was changing for a reception. "Daddy, I became engaged this evening to Galeazzo Ciano, the son of Costanzo," she exclaimed. Mussolini stared incredulously for a moment, then dashed through the house calling to his wife, "Rachele, Rachele, Edda is engaged! This time it's true! And I certainly approve of the young man!"[1] In a letter to a cousin, Edda described her feeling for Galeazzo as "a real thunderbolt" and said, "My destiny is now decided and frankly it could not be decided better."[2] This was the beginning of a love affair, a marriage and a career that would in a few years become part of European history. The beginning, too, of a family tragedy of epic proportions. Ciano was then serving as a junior diplomat in Italy's Embassy to the Holy See. When he broke the news of his engagement to his colleagues, one of them observed: "You have found an insurance policy for life."[3]

There seemed little reason to doubt that. The regime that Mussolini created in 1922 already had blood on its hands, but it was still widely admired in Europe and the United States, and marriage to Edda seemed to assure Ciano a glittering future. At a time of world depression, many noted with approval that the Italian economy was growing. Mussolini had

---

* Pronounced Chah-noh.

instituted ambitious public works projects, set up a social security system, drained the Pontine Marshes, preserved the monuments of ancient Rome, and made the trains run on time. He was bringing order and discipline to Italy, compelling his countrymen to abandon their languorous Latin way of life and become part of modern Europe. A few journalists, such as the American John Gunther, might raise questions about Mussolini's human rights record, but many people rationalized their support for Mussolini on the grounds that the backward Italians needed the lash of dictatorship. The country, after long years of poverty and decline, finally had a ruler of iron determination who felt he had a mission to restore it to the glory it had known under the Caesars. Mussolini's ambitions would coincide with a gradual unraveling of the European order established after World War I, and amid the discontent of the European masses, Hitler, Franco and Salazar would soon vault to power. Winston Churchill praised Mussolini's fight against European Socialism, called him "the greatest living legislator" and declared that he would have donned the Fascist black shirt if he had been an Italian. David Lloyd George and George Bernard Shaw counted themselves among his admirers. President Roosevelt and members of his Cabinet joined the chorus of praise. Cardinal O'Connell of Boston said Mussolini was a genius given to Italy by God. *The New York Times* called him a defender of peace, and a university in Hungary wanted to nominate him for the Nobel Peace Prize.[4] He was widely compared with Caesar, Napoleon and Cromwell. Little wonder that the young, impressionable Galeazzo Ciano soon fell under the spell and indulged in boyish hero-worship of his father-in-law.

The adulation of Mussolini reflected a moment of naiveté in world affairs that was about to end forever. Perceptions outside Italy would change dramatically after his invasion of Ethiopia in 1935 and the brutalities that followed, including the use of poison gas. That act of aggression would provoke the League of Nations to impose economic sanctions against Italy, leaving Mussolini isolated and reviled and helping to drive him into a fatal partnership with Hitler's Germany. It would be followed by Italian intervention on the side of the Fascists in Spain's civil war, by a deepening bitterness on Mussolini's part toward the European democracies, and by Italian military disasters in Greece, North Africa, East Africa and the Soviet Union. Many who had thrilled to the sight of Mussolini, legs spread apart, hands on hips, jaw thrust upward, as he addressed crowds from the balcony of the Palazzo Venezia now saw his gestures as comical. Admiration gave way to ridicule and contempt.

Within six years of his marriage to Edda, Galeazzo Ciano would become Italy's Foreign Minister. As such he emerged as the chief accomplice of

Mussolini's misdeeds, the dauphin of the regime, the Duce's principal emissary to Hitler and his Foreign Minister, Joachim von Ribbentrop, and one of the principal players in the central drama of twentieth-century history. Over the nearly seven years Ciano served as Foreign Minister, Italy would go to war against Ethiopia, enter into its doomed Axis partnership with Germany, seize control of Albania, join Germany as an aggressor in World War II and launch a disastrous war against Greece. Later, it would be forced into a humiliating surrender to the Allies while German troops occupied the country. After Mussolini himself, no one in Italy played a more important role in the history of fascism and its embrace of Nazi Germany than Ciano. He signed the Pact of Steel and the Anti-Comintern Pact that bound Italy into its partnership with the Nazis. In addition to representing the regime in discussions with Hitler and Ribbentrop, he sat in on nearly all of Mussolini's meetings with the Führer. But in the end he would stand apart from the gaggle of ruffians, psychopaths and buffoons with whom he had been associated, for he would break with the man he had adored, struggle to keep Italy out of the war, and try to stave off the catastrophic consequences he had helped to set in motion. He failed to stop the march to war, of course, and to that extent his influence was negligible. But in other respects, he helped to shape the course of history. The adventures in Albania and Greece were largely undertaken at the instigation of Ciano, and the Greek debacle made him, justifiably, the most hated man in Italy.

As a chronicler of the history in which he participated, Ciano was a figure of considerable significance. He kept a diary during his years as Foreign Minister which was one of the most valuable documents to come out of World War II, a diary replete with often unique and surprising insights into the inner workings of the regime, fascinating vignettes of Hitler and his cronies, revelations about Mussolini's vacillations and conflicting attitudes toward Germany and disclosures about Germany's callous treatment of its ally. The diary was a goldmine for historians of fascism. It exploded any notion that the Nazi and Fascist dictators marched in perfect lockstep toward their evil goals, guided by a harmony of purpose. It revealed the huge gulf of mistrust that separated them behind their facade of iron determination and unity and, perhaps more surprisingly, it made plain how often decisions affecting the lives of millions were determined by petty jealousies, personal vanity and point scoring. It may be ever thus in the lives of statesmen, but there is an infantile quality to the relationships between the Nazi and Fascist leaders that is sometimes truly breathtaking, and no one documented this better than Ciano.

At the height of his celebrity, he and Edda were the talk of Europe, and their faces graced the covers of leading American news magazines. Ciano, with his dark hair combed straight back and a friendly smile on his face, could appear rather dashing in the military uniforms he initially favored. But the overall effect was spoiled by a high-pitched, nasal voice, a flat-footed, slightly comic walk, and an attempt to ape Mussolini's gestures of chin thrust out and chest pushed forward. Edda, acutely intelligent but politically naive, was a thin, nervous woman with sharply chiseled features and a personality that was often acidic. But, despite their unprepossessing appearance, Ciano and Edda moved in an aura of youthful glamour and power in the early years of their marriage, and the fascination grew as they drifted apart and openly flaunted their extramarital affairs in a manner that recalled the licentiousness of the Borgia court. For all his flaws, Ciano possessed admirable qualities. He had more intelligence than was sometimes credited to him, and he was warm-hearted toward his friends and generous in his eagerness to do them favors. He was a devoted, if sometimes overly strict and frequently absentee, father to his three children. He displayed a charm and sense of humor that not only attracted adoring women but won over Allied diplomats who dealt with him, sometimes behind Mussolini's back. Americans ranging from Sumner Welles, President Roosevelt's under-secretary of state, to William Shirer and Clare Booth Luce, found him likeable, but Joseph Kennedy, the father of President Kennedy, dismissed him as a pompous ass. He had the reckless courage of youth, and in the crucial drama of his life that drew him and Edda together again, both displayed an exemplary courage that partially redeemed their past.

But Ciano, inordinately vain, arrogant and frivolous, had a darker side. He plotted murder on more than one occasion, and may have had it carried it out at least once. His judgment in international affairs was often faulty, spectacularly so during the Greek affair. No doubt he was corrupted by too-easy success at too early an age, and by the misfortune of having been born in Fascist Italy. For, as the English writer Malcolm Muggeridge observed, he would undoubtedly have been a staunch democrat under a democratic regime. Essentially he was apolitical and a careerist, a man without fixed beliefs or a moral compass, convinced only of his own destiny and ultimately undone by that conviction. Whatever may be said in mitigation of his record in office, he stands condemned before history as a participant and arch-conspirator in criminal enterprises of the gravest sort, that is, crimes against humanity. For Italians, the fascination that Ciano has exerted over their imaginations for a half century is less political than familial. His story, as literature, would be worthy of an Aeschylus, or a Shakespeare; it is a story of intrigue, betrayal and death in a powerful family of clashing personalities and will, often called a modern Greek tragedy. Ciano was the creation of his father-in-law, and it was Mussolini who destroyed him, in the process sundering the ties that bound the Duce and his beloved daughter. This was family conflict played out not in private but as a page of history. But Ciano triumphed over the man who manipulated his fortunes so disastrously, for there was an element of heroism in him that manifested itself at the end, a quality singularly lacking in the human wreck that Mussolini had become. Both men were deeply flawed; but one retained a spark of human decency while the other, just before the final curtain, sealed an ignoble life with a shameful and cowardly act. Tragedy requires a hero, and Ciano's final heroism revealed the kind of man he might have been, had he not become embroiled in a family, and a regime, that corrupted him.

Postwar Italy has understood the poisonous legacy of the Mussolini years, but remains ambivalent about the family. Thus a Mussolini granddaughter has been able to win election to Parliament on the strength of her name alone. It is hardly conceivable, of course, that a Hitler granddaughter, if one existed, could achieve the same in Germany. It goes without saying that Hitler was an infinitely more scabrous individual than Mussolini, but both men bear responsibility for one of the most sordid chapters in human history, and many Italians still have not fully come to terms with that. Ciano's role in all this had its good moments and bad, tawdriness mixed with exemplary conduct, but, above all, the tangled web of his life and Edda's entered the realm of high drama. They were the principal characters in a political thriller that happened to be true.

The romance between Galeazzo and Edda that blossomed in 1930 hardly came as a surprise to Mussolini; in a sense, he was the matchmaker. Edda, independent and headstrong, and known in the family as *la cavallina matta*, the wild filly, had been a worry to her parents for some time. Her boyfriends tended to be the Latin lover, gigolo type, and her parents could never be sure she would not rush into a disastrous and possibly even scandalous marriage. The police, who monitored her activities for Mussolini, reported in 1929 that she had sneaked off to Bologna to meet the son of a rich industrialist who was a cocaine addict and suffered from syphilis. Another boyfriend, the police reported, was an unemployed womanizer who often posed as a count or a marquess and kept bad company.[5]

Edda's aunt Edvige attempted to arrange a match with Pier Francesco Orsi Mangelli, the twenty-seven-year-old son of a noble family from Forli. Edda was less than impressed when they met and took a new boyfriend, a young Jew who was the son of an army colonel. When she wrote to her father that she wished to marry him, Mussolini was horror-struck. He urged Edvige to warn Edda that marriage between the daughter of the Duce and a Jew would "fill the world with talk."[6] Mussolini sent his brother Arnaldo to the young man's parents to inform them he would not permit such a marriage. The parents, as observant Jews, were indignant and informed Arnaldo they never would have allowed their son to marry Edda. Reluctantly, she gave him up and went off to Spain with Mangelli, his parents acting as chaperones. The trip was intended to allow them to become better acquainted, but Edda did everything she could to turn her intended and his parents against her. She drank, smoked, used coarse language and affirmed she would never have children because she wanted to preserve her figure. None of this quelled the ardor of Mangelli, and under family pressure she eventually accepted his proposal of marriage. But he made the mistake of asking Mussolini what kind of dowry Edda would bring to their marriage. The Duce, enraged, ordered his daughter to break off her engagement.[7] Edda was overjoyed, but sympathized with Mangelli. "Poor little thing," she told Edvige. "He is not to blame. His father forced him to make such a gaffe."[8] Ten days later, she met Ciano. He was the son of Admiral Costanzo Ciano, a leading Fascist and World War I hero whom Mussolini had once named as his successor.

Gian Galeazzo Ciano was born on March 18, 1903, in the Tuscan coastal city of Livorno. His sister Maria, the couple's only other child, was born three years later. Costanzo had followed his father into a naval career, and at an early stage headed a signalman's and radiotelegraphist's school at La Spezia, where he became a close friend of Guglielmo Marconi, the inventor of radio. He was ambitious, courageous, stern with his children and, ultimately, corrupt. Galeazzo had a deep admiration for his father, and suffered from his frequent absences due to his naval career. "When he saw him leave . . . his eyes filled with tears and sometimes he threw himself on the floor, crying desperately," his mother Carolina said.[9] Later Edda described her father-in-law as a strict disciplinarian and said he "believed more in the persuasive force of a good thrashing than in the virtue of a moral lesson."[10] He made his son wear a sailor suit cut down from one of his discarded uniforms, and a sailor's beret instead of the straw hat worn by his schoolmates. When one of Galeazzo's friends asked why, Costanzo replied, "Because I want him to find it impossible to accompany you and the others to the whorehouse."[11] As a young man, Galeazzo neither drank nor smoked and had a strong aversion to gambling, all values inculcated by his father that remained with him throughout his life. But Orio Vergani, a childhood friend who became a famous journalist, said Ciano's father also encouraged him "along the road to Fascist virility," meaning that Costanzo passed on to him an attitude toward women that may have accounted for his numerous affairs in later life.[12]

Costanzo was awarded four silver medals for valor for his daring exploits against the Austrian navy in World War I, and Mussolini later gave him a gold medal. In 1925 King Victor Emanuel III named him the Count of Cortellazzo in recognition of his military heroism. Many other military men were ennobled at the same time, because Mussolini had persuaded the king it was necessary to create a new aristocratic class based on Fascist values. Immediately after the war, Costanzo was nominated by Giovanni Agnelli, grandfather of the later Fiat chairman of that name, to head the shipping company Il Mare, and the family moved to Genoa. In 1919 he was an unsuccessful candidate for the right-wing, Democratic Union, but he later joined the Fascists and in the spring of 1921 became one of thirty-three Fascists to win a seat in Parliament. He resigned the presidency of Il Mare and moved the family to Rome to become a full-time politician.

When Mussolini came to power in 1922, he named Costanzo under-secretary of the Navy and commissioner of the Merchant Marine, elevating him the following year to membership of the Fascist Grand Council, the most powerful political body in the country. He was named Minister of Posts and Telegraph in 1924 and, two months after that, Minister of Communications. In that post he had control of railroads, the merchant marine, the automobile industry and trams. Costanzo and his brother Arturo, who worked for him in the Ministry of Communications, became wealthy men. His Fascist critics said Costanzo received a large, annual payoff from Provvida, a consumer cooperative for state employees that was managed by his ministry. In 1925–6 Arturo Ciano and a group of his friends had a contract for the distribution of hundreds of thousands of tons of coal delivered to Italy by Germany as World War I reparations, and a part of the proceeds was assigned to the minister. He was also reported to have made large sums of money from the nationalization of the telephone and broadcasting industries. In 1930 Fascist Party Secretary Augusto Turati openly accused Costanzo of giving favors to industrialists and financiers in return for money. After the fall of fascism in 1943, a government commission found that Arturo Ciano owned 1,025 acres of cultivated land in Tuscany, and numerous apartments and villas on the Tyrrhenian coast, including a grand villa with park and stables at Ponte a Moriano, near Lucca. Costanzo benefited politically from the crisis over the murder of Giacomo Matteotti, one of Mussolini's ablest opponents, by Fascist *squadristi* in 1924. The uproar that followed shook the regime, and some Fascists abandoned Mussolini, but Costanzo stood by him throughout. He was rewarded when Mussolini, in an unpublished document, designated him in 1926 as his successor in case of his sudden death.

Galeazzo, timid and studious, was a star pupil in school, finishing second among all high school graduates in Italy in his final exams in classical studies. His friend Tito Torelli said Galeazzo sometimes was punished for having copied work from his fellow pupils when in fact he gave his homework to them to copy "because he was superior to all of us in most subjects."[13] Torelli said Galeazzo also lost his temper easily, and was once expelled from school for having thrown an inkwell at a professor who infuriated him. When he was older, Costanzo forbade Galeazzo's friends to take him to a Fascist cell meeting because he did not want him involved in politics. In high school, Galeazzo had a platonic love for a Jewish girl, but her parents opposed their friendship on religious grounds. After graduation, he enrolled in the Faculty of Law at Rome University but his interests lay elsewhere. He was part of a group of young men known as the "jackals," who frequented the theater and made sport of booing the performances. Fabrizio Sarazani, a friend, remembered Ciano mostly for "the hoarse voice, the flat feet and a great wish to be taken seriously intellectually." He said Ciano liked to pick up the "easy" girls he met at night in the Gallinaccio Café in the Largo del Tritone in Rome. "In the Ciano of those years," he wrote, "the man he became was not recognizable or predictable . . . Ciano, a young man of good family, had not yet contracted the illness of Roman snobbism."[14]

Galeazzo's sister Maria, to whom he was devoted, was anorexic. She had a horror of food and, when her father tried to encourage her to eat something more substantial than her usual diet of bread and olives, she would wait until he was distracted and spit her food into a napkin. She married the Italian diplomat Count Massimo Magistrati in November 1930, but the day before her wedding she panicked at the thought of marriage and developed a high fever. A year later, Magistrati went to Costanzo to complain that the marriage was not yet consummated. Maria died of tuberculosis at the age of thirty-three, weighing less than eighty-three pounds.

Several current reference books state that Ciano took part in the Fascist March on Rome, but that was a fabrication of Ciano's personal myth-making. As a university student, he took no interest in fascism. Ten years later, his fortunes altered, he backdated his membership in the Fascist Party to May 1921, a year before his father joined, and listed himself as a member of the Florentine squad "Disperata" that had participated in the march. While still a university student, Ciano began to do parliamentary work for the Rome newspaper *Il Paese*; then, with no apparent qualms about its politics, he went to work for the left-wing *Il Mondo*. When the Fascists came to power, he became deputy theater critic of *Nuovo Paese*, a pro-Fascist paper, later switching to the extreme Fascist *L'Impero*. "As a journalist, he was less than mediocre," said Sarazani.[15] He tried his hand at fiction and wrote six short stories that appeared between 1923 and 1925 in *Nuovo Paese* and *L'Impero*. The theme of all of them was death. More than anything, he wanted to be a playwright. He managed to get two of his plays produced in Rome, but both were spectacular flops and he gave up playwriting. His friend Princess Cyprienne Charles-Roux del Drago said he told her years later: "Thank God I entered politics. I know how to write a short telegram, but I wouldn't have been any good as a playwright or columnist."[16]

After Ciano graduated from university in 1925, his father persuaded him to try for a diplomatic career. The Foreign Ministry was offering thirty-five posts, and Ciano was among six hundred applicants. Another was Filippo Anfuso, a Sicilian poet and war correspondent who later became Ciano's principal assistant, and then Mussolini's last ambassador to Nazi Germany. Anfuso came first in the competition, and Ciano twenty-seventh. Another who entered the diplomatic service through that competition was Massimo Magistrati, Ciano's future brother-in-law. As a new diplomat, Ciano had only schoolboy French. But he later perfected his French, learned excellent English and spoke Spanish rather well. The Foreign Ministry posted him as vice-consul to Rio de Janeiro, where he became involved with the daughter of an Italo-American millionaire. The girl's father feared he was a fortune hunter and sounded out Italian Ambassador Giulio Cesare Montagna, who told him: "He is the son of a *squadrista* and a count. He will not get very far."[17] Ciano disgraced himself at a reception in Rio, smiling and saying to a Brazilian whom he mistakenly believed did not understand Italian: "And the very best to you, you old ass kisser." He was then transferred to Buenos Aires as second secretary, and hated it there. Maria Rosa Oliver, a writer who would become a Communist and win a Lenin Prize in the 1950s, made friends with him in Buenos Aires. She asked him if he wanted to be another Mussolini and he replied, "Why set any limits?" She also remembered that he disliked Germans in those days, and once threatened to punch a secretary of the German Embassy.[18] He was happy to leave Buenos Aires, partly to get away from an importunate Spanish lady who was threatening to leave her husband for him. The Foreign Ministry sent him to Peking as secretary of legation in May 1927 and he moved into an apartment previously occupied by Magistrati.[*]

---

[*] It is widely believed in Italy, and frequently published, that Ciano had an affair in China with

Ciano had been two years in China when he was recalled to Rome. Mussolini's brother Arnaldo, looking around for a suitable husband for his niece, spoke to a Sicilian politician who suggested Galeazzo would be an ideal candidate. Arnaldo raised the matter with Mussolini, and the Duce was delighted. He ordered the Foreign Ministry to recall Ciano. The young diplomat sailed on the SS *President McKinley* and stopped in Seattle on August 11, 1929, the only time he set foot in the United States. Even though he was a diplomat of no importance, his title was sufficient to attract coverage in the Seattle *Post-Intelligencer*, which reported: "Not all counts are bewhiskered individuals with monocles and a penchant for soft jobs. Count di Cortellazzo (sic) is a pleasant, clean-shaven young fellow, still in his twenties." Ciano traveled on to New York and took another ship for home.

Mussolini the matchmaker had done his work, but Galeazzo and Edda actually met by chance when she accompanied Maria Ciano to a reception. Maria already had shown Edda a photograph of her brother, and Edda thought he was handsome. When they met, she said to him, "They tell me you are very intelligent." Galeazzo merely smiled. They were both smitten. They danced together all evening and, when they parted, promised to meet again soon.[19] "I had a good sense of humor and a vivid imagination, but was extremely timid," Edda said of herself later. "Galeazzo had tasted most of life's pleasures and was a man about town who attended all the most fashionable social functions." She discovered that he was more emotional and warm-hearted than the Mussolinis, herself included, whom she judged to be rather cold.[20] They began seeing each other frequently, either alone or in the company of Maria. Edda's older brother Vittorio said, "Edda went out more often. At home she was happier, listened to records for hours and, in a word, showed all the symptoms of a girl in love."[21] Edvige also noted a change in Edda. "Her habitual disposition, perhaps a little exhibitionist, jokey and carefree, gave way to an unreserved warmth, to a true and proper romantic impulse," she said.[22] Costanzo was ignorant of the developing romance, and was not entirely pleased when the Rome police chief came to warn him that the police had to report the young couple's meetings to the Duce. Costanzo confronted Galeazzo and demanded an explanation. Galeazzo laughed. On that very day, he and Edda had become engaged.

Wallis Warfield Spencer, later Wallis Simpson, for whom King Edward VIII gave up his throne. Various authors have claimed that Mrs. Spencer, then the unhappy wife of a drunken and abusive American naval officer serving in China, became pregnant by Ciano and had an abortion that resulted in lifelong gynecological problems, leaving her unable to have children. While Ciano did know her, and he and Edda once received a present from her, this story has never been substantiated and Edda later insisted to friends, presumably on the word of her husband, that it was untrue.

Edda was the first-born child of the Mussolinis, and the one he loved the most. That may have owed a great deal to the resemblances between them. She shared his headstrong nature, and could intimidate and control those around her with the piercing, hypnotic eyes she inherited from him. Mussolini used to come home late at night and play his violin over her cradle and he recalled that, as a little girl, she once slapped him twice while refusing to take her medicine. She was born at a time when Italian women were expected simply to get married and produce children, but she was always testing the constraints of traditional society. She was one of the first women in Italy to drive a car and to wear slacks. At the beach she wore short bathing suits while other girls still covered their legs. She liked to use foul language, play poker and drink whisky and gin, and she shocked her father by smoking. Edda once recalled, "Daddy with all his anti-bourgeois attitudes was in certain things more conformist than a retired colonel. He forbade me, for example, to paint my lips . . . He also didn't want me to smoke. One day, during a reception at the Palazzo Venezia, I saw him coming toward me suddenly with his finger pointed and a threatening look fixed on the cigarette that I had lighted in that moment. 'You smoke . . .,' he exclaimed, incredibly stunned, as if he couldn't believe his own eyes. 'Yes,' I replied calmly, 'the desire came upon me.'"[23] In later years Rachele described the relationship between her husband and daughter: "They fought often, due to their very similar temperament and their combative ways. So much so that Benito once said jokingly to me, 'I succeeded in bending Italy, but I will never succeed in bending Edda.' And yet for her he had a true adoration."[24] Edda's brother Romano, famous in Italy as a jazz musician, recalled Edda with fondness in 1996. "My sister was a very cultivated woman," he said. "She was an aristocrat born into a family of peasants. Edda had a true nobility that none of us had. She read books, and American and French magazines. She had good table manners, and she spoke English and French while we still only spoke Romagnolo.* She had friends in the nobility. And she was a courageous woman. I was always very fond of Edda."[25]

Edda was born at 3 a.m. on September 1, 1910, in Forli, where her unmarried parents were then living in dire poverty. Her father called her the "child of misery." She was christened Edda Rosa Edvige. Rosa was the name of Mussolini's mother and Edvige the name of his sister. The unconventional name Edda was inspired by Mussolini's love of the theater. Once in Milan he had seen a performance of Ibsen's *Hedda Gabler*, was entranced by its central character and determined he would some day name a daughter for her. Throughout Edda's life many Italians, and espe-

---

* The dialect of Emilia-Romagna, the province from which the family originated.

cially political opponents of her father, speculated that she was not in fact the daughter of Rachele but of Angelica Balabanoff, a Russian Jewish émigré whom Mussolini had known in Geneva and who later worked with him on his newspaper *Il Popolo d'Italia*. This was because Mussolini, in registering her birth, listed himself as the father but wrote that the mother was unknown. He did so because he and Rachele were not then married and were not, in fact, wed until four years later. Under Italian law, only the father's name could be mentioned in such circumstances. Mussolini added to the confusion by telling some of his Socialist friends that Edda's mother was really an English girl named Gibson whom he had met in Switzerland. He said he had imposed the infant upon Rachele.[26] Edda herself later said no one, not even her father, could have forced her strong-willed peasant mother to raise another woman's child and pretend it was her own. After Mussolini came to power in 1922, he enrolled Edda in one of Italy's most exclusive private schools, the Poggio Imperiale College in Florence. The daughters of a number of Europe's royal families, including Marie José of Belgium, the future wife of Crown Prince Umberto of Italy, attended the college, as did the offspring of rich Americans and the English. Edda made few friends there, and proved so difficult to control that the school authorities once summoned Mussolini with a view to having her removed. But she completed a year and, if nothing else, acquired the polish that later would cause people to comment on her aristocratic bearing.

On February 15, Ciano came to the Mussolini home, Villa Torlonia, to ask officially for Edda's hand. Wearing a gray suit and carrying white gloves, he was ushered into Mussolini's study while the Duce sat with his face buried in his papers. He looked up and pretended to discover by chance that Galeazzo was there. The two men remained closeted for several minutes, after which Mussolini called in Edda and her mother and informed them he had agreed to the wedding. Galeazzo took out a small jewel case, removed a ring and placed it on Edda's finger. Rachele embraced Galeazzo and, to her daughter's horror, told him, "You know, Edda doesn't know how to do anything. She can't sew, cook even an egg or run a household. As to her character, I won't even speak of that. But I'm her mother, and I wanted to warn you."[27] Galeazzo and Edda exchanged their first real kiss on the staircase as he departed. Later she sent him a ring in an envelope delivered by a member of the Italian security service. Galeazzo wrote to her, "I knew that I could expect anything of you, but you will never fail to surprise me. Your sending me a ring by way of a policeman does not lack originality."[28] Galeazzo did not suffer quite the misfortune that Mangelli had with his prospective father-in-law, but he did have one bad moment when Mussolini discovered he had taken his daughter to a nightclub. It was one of the more respectable clubs in Rome, but the Duce gave him a severe dressing-down. Edda observed, "Cabarets, nightclubs and other places of amusement were, to his mind, simply the antechambers of whorehouses."[29]

Galeazzo and Edda were wed on April 24, 1930, in the Church of San Giuseppe, near the Mussolini home. Cyprienne Charles-Roux del Drago said of Edda, "I have never seen anything more elegant. Her figure was so extraordinary that everything suited her. She had long legs, good shoulders, she was not too tall and she had very narrow hips. She would not have been a beauty under Louis XV or Louis XVI of France. But she would have been a beauty during the Renaissance, because of the bones of her face, her shoulders, her hands and her minute feet. Anything you put on Edda would suit her."[30] From the church the wedding party drove to St. Peter's Basilica for a tradition observed by nearly all Roman newlyweds: they kissed the foot of a bronze statue of St. Peter, a gesture meant to assure a happy marriage. Only Mussolini declined to participate. In the early evening Edda, with Galeazzo beside her, drove off in her Alfa-Romeo toward Naples, where the couple planned to take a boat to Capri for their honeymoon. Mussolini, suddenly feeling the loss of his favorite daughter, jumped in his own car and, with Rachele beside him, set off in pursuit. Several police escort cars followed. About twenty kilometers outside Rome, Edda saw his car, veiled in dust, and pulled over to the side of the road.

"Where do you want to go, daddy?" she asked. "It's ridiculous of you to follow us like this."

"I just wanted to accompany you part of the way," he replied lamely. She told him to go home and stop worrying.[31]

At the Hotel Quisisana in Capri, Edda suffered an attack of nerves during dinner in the honeymoon suite. "I didn't succeed in eating even a bite of dinner, so paralyzed did I feel, but I continued to order new dishes so as to detain as long as possible the *maitre*," she wrote. "For the first time in my life I found myself alone at a table with a man."[32] After dinner she hurried into the bathroom, locked the door and threatened to jump into the sea from an enormous rock outside the window if Ciano came near her.

"I know you are capable of doing what you say," Galeazzo shouted through the door. "I wouldn't dream of preventing you from doing whatever you wish. But just explain one thing to me. How will you climb to the top of the rock so as to leap into the sea?" Edda came out of the bathroom, looked at the rock and then looked at Galeazzo. Both of them burst out laughing, and her panic was over.[33]

Chapter Two

Diplomat to Bomber Pilot

Shortly after the honeymoon, the Cianos set sail for China and a new diplomatic posting for Galeazzo first as consul-general in Shanghai, later chargé' d'affaires, then to Peking as envoy extraordinary and minister plenipotentiary. He presided over a League of Nations commission of inquiry charged with settling the Sino-Japanese conflict, and became friendly with the Chinese leader Generalissimo Chiang Kai-shek, who remembered him warmly years later.

Before leaving for China, Ciano had not distinguished himself at the embassy to the Holy See. The ambassador, Cesare Maria De Vecchi, said, "At first Galeazzo made an excellent impression on everyone. It seemed to me he had freed himself from that patina of superficiality that was typical of his character. I quickly realized, however, that I had expressed a slightly hurried judgment because, after a happy beginning, Galeazzo went back to being what he had been, vain, a gossip, iconoclastic and frankly a loafer."[1]

In China Edda, with time on her hands and far away from the constraints of family, took up gambling. Once she sent Galeazzo a telegram from Pei Tai-ho, confessing that she had lost four thousand Mexican dollars at poker. "Am going to kill myself," she added. He telegraphed back: "I have sent you four thousand dollars. Little girls don't play poker and above all do not kill themselves. These things are not done."[2] The diplomat Roberto Ducci said that in the Shanghai of that time Europeans engaged in a *douceur de vivre* without parallel in Europe or America. "If the opium could be the temptation of an evening, a certain promiscuity was tolerated and even made easy,"[3] he said. He claimed the Cianos began living separate lives at that period, but that appears not to have been the case. The first of the Cianos' three children, Fabrizio, was born in China on October 1, 1931. Edda referred to him as "the little Chink," but within the family he acquired the nickname Ciccino. Edda loved nicknames. She shortened her husband's name to Gallo, which happens to be the Italian word for rooster. He gave her the nickname Deda. The Cianos' stay in China coincided with Hitler's appointment as German Chancellor. When the news was announced, Edda exclaimed, "How wonderful!" Ciano replied, "My God, it's a catastrophe." Later Edda wrote, "I found it normal that two dictators should be allies. And this all the more so since, as soon as he took power in 1933, I had begun to consider Hitler a veritable hero." She said she admired the way he stood up to the great powers.[4]

In early 1933 the Cianos returned to Italy, Edda now pregnant with her daughter, who would be named Raimonda and bear the nickname Dindina. Edda had initially expressed a wish to have a lot of children, but after Fabrizio's birth she decided she wanted no more. Both Raimonda and Marzio were the result of accidental pregnancies. The Cianos lived for a time with his parents in Rome, but Edda could hardly bear her mother-in-law Carolina, privately referring to her as "the ape" (*bertuccia*). In her memoirs, she wrote that both Mussolini and Costanzo Ciano became famous because of a desire to escape from their wives. Costanzo, she said, preferred the cannons of war "to the sharp reprimands and sour remarks of his wife."[5] Later Galeazzo and Edda moved to their own residence in the fashionable Parioli district of Rome. They bought apartments on two floors; their children, with a German governess, lived on one floor and they lived above. In her memoirs, Edda noted that the couple became the target of public criticism, with their enemies suggesting that Galeazzo was not cultivated, had only an average intelligence and never read, while she supposedly read only American scandal sheets. "We were, in sum, according to them, the perfect couple—he imbecilic and I trivial." She said Ciano had a lively intelligence, an unparalleled sense of humor and already spoke French, English, Spanish and Portuguese when they met. She went on to praise his taste in decoration, books, paintings and jewels. "He was a gourmet and extremely elegant," she wrote. "He was highly admired in the best Roman society and he was invited because he was Galeazzo Ciano rather than because he was the husband of Mussolini's daughter."[6] Her admiration of his social graces was shared by her mother. Rachele once commented on what a poor table King Victor Emanuel offered and said, "Galeazzo, for example, didn't worry about costs. He was a perfect host: the flowers were never missing, the tablecloths were marvelous, the wines exquisite."[7] Edda dismissed suggestions that her husband was frivolous. "I have never met a man so organized, so methodical, so punctilious in all domains," she said. As evidence of this, she cited the arrangements he made for their apartment in Rome and the thirty-room, prefabricated villa they inhabited on Capri. "It was because of his impeccable taste that our homes were a pleasure to live in," she said.[8]

Galeazzo waited months in Rome for a new assignment and, growing restless, went to Mussolini to demand he give him something to do. Mussolini sent him to London in June 1933 as part of a delegation to an international monetary conference, and afterward named him to head his press office. In September 1934 he elevated the office to the level of an under-secretariat for press and propaganda, and nine months later made it a ministry. Thus, at age thirty-two, Ciano became Europe's youngest minister since William Pitt the Younger was made Britain's Chancellor of the Exchequer at the age of twenty-three. Ciano's job, which brought him into almost daily contact with his father-in-law, was to make sure that the tightly controlled Italian newspapers glorified Mussolini, sang the praises of the regime, denigrated hostile foreign governments and avoided any reports that might reflect badly on Italy. He also tried to influence foreign correspondents to see the regime in the best possible light.

Despite his initial reaction to Hitler's appointment, Ciano was resolutely pro-German at that point, and he undertook with great enthusiasm his first important assignment as the regime's propagandist—directing press coverage of the initial encounter between Mussolini and Hitler at Venice on June 14, 1934. Mussolini did not fully share his enthusiasm. He was wary of the German dictator, and that wariness never completely left him. Mussolini saw Germany as simply a counterbalance to his relationship with France and Britain. He also assumed that, as the elder statesman, already twelve years in power, he would naturally play the leading role in relations with Hitler and that Italy would be the dominant nation. Furthermore, he was suspicious of German intentions toward Austria, and that was his primary purpose in arranging the Venice meeting. After World War I, the Austrian South Tyrol had been ceded to Italy and renamed Alto Adige. German designs on Austria would, in Mussolini's view, simply awaken separatist sentiments among German speakers in the Alto Adige that might be encouraged by Germany.

Hitler assumed the meeting would be a quiet, private discussion, and arrived in a suit and ill-fitting raincoat. Mussolini greeted him in a resplendent military uniform and put on an elaborate ceremonial welcome before two hundred journalists from around the world. The meeting quickly produced a clash of views on Austria and Ciano made sure the assembled journalists learned of Italy's reaction. That evening, over a glass of tomato juice at the bar of the five-star Danieli Hotel on the Grand Canal, which was crowded with journalists, Ciano sounded off to his friend Orio Vergani in a voice evidently intended to be overheard. Hitler, he asserted, was a madman. "He says it is necessary to catch Europe by surprise now that it is not prepared in any way for war," Ciano related. "How? He would like, for example, to invade France. He is sure he can do it in twenty-four hours if we help him. It is enough that we guarantee to be firm. It seems he has I don't know how many thousands of men on motorcycles with machine guns. Crossing the Rhine bridges by surprise and without a declaration of war, they could arrive in Paris and in the major centers of France in less than eight hours, before Paris has time to mobilize and before the barracks can give the alarm . . . Mussolini himself was astonished. He pounded the table with his fist and said no. Hitler has just one aim, war and vengeance. For his people he is a kind of Mohammed with, at the same time, the plans of Genghis Khan."[9] It seems likely, in view of Ciano's earlier enthusiasm for Germany, that he was put up to this performance by Mussolini. The Duce's concern about German military aims was evidenced again in 1935 when he joined British and French leaders at a conference in Stresa, Italy, which sought unsuccessfully to respond to an announcement by Hitler that he would rearm Germany despite the prohibitions imposed by the Versailles treaty.

As Minister for Press and Propaganda, Ciano began through his control of newspapers to try to prepare the public for the invasion of Ethiopia, Mussolini's overriding concern at the time. The Duce had once scorned colonial ventures as a waste of the nation's resources, but by 1922 he had changed his mind and had begun to develop a plan to establish a protectorate over Ethiopia. He believed an Italian empire in Africa would solve the country's economic problems, but the war must be carried out before growing German strength posed a threat to Austria and forced him to amass troops on the Austrian frontier. To officials who argued that Italy lacked the economic capability to expand its colonies, he turned a deaf ear. By 1932 preparations for war were under way, even as Mussolini sought to assure other countries that Italy had no aggressive intentions. More than a half million soldiers and civilian workers were sent to Italian colonies in Somalia and Eritrea to prepare for the coming conflict.

In 1935, Mussolini's son Vittorio was among those who volunteered for military duty, along with Vito, the son of the Duce's late brother Arnaldo. Bruno, the Duce's seventeen-year-old son, was taken out of school and given a quick course in pilot training. In the circumstances, Ciano too felt compelled to volunteer. He was not lacking in enthusiasm—it would be his opportunity to match his father's heroism in battle. He entered the air force with the rank of captain, and sailed for Africa. In Asmara, Ciano assumed command of the Fifteenth Bombardier Squadron, although his flying instructors had judged him a mediocre pilot. His unit was called La Disperata, after the Florentine Fascist squad of which he had earlier claimed membership.[10] At 4 p.m. on October 2, 1935, the outbreak of war was proclaimed in Italy with the tolling of church bells and the wail of sirens. It was to be among the most brutal conflicts of a brutal century of warfare, one in which the Italians indiscriminately bombed Ethiopian civilians and killed thousands with poison gas. Ciano, Vittorio and Bruno all took part in the initial air raid, directed at the town of Adowa. As his plane flew over Adowa, Ciano gave a signal to his friend Alessandro Pavolini, who had gone to Africa as Ciano's "personal journalist" for the Milan newspaper *Corriere della Sera*, and Pavolini released the first bomb on Ethiopia. Vittorio Mussolini later wrote that it was "very amusing" to see bombs fall on groups of Ethiopians.[11] Even though the slow, three-engine Italian bombers offered a good target to the enemy, Ciano liked to come in at low altitude for bombing and machine-gun runs. On October 14, just twelve days into the war, one of his engines was hit and he had difficulty getting back to Asmara. Four days later, one of his fuel tanks was ruptured by enemy fire and he made a forced landing in a field. In a note to Pavolini, Ciano wrote after one bombardment: "We have carried out a slaughter."[12] Pavolini quoted this approvingly in a book he wrote on the squadron.

Despite his evident enthusiasm for his mission, Ciano was rapidly disillusioned by the war and the turn of diplomatic developments in Europe. Italy's aggression had prompted the fifty members of the League of Nations in Geneva to condemn Italy unanimously and to invoke economic sanctions. Talking to under-secretary of colonies Alessandro Lessona in late 1935, Ciano said, "A military victory can be ruled out, because in this mountainous terrain there cannot be rapid solutions. Meanwhile we will be strangled by sanctions. We must have diplomatic talks with England, and immediately. I see black clouds on the horizon."[13]

At the end of 1935 he had to go to Rome for surgery because of a nasal infection. He had been afflicted with nose and throat problems from the time he served in China, and these were made worse by flying conditions. He had developed asthma in China in 1932, and this so aggravated his ear condition that he sometimes was forced to sit with his mouth wide open, taking deep breaths to dissipate his temporary deafness. Once Edda started to imitate him and Ciano, in a rage, threw an ashtray that only missed her face by inches. Ciano repeated to friends in Rome that military victory was impossible. Asked why he didn't tell Mussolini, he said, "You can't reason with the Duce. I have told him everything. You know what he said to me? 'Be calm. You will see that before Easter Badoglio* will have won.'"[14] It was the first serious disagreement between the Duce and Ciano. There would be many more.

* Marshal Pietro Badoglio, the Italian commander in Ethiopia who initiated the use of poison gas against the population.

At this time Mussolini began receiving anonymous letters denouncing Ciano's private life. One writer sent a series of "bulletins" entitled "Thoughts of the People." One bulletin said: "It is simply nauseating to have to note that a superminister . . . who, after having been decorated with three columns of newspaper coverage, leaves the front to hang out in the Roman salons and, worse still, shows himself in public until 3 a.m. in a close embrace with Delia Di Bagno . . . And that while his comrades in arms risk their lives and die and are decapitated."[15] Another anonymous letter advised Mussolini: "Put an end to the affair of your son-in-law with Berlingieri Giovanelli. This lady's costs come to hundreds of thousands of lire in jewels, dressmakers' bills and furs. In Rome everyone laughs at your disgraced daughter."[16]

Ciano returned to Ethiopia in mid-February 1936. On April 13 his plane was damaged and he made another forced landing. Despite his gloomy predictions, the Italians were on the point of victory and on April 30 their troops were within sixty miles of Addis Ababa, the capital. Ciano flew over the capital to check out enemy defenses. He still had not managed to emulate his father's audacity, but now was his chance. He decided to land at Addis airport, capture some flier or soldier to obtain information about enemy defenses, then zoom away again. The plan was audacious but, unlike his father's military exploits, foolhardy in the extreme. His plane actually touched the runway grass, but enemy machine guns opened up and the plane was hit twenty-five times. Ciano pulled up and continued flying over the city for forty-five minutes, even though two of his fuel tanks had been hit and he eventually had difficulty returning to base. Before leaving Addis, he dropped a Disperata pennant on the main square of the city. He won a silver medal for valor, his second of the war, and the Italian press trumpeted his heroism. Mussolini telegraphed: "I am very proud of your flight over Addis Ababa."[17] As a souvenir of his adventure, Ciano took home with him a seat from the plane that was riddled with bullets. The press attaché of the British Embassy in Rome, in a report to the Foreign Office that was intercepted by the Italians, said, "The comments of the newspapers render the most disgusting homage to the war service of Count Ciano."[18] Ciano realized that the press was overdoing it and ordered Dino Alfieri, who had replaced him in the propaganda job in Rome, to reduce the number and tone of articles about him.

Addis Ababa was occupied on May 5. Shortly afterward Ciano returned to his ministerial post in Rome, and Mussolini soon rewarded him by making him a member of the Grand Council. Ciano told his friend Orio Vergani that, when he eventually left his propaganda job, he wanted to be a diplomat again but did not want to go to Berlin. "I would prefer

America," he said. "It isn't necessary to arrive in America with the mentality of enemies of democracy . . . Italy must make friendships in the world."[19] On May 22 Ciano spoke to the Chamber of Deputies, threatening to crack down on anyone who, under the pretext of art or science, offended the values of fascism. He promised that offending publications would be "eliminated without pity."[20] Mussolini joined in the applause. He was about to give Ciano another promotion.

Chapter Three

Europe's Youngest Foreign Minister

On June 9, 1936, Prince Marcello del Drago, aide to Foreign Undersecretary Fulvio Suvich, learned that his boss was about to lose his job and immediately went out to the beach at Castel Fusano, near Rome, to deliver an important message. "There, squatting heavily among a group of feminine admirers, sat Ciano," del Drago later recalled. "I took him aside and told him, 'Tomorrow you will be Foreign Minister.' He was very moved and repeated, 'Ah, I knew it, but I didn't know how or when . . .' "[1] Ciano, with the support of Edda, had been angling for the job for some time. Mussolini was then his own Foreign Minister, having moved Dino Grandi out of the job to become ambassador to Britain. Suvich ran the day-to-day affairs of the ministry, and Ciano had come into conflict with him, once telling Mussolini that the directors of the Foreign Ministry must be replaced because they were not faithful to the regime. The German Embassy, reporting this to Berlin on February 13, 1936, commented, "This attitude of Ciano is all the more interesting, in that the present Minister of Propaganda would not be at all averse to his nomination as Minister of Foreign Affairs."[2] Suvich was known to be hostile to any alliance with Germany, and Ciano's appointment was widely interpreted in Europe as a move by Mussolini to draw closer to Berlin.

Ciano was now thirty-three years old, making him the youngest Foreign Minister in Europe. The appointment did not go down well with ordinary Italians, and there were sneering references to "the son-in-lawissimo" and "the cretin *arrivé*." Ciano was also unpopular with the Fascist Old Guard, whose members resented his rapid rise and attributed it solely to his marriage. Grandi noted that Ciano was jealous of the older generation of Fascists, and said Mussolini "made use of this defect and encouraged it. Through Ciano, Mussolini thought to rid himself, one after the other, of the men of the old fascism." The Duce "favored the defects of his nature, made use of them, made of him the instrument of his personal policy. The Germans did the rest. They enveloped him, made of him a soft, easy instrument in their power . . . A world of pleasures surrounded him and completed the work of corruption started by Mussolini and the Germans."[3] But Grandi's view was perhaps overly cynical, for initially Mussolini admired Ciano and made him his closest confidant after the death of his brother Arnaldo in 1931. It was a father–son relationship, between men not merely of different generations but of different milieux. Mussolini grew up in poverty, the son of a village blacksmith. Although he later became a teacher and a journalist, he was largely self-taught and liked to boast of his peasant origins. Ciano, by contrast, was born into a well-to-do family, was well educated and moved in more rarefied social circles than Mussolini ever did. Having lived in South America and China, he naturally had a more worldly outlook than Mussolini. They were alike only in their views on Italy's place in the world, but when that ceased to be true there was no common ground and they were inevitably headed toward a fatal collision. The seeds of conflict were there from the beginning. Mussolini, with a quick mind that was not trained, often acted on instinct, emotion and prejudice. He despised the Vatican and everything to do with the Catholic Church. He hated the monarchy, the "soft" Italian middle class and the aristocracy. Ciano cultivated ties with Vatican officials and with King Victor Emanuel III, identified with the bourgeoisie and drew his circle of friends and lovers from the aristocracy.

Even if he had had reason to doubt that he got there through merit—and Ciano had no such doubts—his sudden rise to eminence would have turned the head of almost any young man. Ciano became pompous, sometimes ridiculously so, but his subservience to the leader he hero-worshipped could not have been more complete. Filippo Anfuso once told an associate that Ciano's attempts to imitate his father-in-law was a forbidden subject. "You can tell him everything except this," he said. "You can tell him he is a poor man of letters, that women don't like him, that he will become fat like his father. But you cannot let him know he imitates Mussolini. He does not perceive it. He knows that to imitate Mussolini would be an unpardonable gaffe and above all a gross lack of taste in one who, like himself, believes he is a perfect diplomat."[4] That might be true of his associates, but the foreign press commented on his imitation of Mussolini so frequently that he could hardly fail to be aware of it. His gestures were so blatant that even Mussolini was troubled. After watching a film of a Ciano speech in Florence, the Duce said, "Galeazzo should know how to see himself. Those one hundred meters of Florentine film are dangerous, because the voice and gestures are not really comforting for him . . . In Florence they have good eyes and long tongues . . . The ridicule is terrible, there is no appeal from it."[5]

Soon after he took office Ciano began keeping a diary, usually making entries in the evening before leaving work. This is the document that Edda smuggled out of Italy in 1944, and it remains Ciano's most enduring contribution to history, a primary source book for biographers of Mussolini and historians of the Fascist era. "I believe it to be one of the most valuable historical documents of our times," Sumner Welles wrote after the war. "Those who will read the Diary in its complete text will obtain an opportunity to gain a clearer insight into the manner of being of Hitler's Germany and of Mussolini's Italy, and a far more accurate understanding of the degradation of the peoples subjected to Hitlerism and to Fascism during the years when almost the entire world trembled before the Axis partners. They will find in the Diary a hitherto unrevealed picture of Germany's machinations during those fateful years."[6] Malcolm Muggeridge observed, "The great quality of Ciano's Diary . . . is . . . that it records the mental processes, sudden rages, lechery and sentimentality, flashes of insight, inconceivable stupidities, ingenuousness and shrewdness of the buffoon who for a quarter of a century imposed himself on the Italian people, and for the greater part of that time on Europe, as a considerable statesman. No picture of Mussolini hitherto available has come near to this one for verisimilitude . . . Whoever at any time is interested in Mussolini will turn to Ciano. There the man is in all his folly and humanity."[7]

Ciano kept the diary in a small safe in his study. He sometimes talked to Mussolini about it, and occasionally the Duce advised Ciano to be sure to include something that happened that day. Ciano once read passages to Welles, and he discussed it with various friends and associates. The Germans evidently learned about it from some of these individuals, and were aware that it contained critical and compromising references to Germany's dealings with Italy. The diary also contains an excellent record of Ciano's shifting moods, his intemperance and, occasionally, his sense of humor. On December 31, 1937, he met the Norwegian minister to Italy and recorded, "He spat copiously. All that induced me to cut short the conversation. He is an old man in his seventies, who preserves traces of a notable stupidity."[8]

Once Ciano asked Dino Alfieri, who had been president of the Society of Authors and Publishers, how much he thought he could earn from publication of the diary. Alfieri guessed millions of dollars. Ciano was pleased, but said the diary would not be published until after his death. Then he burst out laughing and said, "Think what a bomb would explode if I published the diary now! But my children will see to that. I leave them this task that constitutes, in effect, a fine inheritance."[9] He also talked about the diary to Vergani. "I think the Americans would be very happy if they could read it," he said. "What do you think an American agency would pay for it? . . . The Germans think that I don't have the diary with me. Without doubt they think that I hide it, page by page as I write it, in Switzerland, or even in America. It's a little like the story of *The Purloined Letter* of Poe . . . "[10] Vergani asked if Mussolini knew of the diary. "He knows and he doesn't know, as he does for everything," Ciano said. One striking thing about the diary is that there are scant references to Edda, and those that appear would not necessarily have been pleasing to her. On September 27, 1937, Ciano wrote, "Buffarini . . . intimated that yesterday at Lucca Edda didn't have a warm reception. I am sorry. She is an excellent girl, but lacking in the right manner and she doesn't love the crowd. So she is not loved. A pity, because she has great and singular qualities."[11]

Ciano's diary bequeathed to historians a rich storehouse of memorable Mussolini quotations—some pungent, some spiteful, some egomaniacal. Here are a few examples:

> December 19, 1937: "This is the epitaph I want on my tomb. Here lies one of the most intelligent animals who has appeared on the face of the earth."
> January 31, 1938: Mussolini complaining about the reaction of the king, who stood barely over five feet tall, to his introduction of the goosestep in the Italian military: "It's not my fault if the king is physically a runt. Naturally he can't do the parade step without appearing ridiculous. He will hate it for the same reason he has always hated horses; he needs a ladder to climb onto one. But a physical defect in a sovereign is not a good reason for stunting, as he has done, the army of a great country. They say the goosestep is Prussian. Not at all. The goose is a Roman animal, if it is true that it saved the Capitol. Its place is with the eagle and the she-wolf."
> March 20, 1938: After world indignation caused by Italian air raids on Barcelona: "[Mussolini] said he was delighted that Italians succeed in arousing horror by their aggressiveness rather than pleasure as mandolin players. That, in his opinion, will cause us to go up in the estimation of the Germans, who love total and ruthless war."
> May 13, 1938: The Duce "is more and more anti-French. He says they are a people ruined by alcohol, syphilis and journalism."[12]

Ciano's groveling flattery of Mussolini even carries over into the diary. In his entry for July 4, 1938, he says he began "to cry like a baby" while listening to Mussolini speaking on the radio. He described Mussolini as having "an infallible instinct," a "steel intransigence," a "great spirit, always ahead of events and men." The Duce was "always right," "always his vision is clear." Like a puppy that goes into raptures when stroked on the head, he wrote, "The Duce has telephoned me his satisfaction. This is the prize that counts more than any." And again: "The Duce praised me several times—this so overwhelms me that I am incapable even of thanking him. The truth is that one only works in order to please him—to succeed in this is the greatest satisfaction." In one of his first diary entries after having been made Foreign Minister, he wrote, "Fundamentally, the Duce and I have the sole responsibility—I should say, the sole merit. One day people will realize what they owe to us."[13]

Giordano Bruno Guerri, in his biography of Ciano, noted his tendency not merely to mimic the Duce's physical gestures, but to use phrases that were more typical of the earthy Mussolini than of Ciano himself. He gave these examples:

"I envy the French their Gallery of the Invalides and the Germans their Military Museum. No picture is worth a flag taken from the enemy." That passage is pure Mussolini; the Duce was often disparaging about Italy's art treasures.

"I mistrust foreigners who know Dante. They want to screw us with poetry."

"Our frontiers, the Brenner included, are defended not by treaties but by the breasts of forty-five million Italians. This being so, we have nothing to fear."

"The revolution must impinge upon the habits of the Italians. They need to learn to be less 'sympathetic' and to become hard, relentless and hateful–in fact, masters."

To Guerri's list might be added this diary notation during a visit to Poland: "Too many painters, sculptors and architects have represented Italy in Poland in the past . . . They love in us the poetry of the pen rather than the strength of our arms, in which they still do not completely believe. We must work hard to correct the bad name they have given us for centuries."[14]

There is little doubt about the overall level of accuracy in the diary. Ribbentrop tried to claim, when he stood trial on war crimes charges, that it had been altered and falsified, but the diary entries correspond closely with official records. However, either Ciano himself, Edda or his Italian publisher did remove some pages that showed Ciano in an unfavorable light. The principal changes were made in Ciano's own hand after February 1943 and concerned his shameful role in the Italian aggression against Greece. For example, he removed a page that bore the entry for October 27, 1940, on one side and that for October 28 on the back. To try to hide the excision, Ciano corrected the dates on the pages for October 26 and 29 to read October 27 and 28 and wrote some insignificant lines. The Italian attack on Greece was launched on October 28. Nine pages in the notebook of 1938 were also removed, covering various dates in January, March, June, July and December. As nothing of great significance occurred on those dates, and they cover a period when his relationship with Mussolini was excellent, this is a puzzle. Some have speculated that Ciano or Edda removed pages embarrassing to themselves, either concerning their personal lives or Ciano's questionable business dealings. Several phrases that related to Ciano's plans to have King Zog of Albania assassinated were removed from the pages for 1938 in the Italian edition of the diaries just before they were published by Rizzoli in 1946. Other passages were moved from one day to the next, but these changes were corrected when Rizzoli later brought out a one-volume edition. Some material that presumably was judged of little interest to English readers was eliminated in the English edition of the diary. The most complete and accurate edition was the French one.[15]

Sumner Welles said Ciano was "wholly subservient" to Mussolini. "Count Ciano was a man who lacked neither personal dignity nor physical courage, and yet I have seen him quail at an interview with Mussolini when the Dictator showed irritation," he said.[16] William Phillips, the American ambassador to Italy, was even more unflattering. Describing one meeting with Mussolini, he recorded: "During the entire discussion, Count Ciano remained standing and offered no comment or suggestion. He might as well have worn a livery!"[17] Dino Alfieri remarked on the pleasure Ciano took in being favored by the Duce. "During the first years and for a long time afterward, Mussolini had esteem, confidence and sympathy for Ciano," he said. "After the usual daily report of the morning, he often kept him with him to speak confidentially of various things. Often he called him in the afternoon to Palazzo Venezia to comment on the most recent international events, to bring him up to date on his projects, to consult him about the changes in high positions of state and party . . . It usually happened that, when Mussolini left meetings and public rallies, the police lined up in front of his automobile while all around the applauding, surging crowd often broke the police cordons. Then he, with a friendly gesture, called Ciano and had him get in at his side. Ciano didn't manage to hide a smile of pleasure, as if he wanted to say, 'See, I am the favored and designated one.' "[18] Speaking of Mussolini to Roberto Cantalupo, Ciano once remarked, "You know, he has tasted great glory and from on high he sees the rest of us, very small. He lives in his own world. Perhaps it is better if we leave him on Olympus. He will be able to do great things.

As for us, we respect the concentration of his spirit and we look after the affairs of this world."[19]

Ciano's career as Foreign Minister virtually began with a shameful act. On June 30, 1936, he ordered Italian journalists in Geneva to whistle during a speech to the League of Nations by the Ethiopian Emperor Haile Selassie, ousted from his country by Italian aggression. The idea came from Mussolini, but Ciano added a refinement: he ordered the Italian diplomatic delegation to pass out noisy metal whistles to the journalists. The League had no police force, and the whistling continued for fifteen minutes before Swiss police stepped in and arrested the journalists. They spent the night in jail, were expelled the next day and were received in Italy as heroes.

But Ethiopia was an episode that was past. Ciano's attention quickly turned to more important matters: Italy's relationship with Britain, France and Germany, and civil war in Spain. Little more than a month after Ciano took office, General Francisco Franco began the uprising in Morocco that touched off the Spanish war. Franco needed planes to get his troops to Spain, and relayed a request for them to Italy. Ciano favored sending the planes, but Mussolini was resolutely opposed and only gave way later because he feared a leftist government in Spain would bring the Soviet Union into the Mediterranean. He believed this gesture would be enough to secure a quick victory, but in this he was wrong and Italy gradually became more and more embroiled in the conflict. Mussolini initially sent Fascist black shirts as "volunteers" to Spain, but many were poorly trained and eventually troops had to be dispatched. The Italians occupied the Balearic Islands, and a particularly brutal militia leader, Arconovaldo Bonaccorsi, was sent there as proconsul. Bonaccorsi, known as the "Conte Rossi" because of his red hair and beard, carried out a reign of terror, arranging the murder of about three thousand persons. Then he emptied the prisons and had the prisoners shot. In a message to Ciano he said, in terms that much later would become familiar in Bosnia, "The number of prisoners that I found on my arrival is greatly reduced. Daily radical cleansing of places and infected people is carried out."[20] Ciano never reproached him for his crimes. On the contrary, Bonaccorsi was made a general and sent to Ethiopia, and at one point Ciano telegraphed that he was trying to get more honors for him.

At the time of Ciano's appointment as Foreign Minister Edda happened to be in Berlin visiting her sister-in-law Maria, whose husband Massimo Magistrati was on the staff of the Italian Embassy. Edda noticed that the Germans suddenly began treating her with special consideration. She was introduced to Hitler at a tea hosted by Goebbels at his villa on an island in the Wannsee, and she and the Führer took "a charming boat trip together." He played with the Goebbels children, who called him uncle, and Edda was captivated.[21] Edda later wrote of Hitler that she had gained an impression from films of a man who was a marionette, with abrupt gestures and a raucous voice that made him seem slightly ridiculous. "The impression in the flesh was different," she said. "From the physical point of view, Hitler was no longer the timid, awkward man who had visited Venice two years earlier ... In 1936 he was dressed with a certain elegance; he was more self-assured and behaved like an amiable and cultivated man of the world. His blue eyes were charming, although I did not sense the hypnotic power they were said to possess. His voice was low and agreeable, less warm than my father's and not particularly beautiful, but it could be listened to with pleasure. He spoke calmly, listened attentively and had a pleasant sense of humor. Even his Chaplinesque moustache, which had once seemed so amusing, now fitted his face and gave it a certain personality of its own." She met him several times in later years and was "always struck by his extraordinary kindness and affection toward me as well as by his patience."[22] Only toward the end of the war would Edda overcome her infatuation with the Nazis. She often expressed the hope she might see the White House destroyed by Axis planes.

Edda stayed a month in Germany, being entertained at one party after another, and the French ambassador said in a report to Paris that her conduct had "aroused profound consternation."[23] Grandi said Edda had been received like a queen and returned so "inebriated" as to become "one of the most active propagandists of the Italo-German alliance." He said Ciano did not fail to be jealous of the political position his wife had acquired in German eyes.[24] Ciano was jealous in a more conventional sense as well. After hearing reports of her social life in Berlin, he confronted her upon her return to Rome. "Look me in the eye, and if you are a true lady, tell me the truth: Have you betrayed me?" he asked. Edda replied calmly, "No, Galeazzo." He related this incident to a friend and said, "You cannot imagine how ardently I wanted in those few seconds for my wife to answer 'no.' "[25]

Mussolini's initial wariness of Hitler had by now become modified. Italy's aggression against Ethiopia, and the resulting League of Nations sanctions in which France and Britain participated, had embittered him toward the democracies. Hitler, on the other hand, supported Italy over the sanctions issue, and the grateful Duce began moving toward a partnership with Germany. Ciano made his first official visit to Germany in October 1936, to sign with Foreign Minister Konstantin von Neurath a secret protocol of reciprocal consultation and collaboration with Spanish nationalists, and to confirm the existence of what Mussolini already was calling the Italo-German axis. Ciano came away from the visit with a far different impression of Hitler and the other Nazi bigwigs from the one Edda had gained. In a word, he found the Germans boring. He took an instant dislike to Ribbentrop, referring to him as "a fool," and was surprised by the ostentation of Göring. "Even if I described it minutely to Mussolini, I wouldn't succeed in reproducing the phenomenon exactly. Such a thing would not be possible among us."[26] After the visit he told two Italian journalists who were part of his inner circle: "I found the Germans very much more pliable and malleable than I might have imagined. Von Neurath thinks he's an old fox, but in reality he is a mediocre man and only a diplomat with a certain routine. I handled him easily. Göring is a fat, vulgar ox. But he is a capable man. I think it's right when they say he thinks mainly of grasping money and decorations. He is very well disposed toward us, and has an unlimited admiration for the Duce. I don't like Goebbels. He doesn't have the stupid frankness of his colleagues. Hitler—well, it is just incredible to me how such a man has been able to drag the whole German people after him. He is a man of fixed ideas, about which every so often he becomes excited and makes endless long-winded speeches . . . He's a real madman, a new Parsifal. One can't speak even of a distant comparison between the Duce and Hitler . . . Germany is in the hands of men of very inferior quality whom we must exploit."[27] During his visit, a Berlin journalist asked an official of Goebbels' Press Ministry, "Should we really believe Ciano is a great man?" The answer came back, "Not at all, but he must think we think he is."[28]

Hitler received Ciano at Berchtesgaden on October 24, and Ciano turned over to him thirty-two English documents intercepted by the Italian secret service. The documents demonstrated the aversion of London to Germany, and Mussolini hoped to use them to try to convince Hitler that Britain was preparing for war against Germany and Italy. Hitler told Ciano that Mussolini was "the leading statesman of the world, to whom no one has the right to compare himself, not even from far away." He said the understanding among the democracies must be countered by an Italo-German alliance tactically based on anti-communism.[29] Thus the Axis began to take form. Germany was ready to consider recognition of the Italian empire. Hitler also observed that Germany would be ready to go to war with England in three years, but a period of four or five years would be better still. It was the beginning of Hitler's deception toward his ally; he had no intention of waiting so long, but knew the Italians wanted more time to prepare for war. Hitler gave Ciano an autographed copy of *Mein Kampf*. Anfuso wrote of this meeting: "To say that Hitler was with Ciano sugar and honey is too little; in his sober uniform of night porter of a hotel, he met the Italian Minister and caressed his hands . . . The interpreter Schmidt poured on Ciano rivers of Hitlerian eloquence."[30]

Later that year, from November 9 to 16, Ciano and Edda visited Vienna and met Chancellor Kurt Schuschnigg, who complained that the Nazis were interfering in the country. This fed Italian suspicions that those ethnic Germans in the Alto Adige campaigning for union with Austria had been given encouragement by Germany. The Cianos got a cold reception from the Austrian people, and Edda called Schuschnigg "the most boring man I have ever met." She also bemoaned the rigid program laid out for her. "Every morning at 8, in front of the entrance of my hotel, the black limousine of the Princess of Starhenberg, my austere escort, was stopped," she said. "Less affable than an automaton, rigid and detached, the princess escorted me from one charity institute to another, to schools, museums and asylums. And everywhere I was received with icy coldness . . . When, at a certain moment, crossing the courtyard of a severe building, I saw men and women who frantically waved their arms at our passage, laughing and jumping, I felt liberated from a nightmare. Finally, I thought, someone who fetes me, who has recognized me and wishes well to Italy. Ahem, as one reads in the melodramas, I was deceiving myself, unfortunately. We were in an insane asylum."[31]

In May 1937, Ciano again met Schuschnigg in Venice with Mussolini and committed a major diplomatic gaffe. Virginio Gayda, director of the *Giornale d'Italia*, wrote on Ciano's orders that the Chancellor had promised to take Austrian Nazis into his government. The report was untrue and highly damaging to Schuschnigg, who was under pressure from Germany to do just that. At Schuschnigg's outraged insistence, Ciano had to get Gayda to write a denial. Ciano dismissed Schuschnigg as "crafty, hypocritical, impossible to deal with, flighty, complicated, tortuous."

Ciano's enormous ego continued to swell as he stepped into his role. He preened himself before his friends, and surrounded himself with flattering admirers. Elisabetta Cerruti, wife of a distinguished diplomat, said of him: "Although he was not attractive, being too fat for his age and somehow unhealthy, he had a certain unrefined handsomeness and thought himself quite irresistible to the ladies. They did nothing to correct his impression. The prettiest women blatantly pursued him, vying with one another for one of his smiles. It was painful to watch."[32] He had himself pictured constantly in newspapers and the newsreels. The American ambassador and his wife gave a large dinner dance each winter with Count and Countess Ciano as the principal guests. "On such occasions we were expected to invite his youthful favorites among the opposite sex, of whom there were many," Phillips said. "He devoted his evenings exclusively to them, paying little or no attention to ambassadors and their wives or to the distinguished Italians present. Countess Ciano had much the same attitude towards the young Roman gallants who paid court to her. This behavior on the part of a Minister of Foreign Affairs and his wife shocked the elder members of Roman society but was accepted by the younger set as natural under the circumstances. After all, Ciano was the son-in-law, she the daughter, of a great man. They could do as they wished. It was not considered wise to criticize openly."[33]

On February 1, 1937, British Ambassador Eric Drummond (later Lord Perth), an elderly diplomat who became an admirer of fascism, gave a reception on the occasion of the marriage of his daughter Margaret. Ciano came, the first time an Italian official had entered the British Embassy since sanctions were imposed. Ciano's gift to the newlyweds was a costly tortoiseshell toilet set, monogrammed in diamonds. When he learned that the Drummonds had decided not to display the wedding gifts, he made his disappointment so clear that the presents were hastily brought out and his offering was given pride of place.[34]

Marcello del Drago, after a tour of duty in Washington, returned to Rome and was warned by Leonardo Vitetti, another Foreign Ministry official, not to get too familiar with Ciano. "He never forgets he is the Minister and does not appreciate others who forget it either," he said. Del Drago said Ciano would throw inkstands and other objects at Anfuso, his closest friend in office, and would storm at other people. Once a diplomat opened a letter to him by mistake and Ciano, in a fit of rage, ordered the man transferred to Prague.[35] On another occasion Roberto Ducci happened to be at a dance when Ciano arrived with several beautiful women. Ducci got to his feet, but felt it was inappropriate in that setting to give the Fascist salute. Ciano was clearly irritated and, the next day, suggested to an aide that Ducci had been in the Foreign Ministry long enough. He was soon posted to Canada. Giuseppe Bastianini, who was moved from ambassador in Warsaw to become Ciano's under-secretary, said, "He didn't give the minimum satisfaction to those diplomats who were not to his taste. To those who might have in some way, even without wanting it, touched his susceptibility or that of Mussolini, he made his own aversion felt severely, such as showing to diplomats of small countries that he held them in scant consideration."[36] Ciano boasted to the diplomat Vittorio Cerruti that he never allowed foreign ambassadors or ministers to be invited to parties he attended, thus cutting himself off from contacts that might have served his own interests.[37]

Cantalupo, on returning to Rome after service in Latin America, found a different atmosphere in the Foreign Ministry under Ciano: diplomats living in fear of the minister, ambassadors abroad belittled, the ministry pervaded by irony, skepticism and snobbish cynicism. "Instead of the Ministry there was the Minister, that is, no longer an organism but a man . . . and that man was . . . a willing worker and intelligent executor but immature and overbearing, unprepared and too hasty, corrupted by undeserved honors and an absurd fortune, by an unlimited impunity and a monstrous power."[38] The diplomat Mario Luciolli said that Ciano refused to read a note longer than one page, did not receive foreign representatives and allowed the administration of the Foreign Ministry to ossify.[39]

Ciano's arrogance was sometimes mixed with intolerance. Party secretary Achille Starace once overheard Egilberto Martire, a Member of Parliament and one of the leaders of the Catholic Party, remark that Ciano had the evil eye. Starace had Martire handcuffed and sent to jail. Ciano approved Starace's action and said it had "proved the Duce's favorable attitude toward me, since he reacted with a violence . . . he had never shown before." Mussolini spoke to Ciano about Martire and "expressed his regrets for not having been able to break his ribs personally."[40] Ciano also did not hesitate to interfere in affairs of party and state that were outside the scope of his responsibilities. Guido Leto, director general of OVRA, the Italian secret service, said, "There was not a nomination of a certain importance, from general commanding the Carabinieri to high magistrates to prefects to representatives of big economic agencies, that was not . . . approved by the Minister of Foreign Affairs. Military affairs also were under the high protection of Ciano."[41] Police chief Arturo Bocchini and his successor, Carmine Senise, made weekly reports to Ciano. He wanted to be kept apprised of the secrets they held about his enemies, real and potential, and his rivals for power. "Ciano's interferences in the affairs of the police were continuous and his word was law," Bocchini said.[42] By 1939, according to Grandi's estimation, Ciano was "the effective boss of Italy," spending most of the day receiving officials from outside his ministry and transmitting orders and directives to the leaders of the armed forces. "Ciano was the deputy dictator," Grandi wrote. "The fact that Mussolini . . . not only tolerated but even openly supported these progressive concentrations of powers of the dictatorship in the hands of his son-in-law, the man most hated by the nation, had led everyone by then to believe that the dictator had already chosen his son-in-law to succeed him as Duce No. 2."[43]

That estimation, however, contrasted with views Mussolini expressed in a conversation with Ciano in April 1938, when the Duce was recovering from an illness. Nino D'Aroma, who was present, said Ciano rather brazenly told Mussolini that, during his illness, some people had thought of "a sudden vacancy of power" and urged him to leave written directives about the succession. D'Aroma recounted what followed:

> "Never," Mussolini responded categorically, regarding him with obvious rancor. "Never . . . because I hate political wills, I detest designated heirs and I cannot think that a people and a party, simply for the fact they chose me or followed me, must then supinely accept with closed eyes my order in such an important, delicate matter."
>
> "Well then?" asked Ciano, with an imperceptible tremor in his hands.
>
> "Then," responded Mussolini, "the one who knows how to dominate men and things will take power . . . Who wins . . . wins!"[44]

Elisabetta Cerruti said Ciano was surrounded by friends who seldom, if ever, told him the truth and led him to believe he was trusted and beloved by the Italian people and generally accepted as Mussolini's successor. Sumner Welles noted: "Whether he was personally responsible for the assassination of several enemies of the regime in the earlier years of his tenure of the Foreign Office, as has often recently been alleged, I have no conclusive evidence. But I am inclined to the belief that Count Ciano possessed many of the qualities of the men of the Italian Renaissance, and that such crimes would have by no means been outside the bounds of his toleration."[45]

The crimes to which Welles referred were the murders on June 9, 1937, of the brothers Carlo and Nello Rosselli, leading figures in the exiled opposition to Mussolini.[46] There is strong circumstanial evidence linking Ciano to their deaths. The Rosellis were Reformed Jews, born into a wealthy Florentine family. Of the two, Carlo was the more dynamic personality. Born in 1899, he fought in World War I, then later became active in Socialist politics and would go on to become one of the heroes of the resistance to Fascist rule. He was married to Marion Cave, a young instructor at the British Institute in Florence. Nello became a historian devoted to the study of left-wing currents in the Italian Risorgimento. Carlo later broke with the Socialists and launched a "supraparty" movement called *Giustizia e Liberta*, which he hoped would unite the non-communist opposition to Mussolini. The Italian Directorate of Public Security, in a document dated November 17, 1936, said Carlo enjoyed great popularity among anti-Fascists and had been designated by them as "the only possible successor to Mussolini." In early June 1937 Carlo went to the Normandy mud-bath resort of Bagnoles de l'Orne to be treated for phlebitis that he had contracted in Spain, and Nello later joined him. On June 9, they drove Marion to Bagnoles station so that she could catch a train to Paris and, after seeing her off, they drove back through the Couterne forest along an isolated road. They never reached their hotel. The following morning, their bodies were found in a ditch in the forest. They had been repeatedly stabbed, and a French military knife was left next to the bodies.

The murders caused a sensation throughout Europe. Two hundred thousand people followed the Rossellis' funeral cortège in Paris. The Italian press variously ascribed the murders to anarchists, Communists or friends of the Rossellis who were worried that Carlo might betray the anti-Fascist cause and return to Italy. Then the Rome newspaper *La Tribuna* came up with a new twist. It explained that Masonry had a particular style of killing: the murderer always takes care to leave a knife at the site of the crime. The brothers were killed, it said, because Carlo and Nello were Masons and the secret order feared they were about to betray Masonry. In fact, the brothers had never been Masons. Vittorio Cerruti met Ciano afterward and Ciano, slapping him on the shoulder, smiled and said, "You must admit that the idea of the knife was truly an idea of genius."[47] Some of the worst lies about the case appeared in the Livorno newspaper *Il Telegrafo*, owned by Ciano.

Six months after the murders, French police determined they were carried out by the French Fascist organization *Comité Secret d'Action Revolutionnaire*, more commonly known as the Cagoulards. One of the Cagoulards, who kept a diary about the *Affaire Rossignol* [Nightingale], as he called it, said the murders had been commissioned by Major Roberto Navale, an Italian military intelligence attaché in Turin, and by Lt.-Col. Santo Emanuele, head of counterespionage for the Italian secret service.

In September 1944, after the fall of fascism, an Italian magistrate investigated the murders. Emanuele implicated Navale and Anfuso, and said the initiative had come from Ciano. "The criminal decision was evidently taken by Ciano alone, who at that time directed every military and political service relative to the war in Spain," he said. Anfuso, Mussolini's last ambassador to Germany, sent a deposition to the magistrate from Berlin, dated February–March 1945, claiming Emanuele had offered to arrange the murders but these approaches "were instinctively rejected." After the killings, he said Ciano called him in and, referring to Emanuele, asked, "You don't think it was that madman?" Anfuso said he replied, "Impossible. What reason would he have to do such a thing?" But, he added in his deposition, "I didn't succeed in quelling that very suspicion in myself."[48] General Giacomo Carboni, at one time head of Italian military intelligence, said Ciano once remarked to him that Emanuele had "the great merit, as far as the Duce is concerned, of having been the author of the elimination of the Rossellis." Later, he said, Ciano observed that the murder of Carlo Rosselli was a mistake. "Rosselli, by contrast with most of the exiles, was a man of worth and good faith, who could always have done good for Italy," he said. "Mussolini himself is convinced it was an error." Carboni himself was convinced that responsibility for the murders rested with Emanuele, Anfuso and General Mario Roatta, Emanuele's boss.[49]

At the trial in Rome Emanuele was sentenced to life on March 12, 1945, along with Anfuso, Navale and Roatta, all fugitives. Later the Supreme Court of Cassation annulled the sentences and ordered a retrial. The defendants were acquitted by a Perugia court on the extraordinary conclusion that the crime could have been committed by anti-Fascists abroad. The court offered nothing to support that thesis. That was the end of the Rosselli affair. There was never anything definite tying Ciano to the murders, but Anfuso's account appeared hardly credible, and the circumstantial evidence that Emanuele had received the order from Ciano appeared to many to be compelling.

Chapter Four

Ciano and the Germans

In 1937 Ciano told Roberto Cantalupo, "I am an Anglophile." Later he elaborated on that: "As long as I remain in this post, we will be friends of the English."[1] That same year, he wrote in his diary: "No one can accuse me of hostility to the pro-German policy. I initiated it myself." But five years later he wrote: "No one can accuse me of being a Germanophile."[2] During his seven years in office Ciano, as in everything else, veered from admiration to disdain for the British, from pro-German to anti-German sentiments, from contempt for Hitler to unstinting praise. He never sought to justify these contradictions. He wrote, and talked, as though they did not exist, as though his most recent attitude was the one he had always held. But that was true of his attitude on almost every other subject as well. Ciano's political schizophrenia toward Germany was never more apparent than in the last months of 1937 and the fateful year of 1938, the year of the Nazi take-over of Austria and the British and French sellout of Czechoslovakia at Munich. He praised the Nazis and Hitler one moment, damned them the next. But his equivocations at least gave an indication that German behavior could eventually drive him into unreserved opposition. Despite his initial enthusiasm for the alliance with Germany, Edda said he never liked Germany or the Germans, "not for political reasons in the beginning, but simply because he was a true Latin and therefore not attracted to their mentality . . . He considered that they lacked a sense of humor (not always true), warmth and levity. He felt much closer to the English, the Spanish, the Portuguese and above all the French, whose language he spoke easily and well." She said Ciano looked on Germany's growing strength under Hitler with mistrust and apprehension, while Mussolini increasingly admired what the Führer was doing.[3] Cyprienne del Drago said her husband Marcello and Ciano had one thing in common: they couldn't hide it when they were bored. "And Galeazzo was always bored in the presence of Germans," she said.[4]

But Ciano was his master's voice. On May 13, 1937, he addressed the

Chamber of Deputies for the first time as Foreign Minister, and said Italo-German friendship had "profoundly permeated the social strata of the two countries."[5] Ciano and Mussolini were involved in a delicate balancing act. Mussolini both admired the Germans and feared their strength, and was anxious to make sure Hitler did not enter into agreements with Britain. For his part, Hitler was determined that Italy and Britain, at odds ever since the Italian invasion of Ethiopia, should not renew friendly relations at his expense. Thus the two dictators, while outwardly professing friendship, viewed each other with some mistrust. On September 10, 1937, the British angered Mussolini by signing an agreement with France to protect merchant shipping in the Mediterranean, where Italian submarines had been attacking and sinking merchant ships on behalf of Franco's forces in Spain. But in 1938 Ciano entered into negotiations with the British to try to normalize their relationship, and before the year was out the French would also be making overtures to the Italians.

Ciano accompanied Mussolini to a meeting with Hitler in Berlin on September 24, 1937. "Germany is only a field of maneuver for me," he told Education Minister Giuseppe Bottai. "I mean, for us. Now I must put the brakes a little on the chief, who is prone to get excited by the spectacle of German military organization. In his soul, this is the moment of the military men."[6] But Anfuso, who was in the Italian delegation, said, "When we left Rome to go to Germany, the most pro-German was Ciano . . ."[7] Mussolini used the visit to affirm publicly his warm friendship for the Hitler regime. A journalist friend of Ciano's who covered the visit wrote of the minister: "In Germany he felt isolated. A critical Latin spirit, he didn't succeed in pleasing the Germans. He laughed at their mechanical attitudes and their blind faith in immutable destinies. He despised Goebbels and was detested by him . . . In the German world . . . it wouldn't be long before he would be considered a dangerous enemy."[8] But he told his brother-in-law Magistrati to keep an eye on Ambassador Bernardo Attolico, one of Italy's most distinguished diplomats and a resolute anti-Nazi; he didn't trust him. Back in Rome, Ciano confided to Bottai: "From Nazi Germany will arise again one day the latent strength of anti-human Germanism, which we will have to confront. But it is a day far away . . . Now we must bring down the political-cultural supremacy of France."[9] Only later would he see what should have been clear to any diplomat at the time: that Italy had everything to fear from a powerful German behemoth dominating Europe, and nothing to fear from France. He told Bottai it was wrong to depict Italy as playing second fiddle to Germany. "The truth is that we direct the game," he boasted. "Mussolini said to the Germans: 'You direct the war; let me direct the politics.' "[10] The Germans, of course, were having none of that. Ribbentrop, then an ambassador plenipotentiary, came to Rome on October 22 and persuaded Mussolini that Italy should attach its name to the Anti-Comintern Pact that Germany had previously signed with Japan. The pact was signed on November 6 by Ciano, Ribbentrop and the Japanese ambassador Hotta. Ciano was then in one of his more bellicose moods, and observed that the three nations had perhaps embarked on the road to combat. "Italy has broken out of her isolation; she is at the center of the most formidable political–military combination that has ever existed," he wrote.[11]

On December 18, Edda gave birth to the couple's third child, a son. They named him Marzio, the Italian for Mars, the god of war. In his diary, Ciano commented that people "wanted to give to the choice of the name of Marzio a political and prophetic flavor: war." But he said a solution to Europe's problems could not await "the armed youth of Marzio . . . I wonder sometimes if it is not up to us to force the pace and light the fuse."[12] Marzio's nickname would be Mowgli.

Ciano was extraordinarily hostile to Ulrich von Hassell, the German ambassador to Italy, describing him as "unpleasant and treacherous."[13] He suspected von Hassell was not sufficiently pro-Nazi, and in that he was correct. Von Hassell was a distinguished, veteran diplomat who had been appointed to the Rome Embassy in 1932. He was allowed to remain in Rome when Hitler came to power at the end of that year, but he was repelled by the policies of the new government, particularly its persecution of Jews. After he returned to Germany, he lent support to groups that were working to bring down the Führer and was implicated in Claus von Stauffenberg's failed attempt to assassinate Hitler on July 20, 1944. The SS found documents indicating that the plotters planned to install von Hassell as Foreign Minister of a post-Hitler government; he was arrested and hanged. His daughter Fey, then living in Italy and married to an Italian, was arrested, put in various concentration camps and released only at the end of the war.

Fey von Hassell now lives in Rome, and recalls the relationship between her father and Ciano. "Ciano was considered by my father to be superficial and vain," she said. "He flirted to the right and the left. He didn't mix much in politics; he wanted the Foreign Ministry. He wanted to get pacts, which my father did not want. When he signed the Anti-Comintern Pact, then the Pact of Steel, with the Germans, my father said, 'It's completely wrong. That means war.' " "My father saw what Hitler was," she said. "With Mussolini, he had some hope. He found Mussolini was realistic, and listened. He often expressed good opinions. Ciano hated my father. He was jealous of him because Mussolini liked him and would call him to have a chat with him. So Ciano was furious, and thought von Hassell overstepped the rules. Another factor was that Ciano didn't feel that secure with my father, who was older and more experienced."[14]

Von Hassell did not get along with Ribbentrop either. Fey von Hassell's diary has this entry for December 20, 1937: "My father says that it is already all over for him. Ciano and Ribbentrop are clamoring for his dismissal because he stands in the way of their warmongering policies."[15] Fey said one of her father's shortcomings was his imprudence. "He made a lot of anti-Fascist remarks," she said. "The waiter at our residence, we discovered, spied on us and told Berlin what father had said at lunch and dinner."[16] In February 1938, after Ribbentrop became Foreign Minister, he recalled von Hassell and fired him. Protocol demanded that Ciano give a farewell lunch for the ambassador. He did so, but read a speech that contained no personal or friendly word for von Hassell. In his diary he described their final meeting: "Cold, hostile, brief conversation. I do not feel the least remorse for having engineered the departure of this individual . . . He belongs, fatally and inexorably, to that world of Junkers who cannot forget 1914 and who, basically hostile to Nazism, have no feeling of solidarity with the regime. Besides, Hassell knew Dante too well. I mistrust foreigners who know Dante. They want to screw us with poetry."[17] He had just helped destroy a man whose views he would come to share. Whether he felt any retrospective remorse is not recorded in his diary, but Ciano was never one for self-reproach.

Ciano had privately called Ribbentrop a fool after his first visit to Berlin, but he described as "very good" his appointment as Foreign Minister.[18] That sentiment also proved fleeting. Ciano and Ribbentrop, two men who were similar in many ways, came to detest one another. Ribbentrop, ten years older than Ciano, had been a champagne salesman in New York before he entered the service of the Nazis, and in 1920 had married the daughter of the owner of the Henkel champagne company. Like Ciano, he was vain and frivolous. Unlike him, he was not very bright. Count Otto von Bismarck, who served as counselor in the German Embassy in Rome, once said of him: "He is such an imbecile that he is a miracle of nature."[19] Hitler appointed him ambassador to Britain where he made numerous diplomatic gaffes, leading some of his fellow diplomats to christen him Brickendrop. Ivan Maisky, the Soviet ambassador to Britain, called him "an obtuse maniac, with the mentality and habits of a Prussian corporal."[20] But he remained close to Hitler, and was rewarded for his loyalty. "Ribbentrop was more important than I ever thought," Fey von Hassell said. "Hitler had the last word on foreign policy, but he was easily influenced by Ribbentrop."[21] Ribbentrop's English biographer, Michael Bloch, says

Ciano and Ribbentrop actually had much in common: "They were both vain, cynical, touchy, ostentatious; they both made great play of aristocratic attributes that were of suspiciously recent origin; they were both new men who challenged the ways of the old diplomatic order; and they both depended for their position on a close personal relationship with their respective leaders. Ciano, however, apart from being more glamorous and seductive than Ribbentrop . . . was also more quick-witted and perceptive." Bloch says the dislike between them sprang partly from Ciano's "ill-conceived contempt for Ribbentrop's clumsiness and intellectual mediocrity and unquestioning servility to Hitler."[22] Lord Vansittart described Ribbentrop as "always showy, a presentable fellow with cold eyes, common as Ciano but without Ciano's attraction for women and occasional sense of absurdity . . . It was hard to think much of Ribbentrop, for he never had an original idea."[23]

Once Ribbentrop took Ciano for a walk along the Fuschl lake near Salzburg, with his wolfhound following. Ribbentrop threw a stick into the lake and ordered the dog to fetch it. "But the dog didn't move," Ciano later recounted delightedly. "He looked at him, he looked at me, he looked at the stick, he barked but he didn't move. Ribbentrop shouted and the dog did not move. I would have liked to have embraced that dog . . ."[24] In his diary Ciano wrote: "Is it possible to be more piglike than Ribbentrop?"[25]

Ribbentrop came to office just one month before Germany's invasion of Austria on March 13, 1938. This was a sensitive issue with the Italians, because of their long-standing fear of having German troops on the border with the Alto Adige. Hermann Göring had come to Rome in January 1937 to try to persuade Mussolini to give the Germans a free hand in Austria, but Mussolini had temporized. Göring, incidentally, had recommended to von Hassell that he should not speak to Ciano about Austria. Even at that stage the Germans, aware of the scandalous nature of his private life, did not trust him. Hitler had referred to him privately as "a Viennese café ballerino." He said Ciano had "no secrets from the women who flutter about him like butterflies."[26] Later he called him *der abscheuliche Knabe*, "the repulsive boy."[27]

As the Anschluss approached, the Italians were in negotiations with the British for a settlement of their differences, and Ciano asked Dino Grandi, then ambassador in London, to speed up the talks. Chamberlain was favorable, but Foreign Secretary Anthony Eden was resolutely opposed to trying to reach agreements with the dictatorships. His differences with Chamberlain over Italian policy led to his resignation on February 20, 1938. Ciano wrote in his diary: "Strange case: the English Minister to the Holy See, Osborne, wanted to congratulate me and drink to the resignation of Eden."[28]

Meantime, Nazi designs on Austria were becoming more apparent and on March 11 Antonio Venturini, the Italian ambassador to the Holy See, told Ciano that Cardinal Luigi Maglione, the Vatican Secretary of State, was worried about what would happen. "Tell his Eminence to try to stop Hitler with holy water," Ciano replied. Mussolini and Ciano were aware there was nothing they could do to prevent the German takeover of Austria, but they insisted that the Germans agree with them on the timing and method. In the event, the Germans did no such thing. Their march across the border caught the Italians as much by surprise as it did the rest of the world. The lack of consultation was to be repeated, humiliatingly for Mussolini and Ciano, frequently in the next few years. Mussolini was able to contain his fury over these slights, Ciano not, but neither was prepared to make too much of an issue of Austria. Ciano, talking to Sumner Welles two years after the Anschluss, said Schuschnigg had once told him that if Germany occupied Austria, the majority of Austrians would be in favor of the occupation, and if Italy sent troops the Austrians would be united as one man with the Germans to fight Italy.[29]

The Anglo-Italian agreement was signed on April 16, 1938, little more than a month after the Anschluss. Although it had no practical effect, because it was contingent on an Italian promise to withdraw troops from Spain that was not fulfilled, Churchill saw it as implicitly giving British approval to Mussolini's conquest of Ethiopia and his intervention in Spain. The accord regulated reciprocal interests of Britain and Italy in the Mediterranean, Africa and Asia. Ciano noted that Italians would accept the agreement enthusiastically because they would see it as a possible means of disengagement from the German embrace. The agreement provoked a request from France for negotiations.

On May 3, 1938, Hitler came to Rome and Ribbentrop offered the Italians a military-political assistance pact. Ciano feared this would create difficulties for Chamberlain, who was prepared to announce recognition of the Italian empire at a meeting of the League of Nations Council. Ribbentrop insisted heatedly, but Ciano stalled him, remarking with feigned sincerity: "The solidarity existing between our two governments has been so clearly evinced during these days that a formal treaty of alliance is superfluous."[30] Hitler and Ribbentrop lulled the Italians into believing they had no designs on Poland, assuring them they wanted to see the power of Poland increased as a means of strengthening the anti-Bolshevik barrier. But they made little secret of their designs on Czechoslovakia, and the Führer left Italy convinced that the Italians would support him on that question. Ciano, however, was unnerved. He noted that Ribbentrop "talks about making war right and left."[31] He also reported that the king, Hitler's host at the Quirinale Palace, was hostile to the Führer "and tends to make him seem a sort of psycho-physiological degenerate." The king told Ciano that on Hitler's first night at the palace he asked for a woman at about 1 a.m. "Great commotion," Ciano said. "Explanation: It seems that he does not succeed in going to sleep if he doesn't see with his own eyes a woman turn back his bed . . . Is it true? Or is it rather slander on the part of the king, who also insinuated that Hitler injects himself with stimulants and narcotics?"[32] But it wasn't just the king who suggested that the Führer was a little odd. After the visit, Mussolini told Ciano he was convinced Hitler put rouge on his cheeks to hide his pallor. Mussolini took leave of Hitler in Florence, and Ciano reported: "The two men were moved. The Duce said, 'Now no force will be able to separate us again.' The eyes of the Führer filled with tears." Ciano was worried that the military alliance with Berlin, which he had worked to prevent, was about to become reality because "Mussolini has made up his mind."[33] Phillips, the American ambassador, came to Ciano to express the same fear. Ciano assured him he had nothing to worry about. Mussolini, puffed up by the Hitler visit, told Ciano soon afterward: "Italy will never be Prussianized enough. I will not leave the Italians in peace until I have two meters of earth above me."[34]

In the summer of 1938, a year after the murder of the Rosselli brothers, Ciano was back plotting against an enemy of the regime. This time it was Emilio Settimelli, former director of the Fascist newspaper *L'Impero* for which Ciano had worked briefly as a theater critic in his youth. Settimelli fell out with Mussolini, was confined to the island of Lipari, then expelled to Monte Carlo. He went on to France and sent a bitter letter to Mussolini. On June 11, Arturo Bocchini, the Rome police chief, and Guido Buffarini-Guidi, the Interior Minister, told Ciano they were "very alarmed about the activity that Settimelli proposed to undertake in France," including plans to publish a "scandalous book" about the regime. Ciano began plotting the kidnapping of Settimelli by motorboat, but Mussolini vetoed the plan.[35]

On June 23, 1938, Ciano was in Cologne to hear a speech by German minister Hans Frank. Bottai was there too and noted: "Frank speaks of the Führer as an institution, no longer transient and belonging to the person of Hitler, but permanent . . . Galeazzo leans forward on his seat and, pleased, whispers to me: 'He's right!' "[36] In August, talking to the Italian military attaché in Greece, Ciano described Hitler as "a statesman and politician of the very highest class." He added that England had aged and would not make war "even if they pay them."[37]

The Cianos spent much of that summer at the seaside town of Forte dei Marmi, near Livorno. One evening, Ciano seemed to reveal a bad conscience, or a presentiment. Inadvertently approaching a wall at the Sea Club in Livorno, he told some friends, "Let's move away. I cannot get near a wall without having a shiver run down my spine." To their surprise he explained: "Every time I am alongside a wall, I always think the firing squad is about to shoot me."[38]

While the Cianos frolicked by the sea, Hitler was planning the take-over of Czechoslovakia, using the pretext that Germans living in the Czech Sudetenland had been denied their full human rights, including their right to autonomy. In vain Ciano asked the Germans to clarify their intentions, while Mussolini gave public support to the claims of the Sudeten Germans for greater autonomy. Ciano, fearing war, confided to his diary: "May God protect Italy and its Duce."[39] He asked Phillips what the United States would do in the event of a general European war. Phillips said that was impossible to predict, but final victory would lie not with those nations with the greatest ability to strike, but rather with those that had the greatest capacity to endure. He thought Ciano was completely ignorant of American affairs, was inclined to believe the United States was too far away to count and believed the country was "going Communistic anyway."[40]

At 10 a.m on September 28, as Hitler issued an ultimatum to the Czechs, Lord Perth telephoned and asked Ciano to receive him urgently. Perth appeared deeply distraught. He brought a telegram from Chamberlain asking Mussolini to obtain a postponement of military action by Hitler. The British saw Italian mediation as the last chance to save the peace of Europe. Ciano asked Perth to wait in the Foreign Ministry while he went to Mussolini. The Duce telephoned Ambassador Attolico in Berlin and instructed him to go to Hitler to obtain a twenty-four-hour delay, assuring the Führer that in any eventuality he would be at his side. Ciano returned to the Foreign Ministry and informed Perth that the German action against Czechoslovakia was scheduled for 2 p.m. and Italy would be at Germany's side. "It is no longer a matter of looking at the calendar, but of looking at the clock," he said.[41] Perth's face trembled and his eyes reddened. Then Ciano told him Mussolini had proposed a postponement, and Perth returned to his embassy to telephone London. He was back shortly with a message from Chamberlain, which also had been relayed to Hitler, asking for a meeting of the British, German, French and Italian heads of government to reach an accord within seven days. Ciano returned to the Palazzo Venezia, and Mussolini telephoned Attolico again, asking him to convey to Hitler his support for Chamberlain's proposal. At 3 p.m. Attolico phoned back to say Hitler was agreeable, but only if Mussolini personally attended the conference. He left it to the Duce to decide whether the meeting would take place in Frankfurt or Munich. Mussolini chose Munich, and at 6 p.m. he and Ciano departed by train.

On the morning of September 29, Hitler met with them in their train compartment at Kufstein on the Austro-German border. The two leaders agreed that either the conference would succeed quickly (Mussolini specified that same day) or the problem would have to be resolved by force. In a conversation with Ciano, Hitler commented that the day was coming when Italy and Germany would have to fight the Western powers. "All the better that it should happen while the Duce and I are at the head of our countries, and still young and full of vigor," the Führer added.[42]

The conference began at 12.30 p.m., and Hitler openly threatened military action if there were no quick agreement. Then Mussolini presented a five-point plan that provided for the Sudetenland to be handed over to Germany. Chamberlain immediately accepted, but French Prime Minister Edouard Daladier wanted the document translated before making a commitment. The conference adjourned at 2.45 and resumed at 4.30 p.m. The British and French leaders quickly gave their assent, and it only remained to work out a few details. Ciano recorded Mussolini's demeanor: "The Duce, slightly annoyed by the vaguely parliamentary atmosphere which conferences always produce, moves around the room with his hands in his pockets, and with a rather distracted air. Every now and then he joins in the search for a formula. His great spirit, always ahead of events and men, has already absorbed the idea of agreement and, while the others are still wasting their breath over more or less formal problems, he has almost ceased to take any interest. He has already moved on and is meditating other things."[43] Mussolini wasn't alone in that. During the conference, a bored Ciano took aside the German SS Colonel Eugen Dollmann and begged him, a native of Munich, to show him the city's night-life. At 1 a.m. on September 30 the accord dismembering Czechoslovakia was reached, enabling Chamberlain to return to London proclaiming he had achieved "peace in our time." He had, of course, achieved the opposite. The shameful British and French sellout of Czech sovereignty convinced Hitler that the Western allies did not have the stomach for war and led directly to Germany's invasion of Poland a year later. Ciano remarked in his diary: "Everyone is satisfied, even the French—even the Czechs, according to what Daladier tells me."[44] Mussolini and Ciano, accompanied to their train by Hitler, left Munich, cheered by a large crowd.

But the king later told Ciano the Germans were untrustworthy and dangerous, and expressed sympathy for the British.

At the end of October Ribbentrop came to Rome to push a proposal for an Italo-German-Japanese military alliance that he had first broached with Ciano in Munich. Ciano depicted the German minister as "vain, lightweight, loquacious . . . He has fixed in his head the idea of war, he wants war, his war."[45] Mussolini told Ribbentrop he liked the idea of an alliance but needed time to prepare Italian public opinion. Ciano agreed, but Mussolini evidently had become aware of Ciano's lack of sympathy for the Germans. He told a visitor: "It will be necessary one day or another to go with a twig broom to Piazza Colonna to clear that place [the Foreign Ministry] of certain Britannophile filth that Galeazzo protects."[46]

Meantime the Hungarians had expressed unhappiness at territorial concessions made to Czechoslovakia, and asked Rome and Berlin to arbitrate. Ciano and Ribbentrop met in Vienna on November 2 to carry out this task. Ribbentrop took the side of the Czechs but Ciano supported the Hungarian claims. "Dear Ribbentrop," he said, "you cannot put the same enthusiasm into the defense of Czechoslovakia that a month ago at Munich you put into destroying it."[47] The two ministers used big pencils to correct a border traced by a German–Italian commission of arbitration. Ciano exclaimed to Ribbentrop at one point: "If you continue to defend Czech interests in this way, Hacha* will give you a medal."[48] Paul Schmidt, the interpreter, said Ciano appeared better prepared than Ribbentrop, and he prevailed. Hungary got 12,000 square kilometers of territory. To a journalist friend Ciano commented: "In the past, my ignorance made me think that to change the borders of a European state was a very serious thing, one that could not be carried out without war. Now I have seen that . . . one can cut slices of territory from one and assign them to another without any great power moving and without disturbing international public opinion."[49]

Ciano and Mussolini were, at that time, captivated by the idea of cutting slices of territory from France and adding them to Italy. The new French ambassador to Italy, André François-Poncet, arrived from his former post in Berlin on November 8, carrying with him the news of French recognition of the Italian empire. This might ordinarily have been welcome, but Mussolini already had decided on confrontation with France. On November 30 Ciano spoke to the Chamber of Deputies, and deputies rose applauding and chanting, "Tunisia, Corsica, Nice, Savoy!" These were the territories Italy wanted from France, and the demonstration continued for some time. Ciano later claimed it was spontaneous, but in fact it had been

---

*   Czech President Emil Hacha.

orchestrated by Achille Starace, the Fascist Party secretary. François-Poncet protested, but Ciano took delight in the rumpus he had stirred up.

The Nazi takeover of Austria and the sellout of Czechoslovakia dominated events in 1938. It was also the year in which Mussolini embarked on a formal policy of anti-Semitism, partly out of personal prejudice but more as the result of cynical opportunism, a way of ingratiating himself with Hitler. In Ciano, of course, he had the quintessential opportunist at his side. Neither man was a racial fanatic in the mold of the Nazi leaders, or even of some of the more extreme Fascists, such as Roberto Farinacci. But both, to varying degrees, harbored anti-Jewish attitudes and Mussolini, with no evident dissent from Ciano, adopted racial laws discriminating against Jews in employment and education and forbidding the marriage of Jews with other Italians. This shocked the Vatican and the democracies, to the clear delight of the Duce. Just four years earlier he had expressed his "sovereign contempt" for Nazi racial doctrine.[50] He was offended by the idea of a superior race confined to Nordic blue-eyed blonds, and therefore excluding Italians, but he had long entertained notions of Italians as belonging to a superior Aryan race. Africans were without question inferior people, thus he had no qualms about ordering the execution of prisoners of war in Ethiopia or gassing entire villages in Ethiopia and Libya.

Many of Mussolini's close colleagues in the Fascist movement were Jews, and for a time he encouraged Zionism in the hope of using it for anti-British purposes. He favored a Jewish homeland, but not in Palestine because he did not want to damage his efforts to build ties with Arab governments. At one point, he instructed Ciano to inform the Germans he would not permit so much as a square inch of Ethiopian territory to be made available for Jewish settlement, but he thought a Jewish homeland could be established in Russia, Brazil or the United States, all countries with lots of wide open spaces.

By the beginning of 1938, the Italian press was encouraged to tell its readers that Jews had wormed their way into strategic positions. In July Mussolini announced his Charter of the Race, a blatantly anti-Semitic document, which was followed by laws forbidding the marriage of Italians with those of non-Aryan race without special permission. Foreign Jews who had come to Italy after January 1, 1919, were to be expelled. No Jew was allowed to be a teacher, lawyer, journalist, banker or member of the Fascist Party. Jewish children were to be segregated in special schools. Marriage and fornication with Africans were to be punished with imprisonment. These measures were draconian enough, but mild, of course, by comparison with what was beginning to happen in Germany. Ciano said Italy had embarked on a "rose-water style" policy toward the Jews. He himself succeeded in procuring the elimination of one article of the draft racial laws that would have forbidden Jews from participating in the annual general meeting of companies in which they held more than one-third of the shares.[51] To carry out his racial policies, Mussolini appointed Giovanni Preziosi, a journalist and renegade priest who edited the anti-Semitic review *La Vita Italiana.* He was the leading anti-Semite in Italy, one who shared Hitler's view that all Jews should be expelled from Europe. Later, Mussolini was aware that Jews were being exterminated in Germany, but he sometimes gave orders that Italian Jews should be handed over to the Germans. Eventually Italian Fascists joined the Germans in operating an extermination camp at San Sabba, near Trieste. But when Mussolini discovered that some Jewish engineers who had been fired as a result of his policies possessed knowledge vital to his war effort, he begged them to return to their jobs. At a late stage he sometimes admitted that his anti-Semitism had been purely opportunistic and might even have been mistaken.[52]

Ciano was less stridently racist, but he acquiesced in the policies. And if he was troubled by the fact Italy had allied itself with a nation carrying out the most brutal policy of genocide in history, he never revealed it. In fact, his references to Nazi racial policy in his diary are entirely benign. For example, on November 20, 1937, he wrote, "The secret of dictatorships of the right—and their advantage over other regimes—consists precisely in having a national formula. Italy and Germany have found theirs. The Germans in racial ideology. We in Roman imperialism."[53] The early sections of his diary are replete with disparaging references to Jews and other races. Later, he barely mentions the subject of race at all. Livorno, his birthplace, had perhaps the highest concentration of Jews of any city in Italy. And, as has been noted previously, Ciano as a young man fell in love with a Jewish girl. Later he had many Jewish friends and business partners. That may have tempered his attitude for, on this as on other matters, he was inconsistent. He telegraphed to Germany on March 21, 1937, asking clemency for a Viennese Jewish scientist who had been thrown into prison at the age of nearly eighty. He met the Zionist leader Nahum Goldman on May 4, assured him Italy was not hostile to Zionism and said anti-Jewish polemics in certain newspapers in no way reflected the official Fascist attitude. A month later, he had a "long and cordial talk" with David Prato, chief rabbi of Rome, and assured him Italian policy toward the Jews was unchanged, despite anti-Semitic outbursts in the press. He added, with no apparent sense of irony, that "my best friends are Jews."[54] He told the American ambassador there was no Jewish problem in Italy because there was such a small number of Jews in the population.[55]

In one of the first entries in his diary, just three months later, Ciano recounted a conversation with Mussolini on September 6, 1937: "The Duce let fly at America, a country of niggers and Jews, the forces which disintegrate civilization. He wants to write a book: *Europe in 2000*. The races playing an important role will be the Italians, the Germans, the Russians and the Japanese. Other countries will be destroyed by the acid of Jewish corrosion."[56] On December 3, 1937, he took a more indulgent view toward Jews. "The Jews are flooding me with insulting anonymous letters, accusing me of having promised Hitler to persecute them. False. The Germans have never mentioned this subject to us. Nor do I believe that we ought to unleash an anti-Semitic campaign in Italy. The problem for us doesn't exist. There are not many Jews and, with some exceptions, there is no harm in them. And then the Jews should never be persecuted as such. That produces solidarity among Jews all over the world. There are so many other pretexts for attacking them. But, I repeat, the problem doesn't exist here. And perhaps in small doses Jews are necessary to society, just as yeast is necessary to bread."[57] Preziosi tried to enlist his support for an anti-Semitic campaign, but Ciano refused. "I have no love for the Jews, but I see no cause for action of this kind in Italy. At least not for the present," he commented. Mussolini agreed, promising to "pour water on the flames, though not enough to suppress the thing altogether."[58]

On February 16, 1938, the regime issued *Informazione Diplomatica No. 14* on the Jewish question. This series of papers was intended to outline various aspects of foreign policy, and they were usually written by Mussolini or Ciano. Michele Sarfatti, an Italian Jewish scholar, said Ciano wrote the first draft on February 9 and Mussolini rewrote it.[59] The paper denied that Italy planned to inaugurate an anti-Semitic policy and affirmed that the Jewish problem would be resolved only by creating a Jewish state, but not in Palestine. It went on to say that Italy, with just fifty thousand to sixty thousand Jews in a population of forty-four million, did not have a Jewish problem. But the regime promised to "keep watch over the activity of Jews."[60]

The Jewish scholar Meir Michaelis said that, while Bottai and Interior Minister Buffarini-Guidi outdid each other in anti-Jewish zeal at a Grand Council meeting on October 6, 1937, Ciano took no part in the campaign which culminated in the enactment of the 1938 racial laws. "He was . . . averse to the adoption of anti-Jewish measures on the German model," he said. "Nor is there any evidence that the Jewish problem was ever touched upon in his conversations with the German leaders."[61] Yet, despite his assurances to the American ambassador a year earlier, Ciano now admitted Jews were about to face "troublesome times." There would be no persecution, he said, but they would be segregated from all political and social life.[62]

In August, the Duce had become "very worked up" about the racial question, and ordered Ciano to strike all Jews off the Italian diplomatic list and begin recalling them to Rome. Ciano carried out the order, and gave instructions that Jews employed locally in Italian missions abroad were to be fired.[63] The Prince of Hesse came to him in September 1938 to ask him to intervene with Mussolini on behalf of Queen Margherita. The queen and king, he said, were indignant because their Jewish doctor, Stukjold, had been expelled. Ciano did not fail to see the irony in this approach. He pointed out that Hitler would hardly approve of a mission of this nature being entrusted to the prince, a German and a Nazi. "He turned pale," Ciano said.[64] The Jewish question took a personal turn on November 11 when a Jew who had been at school with him appealed for help. Ciano was not overly sympathetic. "I remember him as a vain and impudent boy, with the arrogance of wealth," he wrote. "He is now a sad, crushed man. Individual cases are distressing, but it is disastrous to consider a great social and historical phenomenon from the point of view of personal suffering." Nonetheless he telephoned Buffarini to urge special treatment for the man, pointing out the mitigating factor that he had an "Aryan wife."[65] Edda said Ciano also intervened, at her request, to save her former Jewish boyfriend and his father, who had been sent to a concentration camp. "He did so immediately, not only to please me but also because he felt that they had done nothing against Italy and should be freed," she said.[66] Later, when Italian officials resisted German attempts to have Jews in occupied Croatia and France turned over to them for extermination, Ciano played some part in helping to save Jews, but the extent of his involvement remains unclear.

Chapter Five

War in Albania

Hitler had won the Sudetenland at Munich, but that was not enough; he wanted all of Czechoslovakia. On March 15, 1939, German troops crossed the Czech frontier into Bohemia and seized control of yet another country. Once again, the Italians had not been informed. But Ciano implied to the American ambassador that Italy had been in agreement with the Germans, or at least had been informed. "It is so unpleasant to lie!" he wrote in his diary afterward.[1] Mussolini was furious at the lack of advance notice. Just five days earlier he had told Ciano, "The Germans are a military people, but not a warrior people. Give the Germans a great deal of sausage, butter, beer and a cheap car and they will never want to risk their skins."[2] But, piqued as he now was, he refused any thought of breaking with them, merely observing bitterly, "Every time Hitler occupies a country he sends me a message."[3] But on March 19, changeable as always, he decided a military alliance with Germany would be impossible. "The stones would rebel against it," he told Ciano.[4]

Ciano expressed dismay at a Germany "that acts at its exclusive initiative and with very little regard for us." He noted Hitler's claim that he acted because the Czechs had failed to demobilize their military forces, maintained their contacts with Russia and mistreated Germans. "Such pretexts may be good for Goebbels' propaganda, but they should not use them when talking with us, whose only fault is that we deal too loyally with the Germans," Ciano said. "The events of these days have overturned my judgment of the Führer and of Germany: he too is unfaithful and treacherous and we cannot collaborate with him. I have also worked today with the Duce for an understanding with the Western powers."[5] But on March 20 Mussolini told Ciano: "We cannot change our policy now because we are not whores."[6] The following day he affirmed to the Grand Council the necessity of adopting a policy of uncompromising loyalty to the Axis. "He made a marvelous speech, polemical, logical, cold and heroic," Ciano wrote, ignoring his own disagreement with such a policy. General Italo

Balbo, one of the Fascist grandees, objected: "You are shining Germany's shoes." Ciano, still loyal to Mussolini, protested heatedly.[7]

Ciano might not like what the Germans had done, but for him German perfidy provided an opportunity. He had long favored an Italian takeover of Albania, but Mussolini feared such a step would provoke Germany to occupy Croatia. Ciano kept urging action, and Mussolini told him nothing could happen until the war in Spain was over and Italy had an alliance with Germany. But in May 1938, Mussolini finally gave his approval for a takeover the following year.[8]

Italy's relationship with Albania had been a special one for some time. A London agreement signed at the outbreak of World War I in 1914 called for Albania to be divided after the war between Italy, Greece, Montenegro and Serbia, but the agreement was never implemented and Albania became an Italian protectorate in 1917. International pressure, however, forced Italy to restore full Albanian independence in 1920 and support the country's entry into the League of Nations. But in 1926 Albania signed a treaty of defensive alliance with Italy, making the country in effect an Italian feudal holding. Ciano wanted more than that. He wanted Albania as his own fiefdom. (Ciano and his father were widely believed to be benefiting from some Albanian oil well concessions.) One of his first acts as Foreign Minister was to name Francesco Jacomoni as minister plenipotentiary in Tirana, the Albanian capital, and in 1937 he signed a treaty with Yugoslavia that contained a secret clause giving Italy a free hand in Albania. In April Ciano visited Albania and told Jacomoni it was necessary to "eliminate" King Zog. He said he wanted Jacomoni to "conduct a policy such as to force the king within a year to leave" the country.[9]

But in 1938 Zog was still on his throne, and although still a bachelor at the age of forty-five, had decided he wanted to marry. Ciano suggested several young women of the Italian aristocracy, but Zog demurred. Finally he married Countess Geraldine Apponyj, a Hungarian, and asked Ciano to be a witness at the wedding. The five sisters of Zog were antagonistic when Ciano arrived in Tirana two days early to inaugurate the new Tirana-Durres highway, built with Italian money. One princess said to him, "You talk a good game, Excellency. To us this highway seems mediocre. Have you ever traveled on the one that leads from Tirana to Elbassan?" As Ciano well knew, she was referring to a German-built highway. Ciano, disgusted, wrote in his diary: "The royal princesses are peasants, ridiculous and worthy of figuring in an operetta."[10] He sent a report to Mussolini in which he said a cousin of Zog's queen had commented it would be better to have Jews in Albania than Italians. In the same report, he said the situation in Albania was unsustainable, and political or military action was needed to impose effective control over the country.[11] Albania, he said, could accommodate at least another two million inhabitants and needed only Italian settlers and Italian intelligence to make it flourish. As Denis Mack Smith has pointed out, during their years as a protecting power the Fascists had done nothing to make a geological survey of the country, nor had they even built a proper road between its two main towns.[12]

Jacomoni, acting on Ciano's instructions, was arming groups of bandits and mountain warriors to undermine Zog. On October 27, Ciano confided to his diary: "The action begins to have a clear profile: killing of the king (it seems that Koci will be charged with it, with a payment of 10 million), riots in the streets, descent from the mountains of the bands loyal to us . . . , appeal to Italy to intervene politically and if necessary militarily, offer of the throne to the King Emperor [of Italy] and a little later annexation. Jacomoni guarantees that everything can happen regularly with a month's warning."[13] Jake Koci, an Albanian minister of state and confidant of the king, was recruited to assassinate him. He in turn recruited one of the king's servants, who promised to put poison in a coffee cup. But the king learned of the plot and called in Koci to tell him, "Try to be calm, Jake. You will never succeed in killing me. If it is necessary, it will be I who kills you!" Koci replied, "You deceive yourself. I will kill you!"[14] Ciano wrote in his diary on December 1: "The Zog regime shows itself always more uncertain and therefore ready to collapse. It is necessary to act with decision and without scruples. For the rest it is humanitarian to cut short a life if with that one can save hundreds and perhaps thousands."[15] He met on December 3 with Jacomoni and Koci, and two days later he wrote: "The disappearance of the king will serve to remove any center of resistance and the movement will have the whole country in flames in a few hours."[16] The assassination never happened. Jacomoni said after the war that the operation was suspended because he tried until the last to reach an accord with Zog. Koci said he did not carry it through because Ciano feared Mussolini would not approve.

In 1939, Mussolini endorsed Ciano's plan for an invasion but on March 16 he suddenly developed cold feet. He ordered Ciano to suspend the operation because he feared this would favor the formation of an independent Croat state under German protection. The next day the German Ambassador Hans Georg von Mackensen reassured Ciano of Germany's lack of interest in Croatia, and Ribbentrop confirmed this in a long letter. Mussolini decided to act against Albania, and on March 23 he and Ciano drew up a proposal for an Italian protectorate which Zog was asked to accept. But King Victor Emanuel, seeing little value in owning Albania, warned the Duce he should not take such a big risk "to capture four stones."[17] Mussolini, nettled by the king's reaction, told Ciano: "If Hitler had had to deal with a shithead of a king he would never have been able to take Austria and Czechoslovakia."[18] On March 28, Madrid fell and the Spanish Civil War was over; one of the prerequisites for an Albanian take-over had been met. Barcelona had fallen on February 22, and many Italians fighting for the Republic had been captured. Ciano had informed Mussolini of this and the Duce ordered all of them to be shot, adding: "Dead men tell no tales."[19]

Ciano learned from Italy's military chiefs that the army was seriously deficient in the arms, equipment and manpower needed for the Albanian operation, such as the hundreds of armored personnel carriers and the thousands of troops required. But Ciano was determined to proceed.[20] He presented a draft treaty for Albania to Mussolini on April 1, and the Duce approved it with slight changes. Jacomoni was to present the plan to Zog the next day and make him understand that either he accepted it, and Ciano would go to Tirana for the signing ceremony, escorted by a large air squadron that would take control of the country, or disorder would break out throughout Albania, requiring immediate Italian intervention. In case of a refusal, the invasion was to take place at dawn on April 7, Good Friday. Ciano told Jacomoni: "Remember, however, that if things go badly, I knew nothing about it."[21] On April 5, Mussolini gave Zog an ultimatum to accept a treaty placing his country under Italian control by noon the next day. Zog, bidding for time to flee the country, promised an answer by 6 p.m. on April 6. No answer came. Italian forces landed on the Albanian coast at 4.30 a.m. on April 7 as Zog and his family escaped to Greece, but the invasion did not go smoothly. Anfuso wrote, "If the Albanians had possessed a corps of well-trained firemen, they would have thrown us into the Adriatic."[22] Italian forces eventually overcame the opposition, and Ciano flew to Durres that day as Italian troops were going ashore.

On his return he met Phillips and assured him that Italy did not contemplate in the least undermining Albanian independence. Phillips wrote: "I wondered only why Ciano had gone to the trouble of giving me and my other colleagues formal assurances that Albanian independence would be respected, when he knew the contrary was about to happen. Certainly he lost the respect of all of us by this futile and unnecessary deception."[23] Ciano flew to Tirana on April 8 and assured the Albanians that Italy would respect their independence. He ordered all political prisoners freed, and distributed money to the poor. On his return from Tirana, he sent top-secret telegrams to the Italian embassies in Paris and London, instructing the ambassadors to let French and British officials know that Italy invaded Albania to counterbalance German influence in Eastern Europe.[24]

Ciano noted in his diary on April 11 that Mussolini had decided to build a mosque in Rome, since six million subjects of the crown were now Muslims. "I do not see any need for such a thing," he wrote. "As for the Albanians, it's necessary to realize that they are an atheistic people, and that they prefer a raise in salary to a mosque."[25] Ciano reported the successful invasion in a speech to the Chamber of Deputies on April 21. Afterward, he telephoned Giovanni Ansaldo, editor of his newspaper *Il Telegrafo*, in an exultant mood. The conversation was recorded by the Italian Secret Service:

> Ciano: Ansaldo!
> Ansaldo: Command me, Excellency!
> C.: What did you think of it?
> A.: Of what, Excellency?
> C.: Of my speech, naturally!
> A.: Ah yes, Excellency. I haven't yet read it. They are passing the papers to me as they are taken down by the stenographer.
> C.: What do you think of what you have read?
> A.: Magnificent!
> C.: Just that?
> A.: Well done, enthralling! It will not fail to arouse a truly worldwide reaction. The exposition is well grounded, brilliant, sublimely logical.
> C.: Fine! I recommend that you point out all that in your comments. Rather, write an editorial about it. Note well that the reception I have had from the public has been truly extraordinary. I've never felt so moved in my life.
> A.: I believe it, Excellency. Any other orders?
> C.: Ansaldo!
> A.: Command me, Excellency!
> C.: I recommend in particular that you do not omit any of the incisions in the text of the speech.
> A.: To what are you alluding, Excellency?
> C.: To the applause, to the comments of the applauding crowd. Do I make myself clear?
> A.: Without fail, Excellency!
> C.: Especially the finale. The final applause! You will see that I have really received a lot. Make it stand out in big type! Don't be stingy with the big type![26]

In the early days of the Italian takeover a group of Albanian exiles proposed Amedeo, the duke of Aosta, as their new king, and Mussolini agreed. The decision was referred to King Victor Emanuel, who made it clear he wanted the crown for himself. This killed off all pretence of Albania retaining its independence. The exiles then met in secret with Ciano and offered the crown to him. Ciano refused, telling them, "I must work in the post that the Duce has assigned to me."[27] He brought in packets of money for the most obdurate Albanians, and a constituent assembly was persuaded to offer the crown to Victor Emanuel. When this was sealed at a Quirinale ceremony, Ciano wrote: "The king responds with an uncertain and trembling voice. Decidedly he is not an orator who impresses his audience, and these Albanians, a hard, mountain, warlike people, look with a mixture of amazement and intimidation at that little old man seated on a great gilded chair, at the feet of which is a bronze giant: Mussolini. They don't understand how that can happen."[28]

Police Chief Bocchini prohibited his officials from concerning themselves in any way with Albanian affairs. "Albania is a fief of Ciano's, and I don't want to break with him," he said.[29] Guido Leto, then head of political services in the Directorate of Public Security, said private police reports sent to Bocchini "were systematically buried because, directly or indirectly, they dealt with things unpleasant for the Ciano clan . . . The power of Ciano grew day by day and Bocchini, who so much clung to his chair, became a true and proper succubus of the Minister of Foreign Affairs."[30]

Emanuele Grazzi also observed that Ciano considered Albania "as his personal fiefdom. He made frequent and repeated visits there, received by the lieutenancy like a sovereign. He had luxurious hunting lodges and game reserves established and the lodges decorated at Albanian public expense. He installed his own people, and even the names of localities . . . were substituted by others, destined to carry into the centuries his glory and that of members of his family."[31] Santi Quaranta became Port Edda. Ciano later referred to Albania as his "grand duchy." Not all Albanians, of course, were quiescent about the Italian takeover, and Ciano took a tough line with dissidents. On May 12, he recorded in his diary, "There is a little flurry in Albanian intellectual circles, a reason for assigning twenty persons immediately to internment. There must not be the least sign of weakness."[32]

Ciano was a shareholder in two Italian oil companies, ANIC and AGIP, but Albanian oil was found to be sulphurous, costly to refine and unprofitable. German spies who later investigated Ciano were unable to find evidence that he profited from the Albanian venture. Italy, in fact, derived no benefits from its takeover, but the backward country of Albania did because Rome poured money into a development program. Two years later, caught up in a war they did not want, the Albanians in the pay of the Italian government had had enough. They asked for and obtained the dissolution of the Albanian Fascist Party, the suppression of the under-secretariat for Albania and the reconstitution of their army.

Jacomoni, after the war, denied there had been any serious plot to assassinate King Zog. He said he opposed the plan violently and it "vanished in the moment in which it was born."[33] A Rome court absolved him, on March 12, 1945, of having plotted the death of Zog, but his trial took place before the publication of Ciano's diary. In December 1939, Ciano noted in his diary that an Albanian official had proposed to have the inconvenient Zog, still living in exile, assassinated. By then Ciano took a lofty, detached view. "The matter does not interest us, and I answer that only the Albanians can be the judges of the life of another Albanian," he wrote.[34]

Chapter Six

An Open Marriage

Ciano might feel on top of the world after the takeover of Albania, but by now he and Edda were living separate lives and there were recurrent rumors she would leave him. At one point she had considered doing so, and had gone to her father to tell him of her intention. She recorded the conversation in her memoirs:

> "Daddy, I want to leave Galeazzo."
> "Why? Doesn't he give you enough to eat? Does he leave you without enough money or let you lack for something?"
> "Oh no, it's not that."
> "Then, is he unfaithful?"
> "Perhaps."
> "Are you in love with someone else?"
> "Not at all!"
> "Then go home, and let's hear no more of this nonsense."[1]

But all Italy talked of the scandalous nature of the Cianos' marriage. Ciano's roving eye, his late working hours and his absence from Rome to fight in the Ethiopian war may all have contributed to the fact that they drifted apart and began living separate lives. He was fascinated by the beau monde of the Italian aristocracy, and took his lovers from among princesses, countesses, marchionesses and baronesses, as well as film stars. Edda scorned his world, preferring the company of athletic young men, such as alpine guides and lifeguards.

The center of Ciano's social life was the Palazzo Colonna, where Princess Isabelle Colonna presided over one of Rome's most important salons. Isabelle, of Syrian origin, was much older than Ciano and married to Prince Marc-Antonio Colonna, an assistant to the papal throne and scion of one of Italy's oldest noble families. Her salon was, according to Roberto Ducci, "the true Court of the capital, the old sovereigns having for years declined to have one." Ciano often went to the Palazzo Colonna in the evening, without Edda, and there met many of the women who came to figure prominently in his life. "It was in one of the rooms of the palace that the favorite of the day was consecrated as such," Ducci said. "Her predecessor retired with a sigh but all in all with good grace, sure that to the one who now triumphed the identical fate lay in store in six months or at most a year."[2] With one important exception, a young countess whom he truly loved, he tired of his mistresses quickly. Elisabetta Cerruti said, "Ciano had one strange peculiarity. He was unable to watch anyone cry without at once shedding tears himself. When he cast a love aside, he would ask her not to cry in his presence, but to take her grief elsewhere."[3] The women cast aside were known as "the widows of Ciano."

Ciano apparently had the sexual appetite of a satyr. Before one trip to Berlin, he telegraphed the Italian consul-general Giuseppe Renzetti: "Provide women."[4] The artist Aldo Raimondi, who painted a portrait of Ciano at the Palazzo Chigi in 1938, said that several times when Ciano was posing for him Anfuso would come in and announce the arrival of female guests. Ciano would then go into a small room with one woman and another would follow Anfuso to a separate room. Joseph Kennedy, then the U.S. ambassador to Britain, visited Rome in 1938 and found Ciano's obsession with women offensive. "I have never met such a pompous and vain imbecile," he wrote. "He spent most of his time talking about women and spoke seriously to no one, for fear of losing sight of the two or three girls he was running after. I left him with the conviction that we would have obtained more from him by sending him a dozen pretty girls rather than a group of diplomats."[5] This was a bit rich, coming from such a notorious ladies' man as Kennedy. Lord Vansittart, who first met Ciano in 1934, had a more indulgent attitude. "He was a bounder. But bounding is no sin in the sun," he said. "He liked women and advancement; others have had the same tastes with less fulfillment. He enjoyed good looks with some good nature and an occasional sense of humor . . . and a *jouisseur*'s repugnance to war is more reliable than a pacifist's because it is more practical."[6]

The other center of Ciano's social life was the Acquasanta Golf Club on the southern outskirts of Rome, where he and his smart circle bantered playfully around the club tables even as the clouds of war were beginning to gather over Europe. Word of this got back to Mussolini, who confronted his son-in-law about his behavior. "I get continuous reports of this golf club," he told him. "Beautiful women and experienced ladies gather too much around the officials of the Foreign Ministry." Ciano laughed. "You're referring to me, to speak plainly?" Mussolini replied, "Exactly." He returned to Ciano a book he had borrowed, Duff Cooper's biography of Talleyrand. "I must conclude," he said, "that when one seeks only beautiful women and one likes terrible books, decadence for a man is certain." Ciano did not reply.[7] The Acquasanta Golf Club had been designed by an Englishman at the turn of the century, and had been run by Englishmen since. The secretary was English, the golf pro a Scot. "Even waiters and caddies talked, thought and swore in English," said del Drago, himself an habitué of the club.[8] Susanna Agnelli, Italy's Foreign Minister in 1995–6, was a friend of Ciano's and expressed some of the ambivalent feelings that many who knew him shared: "Ciano was the social image of power. He played golf and the whole of Roman society took up golf. They gathered at the golf club for lunch, waiting like beggars for Galeazzo's *ciao*.The women behaved with a lack of dignity that was embarrassing. Galeazzo's *favorita* of the moment was adulated, envied, loathed, run after. To hold on to Galeazzo's arm for a moment in public and to be pawed by him was the sign of success . . . Whatever he said, they all doubled up in laughter. I think he hated them all."[9]

Most of Ciano's circle of friends and admirers spoke English and French, and made no attempt to hide their sympathy for the Allies or their conviction that Germans were uncouth. Their viewpoint clearly had a growing influence on Ciano's thinking as his relationship with Mussolini worsened. "The members of the Roman *chiacchiera**, as his coterie was called, were frivolous, promiscuous, irresponsible and as amply endowed with physical charm as they were deficient in intellectual qualities," Eugen Dollmann said. "Matters of moment were settled at the 19th hole or between dips in the swimming pool, and there was no state secret which was not broached and discussed there, as in Marie Antoinette's boudoir at the Petit Trianon."[10]

The only German who formed part of the Ciano circle was Prince Otto von Bismarck, grandson of the Iron Chancellor and counselor at the German Embassy. Dollmann said Bismarck and his Swedish-born wife Ann-Mari displayed a signed photograph of Hermann Göring on their piano, but both were "decidedly anti-Nazi when conversing among themselves and with Ciano and Anfuso."[11] Another couple at the German Embassy, Carl and Veronica Clemm von Hohenberg, also became friends of Ciano's. Many in Italy thought that the Germans, knowing Ciano's weakness for beautiful women, had sent the two diplomats to Rome with the express purpose of having their wives ferret out his confidences. But he apparently kept them at arm's length, and made no secret of his dislike for Countess von Bismarck. Veronica Clemm also came in for Ciano's scorn. Once she told Filippo Anfuso that Germany was entitled to warm-water access and

---

*   chattering classes

would claim Trieste some day. Ciano, in his diary, reported: "Anfuso gave her the twofold advice, not to talk politics, and to dedicate her energies to another occupation in which, as everyone knows, the Baroness is notoriously something of an expert."[12]

Curzio Malaparte described an afternoon at the golf club in 1942 which typified the atmosphere that prevailed throughout those years:

> Count Ciano, standing in front of Brigitte, spoke to her in a loud voice, as was his custom, turning his head here and there and laughing. Brigitte, seated with her elbows resting on the table and her face enfolded between her two hands, looked at him, raising her beautiful eyes full of innocent mischief. Then Brigitte got up and together with Galeazzo went out into the garden, where they strolled around the pool chatting languidly.
>
> Count Ciano had a gallant air, spoke in a loud voice, looking around with his proud and cordial frown. Everyone observed the scene, winking at each other with an air of understanding.
>
> "Ca y est!" said Anne Marie.
>
> "Brigitte est vraiment une femme charmante," said von Bismarck.
>
> "Galeazzo est tres aimé des femmes," said Georgette.
>
> "There is not a woman here who has not had a fling with Galeazzo," said Anfuso.
>
> "I don't know any woman," said Anne Marie, "who has known how to hold his attention."
>
> "Yes, one, but she is not here," said Anfuso, his face darkening.
>
> "Qu'en savez-vous?" said Anne Marie.
>
> At this point Brigitte entered and approached Anne Marie. She was happy, laughing with her rather full voice.
>
> "Be careful, Brigitte," Anfuso said. "Count Ciano wins all his wars."
>
> "Oh, je sais," responded Brigitte, "on m'a déja averti. Moi, au contraire, je perds toutes mes guerres." [13]

Rumors about the scandalous nature of Edda's own conduct became widespread. Sir Percy Loraine, the British ambassador, wrote to Prime Minister Neville Chamberlain and Foreign Secretary Lord Halifax on March 14, 1939, to say that Edda "has become a nymphomaniac and in an alcoholic haze leads a life of rather sordid sexual promiscuity."[14] She made frequent sojourns, alone, to Capri and to the alpine resort of Cortina d'Ampezzo, where in 1934 she met Emilio Pucci, who would become her lover. The world-famous designer of postwar years was then a rather impoverished young nobleman. Edda was also sometimes seen at a nightclub at Forte dei Marmi, near the Cianos' hometown of Livorno, dancing cheek to cheek with various men. Edda herself referred in her memoirs to newspaper articles "that described me as a Messalina,* a debauched woman who liked to visit Germany, for example, to sleep with the Führer's personal guards because they were tall, blond and handsome."[15] Edda's mother-in-law reproved her for her indiscretions, and Edda replied to her letter with sarcasm: "Dear Mamma, you must rapidly persuade yourself that Pompadour, Ninon de Lenclos and Mme. de Maintenon were, by comparison with me, naive little girls worthy of wearing nuns' habits. They say that I am pregnant who knows by whom, and they will say that you are also pregnant, dear Mamma."[16]

Ciano once confessed to Malaparte: "My real enemy is Edda . . . I feel that Edda, for me, is a danger, that I must guard myself from her as from an enemy. If one day Edda left me, if there were someone else in her life, something serious, I would be lost . . . I have tried at various times to make her understand how dangerous certain of her attitudes are for me. But with Edda one cannot speak. She is a hard, strange woman . . . Sometimes she frightens me. I don't know who puts about those stupid rumors about Edda, about her intention to have our marriage annulled so as to marry I don't know who."[17] To Orio Vergani Ciano said, "Edda is the only woman I have truly loved, and she is my only woman friend."[18]

Count Dornberg, the Nazi protocol chief, spoke disapprovingly of Edda's private life to Malaparte. "It's incredible, the people with whom Countess Ciano surrounds herself," he said. "I've never seen anything like it, even at Monte Carlo around the *vieilles dames* with their gigolos." Malaparte quoted the German Princess Agatha Ratibor as saying of Edda: "Her worst enemy is boredom. She spends entire nights rolling dice like a Negro in Harlem . . . She is a sort of Madame Bovary."[19] Malaparte compared Edda with Stavroghin, the tragic figure in Dostoyevsky's *Crime and Punishment*:

> She loves death . . . She has an extraordinary face: some days she has the mask of the assassin, on others the mask of the suicide. It would not surprise me if one day they said to me she has killed someone, or has killed herself . . . Mussolini knows his daughter is of the race of Stavroghin, and he is afraid of it. He has her watched, he wants to know her every step, her every thought, her every vice. He's gone so far as to push her into the arms of a man of the police so he can, even with the eyes of another person, spy on his daughter in moments of abandon. His only enemy, his real rival, is his daughter. She is his secret conscience. All the black blood of the Mussolinis is not in the veins of the father, it is in the veins of Edda. If Mussolini were a legitimate king, and Edda were a prince, his heir, he would cut her down to assure his throne. Basically, Mussolini is happy

---

* Messalina was the third wife of the Emperor Claudius I and was notorious for her many affairs.

about the disordered life of his daughter, about the evil that pursues her. He can reign in peace. But can he sleep in peace? Edda is implacable, obsesses his nights. There will be blood spilled, one day, between that father and that daughter.[20]

Elisabetta Cerruti met Edda only once but commented that few people liked or even approved of her. "Far from minding this, she seemed almost to enjoy it," she wrote. "She made a sport of behaving inconsiderately to elderly, dignified people. She would turn her back on them, declare audibly that they were deadly bores and hastily join the company of her strange friends . . . She always seemed irritated and dissatisfied . . . She knew nothing of the meaning of the expression *joie de vivre*."[21]

It was as well that the Cianos lived on one floor of their apartment building and their children on another, for both were possessed of a temper and they now quarreled frequently. Edda said Galeazzo was always quick to anger and extremely jealous, "so that it was the better part of valor not to provoke him." In the summer of 1934, Ciano went to the beach one day to find his wife wearing a two-piece bathing suit, something considered scandalous at the time. He asked Edda to step into the changing cabin and once inside he lectured her severely, then gave her two hard slaps that made her head spin. "I forbid you to dirty yourself in this way," he said. "Take it off immediately and put on a more decent one."[22]

While there were sometimes rumors that the Cianos would separate, divorce was out of the question, as it was not lawful at the time. "People used to have flirts, then come back to their own families," said Countess Marozia Borromeo d'Adda, a friend of the Cianos. "Everyone made his own life, but the family remained. Edda had a lot of flirts, and he did. But they were nice to one another, and very affectionate to their children. On the whole, they got on quite well."[23] Ducci, who worked for Ciano in the Foreign Ministry, confirmed the attitude of Italians at that time toward adultery. There was a saying, he remarked, that "matrimony was indissoluble but tempered by adultery." He quoted Edda as having told a friend: "It is true that I have lovers, but I make children only with Galeazzo." Not all the grand ladies of that period, he commented, could say the same of their children and their husbands.[24] But Elisabetta Cerruti, said, "This way of living is not Italian at all. The effect they had upon the manners and morals of their contemporaries was definitely harmful."[25]

An anonymous letter sent to Rachele Mussolini on November 3, 1940, claimed that Ciano was having an affair with Delia Di Bagno, one of Edda's friends, and that her husband in turn was sleeping with Edda. In her memoirs, Edda noted Ciano's tendency to speak indiscreetly and said she warned him not to give away secrets. But she was convinced he was often careless, especially when speaking to "pretty women," and his remarks were repeated to the Germans or extreme Fascists.[26]

Ciano not only bedded the women who fluttered around him but used them in his official entertaining. Giorgio Nelson Page observed the role they played:

> If the French nobility, from Louis XIV to the revolution, had only a decorative function at the court of Versailles, the restricted circle of Italian nobles at the court of Galeazzo Ciano had a substantial function. The dinners and receptions . . . involved a very scrupulous dosage of gracious women seated at the table alongside the guests. To the Anglo-Saxons, certain women served to keep the conversation going in good English, to demonstrate that Italian life was imprinted with the tastes of the . . . democracies, to display kinships and friendships with English and American personalities, in short, to create an atmosphere of elegant and perfumed normality . . . With the German guests and those of satellite countries, however, the technique of those women was to show indifference toward the Anglo-Saxon characteristics. It was as if to say: "Look at us well, we are gracious, elegant, perfumed. We have lovers, and we enjoy ourselves. But we speak French with you because you haven't had the ability and the courtesy to speak to us in Italian, nor is it our desire to learn your barbaric idiom."[27]

Chapter Seven

The Pact of Steel

A t the beginning of 1939, Hitler was poised to invade Poland. He had rearmed his country in violation of the Versailles treaty, marched into the Rhineland without a shot being fired, dismembered Czechoslovakia at Munich and swallowed the remainder of it afterward. An air of crisis gripped Europe, for Western appeasement had only whetted the Nazi dictator's appetite and there was general concern over his further ambitions. The pretext for the German invasion of Poland would be a dispute over the historic port of Danzig, formerly part of Germany's West Prussia but now incorporated into Poland. Danzig was separated from the rest of Poland, but the Treaty of Versailles had provided a connecting corridor across West Prussia. Hitler wanted both Danzig and the corridor. Before he undertook this adventure, he wanted to ensure that Italy and Germany were bound together in a military alliance. Göring arrived in Rome in April, uttering threats against Poland and using terms, Ciano noted, that he had previously used about Austria and Czechoslovakia. Ciano expressed reservations about any precipitate action but his words fell on deaf ears.

The Dutch minister came to Ciano on April 24 to ask him about reports that Italy and Germany planned to divide Europe between them, with Germany getting the Netherlands. "They are the ideas of an official who is a little foolish and very frightened," Ciano wrote, "but they are nonetheless indicative of a state of mind that is widespread in the world."[1] The following day, Hitler denounced Germany's friendship treaty with Poland and a recent naval agreement with London. The British ordered military conscription. Mussolini instructed Ciano to define Italy's relations with Germany at a meeting with Ribbentrop at Lake Como the following month. Mussolini wanted to pursue a policy of peace for the time being, but he was now prepared to push strongly for an Italo-German military alliance with Japan.

Ciano was beginning to get nervous about the prospect of an unprepared Italy being plunged into war. He wrote that the Italian military, evidently to please Mussolini, was exaggerating the strength of the armed forces and hiding the deficiencies. "The ammunition depots are short of ammunition," he said. "The artillery is outmoded. Our antiaircraft and antitank weapons are altogether lacking. There has been a good deal of bluffing in the military sphere, and even the Duce himself has been deceived ... Valle* states that there are 3,006 first-line aircraft, while the Navy information service says there are only 982. A gross discrepancy! I report the matter to the Duce."[2]

Ciano and Edda visited Warsaw in February to assess the situation. He acted like a spoiled child, deliberately insulting his host, Prime Minister Colonel Beck, at a dinner following a hunting party by throwing pieces of bread in a display of temper. When Beck mentioned his friendship with Wieniawa Dlugoszovski, the Polish ambassador to Rome, Ciano replied, "Now I can understand, my dear Beck, that it is because of Wieniawa that you have lost your reputation." Beck shot back, "I think your reputation needed no help from Wieniawa to decline."[3] Returning to Rome, Ciano told Mussolini he had the impression the Germans were ready to "burn their bridges" over Danzig.[4] He also told Vergani that Italy could combine with Poland, Hungary and Yugoslavia to stop the Germans. "The only diplomatic action possible for our country is this," he said, "to keep Germany from going to war."[5] Yet his actions belied his words, and never more so than in his conversations with Ribbentrop.

Their meeting was moved from Lake Como to Milan because the French press claimed that the Milanese were in rebellion against a German-Italian military alliance. Ribbentrop and his wife arrived on May 6, and Ciano told journalists in a loud voice: "Certainly we are not going to get ourselves stabbed over Danzig."[6] At an initial round of talks he stressed that Italy needed at least three more years of peace before it would be ready to fight. Ribbentrop agreed that Germany also saw the necessity of maintaining peace for at least four or five years. He assured Ciano: "A strong and independent Poland constitutes a vital necessity for Germany."[7] Ciano relayed this information to Mussolini in a telephone call that evening, and the Duce instructed him to announce that a German-Italian alliance was in existence. Ciano's irresponsibility now reached a level that, in retrospect, seems hard to imagine. He was about to commit his nation to an alliance that could have enormously dangerous consequences, but either through laziness or carelessness he took little interest in the drafting of its terms. The historian Mario Toscano wrote that Ciano "not only agreed to entrust the writing of the project of alliance exclusively to the Germans, but he absolutely failed to discuss and therefore to agree

* Air Force General Giuseppe Valle.

beforehand the general lines of its content . . . Everything was left to the initiative of von Ribbentrop."[8] The diplomat Mario Luciolli said the pact was never submitted to examination by juridical consultants of the Foreign Ministry, and Mussolini also failed to read it closely.[9]

From Milan, Ciano and Ribbentrop went to the Villa d'Este on Lake Como on the evening of May 7 for a celebratory dinner. One guest reported: "All Milan's society beauties were there, and the atmosphere was extremely gay, everyone speaking happily of the new alliance. Ribbentrop, in high spirits, waltzed gaily with the Countess Durini. She alluded to the possibility of another war and asked her partner how Russia was expected to act in that eventuality. Ribbentrop laughed harshly and replied in a half-singing fashion to the tune the band was playing, 'Oh, but Russia is with us, of course,' leaving the Countess quite perplexed."[10]

The new treaty, christened the Pact of Steel, was delivered to Ciano as he boarded a train for Florence on May 13. The first two articles called for consultations on questions of common interest and in case of the threat of hostilities. Article three (there were seven in all) called for automatic reciprocal assistance when one of the parties became involved in war. Ciano's only comment was: "I've never read a similar pact. It is truly dynamite."[11] He later told Mussolini that Phillips had warned him America would not remain outside an eventual European conflict. The Duce was unmoved. Ciano arrived in Berlin by train on May 21 to sign the treaty, and was impressed by the "spontaneous" demonstrations that greeted him. Actually, the Germans had had difficulty rounding up a crowd and had let workers off their jobs to demonstrate. Ciano met Hitler at the Kaiserhof and recorded: "I found him well, quite serene, less aggressive. A little aged. His eyes are more deeply wrinkled. He sleeps very little. In fact less and less. And he spends a great part of the night surrounded by colleagues and friends. Frau Goebbels, who is a constant participant in these gatherings and who feels very honored by them, was describing them to me without being able to conceal a vague feeling of boredom on account of their monotony. It is always Hitler who talks! . . . For the first time I hear hints, in the inner circles, of the Führer's affection for a beautiful girl. She is twenty years old with beautiful, quiet eyes, regular features and a magnificent body. Her name is Sigrid von Lappus.* They see each other frequently and intimately."[12] The pact was signed on May 22 in a solemn ceremony in the Chancellery, with Hitler and other Nazi leaders present. Hitler bestowed upon Ciano the first of a newly created decoration, Germany's highest, the Knight's Order of the German Eagle, in solid gold. A crowd mainly consisting of young Brownshirts acclaimed the Führer

---

*   Actually, Sigrid von Laffert.

and Ciano outside the Chancellery. Lunch followed at the Italian Embassy, and there Ciano gave Ribbentrop the Collar of the Annunciation, on behalf of King Victor Emanuel. This was Italy's highest decoration, and only twenty of them existed. The Collar had to be returned to the monarch upon the death of the holder, and it carried with it the right to be considered a cousin of the king. Göring flew into a jealous rage, so angry that tears came to his eyes. He stormed at Mackensen that he alone was the real promoter of the alliance and that the decoration by right belonged to him. Ciano promised Mackensen he would try to obtain the same award for Göring.[13]

Ribbentrop gave a party for Ciano that night in his villa in the exclusive Dahlem area of Berlin, and invited a number of very beautiful women. Afterward Ciano quoted Hitler as having said of Ribbentrop to Signora Attolico, wife of the ambassador: "Whatever else may be said about him, it must be admitted that this man has a swelled head."[14] Mussolini had once said of Ribbentrop that one only had to look at his head to see what a small brain he had. Before leaving Berlin, Ciano visited the so-called Salon Kitty, a richly furnished private house in one of the most elegant quarters of Berlin, which had been set up by Reinhard Heydrich, the chief of the security police and deputy chief of the Gestapo, as a place where important foreign visitors and leading German bigwigs could enjoy themselves in the company of the opposite sex. Seductive, cultivated women were available, and the rooms to which they escorted the visitors were bugged. Walter Schellenberg, a high official of the Nazi secret service, said the salon, run by Frau Kitty Schmidt, was "of undoubted utility; some guests revealed surprising information . . . that Heydrich, with his usual astuteness, exploited to the damage of Ribbentrop and the Ministry of Foreign Affairs . . . One of the most notable prey was Count Ciano, who went there with other important diplomats."[15]

On May 23, the morning Ciano left Berlin, Hitler told his collaborators: "For the attack on Poland, secrecy is a fundamental requirement of success. The attack must be kept hidden even from Italy and Japan."[16] Five days later, Mussolini gave Ciano a memorandum to pass on to Hitler, specifying that Italy would not be militarily prepared for conflict before 1943. The memorandum, delivered to Berlin by General Ugo Cavallero, the chief of staff, went unanswered. But Ciano was not then worried that Italy would be dragged into war. He told Giuseppe Bastianini after signing the Pact of Steel that it had no implications for Poland, because the Germans "understand very well that Warsaw is not Prague."[17] That mistaken view encouraged Ciano to ignore Attolico's increasingly urgent warnings.

Upon Ciano's departure from Berlin, King Victor Emanuel sent him a telegram, expressing his "warmest pleasure" at his achievement. He had thought to make Ciano a marquis but was dissuaded by Mussolini, who said this could only harm Ciano before the great masses of the party. Later the king noted that it was the first time he had ever sent a telegram to a minister. Why he should want to congratulate Ciano on achievement of the pact is unclear, for he had no illusions about the Germans. "While they need us, the Germans will be courteous and even servile," he told Ciano. "But at the first opportunity, they will reveal what rogues they are."[18] Ciano noted in his diary that the Pact of Steel was more popular in Germany than in Italy. "We must recognize that hatred for France has not yet succeeded in creating love for Germany," he wrote.[19]

On June 26 Costanzo Ciano died unexpectedly of a heart attack, just short of his sixty-third birthday, after having consumed a huge dinner at a Livorno restaurant. He had had a mild heart attack a month previously, but told a friend then that he gave no thought to death. Both the king and Mussolini came to Livorno to pay their respects, and the Duce gave Ciano a document he had written in November 1926, designating Costanzo as his successor in case of his sudden death. Ciano, devastated by his father's passing, devoted a six-and-a-half-page soliloquy in his diary to Costanzo. It was the most personal and emotional entry of the entire diary. On July 10, taking a ship to Spain for an official visit, he reproached himself bitterly, in a conversation with a friend, over his arrogant treatment of his father. Costanzo, he said, had sometimes been eager to know about his work and his meetings with Mussolini, and he had been short with his father and implied that "certain questions were not within his competence." "Is it possible to be more stupid than sons are with their fathers?" he said. "These are things that, when I think of them, believe me, I scourge myself, and they rise in my throat above all now, being here on the sea, in waters where he will have passed so often . . . So many times I failed to give him any satisfaction. So little was required, if there was important news . . . to refer it to him first . . . He would have been happy for a month . . . These are the mortal sins of the sons."[20]

Sir Andrew Noble of the British Foreign Office, who had served in Italy, wrote a memorandum after Costanzo's death which said he was widely assumed to have accumulated a large fortune "by the misuse of official information if nothing worse." He added: "Count Galeazzo Ciano, whose scruples are no more delicate than his father's, may have been inclined to adopt a pro-German policy partly by the prospect of personal profit: I would not put it beyond him. I do not think that Count Ciano's financial operations would bear too close investigation."[21]

Newsweek magazine put Ciano on its cover on March 6, 1939, showing him in military uniform. Reporting on his recent travels, it said: "Behind the scenes his hosts have found him amiable, less of a lightweight than gossip represented and able to discard when required the pompous air he wears as a famous son-in-law."[22] In fact, his crude behavior continued to attract comment and lessen his standing among the Italian people. That very month, at the coronation of Pope Pius XII, he strutted down the center aisle of St. Peter's Basilica, giving the Fascist salute and waving to the crowds as though he were at a political rally. Many were scandalized.

On July 24, it was Edda's turn to appear on an American news magazine cover. *Time* described her as "one of Europe's most successful intriguers and string-pullers." It said the role she had played in recent realignments in Europe "has been half concealed by a regime which refuses to admit women in politics," but offered no evidence to support that fanciful claim. "Of the Mussolini children, Edda is easily the most outstanding in ability, personality and intelligence," the magazine said. *Time* also reported that Edda was not popular with Italians. "Once Edda went to the cinema in Rome during her eighth month of pregnancy, and was publicly applauded," it said. "Doubtful it is if such a demonstration would now occur. The Countess is held by many Italians to be largely responsible for the Nazified laws that Italy has 'imported' from Germany."[23] Journalists were not alone in speculating about Edda's supposed powers. The American ambassador in Paris, William Bullitt, had cabled the State Department four months earlier: "Mussolini's daughter has the greatest influence over him as well as Ciano, and the influence is far from good."[24] The *Time* article was also less than flattering toward Ciano. It said that, before his marriage to Edda, he liked to hang around the Excelsior and Grand hotels, where rich U.S. heiresses generally stayed. It also implied that his father had been corrupt. The Ciano family fortune was small before Galeazzo married Edda, it said, but when Costanzo died "it was estimated one of the greatest in Italy."

Ciano apparently had not blinked when Mussolini told him to have Italian prisoners in Spain shot at the end of the war, but in Vitoria on July 15 he was appalled to find Republican prisoners held in miserable conditions and expressed pity for them. "They are no longer prisoners of war, they are slaves of war," he told one of his aides.[25] He urged Franco to resolve the problem as quickly as possible, but got no satisfaction. Immediately upon his return from Spain on July 18, he was confronted anew by the Polish problem. Attolico sent Ciano a fresh warning of "a new and perhaps fatal crisis," and on July 20 reported that the Germans were preparing to strike at Danzig by August 14.[26] The Italian minister in Prague, Caruso, also reported large-scale troop movements. Ciano couldn't take it in. "Is it possible that all this should take place without our knowledge after so many protestations of peace made by our Axis comrades?" he wrote. "We shall see."[27]

Earlier, Mussolini had outlined a plan to settle the Danzig problem through a plebiscite, but Ciano told him he thought it was "rather utopian."[28] In July, Mussolini proposed to Hitler a conference of the leaders of Italy, Germany, Britain, France, Spain and Poland to resolve the crisis. Ribbentrop assured Attolico that Germany wanted to avoid conflicts, but said the proposal was not acceptable. On July 21, Massimo Magistrati, on the staff of the Italian Embassy in Berlin, assured Ciano that Attolico "permitted himself to be carried away by a not entirely justified fit of panic." Ciano felt relieved, and recorded the next day: "I am skeptical, very skeptical, now about Attolico, who has lost his head."[29] The judgment was not simply mistaken; it showed an astounding lack of confidence in a veteran diplomat who had earned the right to be taken more seriously. Attolico was one of Italy's leading economists at the time of World War I, and helped negotiate the economic clauses of the Versailles treaty. He went on to a distinguished career in diplomacy, first as an under-secretary at the League of Nations, then commissioner of Danzig. When Mussolini came to power, he appointed Attolico as Italy's ambassador to the League, then made him ambassador to Germany in 1935. Attolico was a man of impeccable democratic credentials who despised the Nazi leaders, particularly for their persecution of the Jews. He referred to the German leaders privately as "dangerous clowns who know nothing of the world," and said that in Italy there were "no longer men with a sense of responsibility." He repeatedly told Ribbentrop that he was wrong in thinking that a German move against Poland would not provoke a general war.[30]

Attolico's warnings to Ciano about German intentions were usually hand-delivered by a Carabiniere officer attached to the embassy in Berlin. Despite this precaution, the contents of his reports regularly got back to the Germans. His son, Count Bartolomeo Attolico, thinks the Germans paid someone to look at the reports on Ciano's desk, but it may be that Ciano himself showed them to the German ambassador. In any event, Ribbentrop started to complain to Attolico: "How dare you write such things?"[31] On July 28 Ciano dismissed yet another warning from Attolico about German intentions. "Too bad," he wrote. "This ambassador has done good work. He has let himself be carried away by the war panic."[32] On August 2, Attolico reported that Hitler was planning to act against Poland on August 15. For the first time, Ciano's own conviction was tinged by doubt. "Either this ambassador has entirely lost his head or he sees and knows something that completely escapes us," he wrote. ". . . It is necessary to observe events carefully."[33] The next day, Ciano received a private letter from Magistrati, again minimizing the danger of a German attack. On the other hand, General Mario Roatta, the Italian military attaché in Berlin, informed him of a concentration of forces on the Polish frontier. "Who is right?" Ciano asked. "I may be mistaken, but I continue to feel optimistic."[34] On August 4, with Attolico continuing to bombard him with warnings, Ciano admitted he no longer knew what to believe. "The moment has come to know truly how things stand," he concluded.[35]

Two days later the king informed a startled Mussolini that he intended to give Ciano the Collar of the Annunciation. Mussolini was opposed, and called in Ciano to warn him not to accept it. But a few days later, under pressure from Edda that may have been orchestrated by Ciano himself, Mussolini gave his consent. The award was not popular with the Italian public. In London, Sir Andrew Noble commented in a memorandum that there was reason to doubt "whether the King of Italy really appreciates having to debase the highest order at his disposal by bestowing it on such men as Herr von Ribbentrop and Count Ciano."[36] On the day the king announced the award, Edda was in Venice. During her stay there, Barbara Hutton invited her to lunch along with Elsa Maxwell. Edda asked Maxwell how she liked Venice and she replied, "I've always liked Venice since I came the first time in 1919. But today I like it less because it pains me to hear so much German spoken." Edda laughed and replied, "You are wrong. You must know that the Germans will be with us in the next war. And without doubt you Americans will be with us too when we make war on England, because there are more Italians in New York than in Milan." Maxwell smiled and said, "Let's wait and see. But I fear you don't know America. The Americans would always be on the side of the English, even if they were in the wrong."[37]

Ciano had another talk with Mussolini about Poland on August 6. He wrote afterward that, if war came, Italy would go into it unprepared militarily and economically, its gold reserves reduced to almost nothing along with its stocks of metals. "If the crisis comes we will fight if only to save our 'honor,'" he wrote. "But it's better to avoid it."[38] He proposed a meeting with Ribbentrop to clarify the situation, and Mussolini agreed. Two days later Magistrati again came through with a soothing message. "He does not foresee any immediate aggressive intentions on the part of Germany, even though the Danzig situation is grave and dangerous," Ciano wrote.[39] But his own uncertainty was about to end. On August 11, he arrived in Salzburg for his showdown with Ribbentrop.

Chapter Eight

The Invasion of Poland

En route to Salzburg by train, for what would prove the most important meeting of his career, Ciano, in the company of Mackensen and his own aides, rehearsed what he would say to Ribbentrop. "You all understand that this is no time for war; nobody would gain anything by going to war. Not even Germany . . . She has won the 1914 war without refighting it. But what a fatal mistake it would be to draw the sword!" Ciano expressed confidence that Germany could get Danzig and the corridor without going to war, and could get her colonies back. "We will talk to the English, to the French, to the Poles. We will persuade them," he said. He also drew attention to Italy's unpreparedness. "The ordnance stores are empty, the artillery obsolete, the aviation not ready and scarce, people are tired," he said. "In seven, eight years, then we will see." He abruptly turned to Mackensen and said, "Of course, if Germany wants us to, then we will go for England and for France and break their backs and win." Ciano noticed that Marcello del Drago and Leonardo Vitetti were crestfallen at that last remark. He gave them a wink and said, "But even Germany doesn't want war. I tell you. I know it."[1]

Before his departure from Rome, Mussolini had instructed him to warn the Germans that a war at that time would be madness. "Our preparation is not such as to allow us to believe that victory would be assured," the Duce said. "We must avoid a conflict with Poland, since it will be impossible to localize it, and a general war would be disastrous for everybody."[2] When he arrived in Salzburg, wearing the uniform of a general of the militia, Ciano was asked by an Italian journalist if there would be war. "Well, if I manage to see 'little moustache,' I will remove that idea from his head," Ciano confided.[3] He changed into civilian clothes and proceeded to Fuschl castle, the summer residence of Ribbentrop on a lake twelve miles outside Salzburg. Ciano and Ribbentrop met alone under a trellis in the garden of the villa before lunch. Ribbentrop opened the discussion by telling him the Polish government had clearly repeated its intention of denying Berlin any right to mix in matters concerning Danzig. Ribbentrop expressed his indignation and affirmed that the German reaction must be destructive. Ciano protested energetically. Coming out of the meeting, he whispered to Magistrati, "We've come to blows!" To del Drago he said, "It's going badly."⁴ The two ministers went into lunch with their aides, but the atmosphere was icy. Ribbentrop, to fill the void, began talking about hunting and fishing. At 3.15 p.m. the ministers resumed formal discussions in Ribbentrop's study and talked until 6.30 p.m., with a brief break for tea in which Frau von Ribbentrop participated. Ciano asked if Hitler wanted Danzig or the entire corridor as well. "Yesterday perhaps," Ribbentrop replied. "Today we want much more. We want war."⁵ Ciano was startled. The Germans had abandoned their subterfuge; there would be no three- or four-year interval of peace and military buildup. Ciano advanced counter-arguments for a postponement and showed Ribbentrop a communiqué prepared by Mussolini calling for an international conference to settle the matter. But the German was unyielding. He said Italy should take advantage of the situation to settle accounts with Yugoslavia in Croatia and Dalmatia, and hinted at negotiations under way between Berlin and Moscow. "The conflict will be localized," he told Ciano. Even if France and England were to intervene, he added, a German victory would be certain. Ribbentrop became irritated when Ciano argued the point, and said, "Then would you like to bet? If France and England don't move, you give me an antique Italian painting. If instead they should take the field alongside Poland, I will give you a collection of historic arms." Ciano readily accepted.⁶ Paul Schmidt wrote afterward: "Ciano, though he spoke like an angel, and underlined Italy's weakness, made no impression on Ribbentrop, who was like a hound at the leash, raging against England, France and Poland, and boasting grotesquely about the might of Germany."⁷

Nearly sixty years later one of Ciano's aides, now an old man reminiscing over tea in his Roman apartment about that historic meeting, recalled the scene. As Ciano and Ribbentrop ended their talk and started down a staircase—Italian officials lined up on the right side, Germans on the left—the aide saw immediately that Ciano was furious. As Ciano passed, he whispered to the aide, "These people are mad. They want war!" "He was shocked, taken aback," the aide recalled.⁸ The die was cast, and for Galeazzo Ciano nothing would ever be the same again. The Salzburg meeting would alter his thinking about the alliance with Germany, and the course of his life. He had behaved with extraordinary gullibility, and the humiliation he now felt would never leave him.

That evening Ciano, speaking to the journalist Gaetano Polverelli about Ribbentrop, said: "It's useless to talk to that man. I've known him for years. He has few ideas and is as hard as granite. The striking thing about him is that he doesn't understand the real situation and is impervious to the sound reasoning of others . . . I asked Ribbentrop how many submarines Germany has. He didn't know how to answer. Here is a responsible minister who risks war against one of the great naval powers and he is ignorant of the number of submarines his nation can deploy . . . According to him, public opinion in the United States has become favorable to Germany after German propaganda circulated a booklet in two and a half million copies! Can one believe in such miracles?"[9]

The Germans entertained the Italians to dinner at a famous restaurant, the Weisse Rössl, beside the lake of Sant Wolfgang. Ciano sat on the right of Frau Ribbentrop, facing his host, but did not talk to either of them throughout dinner. After returning to Salzburg, Ciano and his aides gathered in his bathroom, hoping it would not be bugged. Attolico suggested breaking off the alliance with Germany but Ciano, knowing full well that Mussolini would not agree, rejected the idea. Ciano said he was determined to prevent Ribbentrop from issuing a communiqué which would bind Italy to fight at Germany's side. Before retiring, he wrote in his diary: "Ribbentrop is evasive whenever I asked him for particulars about the coming German actions. He has a bad conscience . . . The will to fight is implacable . . . I am certain that even if the Germans were given more than they ask for they would attack just the same, because they are possessed by the demon of destruction . . . I do not hesitate to express my thoughts in the most brutal manner. But this does not move him in the least. I understand how little we are worth in the opinion of the Germans . . . I, at least, have a clear conscience. He has not."[10]

Next morning, the Italians met Hitler at Berchtesgaden. Hitler appeared tired, pale, absent-minded and rather nervous. After a quick lunch that proceeded in virtual silence, he and Ciano talked for three and a quarter hours, with Ribbentrop, Dollmann and Schmidt present. Del Drago described it as "the most remarkable gathering of scar-faced villains collected around the one-time, disloyal subject of Kaiser Franz Josef. The sinister-looking, ex-champagne peddler, Joachim von Ribbentrop, was also there, standing alone and aloof like the bad, evil, domineering spirit of the whole place."[11] Hitler, standing before a large table covered with military staff maps, began by explaining that Germany's West Wall was impenetrable. He added that Britain could put only three divisions into France, and Poland would be defeated "in a very short time." Germany could then concentrate one hundred divisions in the West "for the life-and-death struggle which would then commence." Ciano expressed surprise, complained that Italy had not been kept fully informed, and warned that a

Polish conflict would bring Britain and France into a general European war. Hitler interrupted to say he "knew" the two nations would not intervene. "I've never been mistaken," he said. Ciano replied, "I have made many mistakes, and I hope I am mistaken now." He argued forcefully that Italy was not prepared for war and, at one point, Ribbentrop interjected disdainfully: "We don't need you!" Ciano replied, "The future will show."[12] Ciano said one of Mussolini's reasons for wanting to postpone the war was that he attached great importance to holding the World Exhibition of 1942 in Rome. He produced a draft communiqué stating that the meeting of Axis ministers had reaffirmed a belief that peace could be maintained through normal diplomatic negotiations. But it was too late for that. Ciano tried to pin down Hitler on the date of an attack on Poland. Hitler replied that the settlement with Poland would have to be made one way or the other by the end of August. After that, he said, mist and mud would make roads and airfields on the Polish front unusable.[13]

Dollmann has provided the most colorful account of this meeting:

The weather matched the mood. The celebrated view of the Führer's Austrian homeland was obscured by thick cloud, and this was the first such occasion on which the preliminaries, at least, were conducted standing up. Such were the circumstances under which Ciano delivered his great anti-war speech. His remarks were those of a responsible states-man and thus diametrically opposed to what the German side wished to hear at that juncture.

His central theme was the fact that it was impossible, materially and politically, militarily and psychologically, for Italy to participate in a war at this early stage. She had, in effect, been waging war for years on end. What with the intervention in the Spanish Civil War and the conquest of the Abyssinian Empire, the Italian people had been pushed into one armed conflict after another, and the result was a pronounced degree of war-weariness. In addition, these years had virtually exhausted Italy's scanty stocks of material. Her arsenals were empty and her reserves of gold and foreign exchange too slender to permit of an arms buildup . . .

The reaction was predictable. The Count, who remained quite calm and composed, was bombarded with references to German disgrace, German humiliation—and all at the hands of the Poles . . . Ciano responded by asking for a glass of mineral water, a request which I hastened to fulfill so as to avoid the seemingly inevitable storm to come.

But the storm never broke. In the nick of time, as Hitler was pacing nervously up and down and Ribbentrop stood wrapped in antique gran-deur like a Homeric god of war and Ciano was starting to scratch himself—always a sign of extreme agitation—the miracle occurred. The door opened and Hewel of the Foreign Office rushed in. He whispered to his chief, who in his turn whispered to Hitler. Brows cleared and hostilities were postponed.[14]

The German minutes of the meeting stated that "a telegram from Moscow" was handed to Hitler by Hewel, and they quoted the Führer as telling Ciano: "The Russians have agreed to a German political negotiator being sent to Moscow." The "telegram" was missing from German archives after the war, and may never have existed.[15] The Soviets tried subsequently to stall Hitler's demand for negotiations, and the nonaggression pact between the two countries was not signed until August 23. But Hitler's declaration to Ciano served the purpose of convincing the Italian minister that the Nazis could launch war without having to worry about the Soviet reaction. After the private talks, Hitler joined the larger party of Italian and German officials waiting in the garden, cracking jokes and talking of his fondness for vegetables and children and flowers. "About the coming war and Poland not a word was said, and in vain did Ciano try . . . to bring up the subject over and over again," del Drago said.[16] After the meeting Hitler's mistress, Eva Braun, stayed at the window of her room to photograph Ciano with her telephoto lens. She did not hesitate to say later she found him attractive, and wanted to be introduced to him, but Hitler refused. Eva began collecting photographs of Ciano, and admonished Hitler for not dressing with the Italian count's elegance. Ciano saw her at the window, and asked Ribbentrop her name. Ribbentrop's reply was evasive, and Hitler dispatched an SS man to tell Eva to close her window.[17]

Following that first meeting, Ciano confided to his diary: "[Hitler] has decided to strike, and strike he will . . . He continues to repeat that he will localize the conflict with Poland, but his affirmation that the great war must be fought while he and the Duce are still young leads me to believe once more that he is acting in bad faith . . . I feel that as far as the Germans are concerned an alliance with us means only that the enemy will be obliged to keep a certain number of divisions facing us, thus easing the situation on the German war fronts. They care for nothing else. The fate that might befall us does not interest them in the least. They know that the decision will be forced by them rather than by us. And finally, they are promising us only a beggarly pittance."[18] Ciano telephoned Mussolini that evening and told him the situation was serious. Referring to Hitler, he said, "He says he wants a corridor, but he's going to take the whole apartment." Aware that their conversation was probably being overheard by the Germans, he promised to provide more details when he was back in Rome.[19]

Dinner that evening was another difficult occasion. Ribbentrop kept everyone waiting for two hours, and Ciano was furious. Del Drago wrote: "Vitetti would go by a life-size portrait of Hitler hanging in the hotel hall and say 'Schwein' . . . and then pretend to tremble in his pants when I would tell him that the SS had overheard him. Finally and theatrically Ribbentrop was announced and came on stage, I mean, in the room, with a telegram in his hand. He was very excited, with a strange light gleaming in his fanatical eyes. Somehow he missed his cue because he had to wait for Ciano who, managing a little revenge of his own, had gone up to his room." When the party finally gathered, Ribbentrop repeated Hitler's earlier announcement that Germany and Russia had agreed to open negotiations for a political accord, and he would be off to Moscow in a few days to sign it. This came as a surprise to most of the Italians, indicating Ciano had not informed them of what Hitler had said in their *tête-à-tête* meeting. Del Drago recorded the reaction: "A bombshell. Explosions of joy in the German camp. Hell and damnation in ours. Ciano with a wooden face congratulating Ribbentrop. Vitetti pale green behind his spectacles." Ribbentrop produced a communiqué on "the action and common decision of the two countries," but Ciano said, "I can't sign it. I must report to Mussolini. The communiqué involves too important an issue. The Duce must know. It means war for my country." Ribbentrop suggested he telephone Mussolini immediately, but Ciano refused.[20]

The talks with Hitler resumed the next morning on the Obersalzberg, and lasted only half an hour. Hitler told Ciano any communiqué would be inopportune. He repeated much of what he had said the previous day, and announced that an attack on Poland was imminent. Ribbentrop chimed in to say Russia was "perfectly informed" of German intentions toward Poland. Schmidt, who observed that Ciano had stood up to Hitler "very energetically" the previous day, said Ciano now "made no further effort to impress Mussolini's advice on Hitler. He said no more of Italy's incapacity for taking part in hostilities. Quite inexplicably, he folded up like a jackknife. 'You have been proved right so often before when we others held the opposite view,' he said, 'that I think it very possible that this time, too, you see things more clearly than we do.' Ciano did not point out that Italy was entitled, by virtue of her treaty with Germany, to insist upon a common decision on the attitude to be taken regarding Poland."[21]

Schmidt's impression of Ciano's obsequious behavior was confirmed by Dollmann. "Ciano was a changed man," he said. "All the cool decisiveness and statesmanlike discernment of the previous day had vanished. He seemed totally inert, and listened apathetically to Hitler's renewed assurances that England and France would never go to war on Poland's account – assurances which Ribbentrop confirmed with a vigorous nod." The cynical Dollmann said Ciano's "brief moment of heroism" at Obersalzberg was "only a flash in the pan: by the following day all was forgotten. He skated gracefully along the razor's edge, quickly repenting of his sounder judgments in the arms of some Roman duchess or princess." Dollmann saw correctly that Ciano's attitude toward Germany had changed irrevocably. "Count Ciano had never been a friend of Germany," he said. "I do not think he would have understood—or tried to understand—the Germans of the Kaiser's day or the Weimar Republic any better than he understood his National Socialist allies. From the moment of his return from the Obersalzberg, he became an avowed enemy who balked at nothing in his efforts to sabotage the pact which he himself had negotiated."[22]

Hitler ended the conference by telling Ciano he felt fortunate to live at a time when, apart from himself, there lived another statesman who would stand out in history as a great and unique figure. He would always be at the side of the Duce, he affirmed. Ciano and the Germans agreed there would be no communiqué but as he flew back to Rome in the afternoon, the *Deutsches Nachrichten Büro*, the German press agency, put out a communiqué declaring the two sides had reached full agreement. Ciano arrived in Rome at 5 p.m. and quickly telephoned Mussolini. The Italian secret service recorded their conversation:

Ciano: Duce, I would have wanted to send you a coded message, but for reasons that you well know I didn't consider it opportune.
Mussolini: But here there is a communiqé of the *Nachrichten Büro* that speaks of one hundred percent agreement on all problems.
C.: It's false.
M.: How could they say that?
C.: I spoke with my colleague there, who is not only an idiot but also a big blockhead and ignorant. He wasn't even able to respond to the reasons I expounded, in line with what you ordered and we had agreed.
M.: And the other [Hitler]?
C.: He fully recognized our good reasons and has given assurances that he will not ask for our help. Then there was another very brief talk, in which both he and I remained firm in our respective positions.
M.: But the story of the communiqué?
C.: The usual lie.
M.: For the rest, what are their attitudes?
C.: To the extent I was able to understand and detect, that fanatic seeks the excuse of the corridor but intends to expel the inhabitants of the entire apartment. That, perhaps, in agreement with the bear.
M.: Then he is a criminal!
C.: It is not to be ruled out that, immediately afterward, he will address

his desires toward our sister on the left. And it would not even be hazardous to think that, since the appetite must be fed, he also wants a vacation spot on the sea, on the Adriatic side, toward San Giusto.

M.: But that could cause him indigestion.[23]

Ciano gave Mussolini a fuller report that night at the Palazzo Venezia, then recorded in his diary: "I return to Rome disgusted with Germany, with its leaders, with their way of doing things. They have deceived us and lied to us. And today they are about to drag us into an adventure which we do not want and which may compromise the regime and the country. The Italian people will tremble in horror when they know about the aggression against Poland and will most probably want to fight the Germans . . . I think our hands are free, and I propose that we act accordingly, declaring that we have no intention of participating in a war which we have neither wanted nor provoked. The Duce's reactions are varied. At first he agrees with me. Then he says honor compels him to march with Germany. Finally, he states that he wants his part of the booty in Croatia and Dalmatia."[24]

The relationship between Ciano and Mussolini was about to begin its fatal downward course. There would be growing differences over policy toward Germany, and an increasing lack of confidence of the two men in each other. Ciano tried to convince Mussolini that the Germans were traitors, and that Italy should have no scruples about ditching them. At one point Mussolini concluded that Italy must not march blindly with Germany, but argued that he needed time to prepare a break. Three days later he feared that a denunciation of the Pact of Steel might induce Hitler to forget about Poland and attack Italy instead. Ciano drafted a letter for Mussolini asking the Germans to reconsider their plan of attack. But it came back from Palazzo Venezia with a long red pencil mark drawn along its length by Mussolini. "Mussolini's hold over him was finished," del Drago concluded.[25] Ciano, talking to his friend Pavolini, described Hitler and Ribbentrop as "two madmen" who wanted "the destruction of the world."[26] Ciano told André François-Poncet that Poland must give in to Germany's demands and cede Danzig. François-Poncet objected that Danzig was the symbol of European freedom, but Ciano considered France and England impotent. "They will seem like someone who throws a rock at a lion that is about to devour a man," he told the ambassador. "The man, all the same, will be devoured."[27]

During the final days of that gloomy summer, Ciano was in Viareggio, and warned some journalist friends that war would begin at the end of the month. "What is necessary now is to stop Mussolini from throwing us immediately into the affray," he said. "But I know the fanaticism of

Mussolini and above all his fear of not arriving in time. Tremendous days lie ahead."[28] On August 21, Ciano made one of his most energetic attempts to influence Mussolini, telling him: "Tear up the Pact. Throw it in Hitler's face and Europe will recognize in you the natural leader of the anti-German crusade. Do you want me to go to Salzburg? Very well, I shall go and shall speak to the Germans as they should be spoken to. Hitler will not make me put out my cigarette as he did Schuschnigg."[29] Mussolini was, for the moment, impressed. He agreed Ciano should invite Ribbentrop to meet him at the Brenner Pass and should reaffirm Italy's rights in the Axis partnership. Ciano tried to phone Ribbentrop, couldn't get through, and beat his hands on his desk, shouting, "We will never make war alongside these rascals."[30] When he finally reached him, the German said he could not give an answer at once because he was "waiting for an important message from Moscow."[31] Later in the day, the Germans and Soviets announced their intention to sign a nonaggression pact, and Ribbentrop phoned back to say he would prefer to meet at Innsbruck because he had to leave for Moscow to sign the agreement, which would become known as the Molotov-Ribbentrop pact. Ciano decided to forego a meeting until Ribbentrop had returned from Moscow. Suddenly he, the fierce opponent of war, was like Mussolini, thinking of war booty. "There is no doubt the Germans have struck a master blow . . . We must wait, and, if possible, be ready ourselves to gain something in Croatia and Dalmatia," he wrote in his diary.[32] Mario Luciolli said the Molotov-Ribbentrop Pact convinced Ciano and Mussolini that France and England would not dare to go to war against Germany, and that Italy should remain at Germany's side. That evening, he said, Ciano stayed in his office until midnight with two aides, "making projects for the partition of Europe and enjoying the prospect of the new humiliation of the democratic countries." But he said Ciano's enthusiasm for the pact had vanished two days later, and he tried to persuade Mussolini to break the link with Germany as soon as possible.[33]

On August 23, a day of blistering summer heat, Mussolini authorized Ciano to present to Sir Percy Loraine, the new British ambassador, a plan based on a preliminary return of Danzig to Germany, to be followed by negotiations and a great peace conference. Ciano wrote afterward: "I do not know whether it was the emotion or the heat, but it is a fact that Percy Loraine fainted or almost fainted in my arms." But by that evening the volatile Mussolini was once again talking of going to war. General Alberto Pariani, the under-secretary of war, informed him the army was in good shape. "Pariani is a traitor and a liar," Ciano observed in his diary.[34]

Two days later, Mussolini was persuaded by Ciano he should send a message to Hitler announcing Italy's nonintervention. But by the time Ciano had returned to his office, Mussolini summoned him back. He had changed his mind again. When Ciano got back to his office a second time, Mackensen telephoned to say he wanted to see him. At 2 p.m., Ciano escorted Mackensen to the Palazzo Venezia with a message from Hitler, hinting at an early attack on Poland and asking not for Italian participation but for "understanding." Ciano persuaded Mussolini to reply that Italy would go to war only if Germany furnished the war supplies and raw materials needed. Mackensen, according to Ciano, was hostile to Germany's upcoming military adventure and urged Ciano to make out a complete list, hoping this would put brakes on German intentions. On August 26, after a meeting between Ciano and military leaders, the list was ready. "It's enough to kill a bull—if he could read it," Ciano noted.[35] It asked for 17 million tons of supplies and 17,000 vehicles. Attolico, delivering the message to the Germans in Berlin, added a line that he felt confident would ensure a German rejection—he said Italy needed all these supplies "immediately." Hitler reacted as he had hoped. He offered Italy iron, coal and timber, and a few antiaircraft batteries, and said he would annihilate Poland without Italian help, then go on to defeat France and Britain. Mussolini was immediately disturbed at not being involved, but Ciano expressed relief.

The next day, the British government communicated to Italy the text of a German proposal that the Germans had concealed from the Italians. "Hitler proposes to the English an alliance or something like it," Ciano noted in his diary. "I am indignant and say so. The Duce is indignant but does not show it ... Starace, with his intellectual and moral shortsightedness, has the cheek to tell Mussolini that Italian women are happy about the war because they are going to receive six lire a day and will not have their husbands under their feet. How shameful! The Italian people do not deserve such a vulgar insult."[36] Mussolini put an egocentric interpretation on the German proposal. He decided the Germans were seeking an agreement with Britain because they feared he would intervene and settle the crisis at the last moment, raising his prestige and provoking Hitler's jealousy. Ciano's own interpretation was simply that the Germans were treacherous and deceitful. As for Ribbentrop: "Is it possible to be more piglike than Ribbentrop?"[37]

In these last days of August, Prime Minister Daladier and Foreign Minister Paul Reynaud would sometimes telephone Ciano in the middle of the night, urging a conference or anything that would prevent war. On August 29, Warsaw ordered general mobilization, and Danzig proclaimed itself a

German city. Rome experienced its first blackout of the war the following night.

At 10 a.m. on August 31, Giuseppe Bottai telephoned Ciano and said: "I want to let you know, with my voice, that I am close to you." Ciano replied: "The situation is closed. It's a question of hours. We would need a miracle."[38] Shortly afterward, Ciano told François-Poncet that all was lost; the war was unstoppable. But an hour later, at 12.35 p.m., he telephoned to say that Mussolini wanted to meet with the leaders of France and Britain on September 5 in San Remo to examine the clauses of the Versailles treaty that were the cause of the present troubles. It was a last, desperate attempt to save the peace.[39]

At 7.30 that evening, Bottai called on Ciano at his office. Like many Fascists, Bottai, one of the leading intellectuals of fascism, had initially regarded Ciano as an upstart imposed on the movement by Mussolini. But their common concern about the coming war had drawn them together. As he entered a salon in the Palazzo Chigi, Ciano embraced him, put his arm around his waist, drew him to a wall between two closed windows, and seated him on a bench. Bottai could see from his eyes that he had not slept, and perhaps had wept. Ciano fell down heavily beside him and began an extraordinary soliloquy, which Bottai said he heard with a mixture of pain, disgust, irony and apprehension.

"I am here, inert," Ciano began. "At 1 o'clock I telephoned to London and Paris, proposing a European conference. No reply. We, you understand, must not and cannot intervene. We must not. Germany has acted against our agreements. I broke with that madman Ribbentrop at Salzburg. I reminded him that our alliance foresaw a period of rest until 1942. That an immediate action for Danzig would mean a European war. We do not have any obligation to intervene. And I add: no interest . . . Are we in a condition to do it? No, no, no. There are terrible deficiencies. We have thirteen thousand cannon, of which more than four thousand . . . have a range of less than six thousand meters. Valle . . . goes around shouting he doesn't have fighters and can sustain only fifty days of combat . . . Cavagnari* . . . declares that the Italian Navy is ready to get itself sunk: the proportion with English and French ships . . . is 6 to 1 . . . The truth is that we are not ready. You need a clown like Starace to say the opposite. And he says it, unfortunately, he says it to the Duce, falsifying the truth."[40]

---

* Admiral Domenico Cavagnari, the Navy chief of staff.

At one point he looked out into the darkened streets of Rome: Mussolini had not only imposed blackouts but closed restaurants and recalled men to arms, all steps that led the French and British to believe Italy was preparing for war. Ciano told Bottai these measures were stupid. "It would be enough to turn on the lights, and our situation would be clarified. Literally clarified," he said. As he spoke Anfuso entered and announced that France and Britain had cut off telephone communications with Italy. Ciano, angry, stalked off in the direction of Palazzo Venezia accompanied by Bottai. "In the utter darkness, he pants beside me like a man wounded," Bottai noted in his diary. "The first wounded man of the impending war." They encountered del Drago and Ciano ordered him to come along. "I'm going to stop this damn foolishness," he said.[41] Del Drago described what followed:

"Expanding his chest, he strode majestically into Mussolini's anteroom. 'I want to see the Duce,' he said to the attendant. 'He's busy,' answered the man. 'I don't care, I want to see him immediately, do you hear?' . . . Then noticing Alfieri and Starace, who had gotten up from the chairs they were sitting on and were giving him the Fascist salute, he flew at them: 'And you idiots, fools, imbeciles with no more sense than a cow in those dunce heads of yours—you egg him on, you make him do all this.' And then dramatically: 'Don't you know that telephone communications with France and England are cut and that tomorrow we may have French and English planes over us bombing Rome? Just because an old man surrounded by foolish and dishonest knaves has gone back to his infancy.' The pair stood gaping and stuttering like two flunkeys before an irate master. He went on for five minutes. When he had exhausted his bag of insults, without waiting to be called in he opened Mussolini's door and forced his way in like an angry bull."[42]

What happened then is unrecorded. But Ciano went back to the Palazzo Chigi, turned on all the lights, threw open his three big windows facing Piazza Colonna and said, "At least Romans may see some light from here, from my windows." He summoned the British and French ambassadors and told them Italy would not go to war. The phone lines were reconnected and the lights of Rome came on again.[43] Ribbentrop later accused Ciano of having provoked the French and British to go to war with his indiscretion to the two ambassadors.

At 1.50 a.m. on Friday, September 1, French Foreign Minister Georges Bonnet responded to Mussolini's proposal for a conference at San Remo.

France accepted, on condition that Poland would also participate. But it was too late.[44] At 4.45 a.m., German troops crossed the frontier into Poland. In the half light of early morning, the first of the fifty million people who would die in World War II had fallen. Later that morning, Mussolini convened his Cabinet to announce that Italy would not participate in the war. After the meeting, a relieved Ciano told Bottai: "Now we must return to normality. And, in this normality, work. With our merchant fleet we can make money; and, with money, arms. We will outfit ourselves. We shouldn't have any illusions. We will have five or six years of war. We will have to intervene. When and how, we will see. And we will see with whom. If Germany, for example, draws Russia into Europe, the situation will have to be reviewed entirely."[45]

Dino Grandi was, like Bottai, now drawn to Ciano because of his opposition to the war. After the Cabinet meeting Grandi, who had served as ambassador to Britain and was regarded as an Anglophile, called on Ciano and told him he thought Britain shared a responsibility for the outbreak of war. "Ciano does not agree. He defends England energetically. I seem to be dreaming! I, the 'Anglicized,' I, the 'Anglo-maniac,' I, the ambassador driven from London a month ago to please the Germans . . . today I find myself almost being accused of tepidness toward England. And that coming from Ciano, the author about three months ago of the alliance with Germany, the Axis, the Pact of Steel, today suddenly the furious enemy of the Germans . . . Woe today, at Palazzo Chigi, to anyone who says anything bad about the English. One seeks to remedy without dignity the errors committed without dignity."[46]

Ciano had not yet abandoned all hope of avoiding a general European war. The day after the German invasion, he summoned the British and French ambassadors and, in their presence, placed telephone calls to Bonnet and Lord Halifax, urging their acceptance of Mussolini's proposal for a conference despite the fact war had begun. François-Poncet said after Ciano's talk with Bonnet that the reception of the proposal "was excellent and so favorable that we had the impression we had resolved the matter and that peace was saved."[47] At 7.10 p.m., Halifax telephoned Ciano to tell him Britain regarded a German evacuation of occupied Polish territory as an absolute precondition for accepting Mussolini's proposal. Bonnet, evidently having consulted with the British, telephoned with the same message. Ciano was well aware this was unacceptable to the Germans. The last hope of saving the peace was gone. The next day, France and

Britain declared war on Germany. Six years of conflict lay ahead. As the Italian writer Marco Innocenti would note, the Germans would conquer the land necessary to bury their dead.

Chapter Nine

The Break with Mussolini

After the German attack on Poland, the relationship between Ciano and Mussolini began to unravel, and would never be mended. Mussolini remained in a crisis of indecision for months afterward, but could never bring himself to break with the Germans as Ciano now wanted. On the one hand, the Germans had behaved dishonorably toward him; he had every reason to make the break. On the other, he told himself he must remain loyal to his commitments. But to do so would commit the Italian military to a war for which it was not prepared. Yet, if Italy stayed out, it would be denied its share of the spoils from German successes on the battlefield. Mussolini liked to portray himself as a man of decision and iron will. In reality, he was mercurial to an almost pathological degree, making a decision one minute that could be overturned half an hour later, then revived before the day was out. But in the end he was a jackal who lusted after the benefits of the kill. This, of course, would imply a permanent acceptance of inferiority *vis-à-vis* the more powerful Germans. The Duce's illusion that he was the leader of the Axis was shattered, but greed would prevail over any other consideration. All that then remained was to choose the right moment to enter the war at the least cost to Italy.

The oscillations in Mussolini's mood became so violent and rapid during the autumn of 1939 that Bocchini told Ciano he thought the Duce was suffering from a "psychic condition" brought on by a recurrence of syphilis, a disease that had afflicted him as a young man. "It surprised me very much, and I regret that Bocchini should have said this, although I myself must recognize that now the incoherence of Mussolini is really disorienting for anyone who has to work with him," Ciano wrote.[1] To no one more than Ciano himself. Ciano fluctuated between despair at Mussolini's obstinacy and moments of elation when he thought he had won him over to nonbelligerence. As his hatred of the Germans hardened, so did his exasperation with the man he had previously regarded as a kind of demigod.

But still he hesitated to condemn his protector. Seven days after the German attack on Poland, Bottai had a talk with Ciano and wrote in his diary: "He has decisively detached himself from the Axis. He has already crossed the Rubicon, which the real Caesar still doesn't dare to cross. Every mention of the Germans is full of disdain, almost of hatred . . ." Bocchini, encountering Ciano in an antechamber at the Palazzo Venezia, said to him, "You have been a great Italian." Ciano replied in a quiet voice: "I did my duty. Papa, if he were alive, would have told me to act this way."[2]

General Carboni, the head of military intelligence, told Ciano just how badly prepared Italy was militarily: the armed forces had few resources, the command structure was disorganized, there was demoralization among the masses. Then General Rodolfo Graziani presented Ciano with more specific details: The army had only ten first-line divisions. Thirty-five others were under strength and ill-equipped. Mussolini, confronted by Ciano with this information, admitted it was accurate but did not commit himself either way. Over the coming months, various officials hammered home to Ciano the extent of Italy's unpreparedness. Arturo Riccardi, Minister of Exchange and Foreign Currency, told Ciano it was absurd to plan for seventy divisions when the raw materials at hand were hardly enough to arm ten. General Ubaldo Soddu said that, in his view, Italy could not contemplate entering the war before October 1940. The Germans, he predicted, inevitably would be beaten.

The Soviet Union joined the Nazi attack on Poland on September 17, and six days later Berlin announced it had conquered the country. Once again, the Germans acted behind Italy's back as Ribbentrop embarked for Moscow and the Italians learned of his trip only from news agencies. The purpose of his trip quickly became clear: Ribbentrop and Molotov signed a new pact dividing a defeated Poland between them.

Hitler invited Mussolini to talks in Berlin but the Duce declined out of irritation and sent Ciano instead on September 30. Hitler told Ciano he was sure of final victory and planned in his next Reichstag speech to offer peace to France and England. He then appealed strongly for Italy to enter the war. "If Italy were disposed to march immediately with me, I would not even pronounce such a speech and I would without doubt have recourse to force, in the certainty that Italy and Germany united can, in a very brief time, defeat France and England and settle accounts once and for all with these two countries," he said. He said he did not fear American intervention because Germany's submarine defenses would keep her safe.[3] "We must win the war and we will win it," Hitler said. "If we should lose it, however, we would no longer have the least reason for living and I would be the first to kill myself." Giovanni Ansaldo whispered in Ciano's ear: "Why doesn't he do it right now?"[4] Ciano repeated this with pleasure to Edda when he returned home. He confided in his diary: "What most impressed me is his confidence in victory. Either he is bewitched, or he really is a genius . . . Will he be proved right? In my opinion the game will not be as simple as he believes."[5]

On the evening of October 1, Ciano dined with Ribbentrop at his home but could hardly bring himself to speak to the German and addressed himself mainly to Paul Schmidt. "When I translated Ribbentrop's words . . . Ciano fixed his eyes on the plate in front of him without saying a word and remained impassive. It would be difficult for an 'ally' to have been able to express more obviously his disapproval," Schmidt said. In his memoirs, Schmidt later wrote: "I had frequent opportunities of talking to Ciano . . . I came to know and have a regard for this man who, despite his frequently arrogant and somewhat uncivilized behavior on official occasions, perceived the trend of events with great clarity, and did not allow himself to be blinded by Hitler's and Ribbentrop's fine words."[6] Leaving Berlin by train on October 2, Ciano took off his military boots, unbuttoned his jacket and, in conversation with a journalist friend, unburdened himself of his feelings against Mussolini. "He talked on and on, with a corrosive irony that would have aroused the envy of the most ironlike anti-Fascist," the journalist said. But when the train arrived at the first station in Italy, Ciano noticed the hubbub of the crowd on the platform and suddenly changed his manner. Hastily, he put on his boots and buttoned his jacket. He checked his face in the mirror, making sure he wore a properly "ferocious" expression, then got down on the platform to receive the homage of the crowd. "It was very fine," he said when he got back on the train. "The Italians adore me." Then he returned to his original theme: "As I was saying to you, that man is a madman of the first rank. If we don't keep him out of combat, we will all end up against a wall . . ."[7]

Mussolini's vacillations continued. On October 3, he believed France and England would stand firm against Germany. Three days later, after Hitler made his speech offering peace to the Allies, he concluded the war was now over. "I do not share this optimism," Ciano wrote. "I still have too much respect for France and England to believe they will fall into the trap. The war did not end today; soon it will start."[8] Later he told a group of friends, in a relaxed moment: "Between German hegemony and English hegemony, the latter is better; it is the hegemony of golf, whisky and comfort."[9] Mussolini fretted more and more over Italy's nonparticipation. He told Ciano on October 9: "The Italians, after having heard my warlike propaganda for eighteen years, cannot understand how I can become the herald of peace now that Europe is in flames. There is no other explanation except the military unpreparedness of the country— but even for this I am made responsible."[10] Mussolini was consumed with jealousy over Hitler's battlefield successes. After the Führer escaped an assassination attempt in Munich on November 9, Mussolini found it difficult to compose a telegram congratulating him. "He wanted it to be warm, but not too warm, because in his judgment no Italian feels any great joy over the salvation of Hitler. And least of all, the Duce," Ciano wrote. Later that month he said, "For Mussolini, the idea of Hitler's waging war, and, worse still, winning it, is altogether unbearable."[11]

Mussolini announced a big shake-up in his Cabinet and in the military on October 31. The new Cabinet contained several friends and protectors of Ciano and he noted: "The new ministry is called, sotto voce, the 'Ciano cabinet.' Job hunters begin to crowd around me."[12] Goebbels noted: "Ciano is the strongman, even more so than before."[13] But in Mussolini's regime, there was room for only one strongman. By late November Ciano was convinced the chasm separating Italy and Germany was widening, "even in the Duce's mind." When an Italian living in Poznan sent a report to Rome of German atrocities there, Mussolini was indignant. He advised Ciano to see that, through indirect channels, the American and French newspapers learned of the report. "The world must know," he said.[14] The Germans had been guilty of double-dealing with Mussolini; now he was showing he could play the same game.

On November 30, the Soviet Union declared war on Finland. Ciano, in conversation with a friend, said Fascists were volunteering to fight Russia, "the ally of our ally." Then he added: "I am tired. The Duce asphyxiates us. I am very tired."[15] He was depressed because, a month earlier, his sister Maria had died of tuberculosis and anorexia. Ciano paid fulsome tribute to her in his diary and to friends he said, "I have lost the only person who loved me."[16] Mussolini convened the Grand Council on December 8 and described the huge number of cannon, planes and tanks he wanted to have by the second half of 1941. But Ciano concluded that this timetable meant Italy would never go to war; Germany would have collapsed before Italy had the necessary armaments. On December 16, Ciano went before the Chamber of Deputies to deliver one of the most important speeches of his career, a speech that had been approved by Mussolini and reflected the Duce's resentment of the Germans. It was decidedly neutralist, and Ciano revealed publicly for the first time how Berlin had acted without consultation as the Pact of Steel required, and had taken Italy by surprise. He denied Italy would stay out of the war because of unpreparedness, divisions of public opinion or fear. Germany and Italy, he said, would concentrate on military preparedness and internal reconstruction, and in Italy's case this would take three years. Afterward he wrote in his diary: "My speech was a great success, even if everybody did not discern immediately all the subtle anti-German poison which permeated it. The first impression seemed merely anti-Bolshevist, but in substance it was anti-German." Later he commented that the Italian people had understood his remarks and "they consider my speech to be the real funeral of the Axis."[17]

His remark that Italy would not enter the war for three years was designed, of course, to anger the Germans. Phillips saw it as "information to the enemy," and no unintentional slip.[18] In Berlin, Ribbentrop was furious, but Goebbels misunderstood the import of the speech. He wrote it was "positive for us . . . A few minor niggles, but none significant."[19] Mussolini got wind of the negative reactions to the speech in Germany, and wrote Hitler a placatory letter on January 3, 1940, in which he accepted full responsibility for Ciano's remarks. "You know that Count Ciano has been and remains one of the most convinced defenders of Italo-German friendship," he wrote. "I know that in certain German circles parts of this speech were not liked. It is useless for me to tell you that this represents my thought from beginning to end and I find it was absolutely indispensable to explain to the Italian people the genesis of events and the reasons for our current attitude. Having revealed some details of the truth has not harmed the German cause, such as making known that we both desired a long period of peace."[20] Subsequent events suggested the letter made no impression on Hitler; his contempt for Ciano was unbridled.

With all his fluctuations of mood, Mussolini's jealousy of Hitler continued. In late December, he authorized Ciano to inform the ambassadors of the Netherlands and Belgium that Italy had learned indirectly of a possible German attack on their countries. The Belgian ambassador relayed this information to his government in a telegram on January 2, but the Germans intercepted it and so learned of Ciano's "betrayal." Soon Mussolini was in the grip of one of his recurrent waves of pro-German feeling. "Now he would like to write a letter to Hitler to give him some advice (until now his advice hasn't made much of an impression!), telling him that he is continuing to prepare," Ciano wrote on December 31. "But for what? War at the side of Germany must not be undertaken and never will be undertaken. It would be a crime and an idiocy . . . The democracies . . . are the only countries with which one can deal seriously and honestly."[21] John Colville, Churchill's personal secretary, noted in his diary on December 31: "It is increasingly clear that Ciano is now in the Allied camp. He even gives Loraine information which is obviously to the detriment of Germany, and he is a restraining influence on his father-in-law, who hates democracies and cannot forgive or forget sanctions."[22] The previous month, Sir Percy Loraine had told Colville that Ciano was disgusted with the Axis, largely because of the "abominable way" he had been treated at Salzburg.

On January 17, Ciano found Mussolini somewhat hostile to the Germans. "He says: 'They should allow themselves to be guided by me if they do not want to make unpardonable blunders. In politics it is undeniable that I am more intelligent than Hitler,'" Ciano wrote in his diary. He added caustically: "I would not say that the Chancellor of the Reich has until now proved to be of this opinion."[23] The Italian people were now grumbling over food restrictions, and the Duce found that irritating. "Have you ever seen a lamb become a wolf?" he asked Ciano. "The Italian race is a race of sheep. Eighteen years are not enough to change them. It takes a hundred and eighty, and maybe a hundred and eighty centuries."[24]

The Prince of Hesse, husband of Princess Mafalda* of Italy, told Ciano on February 6 that Göring was more than ever incensed at Italy, and especially at Ciano. "That won't keep me awake," Ciano wrote. "The real reason must be sought in the Collar of the Annunciation given to von Ribbentrop when he expected it for himself. He blames me for it. He will calm down when he gets his."[25]

On February 7, Mussolini told a thoroughly dismayed Ciano he had decided on intervention, and forbade Ciano to sign an agreement requested by Britain for the supply of £20 million worth of arms. Ciano broke the news to Loraine, who told him Britain would soon cut off coal supplies coming to Italy from Germany by sea. Ciano wrote in his diary that day: "He [the Duce] says it is good for the Italian people to be put to tests that cause them to shake off their centuries-old mental laziness. He is bitter toward the people. 'We must keep them disciplined and in uniform from morning till night. Beat them and beat them and beat them.' He does not discriminate among the classes, and calls 'the people' all those who abandon themselves to the instincts of a vegetative life."[26] In mid-February, Ciano received a secret report from Bocchini, who was "very pessimistic on the internal situation . . . The unease in the country grows with the increasing difficulties. The prestige of the regime is no longer what it was. But does he say these things to Mussolini? He swears that he does."[27] Ciano told a friend he himself once had influence over Mussolini, but the Duce no longer listened to him. When the British attacked the German steamer *Altmark*, sailing in Norwegian waters with British prisoners,

---

*   She would die later in Buchenwald concentration camp.

on February 19, Ciano surprised Loraine by telling him the action was "absolutely correct and such as to recall the boldest traditions of the Navy of Francis Drake."[28]

While the guns echoed across Europe, Ciano saw no reason to abandon his active social life and his pursuit of women. The Duchess of Sermoneta described a dinner party he gave in the absence of Edda. "The table was covered with a frightening lace cloth and some ugly silver, and the numerous waiters wore disgraceful livery and gloves of white cotton," she said. After dinner the guests began a game of *chemin de fer*. "When I left they were still playing enthusiastically," she said. "With his arm around the neck of a young woman, Ciano spoke in her ear, ruffling her curls, while his other girl friends bent over him; piles of banknotes covered the table; the servants fetched nonstop trays of drinks."[29]

Sumner Welles now arrived in Europe to try to restore peace. Ciano received him on February 26, and afterward wrote in his diary: "He is an American distinguished in appearance and in manner, who carries easily the weight of a mission which has given him much American and world publicity. The conference was very cordial . . . He is anti-German, but makes an effort to be correctly impartial. He was glad, however, when I let him know my feelings and sympathies." But Welles' meeting with the Duce went badly, and he left Mussolini's office more depressed than when he entered it, in Ciano's estimation. The Duce later told Ciano: "Between us and the Americans any kind of understanding is impossible because they judge problems on the surface while we go deeply into them." Mussolini was not impressed by Welles' personality; Ciano disagreed. "I have had too much to do with that herd of presumptuous plebeians who are the German leaders not to appreciate Sumner Welles, who is a gentleman," he wrote.[30] Welles' own account of his meeting with Ciano was largely sympathetic. "He made no effort to conceal his hearty detestation of Ribbentrop," he recalled. "He said, 'If Hitler wants anything—and God knows he also wants enough—Ribbentrop always goes one better.'" Ciano made clear to Welles that he "bitterly resented" the lack of German consultation. He disclosed that the Germans had told him in the summer of 1939 they were trying to conclude a commercial agreement with Russia, and this was merely a *"petit jeu."* But then Hitler telephoned Ciano on August 21, 1939, to announce the Ribbentrop–Molotov Pact, and before Ciano even had time to get Mussolini on the phone to tell him, the news was being carried on radio. Ciano told Welles he was trying to mitigate German brutality toward Poles in the occupied territory. He added: "No country would want to have Germany as a neighbor. Italy now has her as a neighbor and we must do the best we can to get on with her." Welles observed: "Throughout the conversation Ciano revealed not only his contempt and hatred for Ribbentrop but also an underlying antagonism toward Hitler . . . But neither did he show the slightest predilection toward Great Britain and France."[31] In a foreword to the Ciano *Diary* published after the war, Welles elaborated on this meeting: "Of all the men possessing high authority within the Axis governments, he was the only one who made it clear to me, without subterfuge and without hesitation, that he had opposed the war, that he continued to oppose the war, that he foresaw nothing but utter devastation for the whole of Europe through the extension of the war, and that every effort which he personally could undertake would be exerted to prevent the entrance of Italy into the conflict."[32]

Two days later Mussolini, perhaps reacting to what he had learned of the Ciano–Welles conversation, told Filippo Anfuso: "There are still some imbeciles and criminals who think that Germany will be defeated. I tell you Germany will win." Anfuso reported these remarks to Ciano, who commented: "I accept 'imbecile'—if it is for me—but 'criminal,' it is unjust!"[33] On February 28 Myron G. Taylor, President Roosevelt's personal representative to Pope Pius, cabled Washington that the Pope had information suggesting Ciano was against the war. "All classes of Italian people are against the war, and Mussolini is undecided and wavering," he said. A few days later he cabled: "Mussolini has lost popular support in the last year and Ciano is not a statesman of great worth."[34]

On March 1, Ciano noted in his diary that Italy had a deficit of four trillion lire in its balance of payments for the current year. At the golf club, he met Finance Minister Paolo Thaon de Revel, who advanced a bizarre theory that gold would cease to be worth anything and Italy would become rich through the sale of works of art. He dismissed Thaon de Revel as a fool. Nevertheless, he discussed the plan with Mussolini, and observed: "He does not love art objects and above all detests the period of history in which the major masterpieces were produced."[35]

As Loraine had warned, Britain cut off coal supplies coming to Italy from Germany by sea on March 1. Thirteen vessels were interdicted on March 3 alone. Ciano warned Sir Noel Charles, the British chargé, that this would serve to push Italy into the arms of Germany.

Ciano saw the king again on March 5, and Victor Emanuel told him: "I am in the German black book."

"Yes, Your Majesty," Ciano replied. "In first place. And if you will permit me to be so bold, I figure there immediately after you."

"I think so too," the king said. "But that honors both of us so far as Italy is concerned."[36]

Mussolini was now worried he would become the laughing-stock of Europe, faced with one humiliation after another. He promised Ciano his intervention would bring about British defeat. Ciano reserved his comment for his diary: "Perhaps we will enter the war, but we will be unprepared and unarmed." Mussolini was aware of Ciano's attitude and openly expressed his irritation. "England will be beaten. Inexorably beaten," he told him. "This is the pure truth that you—even you—would do well to get into your head." The Duce's severe tone clearly upset Ciano. "During our seven years of daily contacts this is the *first* time that he has gone for me personally," he wrote. "If I clung to my job more than to my conscience, I should be greatly worried this evening. Instead, I am perfectly serene. I know that I am honestly serving my country and him whom I love and to whom I owe so much."[37] So the "madman" of six months earlier was still revered.

Hitler sent Ribbentrop to Rome on March 10 to tell Mussolini that matters could only be resolved on the battlefield, and Italy's place was alongside Germany. Ciano received Ribbentrop coldly, and privately referred to him as "the obsessive idiot." On the drive from the railway station into Rome, Ribbentrop revealed that a German offensive on the Western front was near and said a quick victory was assured. For Italy, he said, it was "either now or never. The victory of Germany will naturally be the victory of Italy . . . Remaining absent signifies renouncing European leadership." Ciano rushed to inform Mussolini.[38] Ribbentrop pushed this theme with Mussolini and sought to overcome the Duce's distaste for fighting on the side of the Soviets, saying Stalin had renounced Communist world revolution. His words had the intended effect, for the next day Mussolini approved the Soviet-German pact and said he was disposed to resume relations with Moscow. He also promised Italy would enter the war, at an opportune moment, with the aim of breaking out of its Mediterranean "prison." Afterward, Ciano said Mussolini had second thoughts and believed he had gone too far in his commitment to fight against the Allies. "He would now like to dissuade Hitler from his land offensive," he wrote.[39]

Ribbentrop's visit spurred the king to a discreet initiative—perhaps too discreet. Count Alberto Acquarone, the Minister of the Royal House, approached Ciano on the golf course on March 14, spoke of his concern about the situation, and assured Ciano that the king was also aware of "the discontent that disturbs the country." Ciano reported in his diary: "His Majesty feels that from one moment to the next the necessity could arise for him to intervene to give a different twist to things; he is ready to do it and with the firmest energy. Acquarone repeats that the King has for me 'more than benevolence, a real affection and much trust.'"[40] These hints could hardly have been plainer, but Ciano apparently gave Acquarone no indication he would be prepared to conspire in the Duce's overthrow. An opportunity was missed.

Welles returned to Rome on March 16, having sounded out the British and French. He told Ciano and Mussolini that the Allies would give in and recognize the *fait accompli* in Poland if they got certain guarantees of security. "If they fight truly on this road, they are on the way toward defeat," Ciano wrote.[41] In Welles' own account, he stressed that Ciano had revealed to him the result of the Ribbentrop visit: the Germans would undertake an all-out offensive in the near future, would not consider any solution short of military victory and, after victory, peace would be by German diktat. Ciano told him the Germans were confident of achieving victory within five months, with France crumbling first and Britain shortly afterward. "Ciano added that he himself was by no means convinced of Germany's ability to win such a victory," Welles wrote. "He said it might well be that the present German regime was like a man suffering from tuberculosis, who looked strong and healthy, but who had within him the germ of a fatal disease which might lay him low at the most unexpected moment . . . Count Ciano went on to say that in his own judgment Hitler was completely under the domination of Ribbentrop who, he said, possessed a fatally malignant influence . . . " Count Ciano then stated that he wanted to remind me that Mussolini was definitely 'pro-German,' " Welles wrote.[42] Ciano suggested a four-power pact involving Britain, France, Italy and Germany, with a guarantee that if one committed aggression the other three would combine against that country. Welles countered with a proposal of progressive disarmament, and Ciano agreed. Ciano dined with Welles that evening, and predicted the Germans would resort to the bombing of cities, including London and Paris, and to a reign of terror, but ultimately the Allies would win. Welles had planned to leave Rome the next day, but Ciano urged him to stay so he could give him an inside account of the forthcoming meeting at the Brenner. Welles agreed.

Mussolini met Hitler at the snow-covered Brenner Pass on March 18 with the intention of learning more about the Führer's aims. Ciano reported: "Hitler talks all the time. He looks physically fit. Mussolini listens to him with interest and with deference. He speaks little and confirms his intention to move with Germany. He reserves to himself only the choice of the right moment." Afterward, Mussolini told Ciano he believed Hitler "will think twice before he jumps into an offensive."[43] On March 19, Ciano lunched with Welles at the golf club. He said Hitler had revealed his offensive in the West would be postponed, but he planned immediately to begin bombing British ports and cities, particularly London. Ciano predicted that, at some point, Hitler might turn against Russia. He encouraged American initiatives for peace.[44]

Ciano confided to François-Poncet that the German offensive was not imminent. François-Poncet asked if it would be safe for him to go to Milan on April 25-26, and Ciano assured him it would. "And May 18 at the Venice Biennale?" the ambassador asked. Ciano hesitated a long moment, then replied: "Yes, probably."[45]

Ciano lunched with the Hungarian ambassador Paul Teleki on March 27. "Do you know how to play bridge?" Teleki asked abruptly. "Why?" Ciano asked. "For the day in which we will be together in the Dachau concentration camp," the Hungarian replied.[46] Ciano's position was indeed becoming more precarious. On March 31, Monsignor Francesco Borgongini Duca, the Vatican nuncio to Italy, warned him: "Excellency, pay attention to your person and don't expose yourself too much."

Ciano replied: "You are right, I always go without guards. Certainly the Germans, if they could, would shoot me."

Borgongini Duca said, "Be careful not only of the Germans, but also of the Italians because among them also there can be some with evil intentions."

Ciano responded: "But the Italian people love me and know the work that I am doing."[47]

However, that evening he wrote in his diary: "Rumors reach me from many quarters that the Duce has it in mind to replace me at the Ministry of Foreign Affairs. I do not believe it. However, if this should happen, I would be happy to leave this post in which I have served for almost four years—and what years!—with my head held high. My every action has been and is inspired with the sole purpose of serving my country and the Duce . . ."[48] In that same diary entry, he noted that Mussolini was indignant toward Welles because the American had told Neville Chamberlain that the Duce looked very tired and perturbed. Mussolini's source was an intercepted telegram sent to the British Embassy in Rome.

Ciano met on April 5 with Phillips, who reminded him that the minister had told him back in February to expect major hostilities in April. Was that still the case? Ciano replied that he had no reason to change his opinion. Four days later, at 3 a.m. on April 9, the Germans landed in Norway and crossed the frontier into Denmark. An hour before the invasions, Ciano was awakened to be given a letter from Mackensen, asking to be received at 7 a.m. The German ambassador arrived at 6.30, looking pale and tired, and announced the latest German acts of aggression. Ciano and Mackensen went together to deliver a letter from Hitler to Mussolini. The Duce, despite the German discourtesy in informing him in this manner, approved wholeheartedly. "This is the way to win wars," he said. "The democracies have lost the race." Ciano noted: "Mackensen went out of the Palazzo Venezia glowing."[49] The next day, Ciano wrote: "News of the German action in the north has had favorable repercussions among the Italian people, who, as Mussolini says, 'are whores and go with those who win.'"[50] Mussolini told Ciano on April 11: "It is humiliating to remain with our hands at our sides while others write history. It matters little who wins. To make a people great it is necessary to lead them to combat even with kicks in the behind. This is what I will do. I do not forget that in '18 there were 540,000 deserters."[51]

Ciano spent the next eight days in bed with a bad cold. On April 20 he noted in his diary: "Rome is filled with rumors about my resignation. Naturally, the German successes have caused many desertions in the ranks of my so-called friends. On the other hand, it was an old anti-Fascist, Alberto Giannini, who took a courageous stand by writing to the Duce, imploring him not to dismiss me, as this would increase the country's confusion. Mussolini was sympathetic and said that he wished, first of all, to do something that will cut short all these rumors."[52] Giannini told Mussolini he had heard rumors that Ciano wanted to go to the United States as ambassador and had proposed Roberto Farinacci as his successor. "What in my opinion is not to be overlooked is the deleterious impression [this] would provoke," he wrote. "I think you should avoid such an eventuality." Afterward, Mussolini told Buffarini-Guidi and Ettore Muti that Ciano enjoyed his full confidence.[53]

But was he being truthful? Evidently not. Later that month, he presented Ciano with an illustrated French magazine article on the end of Ernst Röhm, the former head of the Sturmabteilung, and invited him to read it. The title was, "Röhm, the man who aspired to the succession to Hitler." Röhm had been put to death by the Nazi dictator in 1934 for conspiring against him. Ciano thumbed through the newspaper, and said he already was familiar with the story. But Mussolini insisted he read the article, then dismissed him. His meaning was all too clear, and Ciano took fright. Later, meeting Anfuso at the golf club, he commented, "Perhaps he intends to liquidate me. The possibilities are two: either he keeps me in the government to compromise me, since I signed the Pact of Steel. If things go badly, he wants to divide the responsibility with me. Or, he sends me away because he smells a good wind and wants the triumph for himself, while he doesn't like the fact I make difficulties with the Germans. Should

I go now? Risk opposition? Son-in-law against father-in-law? And what can I do the day I am no longer minister? Simply be the son-in-law? No. It's necessary to try to remain in the government and continue to do as I am, as long as it is possible."[54] Guido Leto said Bocchini told him at one point of a plot by Ciano to poison Mussolini. He said Ciano asked Bocchini to furnish him with a poison that would leave no traces, telling him it was necessary to liberate the country from "tyranny." Bocchini, in relating this to Leto, grew red in the face and swore he would never have lent himself to such a crime. He added that Ciano had suggested turning to Himmler without, of course, letting him understand the purpose for which the poison was intended. Ciano repeated the request some months later, according to Bocchini, who said he rejected it in strong terms. "Naturally I cannot affirm," Leto wrote, "if the intention manifested by Ciano corresponded to a precise will on his part to kill Mussolini . . . or if it was a matter of momentary furies quickly calmed by sentiment and reason."[55]

While Ciano was worrying about his future and the imminence of Italy being dragged into war, he also had to contend with Göring's wounded vanity. Germany might be on the brink of invading France, but the Air Marshal was obsessed with the Collar of the Annunciation he had been denied. Ciano wrote in his diary on April 23: "It seems that the heart of the big Marshal is still afflicted by desperate sorrow, as last May when he saw hanging from Ribbentrop's neck the golden scene of the Annunciation! I speak of it to the Duce. We must not let the voluminous quasi-dictator of the Reich suffer any longer. And Mussolini, who has a feeling of disdain for these honors, authorizes me to write the King a supplicating letter to reveal the pitiful case of the tender Hermann, deprived of his legitimate trinket, and to propose that a suitable Collar be given him on May 22, the sad anniversary of the alliance."[56] Subsequently the king decided to give Göring what he wanted, but unwillingly. Mussolini told the king, "Your Majesty, it is perhaps a lemon that you must gulp down, but everything suggests the advisability of making such a gesture at this moment."[57]

On April 24 Mackensen informed Ciano the Germans would like to see Attolico recalled. Ciano, who had reviled the ambassador and ignored his warnings of Germany's attack on Poland, now wrote in his diary of the German demand: "That is natural. He is an Italian and a gentleman." Back in Rome three days later, Attolico told Ciano that Ribbentrop did not conceal his dislike for the Italian minister and considered him responsible for Italian nonintervention. "I am proud of it," Ciano said. Mussolini named Dino Alfieri as the new ambassador to Berlin. Ciano had recommended the appointment, despite his low opinion of Alfieri. "He knows nothing and he says nothing, but with many words," he wrote.[58]

On May 10, Ciano attended a dinner at the German Embassy that went on until after midnight. As he was leaving, Mackensen told him he might have to disturb him again during the night. The signal for another German invasion? Sure enough, at 4 a.m. the ambassador called to say he would arrive at Ciano's home in forty-five minutes, and had orders from Berlin to confer with Mussolini at 5 a.m. The subject of this latest rude awakening was the German invasion of Belgium, the Netherlands and Luxembourg. Mussolini, once again, expressed wholehearted approval. After Mackensen had left, the Duce told Ciano he planned to intervene. Ciano argued for waiting. "He didn't deign to answer me," Ciano wrote. "My observations serve only to annoy him. During the morning I see him many times and, alas, I find his idea of intervening growing stronger. Edda, too, has been at the Palazzo Venezia, and, ardent as she is, told him that the country wants war, and that a continuation of neutrality would be dishonorable." Ciano added this condescending footnote: "In leaving for Florence, Edda comes to visit me and speaks of immediate intervention, of the necessity of marching, of honor and dishonor. I listen to her with impersonal courtesy. Too bad that even she, so intelligent, doesn't want to reason. She does very well to go to the Florentine music festival, where she will be able more profitably to busy herself with music."[59] Ciano informed François-Poncet of the May 10 meeting with Mackensen, adding: "You will be beaten. The conduct of Italy will depend on military events." The French ambassador said that, a few days later, Ciano told him "his deep sympathies are with us."[60]

The latest German invasions provoked a deepening of the Nazis' already strong conviction that Ciano was a traitor to the Axis cause. Case Yellow, as the Germans had code-named the invasion plan, had been leaked several days in advance by Josef Müller, a Munich Catholic lawyer and friend of the Pope, through the Vatican. The Schwarze Kapelle, a group of German dissidents plotting the overthrow of Hitler, had appointed Müller to set up a contact with the British government through his friends at the Vatican. Müller leaked the plan to Adrien Niwenhuys, the Belgian ambassador to the Holy See, and the ambassador sent two warning telegrams to Brussels, both of which were intercepted by the Germans. Hitler ordered a full-scale investigation to determine the source of the leak. Admiral Canaris, his security chief, appointed Müller to head the investigation. Müller concocted a story that Ciano had learned of the invasion plan from people in Ribbentrop's entourage and had tipped off the Belgians.[61]

A further bone of contention between Mussolini and Ciano arose after the invasion. The Duce was irritated by sympathetic telegrams that the Pope had sent to the Netherlands, Belgium, and Luxembourg. "In these last few days he often repeats that the papacy is a cancer which gnaws at our national life, and that he intends, if necessary, to root it out once and for all," Ciano wrote. "I do not share this policy of the Duce because, if he intends to wage war, he must not provoke a crisis with the Church."[62]

The German invasion sealed the fate of Chamberlain in Britain. He resigned on May 10 and gave way to Winston Churchill. The war between Britain and Germany was about to begin in earnest. Ciano told Phillips on May 12 there was a 90 percent chance Italy would enter the war. "The Duce has practically made up his mind to join with Germany," he said. Ciano added that a large majority of Italian people desired war. That, of course, was a lie; public sentiment in Italy was strongly against going to war. "Did he, I wondered, really think that I believed him?" the ambassador wrote.[63] After Phillips' report reached Washington, the State Department informed the French and British governments of Italy's imminent entry into war, causing "near-consternation in London and Paris," according to Secretary of State Cordell Hull. French Foreign Minister Reynaud asked the United States to sell some overage destroyers to France and Britain because he anticipated Italian submarine attacks in the Mediterranean.[64] On May 13 the Duce informed Ciano he would declare war within a month. Ciano made no reply, but remarked in his diary: "I can do nothing now to hold the Duce back. He has decided to act, and act he will. He believes in German success and in the rapidity of this success."[65] Mussolini pressured the king to hand over supreme command of the armed forces to him, and the king relented after some initial resistance. Roosevelt sent an appeal to Mussolini on May 14 to stay out of the war, but the Duce refused to see Phillips and instructed Ciano to tell him Italy could not remain absent when the fate of Europe was at stake. The Netherlands fell that day, and Brussels capitulated on May 17.

The problem with Göring grew more complicated. The king, while agreeing to give him the Collar of the Annunciation, refused to send him the usual telegram of congratulations, but the marshal insisted. Ciano reluctantly concluded that the king would have to be persuaded to send the telegram. At a meeting on May 21, the king remarked, "This thing has gone badly. To give Göring the Collar is a gesture that displeases me. To send him a telegram is repugnant to me for a hundred thousand reasons." But he did it.[66]

Phillips came to Ciano on May 25 with a message from Roosevelt, offering to mediate with Paris and London on Italian claims to be outlined by Rome, but hinting at increased American aid to the Allies if Italy went to war. On instructions from Mussolini, Ciano rejected the offer. He continued to signal to Phillips that Italy's entry into the war "will happen soon." On the afternoon of May 29, Phillips heard that Ciano, on the golf course, had told an Italian friend that "things would happen" between June 10 and 15. In a report to Roosevelt, he commented: "Ciano has at least been franker with me than with any other of the colleagues, in letting me know the shortness of time left before the zero hour . . ."[67]

Mussolini informed his military leaders on May 26 that he had decided to go to war. Marshal Badoglio, dumbfounded, went immediately to Ciano to see if he had more information. Ciano did not, and kept repeating, "Mussolini is absolutely mad."[68] On May 28, Ciano tipped off Loraine that Italy would soon enter the war. In the critical months leading up to war, Ciano saw Loraine three or four times a day for several days running, and once said to him, "I cannot tell you everything, but I promise never to mislead you." According to the British, he kept his word. In London Sir Robert Vansittart sent a note to Lord Halifax that echoed Bocchini's judgment about the Duce: "Mussolini's decision to go to war is a clear case of syphilitic paranoia," he said.[69] Sir Alexander Cadogan, permanent under-secretary in the Foreign Office, recorded in his diary that, after Loraine had learned of Italy's planned entry into the war, Halifax wondered whether it would be possible to bribe Mussolini to stay out. "But I do not think we could ever have offered him enough to tempt him, and Loraine always disliked the idea of offering anything to Ciano," Cadogan wrote. "He never felt able to hand him £50,000 on the golf links."[70] There is no elaboration in the Cadogan diary of this intriguing suggestion that the British had considered trying to bribe Ciano.

Roosevelt sent a fresh appeal to Mussolini on May 30, warning bluntly that entry into the war would result in an increase in the U.S. rearmament program and a redoubling of help to the Allies. Mussolini brushed aside Roosevelt's message, and told Hitler that Italy would enter hostilities on June 5. Phillips cabled Washington on May 31 that Ciano had told him Italy's entry into war was now only a matter of days away. Hitler asked Mussolini for a postponement to allow him time to attack French airfields, and Mussolini rescheduled the Italy entry for June 11. But the Germans withdrew their objections, and war finally was declared on June 10. King Victor Emanuel, despite his long opposition to the alliance with Germany, approved the declaration of war on June 1. Ciano wrote in his diary: "By now he is resigned, nothing more than resigned, to the idea of war."[71] But in fact the king, eager like Mussolini not to miss out on the spoils of victory, told his aide-de-camp that "most times the absent ones are wrong."[72]

Hitler was in a fury against Ciano. He told an official of the German Ministry of Press and Propaganda, "I don't understand how Mussolini can make war with a Foreign Minister who doesn't want it and who keeps a diary in which he says nasty and vituperative things about Nazism and its leaders."[73]

On June 1 Ciano asked Phillips whether he thought the United States would go to war. Phillips replied that he could not say with any certainty, but Italy's participation would go a long way in leading the U.S. toward war. Ciano said he was definitely of the opinion the U.S. would enter the war. He told Phillips he had a great admiration for the American soldier, with whom he had come into contact in China, and realized the immense power of the United States.[74]

The French tried to forestall an attack by offering to settle Italy's territorial claims, but Ciano told François-Poncet that Mussolini was not interested in peaceful negotiation. He had decided to make war; there would be no reply to the offer. In his brief time in Rome, the French ambassador had seen a great deal of Ciano and, unlike some diplomats, had come to admire him. In his memoirs written after the war, François-Poncet said Ciano represented "the most moderate and reasonable elements" in the Fascist Party. He called him "a Foreign Minister at the height of his abilities . . . hard working, assiduous in his office, punctual and methodical in his work." He conceded that Ciano was "a natural imperialist" who believed in the inevitability of war with the Western democracies. "And yet he was not warlike," he wrote. "Basically, he did not hate England or France. He had too much consideration for these old nations."[75] On the eve of Italy's declaration of war, François-Poncet came to Ciano's office to take his leave, and wept openly. "We embraced with an emotion that neither of us succeeded in hiding," Ciano wrote. "Poncet is a man like us: he is a Latin."[76]

Chapter Ten

Italy Enters the War

The Italy that went to war in 1940 had, in some ways, already been on a war footing for several years. The League of Nations sanctions imposed in 1936 had forced Italians to tighten their belts and to develop substitutes for goods that no longer could be imported. In bars, signs appeared in front of the espresso machines: "No coffee." Gasoline was short, and only those with a special permit could use their cars. Butchers' shops were not allowed to sell meat on Thursdays and Fridays. As leather shoes wore out, people started going about in shoes made of sailcloth. Rayon took the place of silk, cotton gave way to jute and synthetic fibers. In time, foreign liquors were prohibited in bars, but bartenders secretly poured French cognac for their favorite customers and served whisky in coffee cups. Rationing of goods became increasingly severe as the war approached. First sugar and coffee were rationed, then soap, fats, pasta, rice and bread. Just before the outbreak of war, the government requisitioned copper objects from private homes; thus many families were left without pots in which to cook the polenta. Wages were low, many houses were without electric light, the poor were without telephones and, in the countryside, entire villages lacked running water. In short, a poor country was further impoverished by the ambitions of a single man, and was about to embark on disaster. The war would leave parts of Italy in ruins. It would claim the lives of 300,000 soldiers and 150,000 civilians.[1]

In the final days of Italy's tormented peace, Mussolini closed the dance halls, and discouraged the playing of foreign music. "St. Louis Blues" was rechristened "Tristezze di San Luigi," literally "Sorrows of St. Louis." Schools closed for the summer at the end of May, more than a month early. The great windows of Milan Cathedral were taken down and replaced by canvas. Men in uniform filled the streets. No one doubted any longer what was about to happen, but in some ways life continued normally. The soccer season was still under way. People went to the cinema and the seaside, and lovers strolled in the parks amid the first real heat of the summer.

Galeazzo Ciano might oppose the war, but he had no hesitation about fighting for his country. He decided to assume command of a bombing squadron at Pisa, and said he chose to fight there because it was near Corsica and his native Livorno "where my father lies in his eternal sleep."[2] On June 10, wearing an air force uniform, he lunched with a Tuscan friend at the Hotel Ambasciatori on the Via Veneto. Then he returned to his office and, at 4.30 p.m., called in Loraine and François-Poncet to give them the declarations of war. Loraine jotted down Ciano's exact words and said, "I am sorry, Ciano. I hope you haven't backed the wrong horse." Then he shook hands, started for the door but paused there and said, "I have the honor to remind Your Excellency that England is not in the habit of losing her wars. You think the war will be easy and very short. You are mistaken. The war will be long and very difficult. Goodbye."[3] When François-Poncet arrived, he told Ciano that one didn't need to be very intelligent to understand the reason for his summons. After Ciano read out the declaration of war, François-Poncet said, "You have waited until we were on the ground to give us a stab in the back. In your place, I would not be proud." Then, pointing to Ciano's uniform, he said, "And what will you do in the war? Will you drop bombs on Paris?" Ciano replied: "I think so. I am an officer and I will do my duty." François-Poncet said, "Don't get yourself killed." Ciano assured François-Poncet the war would last a short time. "We will find ourselves very soon around a green baize table," he said. The ambassador retorted, "On condition that you are not killed." He told Ciano, "The Germans are hard masters. You, too, will learn this. After the war, European life will start up again. Those who permitted a ditch full of blood to be dug between Italy and France will be very guilty." In his written account the ambassador added: "With these words we parted, both equally moved. We would never see each other again."[4]

In the streets of Rome, loudspeakers announced that Mussolini would address the Italian people at 6 p.m. from the balcony of the Palazzo Venezia. Crowds of people in black shirts began gathering in the vast piazza below the balcony in late afternoon, knowing already what they would hear. Mussolini came out promptly at 6, with Ciano, Giuseppe Bottai and Alessandro Pavolini behind him. A few minutes into his speech, he announced: "The declaration of war has already been given to the ambassadors . . ." The crowd interrupted him with a cheer that went on for a full forty-five seconds.[5] But many noted afterward that the enthusiasm seemed somewhat forced. Yet, even if the Italians did not like the prospect of war, many of them—perhaps a majority—convinced themselves it would be a short one, with Britain quickly defeated. Many soldiers marched off to the front assuring their families they would be home before Christmas. But Ciano wrote in his diary that night: "The news of the war surprises no one and does not arouse excessive enthusiasm. I am sad, very sad. The adventure begins. May God help Italy."[6] At 11 p.m. the first air-raid alarm of the war sounded over Rome, but no planes appeared.

Churchill later said in a broadcast that Ciano had justified Italy's attack on France by arguing that such a chance would not occur again in five thousand years.[7] He cited no source for this, and everything else in the public record suggests it was apocryphal, unless, of course, Ciano engaged in typical boasting with someone he wanted to impress. Del Drago said in his memoirs: "That day Ciano, for his own good, for his personal satisfaction, for his future ambitions, should have resigned. Why didn't he do it? . . . He just could not face the idea of not having bells to push, secretaries to bully, people coming to him to ask for services he invariably rendered in his own grand and generous style; he liked the power and the glamour that went with his charge . . . So he stayed on."[8]

Ciano told Grandi that Mussolini had decided to declare war because the French were ready to ask for an armistice and it was unlikely Britain would continue a "lost" war. "The war is over and Mussolini will not have the satisfaction of firing even a cannon shot," Ciano said. Grandi asked if he was sure the war was over, and Ciano seemed surprised he could doubt it. "It is precisely because the war is over that I think Mussolini has been wrong to declare it," he said. "He has huge illusions about his German friends."[9] Ciano said Mussolini had decided Italy must occupy the territories of the Rhone Valley because he believed Germany planned to occupy Alpine villages near Italy and that would put Turin within range of German artillery.

Two days later British planes bombed Turin, leaving fourteen dead, and French cruisers shelled the Ligurian coast the day after, killing ten people. Ciano left for Pisa on June 11 and participated in a bombing raid on Toulon, the great French naval base, two days later. Back at his base, he telephoned Edda in Rome and their conversation was recorded by the Italian secret service.

Ciano: Edda, this day for me will be unforgettable.
Edda: Why? What happened to you?
C.: I'm just back from my first flight of this war. I have tasted again in full the intoxication of being a flyer. It is magnificent, soothing, indescribable!
E.: I can believe it. But what happened to you? It isn't exactly the first time you have flown in an airplane.
C.: I will tell you everything. Listen.
E.: Fine, tell me.

C.: I led my flock in an impeccable manner in the skies over Toulon, where we carried out a real slaughter . . .

E.: Is that all?

C.: No, dear, it isn't all. Listen. On the way back, while I found myself on the stretch of sea that separates Corsica from the peninsula, I saw a ship that proceeded placidly and majestically from north toward the south-southwest. I point my Zeiss: British flag. Imagine my orgasm!

E.: I imagine it! And then?

C.: It was a magnificent, great, huge ship; it seemed a transatlantic liner, it was so great and bulky. "What a great coup!" I say to myself. I look down at the indicator, in the hope that some bomb, after the raid on Toulon, still remained on the undercarriage. But no! It was really a misfortune: I had used all of them. Imagine my anger: to have there such a magnificent prey under my hand and I couldn't do anything! Then I take a quick decision. I turn up my engines to full throttle and arrive at the base in record time. The commanding colonel of the base where I land comes up to me while I jump down from the cockpit. "Excellency, you have had a good trip?" he asks me. "Marvelous," I reply. And then I tell him about the ocean liner. "I have come to get more bombs and fuel and I leave again immediately," I tell him resolutely. "It will be easy for me to find the ship again because I have taken exact note of its route and speed . . ." The colonel doesn't let me finish. "Excellency," he says to me respectfully, "I am sorry to tell you that it doesn't seem to me opportune that you risk yourself in such an undertaking. Your plane needs cleaning and testing." "But what testing!" I tell him. "Load the bombs and the gas and I will leave immediately!" "Major Ciano," he replies with authority, "don't forget that I am your base commander and as such I do not receive orders from you, but I have the right to give them to whomever I wish." And he adds immediately with an apologetic and respectful tone: "Excellency, outside the field you command and I am ready to execute your orders. Inside the field you will obey mine." At that I stood immediately at attention. I give my military salute and I reply, "Yes sir, yes, colonel. You command!" And thus I remained cut down. For simple reasons of good example and discipline I had to renounce the greatest coup of my flying career. Imagine my anger.

E.: [Says nothing].

C.: How's that, you don't say anything?

E.: [with absent tone] What about?

C.: My adventure! What do you think of it?

E.: Of what? Oh yes! Interesting, interesting! You have done very well . . .[10]

Ciano participated in further bombing raids on two Corsican towns on

June 16 and 17. Then Anfuso telephoned to tell him to return to Rome so he could leave for Munich that evening; the French, their capital occupied, had asked for an armistice, and Hitler wanted to confer with Mussolini. Ciano returned to find Mussolini dissatisfied at the prospect of a sudden peace. "His reflections on the Italian people and, above all on our armed forces, are extremely bitter this evening," he said.[11] Mussolini had decided on June 19 to attack the French in the Alps. Marshal Badoglio and General Graziani were opposed, saying it would take more than twenty days to go onto the offensive in that mountainous terrain. But Mussolini insisted Italy could not make claims upon France without having fought. Ciano was unenthusiastic. "I find it very inglorious to throw ourselves upon a defeated army, and also morally dangerous," he said. "If our army should not overcome resistance during the first assault, our campaign would end with a howling failure. Mussolini listened to me, and it seems that he will limit the attack to a small sector near the Swiss frontier."[12]

At Munich on June 18, Hitler told Mussolini they would have to conclude separate armistices. He advised Mussolini against demanding the surrender of the French fleet, which could scuttle itself or go over to the British rather than fall into Italian hands. But he accepted Mussolini's territorial claims against France: Corsica, Djibouti and the occupation of France from the Alps to the Rhone below Lyon. Ribbentrop and Ciano discussed Algeria and Morocco. "I find an unusual Ribbentrop," Ciano wrote, "measured, serene, pacifist." Of Hitler he said, "He is by now the gambler who has made a big coup. He would like to get up from the table risking nothing more. Today he speaks with a reserve and a perspicacity which, after a victory such as his, are really astonishing. I am not suspected of excessive tenderness toward him, but today I truly admire him."[13]

France asked Italy for an armistice on June 20, but Mussolini ordered an immediate offensive in the Alps. The attack began the next day, in freezing temperatures, rain and snow, but fizzled out in front of the first French fortification which put up some resistance. In Libya meanwhile, an Italian general surrendered to the British, and a humiliated Mussolini told Ciano: "It is the material that is lacking. Even Michelangelo needed marble to make his statues. If he had had only clay he would merely have been a potter. A people who for sixteen centuries have been an anvil cannot become a hammer within a few years."[14] He needn't have been surprised. Ciano had earlier told him: "With an army like this, one can declare war only on Peru."[15] The Duce also had had numerous reports about the country's military deficiencies. Just before the outbreak of war Carlo Favagrossa, under-secretary of munitions, had submitted a report that was left to gather dust in the archives. Favagrossa said the army had seventy-four divisions, of which only nineteen were complete in both men and arms. The army faced serious shortages of armored personnel carriers, fuel, artillery and uniforms. Italy had only established its first armored divisions in 1938, and equipped them with tanks of three and a half tons compared with the twenty-ton tanks of the Germans and British. Italian tanks tended to bog down in desert sand and mud. The army had no jeeps. The navy boasted 576 vessels of various sizes, but no radar, air cover or aircraft carriers. The air force had 1,946 planes, but they were technologically inferior to those of the enemy and included no torpedo planes.[16]

The armistice was signed on June 24 between Badoglio and the French General Charles Huntzinger. "The war is not yet over, rather it is beginning now," Ciano wrote prophetically in his diary.[17] Mussolini, back in Rome on July 2 after an inspection of the war front, claimed in a conversation with Ciano that Italian forces had broken through the Alpine Maginot Line. "In reality, there was no breakthrough," Ciano wrote.[18] His view that the war was just starting did not last long. On July 4 he told Bastianini that in two months at most the war would be ended. "Do you understand how badly one will live in all Europe after the victory of Germany?" he asked. "Can you imagine what those people will ask of us?. . . Even for us it will be difficult to draw from these people some human concession." He advised Bastianini to improve his German. Bastianini replied that the situation was not so dark; the British were building "throughout the empire an imposing military machine," and would not collapse. "And what do they expect to pull them out of it?" Ciano asked. "America? When America enters the war, if it does, there can only be a guerrilla war on the oceans."[19]

Wishing to repair his relations with the victorious Germans, Ciano informed Alfieri that, if officially invited, he would come to Berlin. Ribbentrop extended an invitation and Ciano arrived on July 7. Michele Lanza, an anti-German attaché at the Italian Embassy in Berlin, described the reception at the railway station in cutting terms: "The Minister arrives followed by the usual line of secretaries, officials, aides, hierarchs and hierarchettes wishing to sponge a trip so they can then describe it to their Roman friends. All of this retinue wears the most varied and ridiculous uniforms. The legs of most of our personalities, perhaps in respectful homage to the Minister, are markedly bandy."[20]

Ciano found Hitler "very kind, extremely so. He is rather inclined to continue the struggle and to unleash a storm of wrath and of steel upon the British . . . He is calm and reserved, very reserved for a German who has won."[21] But Hitler was undecided about attacking Britain. Ciano told him the Italians were preparing an attack in North Africa, spoke of the hostile attitude of Greece and said it was necessary to liquidate Yugoslavia, which was equally hostile. Hitler told him it would be a mistake to light a fire prematurely in the Balkans and provoke Russian intervention. Ciano gave Hitler a list of Italian aspirations, which were not modest. Schmidt recalled: "He spoke as if the war was already definitively won, making a show in every way of requests for his country: Nice, Corsica and Malta should be annexed to Italy, which would also have assumed a protectorate over Tunisia and the better part of Algeria, and would occupy strategic bases in Syria, Transjordan, Palestine and Lebanon. In Egypt and the Sudan, Italy should simply take the place of England, and also Somalia, Djibouti and French Equatorial Africa should become Italian territories. Ciano showed no restraint in mentioning all these desiderata; but Hitler paid no attention at all."[22]

Ribbentrop told Ciano: "One must be moderate and not have eyes bigger than one's stomach."[23] That evening, Ribbentrop hosted a dinner for Ciano at the Hotel Adlon. Then Alfieri gave a reception at his villa at Wannsee. Lanza described the occasion with a kind of malicious glee: "Alfieri invited about twenty of the most beautiful women in Berlin and, as in a slave market, has paraded them in front of the Minister. Naturally the acrid comments on the German side have not been lacking. Ciano passed the squadron in review and chose G. von F. Truly very beautiful. As an antipasto he took her in a motorboat on the lake and, having known her barely five minutes, narrated to her how Balbo had been shot down by our artillery. 'And perhaps'—he added with a wink—'not in error.' The lady in question, who is certainly not a nun, was terrified by the liberty of speech and the ways of our brilliant Minister."[24] Marshal Italo Balbo, one of the founders of fascism and a man Ciano had looked upon as a rival, had been killed on June 28 at Tobruk when his plane was mistakenly shot down by Italian artillery.

The exiled Russian princess Marie Vassiltchikov, who later was closely involved with the men who plotted the failed assassination attempt against Hitler in July 1944, was at the reception, along with two girl friends. She understood that Ciano had come to Berlin for a memorial service for Balbo. "For this occasion the Embassy seemed to have invited all the prettiest girls in Berlin," she noted. "Ciano's own entourage turned out to be rather unattractive, Blasco d'Aieta, his chief of cabinet, being the only exception. To us the whole thing seemed pretty fishy. We were whirled around the Wannsee in numerous motor boats in the pouring rain. On getting back, we three decided to take off for home as soon as we could find a car. But when it came to saying goodbye and thank you to our host, we found him and Ciano in a darkened room, dancing cheek-to-cheek with two of the flightiest ladies Berlin has to offer. And this on a day of alleged official mourning! We departed disgusted . . ."[25]

From Berlin Ciano left by train to visit the German-occupied territories in the West, then returned to Rome. Hitler wrote to Mussolini on July 13, suggesting Italian forces were not trained for the technical aspects of an invasion from the sea and therefore would not be useful for his coming attack on Britain. Ciano saw Bottai at the golf club and remarked: "As Goethe said his greatest misfortune was the birth of Napoleon, who obfuscated his glory, so Mussolini can say that his greatest misfortune was the birth of Hitler."[26]

Ciano's own attitude toward Hitler had now gone full circle. Talking to Bottai again on July 16, he said of the Führer: "He is a man of genius. Rather, he is a genius. Every now and then there appear these enormous personalities that rise toward the sky like mountains: Bismarck, Goethe, and now Hitler." Bottai, in his diary, continued: "Galeazzo . . . eulogizes the 'humanity' of Hitler, so attentive with his collaborators of every rank." Ciano dilated upon the way Hitler, busy with conquering Europe, nonetheless found time on his return from a defeated France to go that same day to visit a sick child of Goebbels. And how Hitler's attentiveness to his collaborators entailed "a thousand little courtesies: to this one, according to his custom, a glass of mineral water, to that one cigarettes. Always equal, calm."[27] Hitler had replaced Mussolini as his hero. "The defense of Hitler continues," Bottai wrote with evident distaste. "Always informed of everything and on everything to perfection . . . patient in asking for information." Ciano contrasted that with Mussolini's "journalistic" temperament, "all sudden intuitions and lightning decisions, prone to resolve a situation in a communiqué." Ciano told Bottai: "Mussolini has remained the man of the banner headline."[28] Phillips was surprised to hear Ciano describe the Führer as "a very reasonable man who looked at things from a just and high-minded point of view." Ciano, who earlier had predicted a German defeat, now told Phillips: "If the British choose to continue the struggle they will be smashed to pieces very quickly, for they appear to have no idea of the immensity of the force which will be employed against them."[29]

Ciano returned to Berlin on June 19, at Ribbentrop's invitation, for a speech in which Hitler planned to offer "peace" to Britain. William L. Shirer, the American correspondent and later historian of Nazism, watched Ciano as Hitler delivered his speech to the Reichstag. "I had met him in Rome and had rather liked him despite his pompousness and clowning," Shirer wrote. "There was something human and decent in him underneath all his foolish Fascist strutting. But on this evening in the Reichstag Ciano cut a sorry figure. In his gray-and-black Fascist militia uniform and seated in the first row of the diplomatic box in the first balcony, Ciano kept jumping up constantly like a jack-in-the-box every time Hitler paused for breath and snapping out the Fascist salute with his right arm. It was ludicrous. Even, I think, to the Germans." In another description of this scene, Shirer wrote: "Could not help noticing how high-strung Ciano is. He kept working his jaws. And he was not chewing gum."[30]

Ciano remarked in his diary that he believed Hitler's desire for peace was sincere. That was confirmed in his own mind at a meeting with the Führer the next day. "He would have preferred an understanding," Ciano wrote. "He knows that war with the English will be hard and bloody, and knows also that people today are stingy with their blood."[31] Just before leaving the German capital, Ciano visited Göring at his palatial Carinhall residence. "He looked feverish, but as he dangled the Collar of the Annunciation from his neck he was somewhat rude and haughty toward me," Ciano wrote. "I was more interested in the luxurious decoration of his house than in him and his variable humors. It is an ever-increasing show of luxury, and it is truly inconceivable how, in a country which is socialistic, or nearly so, they tolerate without excessive protests the extravagant luxuries of this Western satrap."[32]

Back in Rome, Ciano found Mussolini disappointed by the pacific tone of Hitler's speech and thirsting for war with Britain. Talking to Bottai, Ciano bubbled with delight as he described how Hitler had called in his generals and high officials and awarded them promotions, and had given a castle to Ribbentrop, who was so moved that two tears fell onto his cheeks. Ciano complained to his friend of the "inconstant hardness" of Mussolini, contrasting the Duce's behavior with that of Hitler. "I know too well Galeazzo is incapable of objective judgments," Bottai commented. "He is always a man of variable moods."[33]

Despite the victory over France, the journalist Alberto Giannini warned Ciano that there was a feeling of drift in the country. Defeatist factions were at work, people talked openly of replacing the Duce, Fascists had become indifferent to attending party meetings and the state machinery was creaking because individuals were not motivated by a sense of duty. Ciano told Giannini: "I do not even have the liberty to draw up communiqués. If you knew how difficult it is to deal with that man with the little moustache! I cannot suppress the reality: Berlin is today the capital of Europe. What can we do?"[34] Mussolini was also discouraged, and fed up with his people. In August he told Ciano the Italians had a tendency toward alcoholism and complacency, adding: "The principal reason for the reforestation of the Appenine regions is to make the climate of Italy more rigorous. This will bring about an elimination of the weaker stock and an improvement of the race." Later he said, "After the war is over, I shall begin my attack on the middle class, which is cowardly and despicable. We must destroy it physically, and save perhaps 20 percent, if that much."[35]

On August 19, Italian troops captured Berbera in British Somaliland, their first territorial conquest of the war. In the same month, British heavy bombers began concentrated attacks on the cities of northern Italy.

Chapter Eleven

Ciano's War: the Attack on Greece

While he was working feverishly in the first half of 1940 to keep Italy out of war at Germany's side, Ciano was busy scheming to drag the country into another war. The prize in his sights was Greece. Even though he knew Italy was unprepared for such a conflict, he managed to delude himself into thinking it could achieve an easy victory. When war came, he boasted that it was "my war," one that would enlarge the borders of his "grand duchy," that is, Albania. But the result was a calamity for Italy, and the war was the most shameful blot on Ciano's record in office, an act that in effect made him a war criminal. At one stage he had described Greece as "a country too poor for us to covet," but he changed his mind.[1] Greece had been in his thoughts ever since the Italian takeover of Albania in 1938. With typical duplicity, he telegraphed the Italian minister in Athens, Emanuele Grazzi, after the takeover and instructed him to go immediately to General Metaxas, the Greek dictator, and assure him that rumors of an Italian action against Greece were false and spread by *agents provocateurs*. But a month later, in his diary, he noted: "The entire highway program (in Albania) is in the direction of the Greek borders. That has been ordered by the Duce, who is thinking of pouncing on Greece at the first opportunity."[2]

In a meeting with Grazzi on April 30, 1940, Ciano casually asked if it would not be possible to find "some Albanian" who would do away with the king of Greece. Grazzi was stunned. "This question was so unheard of that I had the impression it wasn't made seriously and that it was nothing more than one of those *boutades*, not always in good taste, that were customary in him. Still today . . . I refuse to believe that Ciano seriously intended to propose to me to organize an attempt against the king of Greece, knowing full well that I was not a man to lend myself to projects of such a nature. I limited myself to shrugging my shoulders without answering . . . The minister, whatever his intentions may have been in pronouncing those disgraceful words, let the subject drop immediately."[3]

Ciano went to Albania in May 1940, met General Carlo Geloso, commander of the Italian military forces there, and ordered him to prepare for war. He suggested that Geloso move five divisions from the Albanian-Yugoslav border to the Greek border. Geloso protested that he would need at least twenty to twenty-five divisions. "Ciano laughed," according to Grandi.[4] But he was irritated, and upon his return to Rome managed to get Geloso replaced with General Sebastiano Visconti Prasca, the former military attaché in Paris. He boasted to Gaetano Polverelli: "Finally we have a great general. He told me that in war he prefers the offensive, even with a battalion against a regiment, or with a regiment against a division."[5] Visconti Prasca, an effeminate man who wore a monocle and sported tinted eyebrows, actually said something even more absurd than that: "I have given orders that every column of troops, even if down to just one man, must always attack."[6]

Preparations for war began to take shape in the late summer. On August 6, Mussolini told Ciano he wanted to attack Yugoslavia in September, but Ciano began urging the Duce to consider the Greek option. Mussolini later gave Visconti Prasca some vague directives for an action against Greece. But Ciano, behind Mussolini's back, gave the general more precise instructions. He also stoked up an Italian media campaign against Greece. On August 11, Italian radio reported that the "patriot" Daut Hoxha had been killed in Albania by Greeks, who cut off his head to take it to Athens. In fact, Hoxha had been killed on June 14 during a clash with Greek police. Far from being a political figure, he was a cattle rustler with a string of killings on his record. The Italian propaganda campaign put the Greeks on alert, as did the sinking of their old cruiser *Helli* on August 15 by a submarine.[7] On August 17 Ribbentrop relayed word to Rome that an attack on Yugoslavia or Greece would not be welcome in Berlin, and all efforts should be concentrated on the coming attack on England. But Ciano kept pushing for war against Greece, and five days later Mussolini ordered the General Staff to speed up planning for an attack.

Meantime, negotiations between Hungary and Romania to settle a border dispute in Transylvania collapsed, and both nations agreed to accept the arbitration of Ciano and Ribbentrop. Ciano flew to Vienna, where he and Ribbentrop met with the Hungarians and Romanians. Their dispute had been simmering for some time, and much earlier the Hungarian minister Villani had come to Ciano, denounced the Romanians and said his government sooner or later would be forced to go to war with them. Ciano remained silent, and Villani pressed him for an answer. "And what will the Italian government do if we are constrained to march against Romania?"

he asked. Ciano appeared to meditate for a moment, then fixed Villani with a look of utmost seriousness and said, "Dear Minister, I believe we will be obliged to put the news in the newspaper."[8] Before the Vienna meeting, Hitler made it clear he wanted Romania to cede 40,000 square kilometers of territory to Hungary, while Hungary in turn asked Romania for 60,000. Ciano and Ribbentrop agreed to assign the greater part of Transylvania to Hungary. The Hungarians could hardly believe their good fortune, while on the Romanian side of the table there was a loud thud. Foreign Minister Mihail Manoilescu had fallen forward in a faint.[9]

On September 19, Ribbentrop arrived in Rome with a surprise proposal: a tripartite military alliance of Germany, Italy and Japan, to be signed in a few days' time in Berlin. Ribbentrop told Ciano he was convinced America would not dare to enter the war, but Ciano disagreed. Ribbentrop also assured him that English territorial defense was nonexistent, and a single German division would suffice to bring about a complete collapse. In talks with Mussolini and Ciano, Ribbentrop alluded to a possible Axis diplomatic break with the United States, and Mussolini seemed inclined to go along. But Ciano argued that the Axis must avoid a conflict with America at all costs. He said a break in relations would also render "a signal service" to Roosevelt, since he could present himself in the elections that autumn "in the guise of one who has been attacked."[10] Mussolini approved the Tripartite Pact, and Ciano signed it in Berlin on September 27 with Rib-bentrop and Japanese Ambassador Saburo Kurusu, in Hitler's presence. Two days later, Hitler told Ciano that the assault on England had definitely been postponed, given the lateness of the season. Ciano told a counselor at the Italian Embassy: "The Germans have let themselves be drawn into this adventure without knowing or understanding the English. This morning Ribbentrop showed me photographs of Londoners dancing on the ruins of their houses and called them savages. He didn't understand the spirit of these men of strong nerves and iron will."[11] While in Berlin, Ciano detected a depressed spirit among Berliners facing another winter of war. Mussolini and Hitler met at the Brenner Pass on October 4, and Hitler confirmed that the landing in Britain had been postponed. On the return trip, Mussolini told Ciano he detested the king, who was "the only defeatist in the country." Back in Rome, Ciano told Bottai that Hitler had said, "*Der Krieg ist gewonnen.*" Ciano commented that Hitler had an excessive tendency to underestimate America.[12]

Ciano met the king when he returned from Berlin, and again his mind was on Greece. General Puntoni, the king's aide-de-camp, wrote in his diary: "Ciano showed an impatience to give a lesson to Greece for its conduct which, he says, is ambiguous. Driven by his megalomania, he speaks also of an eventual partition of Switzerland. The sovereign limited himself to commenting, 'The Foreign Minister is not very profound in geography.'"[13]

Grazzi and Mondini, the military attaché in Athens, tried to restrain the headstrong minister's enthusiasm for war, sending him reports on how the Greeks were fired up against the Italians and had a well-armed military force. Ciano dismissed these reports, trusting instead his own informants in Greece. He told the diplomat Raffaele Guariglia that "two hundred airplanes over Athens would be enough to make the Greek government capitulate."[14] Ciano's agents in Greece told him he could buy off the Greek military commanders, and he believed them. The agents assured him that people in the border region would rise up against Greece, the Greek army would not fight and a pro-Italian government would be ready to take over in Athens. Polverelli said, "I was told that checks for five million (lire) were issued in favor of Greek personalities by a Rome bank on orders of Ciano. And yet it is uncertain if such sums are effectively collected by high Greek officials for whom they are intended, or whether the emissaries have been deceived with false promises, or whether these agents deceive Ciano with assurances of negotiations that have never been concluded or have been tried in vain."[15] Later, an Italian official told an American correspondent, "The Greeks accepted many millions of lire and then used the money to fight us."[16]

Mussolini's own wavering about Greece ended on October 12 when German troops entered Romania to take control of the country's oil supplies, and again the Duce was not consulted or advised. With a kind of childish petulance, he decided an Italian surprise attack on Greece would show the Germans two could play at that game. "Hitler always faces me with a fait accompli," he complained to Ciano. "This time I will pay him back with the same coin. He will learn from the papers that I have occupied Greece. Thus the balance will be re-established." He added that he would "give my resignation as an Italian if anyone finds difficulty in fighting Greeks." Ciano noted in his diary: "I believe the operation will be useful and easy."[17]

The decision to attack was made at a meeting of Mussolini, Ciano, Jacomoni and military leaders on October 15, with Ciano and Jacomoni taking the lead in pressing for action. "Ciano was the evil genius of this campaign," Marshal Badoglio, chief of the General Staff, wrote afterward.[18] At the meeting, Ciano said: "There is a clear schism between the population and the plutocratic leadership which animates resistance and keeps alive the pro-British spirit in the country. This is a very small, very rich class, while the rest are indifferent to all events, including our invasion." Mussolini suggested an "incident" was needed to provide an excuse for the Italian invasion. "When do you want the incident to happen?" Ciano asked. "The 24th," Mussolini replied. Ciano said: "The incident will happen on the 24th."[19] Mussolini fixed the attack for October 26. He shared Ciano's assumptions about victory, but several times after the debacle that ensued he told him: "If someone on October 15 had foreseen what really would happen afterward, I would have had him shot."[20] On October 17 Badoglio told Ciano the three heads of the General Staff were unanimously opposed to the attack, and General Soddu reported the following day that Badoglio was threatening to resign if it went ahead. Mussolini, in a rage, said he would go personally to Greece "to be present at the incredible shame of Italians who are afraid of Greeks."[21] Badoglio, in a meeting with Mussolini, did not repeat his threat but only asked for a couple of days' postponement.

Phillips learned of the planned invasion and cabled Washington on October 21 that it was set for the morning of October 25. On October 22, Mussolini revealed his plan to Hitler in a letter which he dated October 19. By now he had changed the date of the attack to October 28, but did not inform the Führer of that. Hitler was in France, and received the letter on October 25 in the train taking him home. Ribbentrop, on Hitler's instructions, fixed an appointment for Hitler to meet Mussolini in Florence on October 28, and the Führer's train headed toward Italy.

On October 24 Ciano wrote in his diary: "I examine with Pricolo the plan of attack on Greece. It is good because it is energetic and decisive. With a hard blow at the beginning, it is likely that everything will collapse within a few hours."[22] He told Bastianini that same day, "It will be a military walkover. Everything is arranged . . . It will all go very well." Bastianini objected that the Greeks "will resist like lions," but Ciano made a sign with his thumb and index finger to indicate he had bought them off.[23] Ciano drafted an ultimatum to Greece and showed it to Bottai, who noted in his diary: "Galeazzo repeats a sentence pronounced by Mussolini the other day in the Council of Ministers: 'If we should not be in a position to defeat the Greeks promptly, I would resign from being an Italian.' "[24] During a stop at Bologna station on October 28, Hitler learned the Italian attack was under way. He arrived at Florence station at 10 a.m., and at that point could only offer best wishes. But he was furious. He could not understand the decision to fight after the winter rains had begun, and knew that the war would give British planes a base in Greece from which to bomb the Ploesti oilfields in Romania.

Ciano left for Albania on October 29. The war started badly, with the Italian attack delayed several hours because of heavy rain that prevented the air force from taking part. Italian planners had failed to take account of the rainy season, and no one had thought to equip the troops with winter clothing. Italy's Albanian mercenaries deserted *en masse* to the Greeks. Within days, the Italians were being pushed back with heavy losses. Ciano quickly began shifting the blame, informing Mussolini that the attack had not been prepared adequately by Badoglio and the General Staff.

On November 1, as the weather cleared, Ciano participated in an air raid on Salonica. Two Italian planes were lost, and the attackers failed to damage the port, which was their target, but some bombs fell near a school where the Greek government had placed all the Italian citizens living in Salonica. In his diary Ciano wrote: "On my return I am attacked by Greek planes. All goes well. Two of theirs fell, but I confess—it was the first time I've had fighters on my tail—it is a very ugly sensation."[25] Marcello del Drago said that Ciano, on his return from that mission, was "very excited and very proud of his success . . . He was then in one of the bad moods that made us despair of him and almost give up. For a few days after his flight he was bitter and resentful against the Greeks, abusing them openly and repeatedly . . . He was very friendly with a girl who had a Greek family in Athens. Even in front of her he would disparage Greeks with a complete absence of restraint and good taste . . . But all this blustering did not last long . . . He quieted down, did not talk about Greece any more and even did a lot to help his friend's relations, sending them food and other essentials."[26]

On November 3, Ciano met Ribbentrop in Schönhof, near Karlsbad, to sign a secret protocol by which Spain promised to join the Tripartite Pact later. Then things started to go disastrously wrong in Greece. Italian troops were forced to retreat to the Albanian border because reserves to reinforce them could not be found. The troops, as well as lacking proper winter clothing for fighting in the icy mountains, were poorly armed and fed. Greece, with less than a quarter of the Italian population, proved to have better weapons, better winter clothing and more medicine for its wounded. In the first fourteen days of war, Italy lost 1,700 men. Mussolini replaced General Prasca with Soddu and complained to Roberto Farinacci that even Ciano had given him "inexact information" on the Greek situation. Despite these setbacks, Ciano told Bottai the Italians would be in Athens by Christmas. Bottai was amazed. "It is incredible," he wrote, "how even a man of great and precise responsibilities wants to delude himself to the point of denial and lying."[27] Ciano met Grazzi on November 8. In his memoirs, Grazzi recalled:

At a certain point he asked me how the Greeks had treated the Italians. I had to respond that the treatment was rather hard. Then he said he wanted to inform the Duce immediately about it. He called Palazzo Venezia on his direct line and repeated what I had told him. Then he added: "Grazzi is here with me. He also says that everything will go very well." And he put down the receiver. Faced with such impudence, I don't know how I succeeded in remaining calm. I said to him: "I didn't tell you that." At which the Minister, getting up, replied in a light-hearted way: "You will see, you will see. The General Staff has been foolish; but now we will send to Albania twenty divisions and in fifteen days everything will be finished." And since I shook my head negatively, he asked me: "Why not?" I replied that within a few days the rain would have begun, after which the snow. Thus until the end of April or the first days of May it was madness to think of large-scale operations . . . The Minister then asked me, "Don't you believe that if we carried out a mass bombardment of Athens the Greeks would get discouraged?" I replied that if he wanted to draw upon Italy the aversion of the entire civilized world there was no better means than the bombing of Athens, but an undertaking of this nature would have no other effect on the Greeks than to multiply the fury against us. He replied that he laughed (I use this word out of regard for my readers) at their impotent fury and . . . he dismissed me very coldly.[28]

Goebbels commented in his diary on November 15: "Ciano was responsible for the whole affair, against the wishes of the majority. Another windbag, a companion for Ribbentrop."[29] That same day Ciano noted in his diary: "We lack guns, while the Greek artillery is modern and well handled."[30] Ciano's unpopularity in Italy was now total. The Italians believed their sons had died in a vain war instigated by him to expand his "grand duchy," and many called for him to be fired. There were rumors he would go to Berlin, Moscow or even Brazil as ambassador. In his diary Puntoni wrote: "All the hatred of the people is for Ciano and for his following . . . People don't understand why the Duce doesn't decide to rid himself of him." The journalist Ugo Ojetti wrote: "Universal hatred rains on Ciano."[31] Mussolini received an anonymous report from a Roman *squadrista* saying that military circles, the party and ministries were pervaded by unlimited indignation toward Ciano. The report claimed he had expressed admiration for Royal Air Force pilots and the successes of the Royal Navy, while deriding Axis victories. "The party considers Ciano less than zero . . . a decadent snob, and a man of scarce intelligence," the informant wrote. He went on to say that Ciano was "a national calamity," and was spreading the word that Mussolini was tired, old and had chosen him as his successor.[32] This was the opportune moment for Mussolini to fire Ciano. But he did not act, and the reason he did not can only be a matter of speculation. Perhaps Mussolini preferred to have Ciano as a lightning rod for the unpopularity that otherwise would have beset him as a result of the Greek disaster. There was some speculation that Ciano was saved by the intervention of Edda. But Edda and Ciano were practically living apart then, and there were rumors she intended to leave him for Pucci.

Marcello del Drago said he later told Ciano that one of the causes of his unpopularity was the general belief that he was responsible for the war. Ciano brazenly told him, "I had nothing to do with it. In a country like Italy where you can't even shake hands because Mussolini frowns on the shakers, do you think I could have started a war without his consent or will? I will show you the minutes of the last meeting when the war was decided. Mussolini did all the talking and fixed the date. Badoglio agreed. I said nothing during the whole meeting."[33] The minutes cited earlier in this chapter show, of course, that he lied. Later, Grazzi noted that Ciano called the conflict "my war," in the presence of various persons "who still shudder at the memory."[34] Mussolini, in a speech on November 18, used a curious expression: "We will break the kidneys of Greece." Italians began calling him Elmitolo, the name of a drug used for the treatment of kidney complaints.[35] His popularity, along with that of Ciano, plummeted.

Hitler, meeting with Ciano on November 18 at Obersalzberg, deplored the attack on Greece and the manner in which it had been conducted. Ciano tried to speak, but Hitler cut him off. He warned that in March German troops would come down from Romania through Bulgaria to join the attack on Greece. "His criticism is open, definite and final," Ciano noted.[36] Yet in a report to Mussolini, Ciano claimed the opposite. He said the Führer was "not displeased" about the attack on Greece, nor had he made recriminations. But Hitler made his feelings known to Mussolini in a sealed letter he gave to Ciano to pass on to the Duce. In it he wrote that the fiasco in Greece "has very grave psychological and military consequences."[37]

Ciano met with the papal nuncio in December to discuss the abolition of New Year's Day, Epiphany and St Joseph's Day as national holidays. "It is a personal initiative of the Duce, who is very proud of it," Ciano observed in his diary. "I wonder whether, in moments such as this, it is worthwhile irritating people with inventions of this nature."[38]

By early December, Greek forces had pushed the Italians back into Albania and had even occupied Port Edda. The Italian situation was desperate. In some cases, troops were forced to eat food that had been destined for their mules. One Italian general hinted that Italy should ask Greece for an armistice, but Mussolini responded that it would be preferable for everyone to leave for Albania and be killed on the spot. He fired

Badoglio for having the impertinence to point out that the General Staff had opposed the war. From that moment Badoglio would bide his time and await his moment of revenge. Goebbels wrote of Mussolini: "He would do better to sack Ciano too. He deserves it most."[39] General Ugo Cavallero replaced Badoglio, but Mussolini was now thoroughly discouraged. "There is nothing else to do," Mussolini told Ciano on December 4. "It is grotesque and absurd, but it is a fact. We have to ask for a truce through Hitler." Ciano wrote in his diary: "Impossible . . . Before telephoning Ribbentrop, I would rather put a bullet through my head . . . What counts today is to resist, and to hold on to Albania." Mussolini changed his mind about seeking a truce, but told Ciano: "The human material I have to work with is useless, worthless."[40] Speaking to Ciano on December 6, the Duce returned to his favorite theme of the soft and corrupt Italian middle class. "If, when I was a Socialist, I had had a more than theoretical knowledge of the Italian bourgeoisie . . . I would have launched a revolution so pitiless that, by comparison, that of Comrade Lenin would have been an innocent joke," he said.[41]

Italian troops continued to be pinned down in Albania, while in Libya the British launched an offensive on December 9 against General Rodolfo Graziani's troops. Four Italian divisions were quickly overcome, and 78,000 men taken prisoner. Most of the Italian planes in the area were grounded for lack of spare parts. Mussolini was at first unruffled, then shaken as the magnitude of the disaster became apparent. He told Ciano on December 14, "Five generals prisoner and one dead. This is the ratio of Italians who have military qualities and those who have none. In future we will make a professional army, creaming them from ten or twelve million Italians: those in the Po Valley and in part from central Italy. All the others will make arms for the warrior aristocracy."[42] Over the next two months the Italians would lose the entire Cyrenaica region of Libya and 130,000 of their troops would become prisoners. The scale of the defeat was hidden from the Italian public. Goebbels' diary for December 10 recorded that Mussolini "is sacking one commanding officer after another. He should fire Ciano, and the Führer should do likewise with Ribbentrop. Both are vain poseurs and dilettantes. This becomes all too clear when they are given a great task to carry out alone and unaided."[43]

On December 20, an Italian division on the Albanian littoral was pushed back by a Greek attack. Mussolini prepared a message asking for German intervention in Thrace through Bulgaria. Four days later, as snow fell on Rome, Mussolini looked out of a window and commented to Ciano: "This snow and cold are very good. In this way the runts will die and this mediocre Italian race will be improved."[44] Italian troops on the Greek front had sufficient experience of cold and snow. By Christmas, temperatures had dropped to –20C. Everywhere the war was going badly. December saw the most intense aerial bombardment of the Italian mainland yet. The specter of hunger loomed over the population of the most heavily bombed cities. On December 30, Mussolini named Cavallero the commander of forces in Albania in place of Soddu. "The final straw was when the Duce learned that Soddu, even in Albania, was devoting his evening hours to composing music for the films," Ciano said.[45]

The king expressed his dissatisfaction about the war to Ciano on January 6, 1941. "For too long a chair has been called a palace in Italy, but this does not alter the fact that a chair remains a chair," he said. "Thus our divisions, undermanned and disarmed, are divisions in name only."[46] Alfieri, then the ambassador in Germany, advised Ciano on January 14 that a campaign against him in Germany had had "certain repercussions," but now it was all over. "I am not surprised by this," Ciano wrote. "The Germans have an old grudge for my nonbelligerency, and even when they try to save appearances they cannot entirely conceal—especially Ribbentrop—a degree of resentment . . . My fault was having been right!"[47]

The following month, Mussolini announced that government ministers and high-ranking Fascist officials could sign up for military operations in Albania. Ciano was among those who prepared to go off to war but, before leaving, he accompanied Mussolini to a meeting with Hitler at Obersalzberg on January 19-20. Hitler confirmed the forthcoming German intervention against Greece, restated his old suspicions about Russian intentions and urged Mussolini to intervene with Franco to get Spain into the war. During the meeting, Hitler gave Mussolini a secret memorandum about Ciano prepared by Himmler. Ciano learned of it, and commented to a friend, "Von Ribbentrop has stabbed me in the back. Behind Himmler there is Ribbentrop. It seems that in that memorandum he asked for my head. If Mussolini gives my head to von Ribbentrop, he will show that he is what we all knew: a coward . . . Mussolini will never give my head to anyone. He is afraid. He knows very well that all Italians are with me. The Italians know that I am the only one in Italy who has the courage to stand up to Mussolini. "[48] The memorandum was not to be found in either German or Italian archives after the war. But the German archives contain a note in German from "some old squadristic friends of Germany" which told of suspicions about how Costanzo Ciano had acquired his wealth, and listed Ciano's own riches. It also listed persons classified as homosexuals, Jews, rogues and pimps who supposedly were in contact with Ciano, and discussed at length Edda's habits and her love affairs.[49]

The king too had turned against Ciano. In mid-January, he confided to Bottai his "disgust" for Ciano and said that, in association with a banker named Armenise, Ciano "was conducting a game against him." Bottai, in his diary, did not elaborate.[50] Goebbels was still splenetic about Ciano. On February 12 he recorded in his diary: "Report from Italy: very pessimistic. Corruption and more corruption. Particularly around the Cianos. And defeatism in influential circles." The following day he wrote: "Reports from Italy mention profoundest defeatism. These days, the Führer is their only hope. Ciano is absolutely finished, and the Duce's popularity is approaching zero level . . . We must soon make a move, or Italy will crumble into nothingness." The very next day he added: "To the common people, Ciano is a devil. And he must be incredibly corrupt. The Italians will continue to give us plenty to worry about."[51] In February, Ojetti wrote that a senator had said to Mussolini, "Let Ciano go, and many tempers will be calmed." He said the Duce struck his desk with his fist and replied, "For your guidance, Count Ciano has nothing for which to reproach himself . . . No one can reproach anything in Count Ciano."[52]

Ciano left Rome on January 26 for Bari where, as a captain of the air force, he assumed command of a bombing unit and participated in air operations on the Greek–Albanian frontier for the next three months. Mussolini resumed control of the Foreign Ministry in his absence, not bothering to inform Ciano of developments in foreign policy. On February 12, Mussolini went to Bordighera to meet Franco and irritated Ciano by failing to take him along. "He hates me, there's nothing for it, he hates me," Ciano told a friend.[53] Anfuso had asked Mussolini if he wanted Ciano to attend the meeting and Mussolini, opening his eyes wide, exclaimed: "Count Ciano is an aviator and remains with his squadron. Either he makes war or he is Minister of Foreign Affairs. Count Ciano will remain in Bari."[54] The Mussolini–Franco meeting was widely reported, with a great deal of speculation in the foreign press about Ciano's absence.

Mussolini told Anfuso he had been hearing reports of bad behavior by Ciano and his fellow officers in Bari, such as launching fireworks in the city at night. "These things are intolerable and require punishment," he said. "I have arranged for a severe inquiry that I have entrusted to an air force general. Even Captain Ciano will have to explain his behavior." One night some officers of Ciano's squadron celebrated the success of one of their colleagues in battle with a rowdy, late-night dinner. Although a curfew was in effect, they went onto the streets of the city center, singing war songs. Sad and humiliated, Ciano had to appear before the general conducting the inquiry. Immediately afterward he wrote a letter to Mussolini in which he complained of the procedure and the Duce's lack of confidence in him. "At the end of this letter permit me to tell you, Duce, that you have opened in my heart a deep furrow that nothing will ever succeed in filling," he wrote. Perhaps no other person would have dared to pen such words to Mussolini. "From this moment their relations became tense and remained so," said Alfieri.[55]

Mussolini ordered a spring offensive, confident that this would win the war, and went to Albania on March 2 to show himself the supreme commander at the moment of victory. When Italian forces launched their attack, their communiqués reported steady advances, but in fact they made headway only slowly, suffered heavy losses and, under Greek counterattack, quickly had to abandon many of the positions they had captured. Mussolini grumbled that his generals showed little spirit or initiative. On March 14, the sixth day of the offensive, Cavallero warned Mussolini that if no breakthrough were achieved soon the attack would have to be called off. The following day, Mussolini learned that a British torpedo plane had sunk the hospital ship *Po* in the port of Vlorë the previous night and he rushed to the scene. One of the nurses aboard the ship was Edda. She had failed to complete her two-year training with the Red Cross, and officials there had refused her application to serve on a hospital ship. But she had persuaded her father to make the navy give her a cabin to herself that was separate from the nurses' group. "Then she acted as a nurse; everybody was happy, they all had their own way and nobody lost face," Susanna Agnelli recalled.[56]

Edda's ship was struck by two air-launched torpedos as she was in her cabin reading P.G. Wodehouse. "I remember there was a wonderful moon," she said later. "Incredibly somebody shouted to me to get dressed, though the ship was going down fast and the lifeboats were damaged and could not be launched. I remember wondering whether to grab my overcoat or my raincoat. I saw the head of our group throw herself into the waves and the waves carry her away. I climbed on the rail and let myself fall into the water. 'Santa Rita,' I cried, 'help me,' and began to swim as best I could in the cold water. I tried not to lose strength and meanwhile I felt in my legs the painful circles of cold and feared a mortal cramp. The sea was full of paper. I thought how strange that a ship had so much paper on board. As the ship keeled over I saw my friend another nurse hit and crushed by the mast and many others drowned. In the distance I saw passing the black shadow of a lifeboat loaded beyond belief. I shouted. They didn't want to take me on board, they were overloaded to the point of capsizing. Someone shouted to me to wait and it was then that I believed I was done for. But a powerful arm reached toward me, I gripped it and I was in the heap of people. I trembled from cold. Someone recognized me. A sailor gave me a bottle of cognac, another a jacket. I emptied half the bottle in one gulp and almost immediately felt revived. When my father met me at Valona [Vlorë] he said to me: 'I see you have the tough hide of the Mussolinis.'"[57] Three nurses died in the sinking of the *Po*. Mussolini hurried to telephone Rachele to reassure her their daughter was safe, and Ciano arrived the next day. The famous Italian journalist Indro Montanelli, among the group of reporters who met Edda after her rescue, described her as shy and proud. "After the ship sank, she sat on a seat smoking and sipping a mixture of rum and coffee," he said. "To our questions she responded unwillingly and with a lack of grace. It was clear she didn't like the role of heroine."[58]

On March 16, with Mussolini away from the front, his generals ordered a halt to their offensive. They had sustained 12,000 casualties and gained no ground. Mussolini left Albania on March 21, complaining that the generals had been deceiving him about the capabilities of their forces. Goebbels observed on March 26: "Still great discontent in Italy. Ciano is the main target. But even feeling against the Duce . . . Fascist corruption stinks to high heaven. Ciano has corrupted the entire crew." Later, he dilated on Ciano's corruption. "I tell the Führer a few facts about Ciano, which disturb him deeply. Ciano is a social climber who has lost all respect in Italy. He is also stupid, without manners, tactless and insolent . . . Mussolini should send Ciano out into the wilderness. But who would take his place? Grandi would be even worse, because he has secret pro-English tendencies. But the business with Ciano will end badly . . . Ciano is finished so far as the Führer is concerned."[59] The Italian navy suffered a severe defeat off Cape Matapan (Akra Tainaron) in southern Greece at the end of March. The losses were the worst in Italian naval history. The British lost one plane and its crew.

Ciano, back in his role as Foreign Minister, met Hitler in Vienna on March 25. He had, said Goebbels, "bounced back up from the depths again."[60] Hitler told him it was urgent to ensure Yugoslav neutrality to avoid attacks on the flanks of German troops moving into Greece via Bulgaria, and therefore Germany had persuaded Yugoslavia to join the Tripartite Pact. It was signed the following day, but the mood in Yugoslavia was hostile to the Axis and the agreement provoked the fall of the Belgrade government. Hitler rushed troops to Yugoslavia and prepared to finish the war in Greece that his Italian allies had bungled so spectacularly. The Greeks had contained the Italian offensive by moving troops from their Bulgarian frontier, leaving that sector almost defenseless. The British planned to send 100,000 troops to Greece to bolster the country's defenses, and some of them had already landed when Hitler's armies swept down into Greece at 5.30 a.m. on Sunday, April 6. Three days later the Germans had moved into Salonica, leaving many Greek troops further north surrounded.

Mussolini ordered an Italian advance in Albania on April 10, and two days later the Greeks began evacuating Albanian territory to avoid encirclement by the Germans, who had moved westward to confront them. On April 17, Yugoslavia asked for an armistice with Germany and Italy, and the following day the encirclement of the Greek armies that had fought in Albania was nearly complete. The Greek king gave his consent to the evacuation of British forces on April 29. The commander of the Greek troops on the Albanian front signed an armistice with the Germans on April 20. He wanted to avoid surrendering to the Italians, but on the following day he was forced to give in. The Italians, however, refused to countenance an armistice while Greeks were on Albanian territory and resumed hostilities. This angered the Germans, who sent units forward to stop the Italian advance. As part of their armistice with the Greeks, the Germans had agreed that the defeated troops could go home and their officers retain their sidearms. Mussolini protested in vain against this decision on April 22. Finally, at 9 p.m. that day, the Greeks asked the Italians to accept their surrender and the agreement was signed at 2.45 p.m. on April 23. The Italians announced that in the last, unnecessary days of fighting they had suffered 6,000 casualties, including 400 officers. Mussolini proclaimed victory. The real victors, the German army, entered the outskirts of Athens on April 27 and the city surrendered without a struggle. The entire campaign had cost the Germans 4,834 men killed or wounded. The month of April ended with the Italian occupation of the Greek islands of Corfu, Cefalonia and Zante. The Italian Defense Ministry reported that 13,755 Italian troops were killed in the war, 50,874 were wounded, 12,368 suffered frostbite and 25,067 were missing, most believed dead. Greek losses amounted to 13,408 killed and 42,485 wounded.[61]

Mussolini had wanted to go to Greece to accept the surrender personally and was outraged that the Greeks were allowed to surrender before he could get there. He set about manufacturing a story that the Greek forces had been in headlong retreat even before the German attack, but no one believed him. His regime was totally discredited with the Italian people, and never recovered. The Italian historian Mario Cervi later wrote: "In the Greek campaign the Italian troops were, without any doubt whatever, the worst-led troops in the world. They deserved better of their country."[62]

In a broadcast on April 27, Churchill taunted Mussolini for having been forced to rely on the Germans to save him from defeat, and then claiming victory. "Here surely is the world record in the domain of the ridiculous and the contemptible," he said. "This whipped jackal Mussolini, who to save his skin has made of Italy a vassal state of Hitler's empire, goes frisking up to the side of the German tiger with yelps not only of appetite—that could be understood—but even of triumph."[63] Hitler tactfully tried to suggest the Italians could have won the war on their own. "The Duce . . . was convinced that with the beginning of the fine weather season the war against Greece would be crowned with success," he told the Reichstag. "I was of the same opinion. Thus the German forces were not deployed to help Italy against Greece."[64]

After the occupation of Yugoslavia in early April by German, Italian, Hungarian and Romanian forces, the free state of Croatia was proclaimed by Ante Pavelic, an extreme Fascist who had been in exile in Italy. The formal partition of Yugoslavia took place in Vienna on April 21-22. Ciano wanted to annex the entire Adriatic coast for Italy, but Ribbentrop told him that northern Slovenia was reserved for Germany. Ribbentrop also suggested that Croatia should not be deprived of an outlet to the sea, and the Adriatic coast eventually was divided between Italy and Croatia.

Bastianini noted in Ciano a passivity toward the Germans after the Greek war. "Did they want to transfer thousands of workers to Germany? They took them," he wrote. "Did they want credits of billions with Italian industries? They helped themselves. Did they want entire trains fully exempt from Customs? They got them. Did they practically cancel our commercial agreements with Croatia, Romania, Hungary? Did they in the occupied countries take over Italian companies they found there? They did as they pleased . . . He didn't feel like opposing them uselessly and irritating them."[65] Fascist Italy's collapse had begun. The Italian people seethed with opposition to the war, and criticism of the regime became more widespread and outspoken. Ciano began to plot seriously against his leader.

Chapter Twelve

The Most Hated Man in Italy

On May 19, 1941, Italy lost the jewel of its empire when the Duke of Aosta, viceroy of Ethiopia, was forced to surrender to the British. A few days earlier, a message had arrived in Washington asking how the United States would react to a coup in Italy accompanied by an offer of peace to England. The message suggested that Mussolini and the king would be overthrown, and the king replaced by the Duke of Aosta. The author was Ciano. John Evans, an agent of the American Office of Strategic Services in London, was then instructed by his superior, Colonel Snyder, to go to Rome and arrange to meet Ciano. Snyder told Evans (possibly not his real name) that in the course of conversation with Ciano he should mention the name Marietti. "If he doesn't respond to that, leave immediately," Snyder said. "If he does, try to get more details and reassure him he will find much understanding in the U.S. government for any step toward a separate peace. Then go to Lisbon for further instructions."[1]

In Rome, Evans contacted Giorgio Nelson Page, the Italo-American who had worked for Ciano in the Propaganda Ministry, and Page arranged for him to be present at the Golf Club when Ciano was there. Page approached Ciano and told him Evans wanted to play golf with him. Ciano replied, "They already say that I am pro-English. If they see me play with an American, who knows what will happen? Tell your friend that I authorize him to say he played with me. To please you." But then Evans joined their table, and as the conversation proceeded Evans said there was an Italian golf pro in Philadelphia who had often spoken of Ciano. Ciano asked who he was. "His name is Marietti, Excellency," Evans replied, drawing on his cigarette and smiling at Ciano. Ciano invited Evans to call on him at the Palazzo Chigi for tea that afternoon. At 3.15 the next morning Page was awakened by Evans returning from his meeting with Ciano. "Everything goes for the best," Evans said. "Think, Giorgio, think that perhaps we will succeed. Because Mussolini may be disposed to retire. I believe the two are in agreement. Tomorrow I leave immediately."

Page pressed him for details, and Evans replied that he would return soon with concrete proposals from Washington and "Italy will be saved."

On June 16 Ciano was in Venice for a conference with Ribbentrop. On a gondola ride on the canals, Ciano asked about rumors that the Germans were preparing to attack the Soviet Union. Ribbentrop replied, "Dear Ciano, I cannot tell you anything as yet. Every decision is locked in the impenetrable breast of the Führer. However, one thing is certain: if we attack them, the Russia of Stalin will be erased from the map within eight weeks."[2] Ciano repeated that in his diary. In a fuller official report, he said Ribbentrop told him a crisis with Russia was "more than probable, by now almost certain." Ciano commented: "The tone and the words used by Ribbentrop are such as to leave little doubt about the decision already taken by the Führer to attack Russia soon." He said Ribbentrop cut short the visit, telling him "the new conflict is now imminent."[3] Evans returned to Rome on June 22, the very day Germany declared war on the Soviet Union. Bismarck had arrived at Ciano's house at 3 a.m., bearing a letter from Hitler which announced the declaration of war. Ciano telephoned Mussolini, who was in the Adriatic resort of Riccione, and the Duce quickly responded that he would declare war during the day so that Italian troops could be present on the new front as soon as possible. Ciano was dismayed. He had gathered from Hitler's message that the Führer would gladly do without Italian participation. Mussolini's enthusiasm for a broader war seemed bizarre in that, only a few days earlier, he had told Ciano of his resentment toward the Germans. He called them "rabble" and expressed his disgust because they had made an armistice with Greece without informing the Italians and robbed them of "the fruits of victory." He went on to say he had had his fill of Hitler and his way of doing things. "These talks preceded by the ringing of a bell are not to my liking; a bell is rung when people call their servants . . . For five hours I am forced to listen to a rather boring and useless monologue . . . For the moment there is nothing to be done. We must howl with the wolves."[4]

Evans showed up at the Excelsior Hotel, where Page was living temporarily, on the morning of June 22, carrying a small suitcase and a leather briefcase. "I have the proposals," he said, and asked Page to make an appointment for him. Page went to the Foreign Ministry and, when he was eventually shown in, found the minister frowning. "What do you want?" Ciano asked brusquely. When Page explained his mission Ciano, with evident irritation, asked, "Are you aware of what he wants from me?" "Really, I am not," Page replied. "I know that he was very moved by your courtesies." Ciano got up and went toward the window. "Now don't bore me with this American rogue," he said. "If you need money to pay your gambling debts, find them in some other way. Do you understand? He will do well to go away immediately. And you be careful. Very careful. Now get out. I have work to do."

Page, dismayed, returned to the Excelsior to report to Evans the outcome of his mission. "He looked at me," Page recalled. "He took the morning newspaper mechanically in hand. In big letters it announced the German declaration of war on the Soviet Union . . . The veil fell from my eyes. The attack on Russia indicated the reawakening of all the German power . . . Galeazzo had seen nothing else. He had believed in the German effort. And his every other concrete 'heresy' now frightened him . . . To hell with John Evans and those cursed proposals made in a moment in which it seemed all was lost." Evans shared his analysis. Before leaving, he commented sadly: "It would have been the salvation of Italy, its territorial integrity and the conservation of part of its African empire." But there may have been another explanation for Ciano's volte-face. The journalist Paolo Monelli reported, in a possible reference to Evans' mission, that Roosevelt and Churchill sent an "envoy" to Rome to discuss Italy's withdrawal from the war. He said, quoting a trusted secretary of the Foreign Minister, that Ciano went to Mussolini and told him: "It's the last chance. There won't be others." Mussolini was said to have replied, "You are always pessimistic. But we must go to our goal, to our goal with our ally."[5]

If Ciano underwent a change of heart toward the Germans after the attack on the Soviet Union, it is not apparent from his diaries. He simply expressed concern about the poor state of equipment of Italian troops going to the Soviet front, and continued to record Mussolini's outbursts against the Germans. The Duce feared they were getting ready to ask him for the Alto Adige, and he was belatedly offended by the way Hitler had had him awakened in the middle of the night to be told of the attack on the Soviet Union. "I do not dare to disturb my servants at night, but the Germans make me jump out of bed without the least consideration," he grumbled. Ciano tried to dissuade Mussolini from sending Italian troops, but Mussolini insisted, convinced they were superior to the Germans, both in men and equipment. "His eternal illusions . . .," Ciano confided to his diary.[6]

Bottai lunched with Ciano on July 1. "I follow the slow, discontinuous evolution of the man toward an anti-Mussolini decision," Bottai wrote afterward. "He speaks of the theft of art works that the Germans—and he names Göring and Hitler—are carrying out in Italy, with the approval of Mussolini, who has said he is disposed to give them 'some hundreds of square kilometers of paintings, in order to get some oil.' I, who have tried to resist from time to time, confess my repugnance. 'I would prefer,'

I say, 'not to be the minister who underwrites this.' 'You are right', Galeazzo responds, 'but prepare yourself for worse.' 'What?' I ask. 'If one day the Germans ask us for the Alto Adige.'"[7]

The king, meanwhile, told his aide-de-camp General Puntoni that Ciano was not working with the seriousness and discernment necessary in a time of such intense world diplomatic activity. Although he himself had expressed a strong dislike of the Germans, he now reproved Ciano privately for the same thing. "In the Foreign Ministry, in many Roman salons and in high society he continues to say bad things about the Germans," the king told Puntoni. "It is extremely dangerous because the German government is in a position to be informed of every rumor . . . Ciano . . . doesn't succeed ever in keeping his tongue between his teeth and his mouth closed; not even when it's a matter of questions that should remain secret . . . I've said therefore to Mussolini that I have known rather unpleasant and compromising things concerning his son-in-law. There has been an inventory of the things left by the old Ciano and it results that his patrimony amounts to nine hundred million lire. Even the Duce rolled his eyes and remained breathless. It seemed to me that he was not up to date and that the news surprised him a lot . . . Mussolini listened always in silence, shaking his head every now and then and passing his hand across his forehead."[8]

There is no record of Mussolini having confronted Ciano with the accusations against him. The Duce was preoccupied with the Germans and, on July 6, said to Ciano, "Note in your diary that I foresee a crisis between Italy and Germany as inevitable . . . I now seriously ask whether a British victory would not be more desirable for our future than a German victory . . . Since we shall have to fight the Germans, we must not create the myth of their invincibility. That notwithstanding, I have little faith in our race; at the first bombardment that might destroy a famous campanile or a painting by Giotto, the Italians would go into a fit of artistic sentimentality and throw up their arms."[9] Buffarini-Guidi came to Ciano on July 9 and painted "a very, very dark picture" of the internal situation. "Anti-fascism has taken root everywhere threateningly, implacably and silently," Ciano noted in his diary.[10] The journalist Alberto Giannini, meanwhile, recorded in his diary: "They say that Edda Ciano, having drunk a few glasses of champagne too many, has said in a vein of confidence, 'Let's have fun and enjoy ourselves while we can, because we are destined to end up hanged in Piazza Venezia.'"[11]

On July 11 an Allied air raid on Naples left refineries burning. "I am glad that Naples has had such severe nights," Mussolini told Ciano. "The race will become harder. War will make of the Neapolitans a Nordic people." Ciano observed privately: "About that I am very skeptical."

Mussolini ordered the air-raid alarm in Rome to sound every time there was an alarm in Naples, and ordered anti-aircraft batteries around the capital to fire "to make it more exciting." Ciano asked himself: "Is all this worthwhile?"[12] Mussolini told Ciano he admired an Italian general in Albania who had told his soldiers: "I have heard it said that you are good family men. That's fine in your house, but not here. Here you can never do too much thieving, murder and rape."[13]

But the Duce's eyes were open with respect to the Germans. He told Ciano he had begun to wonder if Italy now belonged among the vassal nations; even if it were not true, it would be true on the day of German victory. "They are treacherous and unbridled," he said, adding that Italy must place thousands of guns along the rivers in the Venice region to forestall a German invasion. "We must hope for two things: that the war will be long and exhausting for Germany, and that it may end in a compromise that saves our independence," he said.[14] The fulfillment of his fears came quickly. On July 21, Hitler asked to take over Italian air and naval commands. Ciano commented: "I do not believe that this request will increase fondness toward Germany in many circles." He told an associate on July 25: "The Germans have lost the war."[15] From late July until September, Ciano was away from his post with a severe throat infection that required an operation on his tonsils. He learned of the death of Bruno Mussolini in an air crash at Pisa on August 7, and got out of his sick bed to be near Mussolini as the Duce prepared to leave for Pisa to mourn his son.

Edda left Italy in mid-August to serve as a nurse on the Russian front. She spent three months at a field hospital at Stalino, in Ukraine. While working there she told Medical Captain Maurizio Alpi, "In Shanghai I was very much in love with Galeazzo. I was also very jealous of him . . . Afterward there remained much affection between us, but little by little love ended."[16] When she returned to Italy, she resumed her old ways. A secret police report described her "dissipated life" in Capri. It said she had lost 2,500,000 lire at poker, and would not let her guests leave until she had succeeded in recovering the sum. The report also faulted her for going about the island in scanty attire, not even respecting the norms of society after Bruno's death. "The Countess does not even give up dancing, as if the Fatherland were not at war," the report said.[17] But for Ciano, Rachele Mussolini had now become a problem. She had complained about the Duce's behavior to Anfuso, and had threatened to come to the Palazzo Chigi and start "shooting up the place." Edda had dismissed her mother's bizarre behavior as due to "the effects of the menopause." Ciano noted in his diary: "For some months, in fact, Donna Rachele has been disturbed and suspicious, and busies herself like a police officer with many things that don't concern her. It even seems she goes snooping around dressed as a bricklayer, a peasant and God knows what else." He met her and reported: "She is in a continuous and unjustified state of over-excitement . . . She could live quietly, but instead embitters her days by futile controversies."[18]

Ciano had a long talk with the king on September 10. He said he wanted to "separate his responsibility from that of Mussolini," as he felt the Duce had been too optimistic about the war situation. "Ciano's selfishness disgusted me, all the more since his father-in-law has always defended and supported him, even when he knew that all Italy was against him," the king told Puntoni.[19]

When he returned to work, Ciano found Mussolini had convinced himself the Italian people were uneasy because they were not participating in the war on the Soviet front on a larger scale. Ciano wrote: "I don't agree with him. There is little feeling for this war, and the hardship that disturbs our people is called lack of bread, fats, eggs, etc. But this aspect of the situation is not the one that disturbs the Duce."[20] He spoke to Bottai on September 16 of Mussolini "as of a man finished."[21] Alfieri reported to Mussolini that there were rumors in Germany that Ciano was pessimistic about the war and contemptuous of the Germans. Mussolini relayed this message to Ciano, who wrote in his diary: "Alfieri had talked to me along these same lines with respect to what was being said about me. I've told off that affected ass, as I frequently do."[22] If he had disliked the Germans before, he had all the more reason to do so now. An Italian attaché in Berlin informed him that, in certain German labor camps where Italians were among those employed, large watchdogs had been trained to bite the legs of workers who got out of line. "If these facts were known to the Italians, they would revolt with a violence that few could imagine," he wrote. He showed the report to Mussolini, who ordered him to take it up with the German ambassador and pretend that the Duce was unaware of it. Later, however, Mussolini brooded over this insult and told Ciano: "I can even wait many years, but I will settle this account. I will not permit the sons of a race that has given to humanity Caesar, Dante and Michelangelo to be devoured by the mastiffs of the Huns." He ordered Ciano to take up the subject with Ribbentrop.[23]

In late September, Ciano learned that German armed units were being installed in the principal Italian cities. "What for?" he asked himself naively. "We must keep our eyes on them."[24] On September 27, with his country being taken over by Germans and his people suffering the privations of war, Mussolini called a Cabinet meeting and spent most of a three-hour speech, according to Ciano, railing against the bourgeoisie. The Duce also promised that the meager bread ration would be reduced further in the spring, "and this delights me because we will finally see signs of suffering on the faces of the Italian people, which will be valuable to us at the peace conference." Grandi accompanied Ciano when they left the meeting, and expressed his horror at what he called the "white Bolshevism of Mussolini."[25]

Phillips paid a farewell call on Ciano on September 30. Ciano noted in his diary that the Italian secret service had broken the American code, and discovered that Phillips' reporting on Italian events "can lend itself to malevolent interpretations."[26] Still, they had a cordial parting. Alberto Giannini told Ciano on October 3 that it might be necessary to reach an agreement with England, which had every interest in avoiding the collapse of Italy. Ciano replied that he could not make such a suggestion to Mussolini, for the Duce "would send me fishing in Livorno." At that time, Giorgio De Chirico was painting a portrait of Ciano and Edda. One day Ciano told Vergani: "If the war continues like this we will be hanged before the portrait is finished and it will be done truly just for posterity."[27] But the portrait was finished. On another occasion the Cianos entertained friends at dinner, and after the meal showed an American film about a Russian duchess. In one scene a butler was attending the duchess and Ciano, pointing to the butler, remarked: "If we are lucky, we can hope to end like that."[28] No doubt Ciano had begun to hear reports of how unpopular he was in Italy, both because of the disaster in Greece and his lifestyle. Foodstuffs became scarce, but rumors spread that the Cianos were living as though there were no rationing. One police agent filed a report in which he told of hearing a woman at a bus stop complaining that she couldn't buy bread, but knew that two freight cars full of flour had arrived at a rail station to feed the pheasants and other birds at Ciano's hunting reserve. She said she also heard the Cianos had a plentiful supply of milk for their dogs. Another police report said the actress Mariella Lotti had boasted to friends she was getting all the pasta she needed through Ciano, and the actress Elsa Merlini likewise said he had kept her well supplied with coffee. Yet another report said Edda, her children and her mother-in-law, while staying at a hotel in Abetone, had pasta and beefsteaks served to them every day, and ignored the looks from other guests. The report said Edda and her family went about in carriages drawn by English horses. It quoted rumors that she was on alcohol and drugs.[29]

Ciano went to Albania on October 8, and learned that the puppet government there intended to offer General Cavallero "a piece of Albanian soil." He thought that meant an urn filled with earth, then discovered it involved a grant of almost 2,500 acres. Ciano refused to allow it. In his diary, he wrote that Cavallero "doesn't understand that for a man such as himself, on whose fame as a strategist people disagree, but on whose reputation as a swindler all agree, the acceptance of such a gift would be the end."[30] He found on returning to Rome that Mussolini wanted to send another twenty divisions to Russia in the spring. The Duce thought this would prevent the Germans, at the moment of victory, from dictating to Italy as to conquered nations. Mussolini told him, "The conquered states will be true colonies. The associated states will be confederated provinces. Among these the most important is Italy . . . Even if they should ask for Trieste tomorrow, as part of the German *Lebensraum*, we would have to bow our heads."[31] The king told Ciano on October 15 he was against sending more troops to Russia. He was also disturbed by internal unrest, and now referred to his nation's allies as "those ugly Germans."[32]

Ciano lunched with Frau Goebbels on October 17 at the home of Attolico and afterward quoted Bismarck's comments about her in conversation with Anfuso: "Frau Goebbels is the typical wife of a Nazi leader. Her first marriage was with a swindler, and she earned money through prostitution. Then she became Goebbels' friend, but this did not prevent her from going to bed with many who frequented party meetings at the Sports Palast. Goebbels married her one evening when he was drunk. They have produced several children together, but it could be also not together, because Frau Goebbels has continued her former ways. Now she goes around looking for men, and when she isn't enough there is her sister-in-law, who is another whore. I am ashamed to think that my wife has anything to do with such people."[33]

Cavallero assured Ciano he would have ninety-two divisions ready in the spring, and Ciano wrote: "A tasteless lie. He knows very well we will not have even a third of that number. But in this way he spurs the Duce's imagination." Mussolini talked of sending fifteen divisions to Russia.[34]

Mussolini was supposed to pay a visit to Hitler, but he was suffering acute stomach pains and sent Ciano in his place. The meeting took place at Hitler's general quarters at Rastenburg, in a dark forest forty miles from the Russian front, on October 25, 1941. "I find him in great spiritual and physical form," Ciano wrote. "He is very courteous, or perhaps I should say chummy." He found Hitler confident of operations against Moscow once the weather improved and disposed to receive more Italian troops.[35] Ciano also met Ribbentrop for a hunting party. Hitler, learning that Ciano had killed 400 wild rabbits chased by beaters, exclaimed: "Four hundred! Would that in the course of his life as an aviator he had brought down only an infinitesimal part of this figure in enemy aircraft!"[36] In a dinner speech, Ribbentrop predicted victory in 1943. "For a man who has always, from 1939 onward, been announcing victory in fifteen days, he has made a big leap," Ciano said. Ribbentrop told him he had given orders to the German press always to write "Roosevelt, the Jew," adding: "I will make a prophecy: that man will be stoned in the Capitol by his own people." Ciano commented in his diary: "I think Roosevelt will die of old age because experience teaches me to give little credit to Ribbentrop's prophecies."[37] During his visit, Ciano was touched by the sight of prisoners of war serving on farms where labor was lacking. A German official told him: "*Chaque allemand a son français.*" It was, Ciano observed, equivalent to saying he had his cow or his horse. "Serfs. Slaves," he wrote. "If they touch a woman they are shot. And yet they have the blood of Voltaire and of Pasteur."[38]

Ciano later showed Bottai a report he had prepared on the meeting with Hitler. The report said Hitler had confessed that for him Russia had been a surprise. "If he had been able even to suspect earlier the huge mass of armaments, he would have hesitated to attack," Ciano wrote. Nonetheless, he said Hitler had confided that in the next two months Germany would turn its attention to England, "which will be subjected to aerial bombardments of a proportion never before reached." Returning to Rome, Ciano found Mussolini convinced the U.S. would not intervene. "Could he be right?" he asked himself.[39]

Shortly afterward Ciano had his first meeting with the new Italian police chief, the fat, jovial Carmine Senise, and reported on the encounter in his diary with evident relish. "He is an intelligent and ignorant Neapolitan, a strange mixture of instinct and investigator, basically a good man but a chatterer, superficial, a gesticulator," he wrote. "He might better have been a minister under the Bourbons." Senise told him Buffarini-Guidi was a hypocrite and a thief because he demanded money for the Aryanization of the Jews, and received money from Bocchini, his predecessor, a bigger thief than he if possible. Senise also confided that the Duce's new secretary, a man named De Cesare, had the evil eye and was an imbecile. "The information is not first class, but I will see him more often because he is amusing," Ciano wrote.[40] Later Senise wrote in his memoirs: "Not a week passed that he did not call me to Palazzo Chigi to give vent to his bitterness about the way things were going in Italy. 'Do the Italian people know'—he asked me one day—'that I have been against the war with all my strength and that I have fought until the last to avert it?' " he wrote. Senise said he replied: "They know, but they don't pardon you for having remained Foreign Minister and having shared in the responsibility." "But Senise, how can you say that to me!" Ciano said. "Don't you know that resignations are not given today? They are accepted only when no one has given them."[41]

The Germans advised the Italians on November 5 that Marshal Albert Kesselring was coming to Italy to assume command of joint German-Italian forces. There was no pretense of obtaining Italian agreement. "Mussolini has swallowed the toad," Ciano observed. The next day, Mussolini told him Italy could do nothing against Germany for the time being. "We must bide our time . . . [Germany] will collapse through lack of internal equilibrium," he said.[42] Meanwhile, Italy's war in the Mediterranean was going disastrously. On November 9 the British sank an entire convoy of seven ships carrying supplies to Libya, along with two or three destroyers. Then an Italian reconnaissance photo showed four British ships moored at Malta, and the Italians issued a war bulletin reporting one of the British cruisers had been hit. Ciano knew better. "This is equivalent to declaring that a man is probably slightly dead because he has gone to live near the cemetery," he wrote. "Clowns, tragic clowns, who have brought our country to its present necessity of accepting, in fact invoking, outside intervention for protection and defense."[43] Two days later another bulletin credited the submarine *Malaspina* with sinking two British steamers. "The only real sinking was that of the Italian submarine, which has been missing from its base for ten days," Ciano wrote. The bulletin said the two steamers had a total of 10,000 tons, but an Italian admiral picked up a pencil, Ciano said, and increased that to 30,000 because "this would create a greater effect." Ciano added: "Comment is superfluous."[44] As another sign of Italy's declining fortunes, Ciano noted on November 13 that the system of paying the salaries of foreign diplomats had had to be changed because the country had no more foreign exchange.

Ciano represented Italy at a meeting in Berlin in late November to renew the Anti-Comintern Pact and accept the adhesion of China, Denmark, Finland and Czechoslovakia to it. Ribbentrop made a speech which an Italian diplomat who was present said "seems the order of the day of a despot to his vassals. Ciano is furious." Ciano told him, "I wanted to answer him in kind. Everybody would have been with me." The diplomat added: "So why didn't he do it?"[45] In his diary, Ciano was more resigned: "Their European hegemony has now been established . . . Consequently, it is best to sit at the right hand of the master of the house. And we are at the right hand."[46] While he was in Berlin, Göring talked to him of Russians eating each other and of their having eaten a German sentry in a prison camp. "He recounted it with the most absolute indifference," Ciano wrote. "And yet he is a man with a good heart."[47]

On the morning of December 3 the Japanese ambassador to Rome told

Mussolini, in the presence of Ciano, that negotiations between Japan and the U.S. had arrived at a dead end and war was probable. Mussolini gave a commitment to declare war on the U.S. in that eventuality, provided Germany agreed to do the same. Despite his disaffection, Ciano made no attempt to warn Washington of the impending attack. But, facing a balcony in the Palazzo Chigi that overlooked the Corso, a main street of Rome, he commented to a visitor: "There we will see the American tanks go by."[48] Three days before the attack on Pearl Harbor, Ciano noted in his diary that bringing America into the war was "less and less liked by the Germans. Mussolini, on the other hand, is glad about it." But apparently he misread the German mood, for Ribbentrop telephoned him on December 8, joyful at what the Japanese had done. "He is so happy about it that I congratulated him, while not being too sure of the final advantages of this," Ciano wrote. "Mussolini was happy. For a long time now he has been in favor of clarifying the position between America and the Axis."[49] The king also expressed satisfaction.

Ciano called in the American chargé George Wadsworth at 2.30 p.m. on December 11 to inform him of Italy's declaration of war against the United States. He described Wadsworth as "a good but rather timid man, with whom I have had little to do. He thinks that I have called him to discuss the arrest of certain journalists, but I disabuse him immediately. He listens to the declaration of war, and turns pale. He says, 'It is very tragic.'"[50] Eleanor and Reynolds Packard, two American correspondents in Rome, reported Wadsworth's own account of this meeting as follows:

"I received a summons this morning from the Foreign Office saying that Count Ciano wanted to see me at 2.30 p.m. about a most urgent matter. Of course, I knew what it was going to be. Count Ciano received me most brusquely, so unlike his usual, promiscuously friendly manner. When I walked into his office he halted me half-way to his desk by rising, making it quite clear that I was not to sit down. With a scowl on his face he recited his piece as though he had learned it by heart, saying in one sentence that he must inform me that Italy considered herself at war with the United States. I bowed my head and said, 'I'm very sorry to hear it.' I then said, despite his forbidding manner, 'May I give you a message before I take leave of you?' Ciano replied coldly, 'I don't think there is anything more to be said.' I then told him that it was a message from Ambassador Phillips. Ciano said, 'In that case I should like to hear it.' I told him that the ambassador wished to convey at this time his appreciation of the collaboration that he had received in the past and the personal kindness that the Foreign Office had always shown him while he was in Italy. Count

Ciano then relaxed somewhat in his manner and said with the suspicion of a friendly smile, 'Thank you.' "

Wadsworth offered the American correspondents this assessment of Ciano: "In his social life he dislikes most Germans and likes most Anglo-Saxons, but this would not prevent his continuing the alliance with Germany if that might seem most profitable to Italy. His ambitions, however, are apt to outrun Italy's potentialities as a military power, as in the case of the ill-starred invasion of Greece. Furthermore, despite his prominence, his abilities are not such as to make it likely that his fellow Fascists would choose him as the new Duce. Ciano's strongest claim is that Mussolini wishes him as a successor, but the public would never have confidence in him."[51]

Ciano's diary for 1941 includes accounts of Mussolini's increasingly bizarre outbursts. On May 28, after a tough speech by Roosevelt against the Axis: "Never in history has one seen a nation led by a paralytic. There have been bald kings, fat kings, handsome and even stupid kings, but never a king who, in order to go to the toilet, the bath or the table, had to be held up by other men."[52] On December 14: Mussolini "got angry about Christmas, Christmas gifts and the gifts of all holidays in general. He says that the offering of gifts is the alibi of the rich to justify their good fortune in the eyes of the poor. The fact is that in these days the people feel the lack of food more than ever, and complain, but Mussolini, as usual when something doesn't go according to his wishes, takes it out even on the Eternal Father."[53] The Duce returned to the attack on Christmas on December 22. Ciano wrote: "He is surprised that the Germans have not yet abolished this holiday, which 'only recalls the birth of a Jew who gave the world debilitating and devitalizing theories, and in particular screwed Italy through the disintegrating work of the papacy.' He has prohibited newspapers from mentioning Christmas."[54]

Ciano recorded on Christmas Eve that Adelchi Serena, the Fascist Party secretary, was out of favor with the Duce, and had intimated that Mussolini gave more than 100,000 lire a month to his mistress, Clara Petacci. "Serena says that the Petaccis have formed a ring around the Duce, which is manipulated in the background by Buffarini,"[55] Ciano wrote. Two days later, Serena was fired. The artist Amerigo Bartoli was doing a portrait of Ciano at that time. While Ciano posed for him, he suddenly erupted and said defeat was now inevitable and someone should speak clearly to Mussolini. But he didn't dare. Bartoli observed that he felt like "a painter who must do the portrait of Napoleon on the day of Waterloo."[56] It was never finished.

Chapter Thirteen

Plotting Against the Duce

The turning-point in the war came in 1942, with the beginning of the German-Italian defeat in the Soviet Union and the Allied victory at El Alamein. As Axis fortunes declined, so did those of Ciano. Increasingly, he was playing with fire in his opposition to Mussolini but, as always, he remained incapable of acting on his conviction that the Duce must be stopped. "Galeazzo appears, and wants to appear, more than ever tired and disgusted with public life, desirous of 'being sent away.' Mussolini seems to him ever more involved in a situation without exit, since the solution in which he believes, victory, is no longer possible." Thus the observation of Bottai in September, 1942,[1] but these words appeared to sum up Ciano's mood throughout that fateful year. At one point Ciano told Alfieri: "I don't want to get mixed up in it any more. I'm waiting for him to send me away." Alfieri didn't believe it. "If he thought it, immediately he developed in his mind the right arguments to persuade himself that Mussolini would never fire him," he said.[2]

Ciano told a general at the beginning of 1942 that he had always been against the war and was opposed to the Fascist corporative system that had harmed the economic life of the country. "Let it be very clear that my responsibilities have nothing to do with the responsibilities of the Duce," he said. "I am devoted to the king and I see in him the only sure leader Italy has." Evidently he thought that, by distancing himself from fascism, he would make himself an acceptable successor to Mussolini if the king removed him. On another occasion, dining with some officials, he said: "I will not end up hanged. I don't have direct responsibilities. I am not the chief, I am only a minister."[3]

Mussolini's own mood remained dark. He told Ciano that Hitler was to blame for the growing debacle in Russia, and had falsified his communiqués. "He has wanted to amaze us with big figures like that dirty beast Roosevelt," he said, "and the results have been sinister. In fact, they are both dirty beasts and the offspring of mules." When the U.S.

urged all South American nations to break relations with Italy, Ciano said Mussolini's impulse was to declare war on all of them at once, thus imposing upon the United States "the burden of military defense on a very vast front."[4] The Duce's grasp of reality clearly was not improving. Grandi, meeting with Ciano on January 22, told him he could no longer contain himself. "I don't know how I managed to pass myself off as a Fascist for twenty years," he said.[5] Bottai, also increasingly disillusioned, later told Ciano that Mussolini was "a self-taught man who had a bad teacher, and who was a worse student."[6]

German behavior toward Italians was becoming insufferable. Ciano reported that Mussolini had the transcript of a telephone call that an aide to Kesselring made to Berlin, referring to Italians as "macaroni" and expressing the hope that Italy would become an occupied country.[7] Göring, whom Ciano had once admired, came to Rome in February and Ciano found himself disgusted. "As usual he is bloated and overbearing," he wrote. "I only regret the servility of our leading soldiers toward him. Following the example of that perfect clown Cavallero, who would even go so far as to bow to the public lavatories if this would help him, the three heads of our military staff acted today in the presence of that German as if he were their master. And he strutted blissfully . . . I swallowed a great deal of bile—more bile than food." When Göring departed he wore a great sable coat, "something between the 1906 motorist and the *cocotte* at the opera," Ciano said. "If any of us did something similar he would be stoned; instead, he is accepted in Germany as he is and perhaps even loved. Because he has a little humanity."[8] On February 20, Mussolini told Ciano: "Among the cemeteries, I will one day have to build the most conspicuous of all, one for German promises. They have given us nothing, or almost nothing, of what they promised . . ." Ciano said Mussolini then took out his rage on the Italian bourgeoisie. "He is sorry not to have physically exterminated [this class] in 1911," Ciano wrote.[9] Mussolini took satisfaction from signs of friction between Germany and Japan. He told Ciano: "Those are not a people with whom the Germans can have the luxury of making the Emperor and Prime Minister jump out of bed at 2 in the morning to announce things already decided and carried out."[10] Later, he told Ciano the Italian people were "not mature or consistent enough" for the challenge of war. "This war is for the Germans and the Japanese, not for us," he said.[11] Ciano observed that he himself still preferred "the white to the yellow race."

In mid-March, Ciano learned of a student plot to assassinate him. A twenty-year-old Trieste student at the University of Rome, Armando Stefani, told authorities he was part of a group of seventy students who were preparing a super-Fascist revolutionary movement. He said their aim was to impose on Mussolini a violently Socialist policy and to eliminate conservative elements of the party—above all, Ciano, whom they wanted dead. Stefani said he himself hated Ciano, but had revealed the plot because he believed it was not in the best interest of the country. "Why does all this happen?" Ciano asked. "Could it not be a beginning of anti-fascism, which doesn't dare to display openly the flag of revolution but seeks to hide it under the protection of the party itself?" He ordered the chief of police to arrest all the plotters. Later, however, he wrote in his diary: "More than their perversity, it is their idiocy which impresses one . . . I think that, except for one, they should be given their liberty with a kick in the behind. They are not worth anything more." All but two of them were subsequently freed. The two were punished because they were soldiers. The leader of the group, journalist Felice Chilanti, was banished to the remote island of Ustica.[12]

Edda decided in April to visit Germany as the guest of Ambassador Alfieri. It was her first visit in six years, and she met Hitler, Göring, Himmler, Goebbels and Ribbentrop. Goebbels and his wife entertained Edda with a party on the evening of April 25. "In contrast to previous visits, she impressed me this time as exceptionally serious and earnest," he wrote. "She is extremely intelligent and when one talks to her at length she reveals herself as the true daughter of her father."[13] Edda returned the compliment, and more, in her memoirs. "I would say Goebbels was the greatest Minister of Information and Propaganda of all time," she said. "Despite his puny aspect, his short stature and club foot, Goebbels was a captivating man because of the intelligence shining in his brilliant eyes. Gifted with an extraordinary power of persuasion and seduction . . . With a wife and six children, he was famous for the number of his female conquests, despite his physique. Few women could resist him . . ." She said Ciano regarded him as "a truly astute fox." One evening during dinner, she said, Magda Goebbels rejoined her and Goebbels in the salon and told her: "If the war should be lost, we will all kill ourselves, including the children. Death is better than the Russians."[14] The entire Goebbels family died in the bunker with Hitler in 1945; the parents killed their children, then committed suicide.

Edda also charmed Hitler, who referred to her as "an intelligent and pleasing lady." Returning the compliment, she said Hitler was "a man full of charm; lots and lots of charm . . . He was not a psychopath or a neurotic. He was human, very human." Göring was the other German she knew best. She described him as "a sort of condottiere who had degenerated into an extravagant satrap . . . One might have thought that

Göring's extravagant behavior would have finally rendered him disagreeable, annoying, even antipathetic. On the contrary, he was exceedingly likeable. Despite his obesity, he was still a fine figure of a man, and his voice was extremely agreeable. I cannot explain why it was so, but he succeeded in inspiring friendly feelings in most people."[15] She said she met Himmler several times and "nothing in his attitude could have been taken as a sign that he was the monster brought to light toward the end of the war." She hated Ribbentrop. "Around Hitler, as around my father, there was a choreography and Ribbentrop was the principal part of it," she said. "When he raised his arm, everybody raised theirs; when he lowered it, everybody lowered theirs. A grotesque thing."[16] She refused a Ribbentrop invitation to lunch because he had blocked her plan to go to Lübeck, a city devastated by bombardments, on the grounds she might be endangered by unexploded bombs. She insisted on going, and he finally gave in. When she returned, she accepted his invitation to lunch. Goebbels wrote in his diary on May 4 that it was "exceedingly unwise" of the Foreign Ministry to have allowed Edda to visit Lübeck and Rostock. "Anything more foolish can hardly be imagined," he said. "I am having a thorough investigation made into this case and am going to protest to the Führer that such embarrassing happenings must not recur . . . Women who dabble in politics are always a nuisance."[17] In her memoirs, Edda said Ribbentrop took his revenge on her later when he met Mussolini and Ciano in Berchtesgaden. "He explained to my husband that my caprices were beginning to make me frankly insupportable and that many people were becoming ill disposed toward me," she said. "Galeazzo was most displeased."[18]

Mussolini, Ciano and Cavallero traveled to Austria on April 29 by train to meet Hitler and Ribbentrop. "There is much cordiality, which puts me on my guard," Ciano wrote. "The courtesy of the Germans is always in inverse ratio to their good fortune. Hitler looks tired. He is strong, decisive and discursive. But tired." The Führer's hair, he noticed, was starting to go white. He said Hitler and Ribbentrop talked of bringing the Soviet Union to its knees. "I am little convinced by it, and say so to Ribbentrop, much to Alfieri's dismay." "Hitler talks, talks, talks, talks . . . On the second day, after lunch, when everything had been said, Hitler talked uninterruptedly for an hour and forty minutes. He omitted absolutely no argument: war and peace, religion and philosophy, art and history. Mussolini looked mechanically at his wristwatch. I thought of my own business, and only Cavallero, who is a prodigy of servility, pretended to listen raptly, and nodded his head affirmatively . . . General Jodl, after an epic struggle with sleep, dozed off on the sofa. Keitel tottered but succeeded in keeping his head up. He was too close to Hitler to let himself go as he would have liked to do."[19] Ciano observed that only women, children, old men and foreign laborers, "the slaves of the earth," appeared on German streets. He said Edda had visited an Italian workers' camp in Germany, and found one man who had been wounded in the arm with a scythe by a brutal guard. She told Hitler, and he "became furious and ordered inquiries and arrests." But Ciano said he doubted that would change anything.

After the talks, Mussolini told Ciano: "The German machine is still formidably powerful, but has suffered a great deal of wear and tear. Now it will make a new and powerful effort. The goal must be reached." On the return home by train, Ciano noted that Mussolini exercised his old magic over the crowds waiting at the Italian stations. "There was no one who, recognizing the face of the Duce, did not give signs of a festive exaltation," he said. "Exactly as before."[20] On May 18, Mussolini telephoned Edda and instructed her to talk to no one about what she had seen in Germany. The king had told him: "All Rome knows that in a German hospital there is an Italian laborer with his fingers cut off, and it also knows that your daughter energetically protested to Hitler." Ciano said Mussolini recognized in the king's remarks "a maneuver to draw out anti-German feelings in the Italian people, using the specific case of a very impressive name."[21]

On April 6, Göring sent Ciano the gift of a painting by Boldini. The two men had previously discussed the return of certain Italian paintings from France to Italy, particularly those which had belonged to Jews. Among the names mentioned was that of Rothschild, who owned many Boldinis. In a letter accompanying the gift, Göring said, "Unfortunately, there was nothing left in the Rothschild house." Ciano commented: "If one day this letter is found, it will seem clear that I instigated him to sack the houses of Jews and he regretted having arrived too late. This is the political finesse of the Germans!"[22]

Blasco d'Aieta told Ciano on April 9 of a conversation he had had with Bismarck, who told him Germany would have to make peace by October and Himmler favored a compromise peace. "Personally, I believe that German capacity for resistance is far greater," Ciano said.[23] On May 30, Ciano addressed the Senate on Fascist foreign policy, promising that Italy, along with the other Tripartite powers, would fight on to victory "at whatever cost, on orders of the king, in the name of the king."[24] But that same evening he left for Livorno and went fishing with the dissident General Carboni, who would later be involved in the anti-Mussolini plotting. "This year I will come often to Livorno for the purpose of meeting with you," Ciano told him. Later he introduced Carboni to Serrano Suñer, the

Spanish Foreign Minister, and said: "Dear Serrano, if one day you will hear it said that Italy has been saved from Germany and liberated from fascism, you know that much will be owed to this general."[25]

Serrano Suñer, later recounting his meeting with Ciano at Livorno, recalled he had once complained of ruining his health for politics, and Ciano replied, "Don't worry. Life has no importance. I assure you that I would not like to die in my bed." Now Serrano Suñer found a different Ciano. After they had walked on the beach together, Ciano told him: "Life is always good and pleasant. I have decided to walk supported by a cane on this same part of the beach and taking this delicious sun, with more than eighty years on my shoulders. I want to die here in Livorno, an old man, and after having watched the passage into the other world of many of my enemies." Ciano criticized Mussolini's private life during the visit, and Serrano Suñer told him in a joking tone that he hardly seemed the best person to do that. Ciano replied, "Nothing wrong with having a swarm of lovers. The serious and scandalous thing, which is prejudicial, is to have just one, and this is exactly the case of Mussolini."[26]

Mussolini's one lover, of course, was Clara Petacci. Clara was thirty years old in 1942. A brunette with green eyes and an ample bosom, she was well dressed and a striking contrast to the more dowdy Rachele Mussolini. She wore heavy makeup and her fingers and wrists were adorned with amber and ivory jewelry. She was an amateur painter and a writer of mediocre poetry. In 1940, she had become pregnant by Mussolini, and longed to bear his child, but she suffered a miscarriage on August 18. Ciano had long harbored a strong dislike for Claretta, as she was known, and was aware that she and her brother Marcello had abused her privileged position and were engaged in corrupt activities. By mid-June 1942, he saw his opportunity to strike at them. Riccardi, the Minister of Exchange and Foreign Currency, told Ciano he had had an open quarrel with the Petaccis, and a violent exchange of words over the telephone. He showed Ciano a report by a Carabinieri officer, who wrote that "a certain individual (whose name I do not remember) is a crook, but is also the lover of a certain Petacci, sister of the Duce's mistress; therefore I can't touch him." But then Riccardi discovered a clandestine traffic in gold with Spain through the diplomatic bag; both Marcello Petacci and Buffarini were implicated. Ciano said Riccardi confiscated eighteen kilograms of gold and gave them to the police.[27] Riccardi, who went to Mussolini on June 24 and told him the story, later informed Ciano that the Duce was indignant and wanted the guilty punished. But then Marcello Petacci struck back, according to Ciano: "Dr. Petacci came out of the shadows to direct to Buffarini, Riccardi and the Duce a violent letter in which he claims for himself the 'Fascist and nationalist merit of the operation'. . . It will be interesting to see who comes out of it with broken bones."[28] But Mussolini took no action against Petacci.

Three months earlier a Fascist official in Turin had come to Ciano with a tale about the Petacci family. Ciano wrote in his diary: "It intervenes on the right, protects on the left, threatens from above, intrigues from below and steals at all points of the compass . . . Without doubt this scandal will spread and involve the person of the Duce. But what can one do to warn him, especially as two of his most intimate colleagues, De Cesare and Buffarini, wallow in this Low Empire environment?"[29] In April Edvige Mussolini came to Ciano to unburden herself about the Petaccis. She said she had proof of shady business transactions involving the Petacci clan and she had made up her mind to confront the Duce with it. Ciano said he was very reserved and reminded her of what she already knew: "my delicate position in the matter."[30] Then on April 27 Marcello Vaccari, the prefect of Venice, told Ciano of the extravagances of Marcello Petacci, of how he had caused a big scandal in Venice and of how Buffarini had suppressed Carabinieri reports which Vaccari himself had given him. Ciano also quoted Petrognano, the director of public health, as saying that Buffarini was financing Clara Petacci with 200,000 lire a month. "Buffarini feels he can act with complete impunity," Ciano wrote. "However, now there is really too much talk about the affair."[31] Later Ciano said one of his informants told him that Clara, while vacationing in the Adriatic resort of Rimini, "hands down judgments, abets and intrigues. Her factotum is a certain Spisani, a third-rate ballroom dancing teacher."[32] Edda was also fed up with the impression the Petaccis were creating, and went to her father in November for a showdown. He told her he was already dealing with the problem, was going to end his affair and was grateful to Edda. "In fact, I did not have much hope that I had really succeeded in my efforts," Edda said afterward. "During the last years, my father and I had grown apart, and we sometimes did not see each other for months. When we did meet we always seemed to argue."[33]

Just after Christmas that year, Princess di Gangi spoke to Ciano about Petacci. She said Mussolini had had enough of the whole Petacci clan, but could not get rid of them because they were "riffraff, ready to blackmail and create a scandal." She said Mussolini told her that Clara "makes him throw up . . . The Princess attributes to the Petaccis everything bad in Italy, including the Duce's illness. That, honestly, seems to me a bit exaggerated," Ciano said.[34] The following month, the "brazen-faced" Marcello Petacci sent Ciano a peremptory letter proposing his business partner Vezzari for the post of ambassador to Spain. Vezzari had been involved in the gold scandal, and Ciano rejected the letter. "Vezzari is an old jailbird, ignorant, a rogue and dirty," Ciano said in his diary.[35]

On August 2, Edda launched a violent attack on her husband, more out of concern for him, apparently, than from anger. She accused him of hating Germans, told him this was known everywhere, and especially among the Germans themselves, who were saying "how I have for them an invincible physical revulsion," Ciano wrote. "I don't understand why Edda has become so heated and who has spoken to her . . . I haven't answered, or barely; after all, she knows very well how I think. And I am not alone."[36]

Princess Marie José, wife of Crown Prince Umberto, met with Monsignor Giovanni Battista Montini (the future Pope Paul VI) at the Vatican on September 3, and asked him to inform Myron G. Taylor that the Italian people were fed up with war and he should avoid negotiating with people around Mussolini such as Ciano "and others like him." She said, "A change in the situation is not possible with the leaders of today. The people will not follow them."[37] Bottai recorded in his diary on September 18 that "the evenings of Galeazzo are long and empty. This man, who doesn't smoke, doesn't drink, doesn't play, has for his vice a kind of sleepwalking among easy women and complaisant men." On September 19, he said he asked Ciano if he planned to approach Taylor. Ciano told him: "It is dangerous to try anything with the Americans, who spill everything in their newspapers. Better, in any case, with the English, more reserved and serious."[38] Taylor informed Washington: "Ciano has no popular following in Italy. He holds himself very ostentatiously apart from current developments. He wants to disappear as much as possible from the scene, but the Duce will not let him."[39]

But Ciano had apparently begun a serious effort toward peace during the summer, using the Polish princess Sapieha, who were known in the British court and the Vatican and resided in the Italian-occupied zone of France. Ciano contemplated sending them to Lisbon to make contact with the British, but they were arrested by German police before the operation could begin. He made another attempt in November through the Italian minister in Lisbon, Francesco Fransoni. Anthony Eden wrote to the American and Soviet ambassadors in London on December 18 that the Italian Legation in Lisbon, through a Romanian intermediary, had conveyed to the British and Polish Embassies its interest in a separate peace. He said Britain had decided not to respond because the Italians in Lisbon were servants of the Fascist regime and this could raise doubts about Allied intentions to destroy fascism.

The Germans knew what Ciano was doing. Admiral Canaris, head of German counterespionage, referred in a report to contacts between Fransoni and American representatives, and said Ciano was "implicated in the affair" together with Prince Umberto. But Mackensen discounted Ciano's maneuvers, telling Berlin in a telegram: "He is by a long shot the most unpopular man in the country. He may not have very clear ideas on his great unpopularity, but he must live on the moon if he thinks he can have some following in the mass of the population, in whose eyes he appears as the major supporter of the Axis."[40]

Blasco D'Aieta reported to Ciano on September 22 on a conversation he had with Bismarck, who was now sure Germany would be defeated but would fight to the "bitter end." Bismarck said Italy would find a way out and Ciano's "measured policy . . . toward Britain and America may contribute to this end." Bismarck also said it was because of this policy that Ribbentrop in particular, and the Germans in general, hated Ciano. If they should win the war, Ciano's head would be the first one they would want. He also revealed that many Italians were denouncing Ciano to the German Embassy as pro-British.[41]

Edda wrote to Ciano in late September, telling him that Mussolini was suffering from stomach pains, irritability, depression and other ailments. She said her mother had let the matter slide, and had attributed his problems to the effects of his private life in recent years. Edda urged Ciano to find a doctor for him, as the Duce's regular doctor was not available. Ciano went to see Mussolini on September 27, after a long absence, and said his appearance "doesn't confirm at all Edda's dark impression."[42] But Mussolini was genuinely ill at the time, and increasingly complained of his stomach condition. On October 13, a doctor reported that he had had a recurrence of an old ulcer.

Himmler came to Rome and had a long talk with Ciano. He wanted to know about the monarchy and the Vatican, and Ciano assured him that the monarchy was loyal. That, at least, was the account he gave in his diary. In fact, he apparently told Himmler the police had had to keep a close watch on Prince Umberto, and said Mussolini had a police folder that made it impossible for the crown to intrigue against the regime without compromising the succession to the throne. "The prince of Piedmont is in our hands," he said.[43]

On November 6, Mussolini asked Ciano if he was keeping his diary in order. When Ciano replied that he was, the Duce said that it would serve "to document how the Germans, in the military and political field, have always acted without his knowledge." Ciano was suspicious. "But what does his strange question really hide?" he wondered.[44]

In early November, General Montgomery scored his impressive victory over the combined German and Italian forces at El Alamein. Rommel began retreating, leaving the Italians in the lurch, and most of them were taken prisoner. Ciano told a friend: "El Alamein is the beginning of our defeat. The hand of fate is against us."[45] After the Anglo-American landing in Morocco and Algeria on the night of November 7–8, Ciano told Vergani it was useless to continue the war, but Mussolini did not agree. Vergani suggested Ciano should resign. "If I were to resign, we would be put in the condition of not being able to act in any way," Ciano replied.[46] General Amé told Ciano that the morale of the army was "dramatically low."[47] Later Vergani pressed him again to resign, and Ciano told him it was too late. "I should have done it on June 10, 1940 . . . When one is in my situation, one can only remain at one's post until the moment that times are right for acting." Vergani suggested he take a plane and get out of Italy. "I don't know with what face I could present myself at an Allied airfield," Ciano replied. "They would consider my gesture as inspired by a spirit of self-preservation. I don't consider myself, in this, a better man than others . . . I have had an excellent wife and children whom I cannot abandon . . . I didn't want the war, I didn't accept it. I must risk something to bring it to an end."[48]

Mussolini sent Ciano to Munich on November 9 to discuss with Hitler the North African landings. Göring, Ribbentrop and the French Prime Minister Pierre Laval also were present. The meeting decided on the immediate occupation of Corsica and all of France to prepare to defend those areas from Allied invasion. The Italian diplomat Lanza observed Ciano at midnight in a room with Hitler. "Ciano is in a corner, confused among generals and Nazi officials; no one seems to pay attention to him," Lanza wrote in his diary. "Hitler lowers his face and closes his eyes. I seem to be attending a spiritualist gathering. Ciano is agitated and says something in a loud voice. Everyone turns on him, irritated and reproachful. Next day, Darlan* goes over to the English. Germans seem to lose their heads." Ciano later had a brief private meeting with Hitler. Again Lanza: "When he comes out he is red in the face and excited. He exclaims: 'We are finished . . . and the Germans still don't understand it! They are frightened to death, but they don't believe in defeat. In April the Allies will be in Italy and we will pay for everything.'" After midnight, reports came in of an American landing in Corsica. Ciano exclaimed in a loud voice: "Oh, they could very well disembark at Rome, at Genoa, where they want. They would not find anyone to receive them."[49]

When Laval joined the talks, Ciano said, Hitler treated him with "frigid courtesy . . . Not a word was said to Laval about the impending action—the orders to occupy France were being given while he was smoking his cigarette

---

* Admiral Jean Darlan, a pro-German French naval commander, vice-premier and foreign minister. He was assassinated in Algeria a month later.

and conversing with various people in the next room." Ciano described Laval as "a disgusting Frenchman—the most disgusting of the French. To ingratiate himself with his German masters he doesn't hesitate to reject his compatriots and to denigrate his unhappy country."[50]

Francesco Fransoni met with Ciano on November 18 and asked him if there was any hope of an Axis military victory. When Ciano assured him there was not, Fransoni suggested that, once back in Lisbon, he should sound out the British about the possibility of a separate peace. Ciano gave his approval, but it was clear to Fransoni that he did so without having even the tacit approval of Mussolini. Fransoni's initiative came to nought, as did another one he attempted in the summer of 1943, because the British refused to deal with anyone associated with the regime, and the Americans subsequently backed that position.[51]

On November 23 the Russians began their counteroffensive at Stalingrad. The Italians were defeated, only part of the army being able to break through the Russian encirclement. The Italian Command had ordered retreat too late. Ciano reported that Guariglia, the Italian ambassador to the Holy See, spoke to Vatican officials on December 13 about removing the Italian Command from Rome to avoid Allied bombing of the city. When Guariglia said to Monsignor Montini that even the Duce would leave the capital, Montini replied: "I believe he will have to make another march on Rome to return here."[52] In another conversation with Vergani, Ciano said, "No one succeeds in making Mussolini move . . . Churchill has gone to visit places bombed by the Germans, and every day has contact with people who suffer and die. Mussolini has commanded three wars but has never seen one of the dead in these three wars . . . He doesn't know what the eyes of the dead are like. It is a terrible nightmare."[53]

Mussolini was summoned to a meeting with Hitler in mid-December but, still suffering stomach pains, he sent Ciano and Cavallero with instructions to support an agreement with Russia or to urge that a solid defensive line be created in the East so that the Axis could concentrate in 1943 on a probable Anglo-American offensive in the West. The meeting took place in the forest of Görlitz. "The atmosphere is heavy," Ciano wrote. "No one tried to conceal from me or from my colleagues the uneasiness over the news of the breakthrough on the Russian front. There were open attempts to put the blame on us."[54] Hitler, Göring and Ribbentrop told Ciano that the inexplicable retreat by Italian soldiers caused the entire German line on the Stalingrad front to fall back. "Ciano . . . was apathetic and indifferent, as he found himself before an irreparable situation," Alfieri wrote. "I tried to arouse in him a reaction, so that he would oppose such ignoble speculation before it became widespread . . . But

1. Edda Mussolini at age 17 with her father Benito, 1927.

2. Galeazzo and Edda Ciano outside the Church of San Giuseppe in Rome after their wedding, April 24, 1930.

3. Galeazzo and Edda Ciano at the beach.

4. Edda Ciano with her children, Fabrizio, Raimonda and the baby Marzio in 1938.

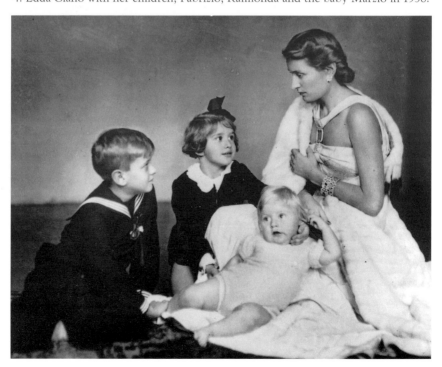

5. Galeazzo Ciano in London in June 1933 as a delegate to a monetary conference.

6. Ciano in his office as Mussolini's undersecretary for press and propaganda, 1934.

7. Ciano assuming the stern visage that he liked to adopt in imitation of Mussolini, 1934.

8. Ciano and Hitler meet at Obersalzberg, October 1936. From left, German Foreign Minister von Neurath and the Italian and German ambassadors Attolico and von Hassell.

9. Signing of the Anti-Comintern Pact in Rome, November 6, 1937. Foreground, from left: von Hassell, Ribbentrop, Mussolini, Japanese envoy Hotta and Ciano.

10. Ciano dancing with Grand Duchess Anna of Austria, January 1938.

11. Hitler and Mussolini review troops in Rome, May 1938. Ciano is between Ribbentrop and Goebbels.

12. The Munich conference, September 29, 1938. From left, Chamberlain, Daladier, Hitler, Mussolini and Ciano.

13. Ciano with Ribbentrop in an open car, October 1938.

14. Italian Fascist women greet Ciano in Berlin, May 1939.

15. Ciano visits his "grand duchy," Albania, 1941.

16. Ciano with his son Fabrizio, Rome, October 1938.

17. Filippo Anfuso, Ciano's chef de cabinet at the Foreign Ministry.

Facing page

(*top*) 18. Ciano and Hitler on the Reich Chancellery balcony after signing the Pact of Steel, May 22, 1939. Ribbentrop at left, Goring at right.

19. Ribbentrop, Hitler and Ciano at Obersalzberg, August 12, 1939, just before the Nazi invasion of Poland.

20. Ciano visits Hitler at the Fuhrer's "Wolf's Lair" in a Polish forest, October 25, 1941.

21. Edda Ciano and a friend on a visit to London, outside the Italian Embassy, on the eve of World War II.

22. Edda's lover and famed postwar fashion designer, Emilio Pucci, 1968.

23. Hildegard Beetz, the SS secretary who befriended Ciano and helped Edda escape to Switzerland.

24. Ciano, in light coat, turns to face the firing squad moments before his execution in Verona, January 11, 1944.

25. Benito Mussolini and Clara Petacci hang by their heels outside a Milan filling
station on April 29, 1944, after being shot by partisans.

26. Edda in later years with her mother Rachele.

. . . he ignored my appeals, saying that by now it was too late and there was nothing more to be done."[55]

Ciano quoted, in English, this exchange between Mario Pansa, deputy head of ceremonial at the Foreign Ministry, and the German official Hewel:

Pansa: "Had our Army many losses?"

Hewel: "No losses at all; they are running."

Pansa: "Like you did in Moscow last year?"

Hewel: "Exactly."[56]

Ciano returned to his train at 9 p.m., nervous and excited, and told his colleagues the situation was extremely grave. The Führer had referred twice to the possibility that the war might be lost. The Germans feared Rostov might fall, and spoke of abandoning all of North Africa. Lanza said, "Hitler insistently urged Ciano to telephone the Duce so that he would 'personally telegraph to Italian soldiers in Russia not to cede an inch of ground . . .' When Ciano spoke of negotiating peace with Russia, Hitler recovered and declared he was 'certain of winning the war.'" Lanza observed Ciano when the talks resumed the next day:

> The speeches of Ciano, brilliant and amusing, are of a disconcerting vacuity and an extreme monotony. The Germans seem to be his preferred target. It amuses him to treat them in the worst ways. Mackensen must be used to hearing these things said in every color because he remains silent in a dignified way about the too-open allusions against his country. Cavallero one doesn't ever see. Ciano, when he speaks of him, calls him "that fool with the short legs." Fool here, fool there; Germans imbeciles here, Germans cretins there; "that delinquent Ribbentrop," "that criminal Führer," and thus it goes on.[57]

Hitler assured this conference session that Germany would be able to hold on to the Russian front, and said it would be impossible to reach an agreement with Moscow. Lanza observed:

> "Ciano gives the impression of having completely lost his nerve. He doesn't stay still one moment. He gets up and sits down. He jokes, then grows sullen. He has outbursts of sudden anger. He tries a reasoned line of thought and ends by cursing. His refrain is always the same: There is nothing to be done, the Germans don't understand reason, the Germans have lost the war. Suddenly Alfieri has an unexpected excess of energy and speaks with sufficient effectiveness of the necessity of trying a break (with Germany). Ciano looks at him with tired eyes (evidently he is already thinking of something else), then lets fall these textual words: 'Nothing, nothing! It remains only to await the collapse.'"

The Italians left at midnight the next day, Ciano "convinced that it's necessary to let Italy fall into catastrophe, sure as he is in the idea that the Allies would then want to entrust the government to him."[58]

Ciano had a conversation at the Golf Club with Malaparte, who later gave this account:

> "Watch out for the old man," I told him.
> "I know, he hates me. He hates everybody. Sometimes I wonder if he isn't crazy. Do you think that one can still do something?"
> "There is nothing more to be done. It's too late. You should have done something in 1940, to prevent him from dragging Italy into this shameful war."
> "In 1940?" he said, and laughed in a way that I didn't like. Then he added: "The war could still go well."
> I remained silent. He felt there was something painful and hostile in my silence, and added: "I'm not to blame for it. It was he who wanted the war. What could I do?"
> "Go away."
> "Go away? And then?"
> "Then? Nothing."
> "That would have served no purpose," he said.
> "It would have served no purpose. But you should have gone away."
> "Go away, go away. Every time we speak of these things, you only say to me: Go away! And then?"[59]

In 1942, Ciano apparently became involved in Italian efforts to save thousands of Jewish refugees living along the Côte d'Azur. But the extent of his role is unclear. In November, after Allied forces had invaded North Africa and the Axis powers took control of the French state, the Italians were assigned the Alpes Maritimes and Var, and six other departements north to the Swiss border. Civil administration in the Italian zones of occupation was left in the hands of the Pétain regime, which had begun in the spring to round up Jews to send them to forced labor in the German-occupied zone. Alberto Calisse, the Italian consul-general in Nice, contacted the Foreign Ministry in Rome when he heard what was going on. The ministry replied: "It is not possible to permit the forcible transfer of Jews. The measures to protect the Jews, both foreign and Italian, must be taken exclusively by our organs." Calisse told the French authorities they must revoke every anti-Jewish measure they had taken.

John Bierman, an American author who studied the question, said: "These instructions, in all probability, came all the way down from Count Ciano . . . Laval and the Nazis both believed this, as documentary evidence indicates. Laval was so incensed at this Italian interference that he called in the Italian ambassador to complain. But the result was the opposite of what Laval had intended: the Italians promptly extended their protection of the Jews to include those in all the departements occupied by their forces—not just the Alpes Maritimes—and the Italian Foreign Ministry notified Vichy in very plain language indeed that only the Italians were entitled to arrest or intern Jews, irrespective of nationality, in the departements they controlled."[60]

In December 1942, the French prefect in the Alpes Maritimes ordered foreign Jews to register at post offices and go from there to concentration camps in the German zone of occupation. When Ciano heard of this, he told the Italian ambassador in France that "measures of precaution with regard to said Jews must pertain solely to Italian authorities without exception . . . the disposition regarding the Jews must be suspended." The historian Renzo De Felice has written: "It is symptomatic that the Vichy and Nazi documents present Galeazzo Ciano as the *deus ex machina*, the 'inspirer,' of the policy of protection of the Jews" in the occupied territories.[61]

Meanwhile in Croatia, the governor of the Italian occupation zone, Giuseppe Bastianini, had reported to Rome in mid-May 1942 that the migration of Jews into the zone had reached alarming proportions and must cease. The Germans wanted the Jews handed over to them. On August 17, Ribbentrop instructed Bismarck to submit a request to the Italian Foreign Ministry for joint action against Croatian Jewry. In doing so, Bismarck secretly warned the Italians this would mean the liquidation of the Jews. Ciano sent Mussolini a memorandum which clearly referred to the possible "dispersion and elimination" of Jews, and Mussolini wrote on the upper right-hand corner: "*nulla osta* . . . M." No objection. How Ciano reacted is not recorded. But General Mario Roatta, the Italian military commander in Croatia, refused to hand over Jews to the German army, and various Italian diplomats and civil servants also refused to obey orders. Jonathan Steinberg, a British writer, noted that the Italians resorted to time-honored bureaucratic obstruction to make sure Mussolini's order was not carried out.[62]

The Germans piled on the pressure, with Ribbentrop appealing directly to Mussolini in a meeting in Rome the following February for the expulsion of Jews from the Italian zone. Again Mussolini gave his consent. Ciano was by then out of office, but other Italian authorities concentrated all Jews in one camp on the island of Arbe, in case the demarcation line between the German and Italian zones was altered. Mussolini's policy was again thwarted. In Greece and Tunisia, Italians also acted to safeguard Jews. Michaele Sarfatti, an Italian Jewish scholar, points out that in these areas, some of the Jews were Italian citizens, and the Fascist regime counted on them to help carry out its expansionist policy in the Mediterranean, in competition with England, France and Germany.[63]

Chapter Fourteen

Into the Cage of the Beasts

On an evening in late January 1943, Allen W. Dulles sat in his comfortable apartment on Herrengasse 23 in Bern, warily facing a visitor who had come in through the protective cloak of the Swiss blackout. He was a bespectacled, six-foot-four-inch Prussian lawyer and civil servant named Hans Bernd Gisevius. A German exile opposed to the Nazi regime had arranged the rendezvous. Gisevius was officially vice-consul at the German Consulate General in Zurich. In fact, he was an intelligence operative, sent to Switzerland by Admiral Canaris, a secret member of the German resistance, to make contact with the Allies. Neutral Switzerland was, of course, an ideal location for Allied spies operating against Germany. There they could recruit agents opposed to the Hitler regime, who had the opportunity to go back and forth across the frontier, and meet with them in secret. They saw people from the occupied countries, and read the mail of Germans that some obliging Swiss turned over to them. The most famous of these spies was Dulles. Officially a special assistant to the American ambassador, he headed the Bern operations of the American Office of Strategic Services, and was a legendary figure widely known throughout Switzerland. After the war, the OSS would be transformed into the Central Intelligence Agency, with Dulles as one of its first directors.

Dulles was necessarily suspicious at his initial meeting with Gisevius. The German could be a plant. The two men sparred and circled one another that evening, then met again a week or so later. "How do I know you can be trusted?" Dulles finally asked.[1] By way of reply, Gisevius drew a black notebook from his pocket and began to read from it. Dulles was astonished to hear the text of a number of coded messages his office had sent to Washington a few weeks earlier. Gisevius had just returned from Berlin, where he learned from his friends in the Abwehr that a German monitoring base near Stuttgart had succeeded in breaking one of the American codes. It was not Dulles' usual code, but the so-called "Burns" to "Victor" code he occasionally used to transmit general political reports.

"Burns" was Dulles; "Victor" was General William Donovan, head of the OSS. One of the messages was a report on the Italian situation which discussed dissension within the government and the activities of the anti-German group that had formed around Badoglio, Grandi, Ciano and others. Gisevius told Dulles this telegram had been laid on Hitler's desk, whereupon the Führer sent it to Mussolini with his compliments. In revealing that the Germans had broken the American code, Gisevius overcame all of the spymaster's doubts. From then on he was OSS Agent 512, codenamed "Tiny" by his new boss. "The incident of the broken code actually brought Gisevius and me closer together," Dulles wrote. "It was strong evidence of his sincerity."[2]

Within days of Mussolini's receiving the intercepted telegram, he fired Ciano as Foreign Minister. The date was February 5. This is Ciano's own description of how it happened:

> At 4.30 in the afternoon the Duce calls me. The moment I enter the room I perceive that he is very much embarrassed. I understand what he is preparing to tell me. "What do you wish to do now?" Thus he begins, and then adds *sotto voce* that he has changed the entire government. I understand the reasons. I share them, and I do not intend to raise the least objection. Among the various personal solutions that he offers me I decisively reject the governorship of Albania, where I would be going as the executioner and hangman of those people to whom I promised brotherhood and equality. I choose the embassy to the Holy See. It is a place of rest that may, moreover, hold many possibilities for the future. And the future, never so much as today, is in the hands of God. To leave Foreign Affairs, where for seven years—and what years!—I have given the best of myself is certainly a hard and painful blow. I have lived too much, in the full sense of the word, between those walls not to feel the anguish of a physical uprooting, almost of a mutilation. But that does not matter. I know how to be strong and look to the morrow, which may require an even greater freedom of action. The ways which Providence chooses are at times mysterious.[3]

Orio Vergani was convinced that this account was false. He met Ciano on the morning of February 6, and said Ciano told him he had learned of his dismissal, not in a meeting with Mussolini, but from a report of the Stefani news agency the previous evening. Ciano said Mussolini had confirmed the news in a telephone call to him on the morning of February 6. It was, he said, "a difficult conversation, more so for him than for me."[4] If Vergani's report is correct, then the meeting with Mussolini probably took place later that day.

Did Dulles unwittingly bring about Ciano's downfall? He himself was not sure. "I was never able to discover whether this [firing] was coincidence or whether this cable was the cause," he wrote.[5] The cable may have finally decided Mussolini to act, but he already had ample evidence of Ciano's lack of loyalty and had grown increasingly suspicious of him. Nearly three weeks after Ciano's removal, the British Embassy in Washington, passing on to London information it had obtained from U.S. officials, said a prominent Italian recently returned to Turkey had reported that the changes in the Italian Cabinet resulted from the discovery by the Gestapo of a plot to put the Prince of Piedmont (Umberto, the crown prince) in power and overthrow the government. "Grandi, the former Italian ambassador to London, and Count Ciano organized the movement with the full cognizance of the Prince of Piedmont," the embassy stated.[6]

Ciano did not hide from Mussolini his desire for a compromise peace. Toward the end of 1942, he suggested he might take discreet soundings to determine British views on the subject, but Mussolini reproached him for thinking such thoughts. Ciano continued to meet with General Carboni, in Rome and in Livorno, and was in regular contact with two disgruntled members of the General Staff, Generals Vittorio Ambrosio and Giuseppe Castellano. All this could not have escaped the notice of Mussolini or, more to the point, the secret police who reported to him daily. "If something happened at 11 a.m., Mussolini knew about it by 1 p.m.," said Mario Mondello, who worked for Ciano in the Foreign Ministry and was his personal secretary when he was ambassador to the Holy See. Mondello said several of Grandi's representatives were coming "three times a day" to the embassy to meet with Ciano.[7]

Many prominent people came to Ciano in January 1943 to ask him to use his influence to obtain a separate peace. "Everyone wanted this impulsive, exuberant, plucky and very-much-in-earnest boy on their side," said Marcello del Drago. "We had to beg him and warn him several times not to talk too much . . . but secrecy and reserve were not his strong points anyway." Ciano became more openly defiant and outspoken. "He would not give the Fascist salute any more, but just raised his hat as in the good old times he had never known," del Drago said. "One day somebody told him that Mussolini was going to have him arrested. It was not true, but enough to make him even wilder and want to fly away to Tunisia or Spain and start a free Italy. We persuaded him not to do it."[8]

Ciano met on January 12 Monsignor Montini at the home of Princess Isabelle Colonna. He talked of the German betrayal of Italy and how he had fought to keep Italy out of the war. The Holy See, he said, would have a role to play in bringing the war to an end, but he did not elaborate.

Finally, del Drago said, a definite plan of action was formulated by Ciano and his fellow conspirators. Trustworthy troops under dissident generals were to be shifted to key positions. The Rome garrison was to be placed under the orders of a well-known anti-Fascist commander. On a given night, Fascist personalities were to be arrested, public buildings seized, wires cut. Mussolini would be taken into protective custody and moved to an unknown destination. Troops would man the Brenner Pass and other border points to hold back the Germans. British and American troops would land at various points to give support. "One day Ciano told me it was all over . . . The king had not agreed and the generals would not do anything against the royal wish," del Drago said.[9]

Mussolini, in a weakened condition from chronic gastric upsets, left Rome on January 12 for a rest at his home in Rocca delle Caminate. While he was away, Buffarini revealed to a friend of the Duce, Angela Curti Cucciati, that Ciano, Grandi and Bottai on the one hand and the pro-Nazi Farinacci on the other were plotting against him. Buffarini said he had not risked telling Mussolini what he knew about the plots, so it was up to her. She wrote immediately to Mussolini to warn him, and that may have provided the initial impetus for his decision to fire Ciano.[10] Ciano went to Rocca delle Caminate on January 20 to tell Mussolini of a report by the Italian Minister in Bucharest, Renato Bova Scoppa. The minister had come to Rome to inform Ciano that Ion Antonescu, the Romanian leader, had asked him to contact Ciano and see if their two nations could not arrange a separate peace together. Mussolini merely repeated his confidence in the ability of German forces to resist on the Russian front, then changed the subject and talked about his intention to replace Cavallero as chief of the General Staff, a move prompted by the imminent fall of Tripoli. Cavallero was a strong supporter of collaboration with Germany. Ciano had been working with several generals to bring about his downfall and have him replaced by Ambrosio. That came about shortly afterward.

The Abwehr branded Ciano a traitor in a report to Berlin on January 24. They accused him of conducting an anti-German campaign with the help of "Jew-tainted Aryans" and other traitors in the Foreign Ministry. "It is certain that this is the real and almost the only organization of traitors which exists in Italy," the report said. It named fifty-seven Foreign Ministry officials, seven of them married to Jewesses or supposed Jewesses.[11]

On January 29, Ciano showed Mussolini a letter written by Anfuso from Budapest, saying the Hungarians were negotiating secretly with the British and Americans. Privately he told a friend he wanted to leave politics. He said Mussolini must resign and make way for a coalition government. "The parties must revive. People must have the right to speak." As for himself, he would refuse to take a post in any government. "These are dreams, but I would like to go to live in my house at Ponte a Moriano, with a book and a picture," he said. "I know there is a million to one chance of this. Who knows where I will be in a month, six months, a year?"[12]

When the ax fell on February 5, Mussolini also fired Grandi, Bottai and Buffarini. The first two were undoubtedly removed because they were known to share Ciano's views. Buffarini was dropped because of his involvement in the Petacci affair. Mussolini could not rid himself of his mistress, but he could dispose of the man who had furthered her brother's corrupt dealings. The Duce took back the title of Foreign Minister for himself, and appointed Bastianini as under-secretary of foreign affairs to run the ministry. That appointment was something of an act of defiance, for he presumably knew Ribbentrop had called Bastianini an "honorary Jew."[13] Afterward, Ciano told Anfuso and Bova Scoppa that their memoranda had caused his ouster. He said to Bova Scoppa, "You caused me to be sent away from the Ministry of Foreign Affairs with your memo in January; the cause of my disgrace was to have supported it and backed it up."[14] Vergani said of Ciano at this time: "He had many times given me the impression of a boy who plays, through the bars of the cage, with the tigers. Now it seemed to me he had entered the cage of the great sleeping beasts armed only with a very thin whip."[15]

Mussolini offered Ciano a choice of three posts: Albania, the Holy See or ambassador to Spain. His mother, whom Ciano telephoned that same evening, was under the impression he would retire from politics and take over direction of his newspaper in Livorno, *Il Telegrafo*. Edda also thought he wanted to leave the political scene. In fact, he told Vergani as he was clearing out of the Palazzo Chigi later: "I take my leave, forever, from political life." But he added: "If I don't retire to the countryside, it is because I have a task from which I cannot and must not withdraw . . . I want to do everything that is in my power to put an end to this disaster."[16]

Edda was convinced her husband had lost his job because of the machinations of the Petaccis. "The firing is also a reprisal against me, since I intervened with my father, proof in hand, to convince him that his relationship with Clara aroused too much gossip and damaged him, while the dubious affairs of her brother do not contribute to improving the situation," she said. "Not being able to do anything against me, they take their revenge on Galeazzo." She said she had "lost the first round," and her father, afraid to face her in person, had profited from her absence from Rome "to knife in the back a man who had served him so faithfully during so many years."[17] She asked Albini, the new under-secretary of the interior, to furnish her with proof of all of Marcello Petacci's misdeeds. Then she went to her father with the incriminating material. He read it, became indignant and told Edda he intended to get rid of Clara immediately. Edda, skeptical, left for Sicily soon afterward to continue her service as a nurse. When she came back, Ciano told her Mussolini had sent Clara away, and all her family and friends were panic-stricken. Then, two or three days later, Mussolini let her return, and the Petacci family was determined to pursue a vendetta against Edda. "The effects began to surface: Galeazzo was accused of infidelity and treason," Edda wrote. He went to Mussolini and asked to be confronted with his accuser. Mussolini told him he paid no attention to such stupid and malicious gossip.[18]

Rachele Mussolini said "Benito had his reasons" for removing Ciano and letting him go to the Vatican. "He thought that, in the worst hypothesis, if he were one day forced to negotiate peace, Ciano would be very precious to him in that circle in which diplomats of all the world lived, side by side," she said.[19] In Berlin, Lanza recorded in his diary that the Germans were suspicious of Ciano's new appointment, fearing Mussolini wanted to start negotiations with the Allies through this channel. But Goebbels, in his diary, made no mention of such suspicions and correctly assessed that Ciano was the only genuine target of Mussolini's government shake-up. "The Duce made a great fuss about it so that the elimination of Ciano should not draw so much attention," he wrote. Later he added: "Ciano was the ringleader against his own father-in-law. He is a scoundrel and a contemptible traitor, unique and unparalleled in all history."[20] Two days after he was fired, Ciano wrote a brief letter to Mussolini in which he said, "It is not without great sadness that I take leave of you as an immediate collaborator, and the sadness in me is particularly acute."[21]

When Ciano told del Drago he had been fired, he asked his advice on which post he should take. "Nothing," Del Drago replied. "Go home to Livorno and fish." But, he said, Ciano couldn't give up "politics and plotting and intriguing . . . He took the Holy See, hoping to remain in Rome and watch from the Vatican windows the Americans march in to the 'Stars and Stripes' and the 'Yankee Doodle'."[22] Mussolini did not believe Ciano would take the post at the Holy See. He had offered it a year earlier to Bottai, and commented: "I refuse to believe that a bold man like Bottai should, at forty-six years, end up as a sacristan."[23] For his part, Ciano feared Mussolini would change his mind and withdraw the offer. Ciano contacted Guariglia, the man he was to replace, and urged him to obtain Vatican consent to the appointment quickly so that Mussolini could not backtrack. Guariglia did so, and half an hour after the Vatican gave its approval, Mussolini telephoned Ciano to say he had changed his mind and wanted to send him elsewhere. But he was too late. "The Duce accepted the accomplished fact with indifference," Ciano wrote in his diary.[24] He told Guariglia, "It is necessary to save Italy. I and several others will begin work and you will have to collaborate. Perhaps we will all meet again in Lisbon."[25]

In his conversation with Vergani as he was packing up, Ciano said:

> I entered this building eighteen years ago as a boy just out of school, and this room seven years ago, at the age of thirty-three. I leave at forty. Perhaps I have committed, in this room, some errors, but probably any other man in my circumstances would have committed them . . . My fate has made me become the man who, more than any other, is disliked by the Italians. I know all the little jokes at my expense, what is said about my private life, my riches, my frivolity. I know that journalists who are friends of mine render me a service when they don't publish my photograph. I know that in the movie theaters they laugh and snigger when they see me in the newsreels. Don't think that I speak like this because of a persecution mania. And I don't claim even to become likeable from one moment to the other. I wish only that one day it will be known that, within the limits of my possibilities, I tried to keep Italy far from the war, and that someone may testify that I did everything possible to bring the war to an end.[26]

Vergani returned to the Palazzo Chigi on Ciano's last evening there, February 7. Ciano remarked, "Do you also smell the odor of death? It's necessary to hurry to remove it because tomorrow it will begin to stink."[27] As he left the palace, Ciano observed that he would have to pay in person for his involvement in the regime, even if his life would be cut short. "Many innocents are dying. Why shouldn't I run the same risk?" he said.[28] Ciano handed over the office to Bastianini the next morning, then went to the Palazzo Venezia to take leave of the Duce. Mussolini told him, "Now you must consider that you are going to have a period of rest. Then your turn will come again. Your future is in my hands, and for this you can feel easy." Evidently Mussolini thought Ciano would draw a salutary lesson from having been fired, and would behave himself in future. Ciano told Mussolini he had all the documents proving German treachery toward Italy, and said he was bursting to make a speech revealing it. "He listened to me in silence and almost agreement . . . He has invited me to go to him often. 'Even every day.' Our leave-taking was cordial. For that I am very happy because I love Mussolini very much, and the thing I will miss most will be my contact with him."[29]

A postscript would come much later, but Ciano's diary ended with those words. About a year earlier, he had taken the first volumes of the diary out of his office safe and turned them over to his mother. When he left the ministry, he took with him sixteen volumes recording the minutes of his various official conversations as Foreign Minister. A friend described him as "a politically sick man hanging on to various strings of numerous plots."[30]

A journalist friend, Yvon De Begnac, visited Ciano at his new embassy, in a magnificent Renaissance palazzo on the Via Flaminia, and found him a changed man. "The Ciano of eight years before had returned," he wrote. "He no longer suffered from nervous hypertension . . . The atmosphere around him had become free."[31] But Ciano's office became a center of intrigue and plotting, and others had a different impression. Susanna Agnelli found him "worried, nervous and plotting like everybody else."[32] Mario Mondello, who himself became ambassador to the Holy See after the war, recalled that Ciano "received every day five to ten generals and admirals, those who made the coup" against Mussolini later. Mondello said Ciano also saw the Pope often. He noted that Blasco d'Aieta, Ciano's No. 2, was a relative of Sumner Welles, and Cardinal Luigi Maglione, the papal secretary of state, often called on d'Aieta. Mondello said these meetings could suggest Ciano was using d'Aieta as a means of making contact with the Allies, but no one knew anything for certain about this.[33] In the case of the Americans, it seems unlikely, principally because the Americans wanted nothing to do with him. Myron G. Taylor ruled out any solution to the Italian political problem based on Fascist dissidents. He judged that Ciano was without a following, and Grandi was too weak. But it appears Ciano did establish contact with the British.

Ribbentrop visited Rome from February 24–28, and gave Ciano a painting by Boldini to mark his coming fortieth birthday. Ciano, having for years reviled him, thanked him for "the delicate thought from a faithful friend."[34] This was not simple politeness; Ciano had undergone another change of opinion. He wrote to Alfieri: "I am very touched by the solicitude of Ribbentrop; I must frankly say that he has held and holds toward me an attitude of real friendship."[35] In that he could not have been more mistaken.

Ciano told Bottai on March 11 that he believed Mussolini was thinking of distancing himself from Germany. But that day Mussolini made a speech asserting he would go all the way with Germany and Japan. He followed that with a letter to Hitler in which he urged a separate peace with Russia. The next evening, Bottai met again with Ciano, who told him Churchill would be prepared to accept an internal solution of the Fascist crisis, involving Ciano and Grandi, but Eden would be strongly opposed to all the men of fascism.[36] Anfuso came to Rome from Budapest in March and found Ciano "immersed up to his neck in the Fascist plot, a watertight compartment of the general plot." He said Ciano "ran from the Vatican to Bottai, from him to Carboni . . . from Carboni to Castellano and without taking an active part in any plot he was aware of all of them."[37] Mussolini was suspicious, but at the same time expressed confidence Ciano would not stab him in the back. Ciano lunched with Bottai on April 13, and predicted the collapse of the regime within a week or two. "There is no bitterness in him, only a poisonous joy, a will of perdition, of suicide," Bottai wrote.[38]

In the spring, a note to Berlin from German police in the Italian zone of occupation in southern France said Italian troops were protecting Jews and added: "The one who inspired this spirit is Count Ciano, presently ambassador to the Vatican, who with his attitude hopes to buy up sympathies for Italy should they lose the war."[39] Ciano's friend Cyprienne del Drago said: "Galeazzo didn't like Jews very much. But he helped save them." She said that, as ambassador to the Holy See, he helped through his Vatican contacts have false papers issued to show that a Jewish man was married to an Aryan woman, or vice versa. In one instance, she said, Ciano invoked the aid of Bismarck in helping a Dutch Jew. When Ciano thanked him, Bismarck was dismissive. "After all, it was only a little Jew," he said.[40]

Mussolini fired Carmine Senise as police chief in April. The Germans disliked him because he had snubbed Himmler and had pointedly avoided attending the funeral of Reinhard Heydrich, the chief of the SS security service assassinated in the former Czechoslovakia. Fascists disliked him because he had always refused to become a party member. Ciano told Senise to keep himself at the ready because he could need him at any time. Ciano also said Edda had gone to the Palazzo Venezia and reproached her father bitterly for firing Senise.

Ciano's old friend Marcello del Drago was transferred to Brussels in April as Minister for Consular Affairs. He and his wife paid a farewell call on Ciano, who told them, "I have no allies. I am a dead man. It is necessary to be realistic. What I did, I did for my country. I must never forget my father was a great hero, and a soldier has to serve his country. But I am a dead man. I am a man cast aside." Cyprienne said many years later: "He still hoped to act. He knew he had to do his duty. He didn't expect anything from the Allies."[41]

On April 21 the king met with a number of politicians who urged him to remove Mussolini, but Ciano apparently was not among them. Meanwhile, Ambrosio gave Castellano permission to prepare a plan for the capture of Mussolini and his closest aides. Castellano showed the plan to Ciano, who gave it to d'Aieta and said, "This is dynamite. You take it. I haven't seen it."[42]

Ciano met Luciana Frassati, the Italian wife of a Polish diplomat, in April. "He spoke to me with great sadness about the Italian situation, which was increasingly disastrous, and of the progressive German arrogance," she wrote in her memoirs. "He foresaw, without enthusiasm, a forthcoming kingdom of the Jews as a consequence of the concentration camps and gas chambers."[43]

Italy was now facing final collapse on the battlefield. On May 12 Mussolini allowed General Messe, his commander in North Africa, to surrender his encircled troops. The last Italian foothold in Africa was gone. That same day, Pope Pius prepared a "declaration" for Mussolini, inviting him to consider the requirements of the situation. Ciano saw Mussolini on May 13, then met with Maglione to inform him the Duce saw no alternative and Italy would continue to fight. Privately, he said Mussolini did not like the papal intervention, and told him he would fight to the last Italian.

Two days later, the Supreme Command informed Mussolini that Germany had sent fresh divisions to Sicily and Sardinia. Mussolini again left for Rocca delle Caminate in bad health, and told Bastianini: "Yesterday I sent for Ciano and asked him if it was true he had willingly called me soft in the head. He denied it indignantly, and I believe him. However, it is strange that, from various quarters, in the most varied moments, I am advised to have him watched."[44] A police report drafted on May 21 must have erased all of Mussolini's doubts, but he did not act on it. The report stated:

> A person worthy of trust has reported that H.E. [His Excellency] Ciano . . . for some time has been criticizing acidly the policy of Germany and the alliance of Italy with the German state. Ambassador Ciano recently, on various occasions in the presence of high prelates, has not hesitated to criticize even the work of the Duce. He criticizes the way in which Hitler and the Germans act toward us, their disloyal way of conducting the war, and the spirit of giving orders and of domination that pervades them.[45]

The German mission in Bern reported to Berlin on May 15 that Ciano had held conversations with the British and Americans, and this had been reported to the Swiss government by its ambassador to the Vatican. But on June 25, the apostolic nuncio in Washington, Monsignor Amleto Cicognani, telegraphed to Maglione: "Allies refuse to treat with any Fascist, including Grandi and Ciano."[46] Which report was true? Judging by the following, the first one was.

Ciano met privately at this time with Ernest Koliqui, the Albanian minister plenipotentiary in Rome, and told him: "I am happy to have come out of the Albanian developments without having soiled my hands with blood . . . I thought of your country also when it seemed that it was less near. I spoke of Albania with the English and I received from them the promise that the land of Scanderbeg will have independence, but with Italian interests safeguarded."[47] This statement, revealing that Ciano had been in contact with the British, was confirmed by Ivanoe Bonomi, a former Italian prime minister, in his memoirs. He said Ciano and Grandi had contacts with the British ambassador to the Vatican, Godolphin D'Arcy Osborne, about an end to hostilities and a compromise peace.[48] Ciano told Gaetano Polverelli: "Mussolini cannot have discussions with Churchill and Roosevelt. He is the obstacle to negotiations. He doesn't want to be persuaded but if it is decided to set him aside, discussions on an equal basis will be possible immediately. Basically, London and Washington look to strike the Germany of Hitler. I am persuaded that not even England is interested in striking Italy. If Mussolini is not put aside, Churchill and Roosevelt will refuse discussions. They will have converging landings, south and north of Rome, and everything will be finished."[49]

Some of the officials who had been fired by Mussolini in February, Buffarini among them, met at the end of May to discuss the situation, but Ciano did not attend. Buffarini, fearing that Ciano had stayed away because he intended to reveal everything to Mussolini, hurried to the Duce to tell him of the meeting. Mussolini did not take the warning seriously, nor subsequent ones he received from the extreme Fascists Giovanni Preziosi and Farinacci.

Edda at this time was in Sicily, still working as a Red Cross nurse. She wrote to her father, telling him how people there were living in misery under Allied bombardment. "It seems the military men give a spectacle of fear worse than the civilians, fleeing like rabbits in the fields," she said. "But this is nothing. After the invasion, instead of rushing to help, they remain placid, by contrast with the Germans who set out to do something. The population that couldn't stand the Germans now not only tolerates but admires them for their organizational and even altruistic sense . . . They tell me that General Fiocca, the military commander, isn't worth a fig."[50] Mussolini sent her 50,000 lire to distribute to the most needy.

At the beginning of June, Edda returned to the mainland, exhausted and ill. By now her sympathy for the Germans had evaporated. Alfredo

Cucco, vice-secretary of the Fascist Party, traveled with her and remembered that, when their car was passing a German truck full of troops that did not want to yield, Edda put her head out the window and raised her arm, making a gesture with the index and little fingers that Italians call a *cornuto*, indicating that those to whom it is addressed are cuckolds.[51]

In the first week of June, various Fascist and anti-Fascist personalities, all opposed to Mussolini, met the king to beg his intervention. Italian forces on the island of Pantelleria surrendered on June 10, with Mussolini's permission. The island of Lampedusa fell three days later, and the king met with Ciano at San Rossore. Ciano said Maglione had informed him that, if the king did not act to change the leadership of the government before Allied landings in Sicily, Mussolini's enemies would recognize a government in exile, headed by Count Carlo Sforza, the former Foreign Minister who was then teaching at the University of California. Afterward Ciano told Giovanni Ansaldo the king had asked him if he had communicated anything of this to Mussolini. "I told him no because the talk with Maglione was private and because I wouldn't have achieved any result except to exasperate the man and make him suspicious," he said. The king told him that even he could not speak to the Duce, but he recognized that the situation was grave. "I have the impression that many people are asking where we are going," the king said. Ciano replied: "Not only that. The most serious thing is that many ask it of your Majesty." He urged the king to replace Mussolini and said Italy must assist the Allied landings and make an armistice. The king remained silent. Ciano told Ansaldo: "He's anything other than his antecedent Carlo Alberto! He is more astute than Carlo Alberto and more Hamlet-like than Hamlet."[52] After Ciano left, the king betrayed him to Mussolini. The Duce then called in Ciano and accused him of plotting against him.

An official report to Mussolini on June 10 quoted unconfirmed information that two railroad cars containing valuable effects had been sent from Rome to Switzerland under the surveillance of the chief official of public security. It said the effects were reported to belong to Ciano and Bottai.[53] In the same month Rachele Mussolini told the SS Colonel Dollmann that Ciano was the "bane" of her family. "He was the one who brought unhappiness into our family," she said. "With him, luxury, social fads and high living take priority over the party and over us all. I am fully aware that his lady friends at the golf club know all there is to know, and I am equally aware that his vanity and ambition mean more to him than his links with our family—but Edda will always be a Mussolini. She is one of us, even though she often seems to have turned into a Ciano under Galeazzo's influence."[54] Meanwhile, German counterespionage agents in Rome prepared a report on June 24, entitled "the Ciano Group," in which they voiced suspicion that Ciano was engaged in spying. The report said his main collaborators, led by Leonardo Vitetti, were in the Foreign Ministry.

Ciano was in the Livorno Prefecture on June 28, after a heavy Allied air raid, when in front of police and officials he launched into a tirade against "that mad tyrant who wanted this war."[55] At that time he was writing a book against Mussolini, but he later destroyed it. Before leaving Livorno, he stopped at a cemetery to put flowers on the graves of his father and his governess. "She used to say, 'Galeazzo, you will end badly,'" a friend recalled. "He had a premonition that things might go wrong."[56]

On the day Ciano left, Emilio Pucci arrived at the Ciano home to visit Edda. By then their affair was over and they were just good friends. But, in any case, Ciano didn't mind, one of his friends said. He remained friendly with Pucci, who had become an air force hero during the war, often mentioned in the war bulletins. Pucci was decorated for bravery several times and was wounded. In a statement he made to the Swiss authorities in 1944, Pucci said he became an "intimate friend" of Edda in the summer of 1941 on Capri. "Count Ciano was aware of my friendship with the Countess, whom I saw very often at their house in Rome and elsewhere," he said.[57]

After Ciano's appointment as ambassador to the Holy See was announced, Prince Erwin Lobkowicz, representative of the Croatian Ustashe government at the Vatican, cabled his government that the appointment had come as a shock in Vatican circles because of Edda, "who is very immoral."[58] Melton Davis, an American correspondent in Rome, reported that Ciano in 1943 was "no longer the exuberant, youthful heir-apparent to Mussolini. The dark circles under his eyes were beginning to be permanent, his robust physique was degenerating into fat, his features thickening, and his cheeks more jowly than ever . . . Still cordial with intimates, he became increasingly distant and haughty with people he didn't like."[59]

Allied landings in Sicily began the night of July 9-10. The Italian navy did not intervene, and the air force was almost nonexistent. Some Italian troops fought, and others fled, but the Germans resisted. In Rome, the plot against Mussolini gathered momentum.

Chapter Fifteen

Collapse of Mussolini's Regime

The Allied landings in Sicily concentrated the minds of all those who had contemplated a coup against Mussolini but had previously dithered. Ciano met in Rome on July 12 or 13 with General Gastone Gambara, the Italian commander of an armored corps in Croatia. They agreed that the situation required the return of the Supreme Command of the armed forces to the king as well as the direction of military ministries by military men. On July 14, Ciano revealed his hand to one of his enemies, Roberto Farinacci. He said either one must think Germany would win the war, in which case all Italians should draw more closely around the king and the generals, or one must think the Allies would win, in which case it would be necessary to conclude a separate peace before it was too late. "From both horns of the dilemma you get, in my way of looking at it, a diminution of the powers of Mussolini, with consequent diminution of responsibility," he said. "In other words, it is necessary to return the Supreme Command immediately to the king and call to government responsibility the men who did not want the war and who can eventually save fascism through agreements with the Allies." He added that the Allies regarded Mussolini as "the true, unique obstacle to peace."[1]

That same day, Ambrosio asked Castellano to re-elaborate his plan for the capture of Mussolini. Former Prime Minister Bonomi met with Badoglio at his house, and agreed to propose to the king that he remove Mussolini and name Badoglio as prime minister with full powers and Bonomi as deputy premier. Badoglio presented this plan to the king the next day. The monarch rejected the idea of a government including politicians but, for the first time, said he was ready to act.

Edda by now had turned against her father. She told Ciano: "If my father can remain in power only with the support of the Germans, it is better that he leave. It is no longer a question of being Fascist or anti-Fascist, but of being Italian. No matter what happens, Italy must be saved."[2] Meanwhile, Ciano was in bed with an ear infection. It was real enough, but his decision to take to his bed may have been an act of political prudence. He had heard that Mussolini wanted to see him, but when he telephoned the Palazzo Venezia the Duce's secretary assured him Mussolini only wanted to know if he were in Rome. Mussolini telephoned on July 17 and told him to stay in bed and get well. Ciano later said that when he received the phone call he was "in sweet conversation with an aspiring film actress."[3]

On the morning of July 19, American planes bombed Rome for the first time, killing many people in the San Lorenzo quarter on the eastern edge of the city and heavily damaging the ancient church of St. Lawrence Outside the Walls. Anfuso, just back from Budapest, met with Ciano that day and wrote afterward: "He was at home with a political illness, linked to the numerous lines of numerous plots. Groups of countesses and princesses came and went in his room. The women didn't say much; it pleased them to see with whom Galeazzo had fallen out. He railed against Mussolini to such a degree that one of the countesses, out of prudence, went to close the window so his neighbor wouldn't hear . . ."[4]

Mussolini called a meeting of the Grand Council for July 24 to face down criticism from within the party. Ciano met with Grandi and Bottai to discuss a common strategy for the meeting. Neither wanted him to vote against Mussolini because of his kinship with the Duce, but Ciano insisted. "If my father were alive, he would be with you," he said. "Would you want to stop me doing what I do in his name?"[5] Farinacci went to Mussolini on July 21 to show him a message he had received from the pro-Nazi Cavallero. It read: "Be extremely careful. Grandi and company are plotting to undermine Mussolini, but their game will be vain in any case because the royal house, with Acquarone, conducts the struggle for its own count and will play off all of them." Mussolini brushed aside the warning. Just that morning, he said, the king had told him: "These are bad times for you, but know that you have a friend in me. And if, to use an absurd hypothesis, everyone should abandon you, I would be the last to do so. I know how much Italy and the dynasty owe you."[6] But then Mussolini's eyes were opened. Carlo Scorza brought him a resolution that Grandi proposed to introduce at the Grand Council meeting, calling on Mussolini to relinquish his military and political powers to the king. Grandi himself had given the resolution to Scorza. Mussolini branded the resolution "vile and unacceptable." Scorza also informed him of an intercepted phone call from Badoglio to Acquarone in which the marshal spoke of "wrapping up the Duce while he leaves Villa Savoia." Mussolini replied that he didn't like thrillers.[7]

Acquarone told Ambrosio the king had decided to act, and it was time to put his plan into operation. On July 23, participants in the plot began a series of feverish contacts. Bottai and Grandi went to party headquarters and found Scorza, Ciano and Farinacci together. All had agreed to support the Grandi resolution.

For some months, Rachele Mussolini had tried to persuade her husband that Ciano was a traitor. She met Dollmann in early July and entreated the Germans "to keep their eyes open and to think in time of how to parry the treason of Galeazzo." Four days before the Grand Council meeting, she pressed Mussolini anew to act. She said she had been given a list of traitors, and told him it was "time to do something about Ciano, Grandi, Badoglio and the rest." He told her he was more worried about American tanks than Italian intrigues.[8] He believed his officials, Ciano included, were incapable of carrying out a coup, and told his police chief, Chierici, that he did not expect opposition at the Grand Council meeting. The council members, he said, were "modest, very modest, in intelligence, vacillating in belief, hardly gifted with courage." "Believe me, Chierici, they do not ask anything better than to be persuaded and it will not be difficult for me to lead back to the fold a Grandi, a Bottai and even Count Ciano who, I believe, begins to exaggerate truly in the notion of succeeding me," he said.[9]

Alfieri, who had come from Berlin, joined those who had agreed to vote for the resolution. Ettore Muti, the thuggish former party secretary, told the other plotters: "You make me laugh with your resolutions. If you want, I will resolve the question very quickly and I will put the Duce out for you this evening."[10] Acquarone, Ambrosio and Castellano went to Badoglio's house to inform him of the king's decision to name him prime minister in place of Mussolini. They showed him a message the king planned to read on the radio, and Badoglio gave his assent. Castellano then contacted Senise and told him to be ready to assume direction of the police. Together they compiled a list of officials who were to be arrested. At 1 p.m. Zenone Benini, a lifelong friend of Ciano's, went to Ciano's house for lunch. Ciano told him, "Everybody's afraid, and it could mean that we'll all finish behind bars." But then, adopting a "fatuous and at the same time serious tone," according to Benini, Ciano added, "You will see that in the end he will go and we can straighten things out somehow." Benini said, "He thought of a kind of triumvirate in which the aspirations for the post of 'Duce' would by tacit agreement be set aside." He said Ciano continued: "Yes, there is the war. Certainly, there is the war, but that can be resolved also if the madman goes away. If we make peace and get the Germans out of Italy we can avoid occupation by the Americans."[11]

The Grand Council meeting was fixed for 5 p.m. As Mussolini prepared to leave Villa Torlonia, Rachele told him: "Have them all arrested before the meeting begins."[12] He said nothing, but kissed her and walked to his car. The members of the council wore black uniforms on this hot and humid Saturday in summer. Grandi went in with two hand grenades concealed under his cloak, and Bottai had one. Grandi later said that, if Mussolini had ordered them arrested, he would have used his grenades. Luigi Federzoni, another plotter, said "not a few" members came well armed. "One of them drew me into a corner and, with a rather boastful air, drew from under his long coat two hand grenades, expressing his wonder that I was not similarly armed," he said. Ciano may have been armed as well. After the meeting, when he was back in his embassy, Anfuso went to see him and found on his desk "two or three hand grenades" that had never been there before.[13] Most of the council members carried concealed pistols, and Umberto Albini, one of the anti-Mussolini plotters, arranged to have two hundred public security agents hidden in the palace. Mussolini's personal guards were kept away, on Albini's orders.[14]

Mussolini opened the meeting with a speech that lasted nearly two hours. Then Grandi read his resolution, and after that it was Ciano's turn. He began by saying it was necessary to hold out against the Allies to the limits possible. Then he recounted how the Germans violated clauses of the Pact of Steel by attacking Poland without prior consultation with Italy, betraying the absolute loyalty of the Duce. He avoided recriminations and was deferential toward Mussolini. Ciano observed that the alliance with Germany had twice been requested by the Germans, starting in 1938, and Mussolini had initially avoided a commitment. He went on to say that, when Italy finally did sign the pact with the explicit reservation about refraining from war for several more years, the German General Staff already had fixed the date of the attack on Poland. "We were not minimally advised or consulted," Ciano said. He added that Italy's "loyal warnings" in 1939 fell into a void. "The Germans lighted the fuse ahead of time, against every pact and understanding with us. And they did not abandon this method during the entire course of the war. All the attacks that followed the one on Poland were equally communicated to us at the last hour: from that on Belgium and Holland to the last one, against Russia . . . In short, our loyalty was never returned. Every accusation of betrayal made by the Germans to us could be incontrovertibly turned back on them. We were not, in any case, traitors, but the betrayed."[15] Federzoni said the quarter hour of Ciano's speech was, for Mussolini, a period "of most bitter exasperation." The Duce's eyes lighted up with a barely concealed anger, and he began working his jaw, "chewing tacit imprecations and sinister promises against the unfaithful son-in-law,"

Federzoni said. Buffarini commented: "The face he made when Ciano spoke cannot be described."[16] Mussolini apparently felt particularly wounded that Ciano had revealed how the Germans had failed to consult him, and thus had demonstrated the evident low regard Hitler felt toward him.

After Ciano spoke, Farinacci introduced an alternative resolution calling for fidelity to the Axis alliance and specifying that Mussolini would hand back only his military powers to the king, not his political powers as well. Near midnight, Mussolini suspended the debate for twenty minutes. In an anteroom, Grandi collected signatures for his resolution. Ciano was ready to sign, but Grandi told him: "No, let it be. We are all grateful for your support and the collaboration you have given us until this evening. Now don't put yourself in too serious a position. No one will mind if you abstain." But Ciano replied, "I have taken some decisions and I have measured all the responsibilities that accompany them. I remember very well your advice, but I remember also that I have made the sign of the cross before the Madonna as a promise not to change course. I want to sign and I will sign. Give it to me."[17] During the break, one diehard Fascist heard Ciano say of Mussolini: "He's like a wounded bear. If we don't defend ourselves, he'll tear us to pieces."[18]

When the session resumed, Ciano intervened again to say it did not amount to an admission of defeat to restore military powers to the king. Afterward he whispered to Farinacci, urging him to propose that all the resolutions be withdrawn so everyone could agree on just one text. Farinacci replied: "It's up to you. You propose it. I will keep mine."[19] Galbiati, seated on Ciano's left, grew nervous and repeated to himself, but in a voice loud enough to be heard by the others, "I don't see clearly what this resolution contains, but I don't like it, I don't like it." Ciano commented afterward: "Seeing him like that, I felt ice in my spine and thought of Fouquier-Tinville, the prosecutor of the French revolutionary tribunal who had sent some of his relatives to the guillotine, and after the Thermidor reaction ended there himself."[20] Mussolini also intervened again, interrupting Bastianini who had spoken of the fracture between the country and the party. "The origin of this fracture can perhaps be found in certain rapid enrichments of some personality," the Duce said.[21] Alfieri claimed he was looking at Ciano as he said this. Mussolini insinuated he might not accept "being decapitated" if the Grandi resolution was passed, and said he was sure of the friendship of the king. "And then I have in hand a key to resolve the war situation," he said. "But I will not tell you what it is."[22]

Bottai made the final speech, one that may have won over those who were wavering. "For two days I haven't eaten and I haven't slept, but if now I were to withdraw my signature from the Grandi resolution I would no longer feel myself a man," he said. Mussolini then called for a vote. Scorza voted no, but six who followed him voted yes. It was now Ciano's turn. As he rose, Mussolini half shut his eyes. He and Ciano exchanged a long and penetrating look. Then Ciano in a strong, clear voice said, "Yes." When the final vote was tabulated, it was nineteen for, eight against and one abstention. Mussolini closed the meeting: "You have provoked the crisis of the regime." He instructed Scorza to omit the salute to the Duce on the part of those who had abandoned him. At 2.30 a.m. on July 25, nine and a half hours after the meeting began, he strode from the room. As he did so, Ciano told Scorza that he was like "a wounded wild boar."[23]

Ciano approached Farinacci and said: "Roberto, we are in two opposed camps, but you must believe me. I act for the good of Italy, as I believe you do." Farinacci did not reply. Antonino Tringali Casanuova, accompanying Farinacci, did, however. There are four versions of what he is supposed to have said:

> "Dear Ciano, from the discussion and vote of this night many troubles will arise for Italy and fascism. Much blood, perhaps fraternal blood, will have to be spilled. May God wish that it doesn't fall on your head."
> "My boy, what you've done this night is not good. It seems to me that you have put your head on the block."
> "Young man, what happened this evening is a crime that will be paid with blood. I wish you good luck. However, I believe your days are numbered."
> "Young man, you will pay for your betrayal with blood."

Among those present, there was no disagreement about Ciano's reply: "I am sorry to have had to vote as I did, but I could not betray my country as you are betraying it, you who are implacably seditious."[24]

Ciano left with Bottai and drove him home. Grandi sent his resolution to the king, inviting him to form a non-Fascist civilian government headed by a military man, Marshal Enrico Caviglia. After Ciano returned home, Benini, Vitetti and d'Aieta rushed there and found him agitated, torn between anxiety and joy. "In a few hours Mussolini will have me arrested," he said. "But then the king will take away his power and I will be let out."[25]

Mussolini drove home after 3 a.m. through deserted streets, accompanied by Scorza. They rode in silence until Mussolini exclaimed, "Even Ciano, Albini and Bastianini." Rachele met him at the door of Villa Torlonia and asked him if those who voted against him had been arrested. "No, I'll do it tomorrow," he answered dully. "Tomorrow will be too late," she said.[26] On the morning of July 25, Mussolini received Bastianini courteously, even though he had voted against him. The Duce commented bitterly that, with Ciano, the traitors had entered even into his own house. Bastianini showed him a report Ciano had prepared on conditions put forward by the British and Americans through the Vatican for recognizing Rome as an open city. Mussolini read it attentively.

Ciano returned to his embassy in the afternoon, met with some friends and read them the Grandi resolution. "This morning I sent it to Maglione," he said. "They are up to date in the Vatican." Anfuso asked him, "Don't you think Mussolini will have you arrested?" Ciano replied, "It's possible." Bonomi had already sent an aide to warn him to beware of Mussolini. "What are you doing here then?" Anfuso said. "Waiting for them to come and take you? Let's get out of here! Come to my house. It's far from the center and they will not think that you are there because I don't live in Rome." Ciano looked at a pair of hand grenades resting on his desk, then tried to use the telephone. He found the line had been cut, grew alarmed and decided to take Anfuso's advice.[27] They drove away together, but he said that first he wanted to stop at Grandi's office. While he was there, Muti arrived and announced that Mussolini had been arrested on orders of the king. He had been arrested at 5.30 p.m. at the Villa Savoia, the royal residence, as he came to call on the king, and taken to a Carabiniere training barracks in Via Legnano. Dollmann later said Mussolini often paced restlessly up and down in the barracks in coming days. "Every now and then he would come to a halt, shake his bald head and roll his eyes furiously, crying: 'Ah, *il quarantenne, il quarantenne!*'"*[28]

Ciano was clearly surprised. "What a mess," he said. "It's the collapse of everything. Now they will handcuff us as well." He took leave of Grandi and went on with Anfuso to his house.[29] When Ciano learned that evening that Badoglio was the head of government, he began making arrangements through General Castellano for the safety of his wife and children, who were in Livorno. Castellano assured him he would get them safely to Rome. Shortly after the radio announced the dismissal of Mussolini, messages from the king and Badoglio were read out, declaring that "the war continues." At 8 p.m. Ciano telephoned Edda from Anfuso's house and told her, "There is a *tramontana* [north wind, an agreed code word between them] not especially for us. I'll be sending the car tomorrow morning. Telephone my mother and make her leave with you."[30] Anfuso's servant, afraid that Ciano would be arrested, urged them to go away. Out in the street, Ciano's driver, Tiberio del Gracco, wailed, "My children! My children! The Count! Everything is lost!" At 3 a.m., Ciano decided to return home, and Anfuso accompanied him. Even at that hour, they

---

* *Quarantenne* means forty-year-old—Ciano's age at the time.

found groups of people in the streets of Rome celebrating the fall of fascism and pulling down party symbols. In Piazza Santi Apostoli, Ciano looked at Anfuso, consternation showing in his face, and said with a lapse into Roman slang, "How boring! Talk about boring, this really is the limit."[31]

Chapter Sixteen

Escape to Germany

After Ciano had telephoned Edda to say he was sending a car, she rang her mother-in-law, who had Marzio with her, and told her to come immediately. She had some difficulty making her mother-in-law understand that she was not to bring her usual huge suitcases and maids. Then she drew Fabrizio and Raimonda to her and told them the news. Fabrizio was immediately alarmed. "What do you suppose is going to happen to us? Shall we all be killed?" he asked. "No," she replied. "Not yet anyhow, but we must be ready for anything. In the best hypothesis your father will lose his job, his fortune will be taken and we will all become private citizens. But it's much more probable that we'll go through the usual routine: prison, death or, if we are lucky, exile."[1] Little wonder that some of Edda's old friends say she was not a good mother to her children; there could hardly be better proof than her chilling frankness in telling her young children about the possibility they would be killed. The rest of her conversation was just as bizarre.

"Does it really matter?" she asked. "Our country is in mortal danger; nothing matters any more as long as our country lives. We have had our gorgeous moments. Now we must pay for it all, especially for the one fatal mistake. And anyway, people like us, in our position, must be ready to take the smooth and the rough when it comes and put a brave face to it. Thank God we are no cowards. One moment at the top of the world, the next at the bottom of the abyss. The *aurea mediocritas* is not for us and if we had it we certainly would not know what to do with it." Edda convinced herself the children understood what she was talking about. As for herself, she said afterward, "I had no illusions . . . At that moment I just knew that the blow had at last fallen; that we were doomed; rats in a trap. But there can be beauty even in the death of a mouse." She said to the children, "Let's have music. It's our last night, let's make a night of it." "It was barbarous and beautiful," she wrote later. "We were drunk with music . . . After a little more conversation we all retired . . . I went to bed, and for one more night, in blissful ignorance, I was still a dictator's daughter."[2]

The car that was supposed to collect them from Livorno the next day did not arrive, and telephone communications between Rome and Livorno were cut. This was the first indication that, with the coup, the military plotters and the royal court had no further use for Ciano. He was, in fact, a liability. The public was unaware of the fact he had opposed the war and saw him only as the author of the disaster in Greece and as a man who had enriched himself in public office. He was publicly reviled, and there would soon be demands for his arrest. Ciano had thrown Mussolini overboard without securing a lifeline for himself. He was isolated and, in the high circles that mattered, friendless and despised.

A Carabinieri captain came to the Ciano house in Livorno during the morning to tell Edda she and the children would have to leave by train. At 2 p.m., as she reached the station, Edda bought a newspaper and learned that her father was no longer in power. During the long, slow journey to Rome, she had to contend with a boil that was causing her considerable pain. The train passed freight cars that had "down with Mussolini" signs on them, and Fabrizio and Raimonda had tears in their eyes. It was nearly midnight when the train arrived, four hours behind schedule. Three Carabinieri officers escorted them to their home and one reproached Edda for not having told her father how the Italian people felt about the war. During the drive through Rome, she thought the city was "decked out as for the conquest of Addis Ababa."[3] Ciano met them in the library of their apartment, and told Edda he never would have imagined the fall of the regime would be so complete or greeted with such enthusiasm. He said he had seen people embracing in the streets and slashing photographs of Mussolini to pieces. "We haven't the least chance of survival if we remain in Italy," he said.[4] Acquarone came the next evening and told Ciano the king wanted him to remain as ambassador to the Vatican. Afterward Edda said to Ciano: "If the Germans react [to the coup], I will serve as a buffer. But if the Allies are the ones who arrive, perhaps then you can do something for me."[5] Two days later Ciano informed the king he thought he should resign, and on July 31 he did so.

He was now under house arrest. Grandi had fled to Portugal, and Bottai would soon take refuge in a monastery under Vatican protection and later fight with the French Foreign Legion. Vittorio Mussolini had gone to Germany. But Ciano had nowhere to go, and armed Carabinieri patrolled the street in front of his house. He and Edda decided they should seek refuge in Spain, and he applied for passports, but there was no reply. Ciano began to talk of suicide; his uncle Arturo had in fact committed suicide after the events of July 25. Badoglio told Foreign Minister Guariglia that public opinion would be scandalized if Ciano were allowed to leave the country, since rumors that he had enriched himself in office were circulating widely.

Edda contacted the Vatican to request refuge, but her plea was rejected. Fabrizio in later years surmised that there were two possible explanations: (1) the Badoglio government advised the Holy See against giving Ciano asylum, since it had decided to arrest him and it would have been embarrassing for the Pope to harbor a fugitive from justice; (2) the Allies advised the Vatican to say no, since Ciano was on their list of war criminals.[6] Either explanation seems highly plausible. Many of Ciano's friends urged him to leave Italy, but he refused to go without his family. "The pilot at the Foreign Ministry was devoted to Ciano. He owed his whole career to him," one friend said. "He could have gotten him out if he had wanted to go."[7] Mussolini, interned on the island of Ponza, received a letter from Edda on August 1. He glanced at it and threw it under his bed, apparently irritated at references to Ciano. He told a fellow prisoner that Ciano was "a truly ignoble person."[8]

A steady stream of visitors, including Ciano's women friends, came to the apartment on Via Angelo Secchi. Alfieri, among his callers, wrote: "As soon as he saw me, he was moved and embraced me. He was more than usually nervous and emotional. When he spoke of Mussolini, he burst into sobs: 'He was a great man, a real genius. He could still do so much good for Italy . . . Why has he treated all of us like this?' Then he calmed down . . . Certainly he did not foresee the worst. 'You will understand,' he said to me, 'that even if I must stay at home for two or three months, it won't be death. Later, we will see how things go . . .'" Edda suddenly appeared in the room. She was "pallid, emaciated, her lips pale, her large, luminous eyes sunken and veiled with sadness . . . For the more than twenty years that I knew her, for the first time she appeared to me a simple and poor woman in her humanity, undefended against the very hard blows of her destiny,"[9] Alfieri wrote. Ciano told one of his visitors: "I have found a help in a person in whom I would never have believed. Edda has shown herself to be an exceptional wife."[10] Anfuso, a less sympathetic observer, was also among Ciano's callers. "If the Fascists of the plot were constrained to abandon him, the countesses instead remained faithful," he wrote. "The countesses were Anglophile and awaited those Englishmen whom Galeazzo had promised them . . . The ground was burning under Galeazzo's feet . . . All those who had promised Ciano a plane to flee to Spain were no longer to be seen."[11]

On August 4 the Badoglio government had announced it was setting up a commission to look into illicit riches of high Fascist officials. This was ironic, since Badoglio was one of the principal beneficiaries of the regime. Ciano possessed documents showing that Badoglio had pulled off some shady deals in Ethiopia and Greece and had approved the murders of the king of Yugoslavia and the French Foreign Minister Barthou in 1934.

Ciano became desperate in his search for a way out. He already had discussed with Edda the possibility of seeking German help, and in July he had told Anfuso: "Go to Mackensen and tell him I cannot continue to live and wait in these conditions. Badoglio will not let me leave and here things are always going from bad to worse." Anfuso warned him the Germans would put him in irons or send him to Dachau. "I spoke of Dachau because it seemed to me the most terrifying place," he said. "I added that it was madness to wind up in Germany after having voted in the Grand Council against Mussolini."[12] But Ciano ignored that warning, and a more explicit one from Baron Dörnberg, head of ceremonial of the Reich, who told one of Ciano's friends: "Tell Galeazzo that he should make sure not to fall into the hands of the Germans; if they succeed in catching him, they will kill him."[13]

Admiral Candido Bigliardi, who had known the Cianos in China, and a Colonel Casero offered to smuggle Ciano out to Spain but said it would not be possible to take his family with him. "For this reason Galeazzo refused. It was a noble act of foolishness," Bigliardi later recounted.[14] Edda and the children would have been safe in Italy, or could have taken refuge in Germany. Edda completed the blunder by helping to persuade Ciano they must appeal to the Germans for help. In early August she asked Bigliardi to get in touch with Dollmann and request his help in getting the family out of the country. Bigliardi replied that she was mad, as the Germans could not bear her husband. Edda replied, "I know that, but they are the only ones who can give us a plane to fly to Spain. You cannot imagine what I must go through to keep up Galeazzo's spirits. It is becoming impossible! I would rather run the risk of facing the Germans, and perhaps my name will help a bit . . ."[15] Bigliardi arranged the meeting for August 11, and that evening she left the house as though going for a walk. Dollmann's car was waiting around the corner. He started the engine, and she climbed in. Dollmann drove to the home of some friends. "Mussolini's daughter behaved precisely as her intimates had expected her to behave when it came to a pinch," Dollmann wrote. "Questionable as some aspects of her married life had been in the past, she now became all wife and mother. Her every thought and emotion were centered on a wish to save her husband and children, and the present fate of her father received only fleeting mention." Dollmann agreed to use his influence with Kesselring to secure a flight from Rome. He said he stressed several times to Edda that the plane "would undoubtedly take them to Germany." Edda, he said, declared that Ciano would be agreeable to this if his first choice of asylum, Spain, was ruled out.[16] That account does not square with Edda's own later insistence that the Cianos had expected to be flown to Spain and were surprised to find, once they were in the air, that they were heading for Munich. Several days later, a German military officer turned up at the Cianos' residence dressed in civilian clothes and carrying a huge bouquet of flowers. His purpose was to fill the pockets of his overcoat with various valuable articles the Cianos were anxious to save.[17] As the arrangements progressed, Edda had a visit from a close friend, Lola Giovinelli. On a hot day in August, Giovinelli left the Ciano house wearing two of Edda's fur coats. She walked calmly past the Carabinieri who, if they found anything odd about her choice of attire, said nothing. Despite the summer heat, Edda lighted a stove in the apartment and began burning papers.

Countess Marozia Borromeo d'Adda called on the Cianos and urged them to go to the Vatican, but she was told "they don't want us." The countess insisted. "You must go and present yourselves at the door," she said. "They won't turn you away." But the Cianos declined to take her advice. "Going to Germany was really idiotic," she later recounted. "It was Edda's fault. She thought because of her father the Germans would have respected them."[18] Susanna Agnelli was another visitor to the apartment. She noted that Edda received her friends in one room, and Ciano received his in another. She found Ciano nervous, and he told her with a snigger that he had neither seen nor heard from many of his old friends since he had fallen into disgrace. "Let's hear you who tell the truth, Suni," he said. "Do you think they are going to kill me?" Agnelli smiled to soften the impact of her words. "Yes, I do, Galeazzo." "And who do you think would kill me, the Germans or the Allies?" "I'm afraid either one." She regretted her answer immediately, and noticed that he turned pale. "Remember one thing, Suni," he said. "If they kill me, they will kill you too." "That may well be." Agnelli took his hand and urged him to go to Spain. But she found him reluctant to leave his family, and kissed him goodbye. "Galeazzo had little sense of reality and was a very poor judge of human beings," she recalled much later. "I would have wanted to help him; he had so many times helped people I had asked him to intercede for when one word from him could change their future from death to life. Now he was surrounded by people who flattered him. They assured him that everybody loved him and that, certainly, his life was not in danger."[19]

On August 22 the Cianos' position in Italy grew more precarious. The Milan newspaper *Corriere della Sera* carried an article on Costanzo Ciano's riches, and on those allegedly amassed by his son. Such charges could set the stage for Ciano's arrest. He sent a letter of protest to Badoglio, saying the supposed billions of his father actually amounted to about 800 million lire, aside from the value of the family-owned newspaper, *Il Telegrafo*. Badoglio did not reply. In the letter, Ciano lied. For one thing, the list of his assets did not include ninety-five apartments that he owned in Rome, or his house in Ponte a Moriano. For another, documents in the U.S. National Archives, which only came to light in late 1996, revealed he had hidden millions of pesos in Argentina and had, along with Mussolini, secreted more funds in Switzerland. David C. Berger, first secretary of the American Embassy in Buenos Aires, cabled the State Department on December 9, 1944, that the Argentine government, while investigating for tax purposes the records of a textile firm called Denubio, uncovered proof that the capital of the firm was owned by Ciano and the German General Hans Guderian. Berger said that, although the capital was two million pesos, the firm made a profit of nine million during the previous fiscal year. "A reliable informant of the Embassy has stated that Edda Mussolini Ciano is endeavoring to come to Argentina to collect the assets of her late husband, Count Ciano, which are reputedly held by Victor Valdani, (I.L.) Editor of the Proclaimed List Italian newspaper *Il Mattino d'Italia*," Berger wrote.[20] In fact, Edda was then still in Switzerland, with little immediate possibility of leaving the country. After the war she did visit Argentina on more than one occasion, but whether she recovered the funds Ciano held there is unknown.

Even during the period Ciano served as Foreign Minister the secret police compiled a lengthy file of allegations about the enrichment of the Cianos. One note that the police received from an informant in Pistoia said the head of a certain family had bought eighteen parcels of land in the Lucca province in a questionable transaction. It said the head of the family was G. Ciano. The police also quoted rumors that he had an interest in several railway companies, the Bombrini-Parodi firm and the Motta company, famed for its candies and cakes, and had acquired various properties in Sorrento, Amalfi and Tuscany. Other reports said he had an interest in a company involved in the excavation of Carrara marble. The Secret Archive of the Vatican received information in February 1942 that Ciano had formed a bogus company with other Italians to acquire from the state the entire area of the military barracks at Castro Pretorio, about seven and a half acres, with a view to demolishing the barracks and developing the land. The report said the state sold the land at barely six lire per square meter when in reality its value was about 1,500 lire.[21] But Mario Mondello, who was one of Ciano's long-time collaborators, is skeptical of suggestions Ciano enriched himself in office. He said Ciano never took his salary as Foreign Minister but contributed it to a charity administered by ministry officials.[22] Of course, it could be argued that if he enriched himself in other ways he did not need his salary. Charity and greed in one man would be inconsistent, but Ciano was, above all else, inconsistent.

Ciano's concern over his position turned to alarm when, on the night of August 23–24, Ettore Muti, who had warned him to leave Rome, was killed at his house in Fregene outside Rome. The official version was that he was shot while trying to escape arrest. Ciano had every reason to be alarmed. After the *Corriere* article appeared, Badoglio gave orders to Carmine Senise, back in office as chief of police, to arrest Ciano and other high-ranking Fascist officials. Edda said Raimondo Lanza, Susanna Agnelli's boyfriend, visited the Cianos the day before their flight and tipped them off about Badoglio's plans. "In a day or two Galeazzo will be arrested and taken to the island of Ponza," he told Edda.[23] But Senise was sympathetic to Ciano. "The public demanded his arrest," he wrote in his memoirs. "I wasn't favorable in that moment. We didn't have means to determine his wealth. Arrest seemed premature, before an inquiry was completed." After receiving Badoglio's order, Senise telephoned to ask if Ciano should be arrested immediately or if it would not be better to arrange his transport to Ponza with the navy minister. Badoglio told him to handle the matter as he saw fit. An hour later, Senise learned that Ciano, his wife and children had fled the country that morning.[24]

The German officials in Rome who had met Edda naturally had to get Hitler's approval for the escape plan. According to Lt.-Col. Wilhelm Höttl, head of the German secret service for Italy and southern Europe, Hitler "had a great affection for Edda." He said he was happy to save "the blood of the Duce" but Ciano could remain "where the pepper grows." When the Führer approved the plan, his orders referred only to Edda and the children. Queried by his underlings in Rome, Hitler reluctantly said Ciano could come too if he wanted, and particularly if his wife set any store by his coming. "Hitler had obviously been influenced by the rumors current in Germany that relations between husband and wife were as bad as they could be," Höttl wrote. "He thought Edda would be pleased at an opportunity to get rid of her husband."[25]

The escape was fixed for August 27. That morning, Edda woke the children early and told them to put on a double set of clothes. Then she motioned to them to follow her out of the house and whispered, "Behave normally. Pretend we are going for a walk."[26] Her maid had lured one of the sentries into a neighboring park by seductive promises. Edda and the children walked to the nearby Piazza Santiago del Chile. As they arrived, a black American car carrying two Germans pulled up, Edda and the children quickly got in and the car sped away. Moments after they left home, Ciano, wearing a pair of large, green-tinted glasses, stepped out of the front door of their apartment building and, before the Carabinieri had time to react, quickly climbed into a slowly moving car that had its door open. Senise later reported that a police inquiry found the family climbed over a wall that separated their house from an adjacent villa, between 9 and 9.30 a.m., and a car with diplomatic license plates picked them up from in front of the villa. Evidently Ciano's servants and the police on duty, who may have been bribed by the Germans to allow the escape, lied to those conducting the inquiry, for this account does not square with those of Edda and the Germans. Senise said Ciano, on the morning of the flight, gave generous sums of money to all his servants.[27]

The two cars carrying the Cianos converged on the courtyard of the Deutsches Heim, where a closed German Wehrmacht truck waited to take them to Ciampino airport southeast of the city. A Junkers 52 military aircraft with engines running waited on the runway. Among those who received the Cianos aboard the plane was Colonel Otto Skorzeny, the man who later led the operation to free Mussolini and spirit him out of Italy. The pilot was SS Captain Erich Priebke, who took refuge in South America after the war and was returned to Italy in 1996 for trial on charges that he participated in the Ardeatine Caves massacre of Italian civilians in 1944. In that incident, three hundred and thirty-five Italian men and boys were lined up and shot in caves on the outskirts of Rome in reprisal for the killing of ten German soldiers by partisans in the capital. Priebke was sentenced to five years' imprisonment in July 1997.

Edda said the first thing she and Ciano did when they boarded the plane was to pin their Fascist insignia onto their lapels again. Höttl reported, "Even before the plane had left the ground, Ciano began to pull gold cigarette cases, bracelets and rings out of all his pockets and to make a first inventory. His little daughter too had a small satchel crammed with jewelry. Before he was rescued Ciano had already sent his valet ahead to Germany with a small leather sack full of the most valuable trinkets."[28] In her memoirs, Edda said they were told the plane would land at Munich for lunch and would fly on to Spain from there, with a probable stop in Berlin to collect false passports. German accounts, however, agree that the Cianos were informed from the beginning that their destination was Germany, and no promises were made about going to Spain.

The Cianos had left their apartment in summer clothes but, flying in an unpressurized plane at 18,000 feet, they were chilled to the bone, according to Höttl. He said Edda and the children swigged brandy that Skorzeny had provided to warm them up, but the teetotal Ciano hardly touched a drop. General Hellstein, the SS commander in Bavaria, and SS General Karl Wolff met the plane when it landed at Munich at 4 p.m. Hellstein told the Cianos they would be receiving ration cards for food and clothing. Ciano turned to Edda and exclaimed, "My God! I think they are counting on keeping us here for some time."[29] Höttl's own version of the arrival: "Ciano got off the plane visibly happy and was conducted by auto, together with his family, to Oberallmannshausen, on the lake of Starnberg. He was put up in great secrecy in a magnificent villa placed at his disposal by Hitler."[30] Mad King Ludwig II of Bavaria committed suicide in the Starnberg lake in 1886. The Cianos had arrived with few clothes, but Höttl furnished them with more and later accompanied them to a Munich department store where they were able to replenish their wardrobes.

Two days after their arrival, Edda received flowers from Ribbentrop and a note from Kaltenbrunner asking to be received. When she met him, she said, "He spoke only to me, and seemed to ignore my husband's existence." Kaltenbrunner arranged for Edda to go to Hitler's headquarters on August 31 to meet with the Führer. On August 30, the Germans took photographs of the Cianos for their false passports, and Ciano wore a fake moustache and glasses. He was identified on his passport as an Argentine of Italian origin and she was named as Margaret Smith, an Englishwoman born in Shanghai. The children were also given false passports.[31] Winston Churchill could not have known at this point of the Cianos' flight to Germany, but in a broadcast on August 31, he reveled in the downfall of Mussolini and Ciano. "See how those who stray from the true path are deceived and punished," he said. "Look at this wretched Mussolini and his son-in-law and accomplice Ciano, on whom the curse of Garibaldi has veritably fallen."[32]

Höttl had several conversations with the Cianos during their first weeks in Germany. At first, he said, Ciano tried to disguise the actions that led him to join in Mussolini's downfall. But not Edda. "Countess Edda made not the slightest attempt to hide the truth," he said. "Her forthright character, which knew no half measures in love or hate, would not tolerate any such evasion. With irrefutable logic she showed exactly where and how her father's policies had been wrong, though her affection for him was still deep. Ciano gradually came to agree more and more with her opinion." Höttl said it was not simply the divergence of views between Mussolini and Ciano on foreign policy that caused their estrangement. "Ciano and his wife repeatedly asserted that with the increasing deterioration of the war situation, Mussolini's rabid Socialist views became more and more apparent." He said the couple referred to Mussolini's "uncouth" attacks on the bourgeoisie and the aristocracy, and expressed concern that after the war Mussolini would set up in Italy "a system which was but little different from that in Russia."[33] Ciano by now shared Mussolini's contempt for the Italian people—but for different reasons, Höttl said. "He felt he had been betrayed, overthrown and driven into exile." Ciano felt so strongly, he said, that he was determined his children would not be brought up as Italians and were never to return to Italy. "As far as he was concerned, he declared, he would rather see them become Cubans," Höttl wrote.[34]

Ciano told the German that Crown Princess Marie José had been the mainspring behind the royal plot against Mussolini. As long ago as 1942 she had told Ciano she would do everything she could to get Italy out of the war. During their talks, Ciano began to discuss his diary, and ended by offering to hand it over to the Germans if they would allow him to go to Spain and South America. Ciano said Ribbentrop would be so compromised by the diary that he would be unable to continue as Foreign Minister. Höttl was intrigued. He decided to bring in his secretary, then in Rome, to act as an interpreter. Her name was Hildegard Burkhardt Beetz, and she held the rank of major in the SS. A native of Weimar, in September she married a Luftwaffe major, Gerhard Beetz, who was then fighting on the Russian front. She spoke Italian faultlessly. A short woman with brown hair and an intelligent face, she had a jovial temperament and for that reason had been nicknamed Felicitas by Kaltenbrunner. She was then twenty-two years old, and later said she was a "fervent Nazi" at the time she met Ciano. "At first he did not make a good impression on me," she said. "He was tall, well-built, physically attractive, sure of himself. He had an intense gaze. But he seemed to me a man too full of himself, vain and frivolous. With the passage of time, however, I was constrained little by little to change my judgment. I perceived in fact that basically he was a good person, a good father of family, very affectionate to his children. Also Edda Mussolini, his wife, did not at first make a good impression on me. But, also in her case, getting to know her better, I learned to appreciate the positive sides of her character."[35]

In his talks with Höttl, Ciano advanced an alternative plan to win his freedom. He offered to go to South America as a distributor of counterfeit sterling manufactured by the Nazis, arguing that that would cause a devastating blow to the British economy. While Beetz continued the discussions with Ciano, Höttl flew to Berlin to meet with Kaltenbrunner, a sworn enemy of Ribbentrop who had ambitions to become Foreign Minister. Höttl found Kaltenbrunner enthusiastic about both of Ciano's proposals, as was Himmler, who was equally hostile to Ribbentrop. Everything was arranged secretly through these two men, according to Höttl. But then Edda made her second serious mistake. Against Höttl's advice, she insisted on asking for Hitler's permission and support. Edda flew through a storm for the meeting deep in the Polish forest that Kaltenbrunner had arranged. Hitler met her at the door of his forest home, held her hands in his and tears welled in his eyes as he led her into a salon to be served tea. "Why did your father convene the Grand Council? What a terrible error he made," were his first words.

"And what will happen to my father?" Edda asked.

"Never fear. He will be liberated. We still don't know where he is being kept prisoner, but we will know very soon. And then, I promise you, I will do everything in my power to rescue him. You can be sure that I will bring him to you safe and sound."

Edda switched the conversation to the plight of the Cianos, and demanded she and her husband be allowed to go to Spain. Hitler replied with a tirade: "The Führer has no intention of keeping you here against your will. However, he hopes that you are aware of the dangers facing you, particularly in Spain. That country is not serious and certainly not loyal. You might be kidnapped by the English." Edda replied that she did not care. During the conversation she also behaved with a foolish lack of tact. After Hitler had explained to her that the Axis would definitely win the war, just as Frederick II of Prussia had won the Seven Years' War despite the coalition fighting against him, Edda replied, "Yes, that's true, but in Frederick the Second's time there were neither Mosquitoes* nor Americans . . . Believe me, the war is already lost, and the only thing to do is to make a separate peace with the Russians." Hitler leaped to his feet. "*Nein! Nein!*" he cried. "Anything but that! I shall never negotiate with the Russians, madam. You cannot marry water with fire. Peace with them is impossible!"[36] Edda commented afterward that, although she sometimes made Hitler angry, he never made a terrible scene with her or reproached her too severely. But Vittorio Mussolini, who was present, told her when they had taken their leave of Hitler: "I don't think you have increased your chances of going with Galeazzo and your children to

---

*   British warplanes.

Spain, after such remarks. You aren't much of a diplomat, my dear sister."[37] But she was convinced Hitler admired frankness.

According to Goebbels, Edda committed an even more serious gaffe. Ciano had brought six million lire with him from Italy, and Edda asked Hitler for permission to exchange this money for pesetas. Goebbels said she "actually offered the Führer the difference in the exchange rate, a tactlessness that nauseated the Führer."[38] Edda's own account of this episode, in her memoirs, merely states that she asked to change lire into pesetas and Hitler told her his secretary would deal with it. If she knew of Goebbels' accusation, she never bothered to comment on it. Goebbels and Ribbentrop, present at the meeting, naturally supported Hitler's views. Ribbentrop later confessed to Kaltenbrunner that Ciano might start a "regular stink" against him if he were allowed to go abroad.[39] Edda stayed overnight in Hitler's train, and the next day, September 1, he came to wish her a happy thirty-third birthday, carrying a bouquet of orchids. Subsequently, Edda said, whenever she and Ciano questioned the Germans about what would become of them, the reply was always the same: they were the Führer's guests, and had nothing to worry about.

"Life at Allmannshausen became increasingly difficult," she wrote. "Bad food, disagreeable personnel, only relative liberty since the SS were always with us. Galeazzo's nerves began to crack from September fifth on, and mine faltered soon afterward. But I still could not believe that the Germans had tricked us." She said an SS Major Otto treated them with particular brutality, and they began to think of suicide once they realized they were in fact prisoners.[40] Much later, Fabrizio Ciano gave an example of Major Otto's cruelty. He said his brother Marzio had found a cat and became very fond of it. But one day Otto killed it with a gunshot. "One doesn't forget people like Major Otto, even after almost a half century," he wrote. Otto had a son who was going blind, and one day Ciano told him he knew his son was ill and he would like to be with him. "I give you my word as an official and man of honor that I will do nothing to escape. Go home to your son for a little while," he said. Otto looked away and did not move.[41] On September 8, the Badoglio government announced its unconditional surrender, and the king and his generals fled to southern Italy and the protection of the Allied armies. An SS officer opened the door of the Cianos' residence with a kick that day and, red in the face, shouted: "Verräter! Verräter!"* Then he went out and slammed the door.[42]

When Beetz saw Ciano in September, a month after their first meeting, she found him a changed man. "He had lost his self-confidence. He was downhearted, prostrate," she said. "Instinctively I felt solidarity with him.

---

* Traitor.

The initial antipathy was transformed into sympathy. At the beginning he continued to mistrust me but then, little by little, he understood that he could trust me. He began to confide in me, to unburden himself. Our relations became ever closer, more confidential. It came naturally to me to try to help him, to bolster his courage."[43]

On September 12, the Cianos learned from a radio broadcast that Mussolini had been freed from the Gran Sasso mountain in the Abruzzi region, and had been brought to Germany. Hitler, in his first meeting with the Duce after his release, told him: "I don't doubt that you will agree with me in believing that one of the first acts of the new government will have to be to sentence to death the traitors of the Grand Council. I judge Count Ciano four times a traitor: traitor to his country, traitor to fascism, traitor to the alliance with Germany, traitor to his family. If I were in your place perhaps nothing would have stopped me from rendering justice with my own hands. But I advise you: it is preferable that the death sentence be carried out in Italy." Mussolini was appalled. "But you're talking of the husband of the daughter whom I adore, the father of my grandchildren," he said. "All the more reason Count Ciano merits punishment in that not only has he failed in fidelity toward his country, but in fidelity to his family," Hitler replied.[44] Eva Braun, who had once admired Ciano, told Otto Skorzeny that Ciano now deserved to die. "He betrayed the Duce, his wife and his children," she said.[45] Later, Mussolini, sick, tired and fearing that he was suffering from stomach cancer, expressed to Hitler his reluctance to head a puppet government in northern Italy as the Germans wanted. Hitler's reply was brutal. "Northern Italy will have to envy the fate of Poland if you don't accept," he said. "In such a case, Count Ciano will naturally not be handed over; he will be hanged here in Germany."[46]

Edda met with obstacles from the Germans when she asked to see her father, but they finally agreed and the meeting took place on September 13. Rachele was shocked when she saw her daughter, "very thin, upset, with feverish eyes in a drawn face and her voice altered by emotion."[47] Edda begged Mussolini to receive Ciano, and he agreed. Several days later, Ciano was allowed to see him at his residence near Hirschberg. "The greeting was warm and they embraced with emotion," Edda said. "Then they were closeted together for some time. Upon leaving my father's office Galeazzo seemed quite serene. He told me that he had explained his role to my father, who had seemed to believe him, and that he had asked to be permitted to return to Italy and work in no-matter-what capacity, including going into the air force. According to my husband, Papa had agreed to this."[48]

Filippo Anfuso, arriving in Germany, said Mussolini could not understand the Italian mood and that of the diehard Fascists who were baying for Ciano's blood. "For Mussolini his son-in-law remained, still at Hirschberg, the boy to whom he had given a hand up in politics: good even if lightweight," he said. Even when he became convinced of Ciano's betrayal, Anfuso said, he never accused his son-in-law of that and always said Ciano had put himself in the midst of people without scruples.[49] Goebbels noted in his diary on September 23 that the Cianos were exerting an "unwholesome influence" on Mussolini. "Edda Mussolini has succeeded in completely reversing the Duce's opinion of Ciano," he wrote. "Ciano has again been accepted in the good graces of the Duce. That means this poisonous mushroom is again planted in the midst of the new Fascist Republican Party. It is obvious that the Duce cannot start criminal proceedings against the traitors of fascism if he is not willing to call his own son-in-law to account . . . If he were a man of really great revolutionary calibre, Mussolini would have asked the Führer to hand Ciano over to him and would personally have taken him to task. This he won't do, and that handicaps him seriously in proceeding against the other traitors of fascism . . . If after all his bad experiences the Duce again puts himself in the hands of his daughter Edda, who is really a vulgar and mean wench, he can't be helped politically."[50] Goebbels said the fact that Edda "gives in so completely to her sexual impulses indicates that the thesis of the Führer, according to which she would be half Jewish, is correct." The Nazis were convinced Edda was the daughter of Mussolini's former Jewish mistress Angelica Balabanoff.

Ciano's attempt to rehabilitate himself in Mussolini's eyes also met opposition from his mother-in-law. "I will spit in his face if he comes near me!" Rachele said. But she was present at the first meeting between the two men. "Ciano defended himself from the accusation of treason, lashing out at Grandi and Badoglio," she said. "Benito listened to him in silence: what he had suffered recently led him to pardon more than to revenge. Besides he loved his Edda too much. Perhaps she was the only person in the world from whom he sometimes accepted advice. I was also disposed, for love of Edda, to suppress my resentment." But a few days later she scolded Ciano severely. "If you didn't like the post the Duce had assigned you, you could have resigned," she said. Ciano said he had always acted in good faith, but Rachele cut him off. "The Duce is not a piece of furniture that you can put in the sunroom when someone is tired of it," she said. "You have erred and it may be that one day you will have to pay for this." She said Ciano admitted that perhaps he had committed an error in supporting the Grandi resolution, but added that he and the others who voted for it had not taken a position against Mussolini. "Mussolini is above everyone," he said.[51]

Later, Rachele said her relations with Ciano had been cold for a long time before this. "I didn't approve of his mania for mixing with certain members of the Roman aristocracy from whom I and Benito had always wanted so much to keep our distance," she said. "Several times he criticized the fact that I 'continued to wear old rags and remain what I was originally, a simple and modest woman.' Therefore we saw each other rarely and during our meetings we limited ourselves to exchanging conventional phrases."[52] Years later Romano Mussolini said, "My mother was a woman of the people, a peasant. Galeazzo was different, had an aristocratic attitude and was ambitious. I think he loved my mother. They quarreled about a lot of things, but he came often to eat at our house. My mother was very hard. Once she made up her mind about someone it was difficult to get her to change her opinion. She was more politically involved than any of us."[53]

Goebbels wrote that Rachele "hates Edda from the bottom of her heart," but said Mussolini trusted Edda more than he did his wife. "If the Duce were a man whose politics were uninfluenced by family considerations, he would have Ciano executed, instead of forgiving him, and would have his daughter whipped," Goebbels wrote. Goebbels' diary also suggests that Ciano put himself in greater jeopardy by letting the Germans know about his diary. "Ciano intends to write his memoirs," he said. "The Führer rightly suspects that such memoirs can only be written in a manner derogatory to us, for otherwise he could not dispose of them in the international market. There is therefore no thought of authorizing Ciano to leave the Reich; he will remain in our custody, at least for the present."[54]

Ciano had another two meetings with Mussolini, again promising he would enter the armed forces if he were allowed to return to Italy. "My husband naturally let himself be affected," Rachele said. On September 19, the Cianos dined with the Mussolinis. During dinner, Romano went into another room and began playing American jazz on the piano. When it was made known to him that American music was not much appreciated, he switched to Viennese waltzes. Rachele said afterward the family dinner heightened German suspicions, and from then onward "they did not stop spying on us."[55] Vittorio Mussolini later described the family gathering:

My father sat at the head of the table, in an old armchair. He wore a dark civilian suit, the knot of his tie done hurriedly and carelessly . . . He was thin, suffering, and only his eyes, deep and imperious, had conserved a little of their strength.

After some minutes the attendants served the soup: a rather thin vegetable broth. Papa took barely a few spoonfuls, without desire. I saw him lost in thought far from us, and perhaps from himself. On his right, my brother-in-law Galeazzo conserved his habitual superior and detached manner that piqued my mother.

He wore a light gray suit, perfectly tailored, and from the pocket of his jacket hung a white handkerchief, with elegant nonchalance. His hair was carefully combed, his fingernails neatly cut. Every now and then he even succeeded in making us smile, commenting to me on the modesty of the meal that, after that vegetable soup, consisted only of a duck, a few boiled potatoes and a slice of horrible synthetic yellow butter. . . Beside me, Edda tried to bolt down some mouthfuls in silence, by now abstracted from any consideration that did not concern the salvation of her husband. Her instinct, more than the resistance the Germans had shown to the plans for a flight to Spain of all the Ciano family, led her to identify in Germany the true and mortal danger that weighed on her family. Galeazzo, immediately after the talk with my father, had tried to give him courage, showing he felt sure of his innocence and therefore of the understanding and protection of the Duce. But in that moment Edda, the Duce, the Führer, the war, the alliance, were words devoid of meaning. To flee, this was the only thing that needed to be done and therefore whoever might have a different opinion became for her, automatically, an enemy: even my father . . .

The modest portion of roast duck and boiled potato was finished and my father, with an habitual gesture, gathered the breadcrumbs. Beside him Galeazzo, after having passed a corner of the napkin lightly over his lips, slowly drank a glass of Mosel wine. Edda and my mother remained silent, staring at them . . .

My father bade farewell to all of us with a tired gesture. He went out, and Edda and Galeazzo got up to return to their villa at Allmannshausen, where the Germans had lodged them . . .

In the great dining room only my mother remained. I will always remember her eyes in that moment. They were fixed in the void, far away, without tears.[56]

Goebbels wrote that Hitler had shown him a copy of a letter that Edda had written to her father. "This letter beats everything," he said. "Edda Mussolini is acting like a wildcat in her Bavarian villa. She smashes china and furniture on the slightest provocation. This time she complained to her father because she could not get through to him on the telephone on one occasion and because she was once denied a car. She uses ridiculous trivialities to threaten her father with blackmail. She states in the letter that unless he helps her immediately and takes her along to Italy, she will involve him in a gigantic scandal . . . It is hard to imagine that the daughter of a great man dares to act thus toward her father." Goebbels and Hitler wondered what Edda and Ciano knew about Mussolini that could so compromise him. Whatever it was, they decided that it contained "the riddle about fascism," the mystery of why the Duce always yielded to Ciano. "The letter certainly bears testimony not only against Edda Mussolini but against the Duce himself," Goebbels wrote. "What sort of upbringing must the Duce have given his daughter if she dares to write him such a letter in the circumstances!"[57]

Goebbels said Edda, at her earlier meeting with Hitler, had told him she wanted a separation from her husband, while Ciano wished to go to Spain to write his memoirs. "Ciano has no special talent as a writer," Goebbels said. "He cannot, therefore, achieve literary success by style or quality. He can do it solely by sensationalism, stemming from his hostility to Germany. I am firmly convinced that this dirty scoundrel would start writing against us before he had been gone a month, and that he would intrigue against us in the most contemptible manner. Ciano is the Satan of the Fascist movement and the curse of Italy. We must safeguard ourselves against him, now that he is in our hands. The Führer doesn't know exactly how that is to be done but, to begin with, he wants to put strong pressure on the Duce to create order at least in his own family." Goebbels added that Hans Johst, a Nazi novelist and dramatist who was a neighbor of the Cianos, had written to Hitler about their behavior. "Johst described conditions at the Villa Ciano as simply grotesque," he said. "But he sees the essential point: Ciano and his wife are absolutely worthless creatures who under normal conditions would be put in prison . . . The Führer would like the Duce to hand Ciano over to him. He would stand him up against a wall immediately and send his wife, Edda, to a house of correction, where she would probably soon come to her senses."

Later, Hitler told Goebbels he feared that Mussolini, facing the blackmail threats of his daughter, might have thought at one time of deserting the Germans. "Edda Mussolini knows some secret about her father which is either of a criminal nature or compromises him socially and politically," Goebbels said. "It is either a question of love affairs or of money. I have heard on a previous occasion that Ciano helped the Duce to transfer large sums from Italy to Switzerland. Such a revelation would naturally be an almost mortal blow to the Duce . . . The whole affair is certainly very strange and it is desirable that we should hold onto the personalities involved so that no disaster may result."[58] While Mussolini was in Germany, he met Fascists still loyal to him and told them he favored condemning Bottai, Grandi and Federzoni for their part in his ouster. Farinacci, who attended the meeting, supported a trial but was against condemning anyone to death. He favored exile from Italy.

Around September 20, Ciano began to talk to Edda about the diary and other documents he had left hidden in Italy, and said he wanted her to go to Italy to recover them. At first the Germans were not disposed to let her leave, but she threatened to go on hunger strike and Mussolini intervened. She was given an *Ausweis* made out in the name of Emilia Santos. On September 27, she took the train to Italy. A few days later, Kaltenbrunner arrived at the Ciano residence and told the children to pack their bags because they were changing houses. They were taken to the castle of Waldbickel, where they found all the Mussolinis except the Duce, who by now had returned to Italy to set up his puppet republic.

On her return to Italy, Edda found a car to drive her to the home of Ciano's uncle Gino at Ponte a Moriano, near Lucca. There she met Ciano's mother Carolina, who told her the documents Ciano had entrusted to Gino had disappeared. Gino had buried them at the foot of a tree in his garden, but someone evidently had seen him doing so and had dug them up. Carolina put the word out in the village that a package containing family papers had been lost, and she was ready to pay 20,000 lire for its return. A few days later, the package was found lying at the foot of the garden gate. True to her word, Carolina left the promised money in the same spot. But Edda still had to retrieve the notes on Ciano's conversations with Ribbentrop, and a file entitled "Germany," which dealt with Italo-German relations. Carolina told her Gino had hidden these papers in Rome. She left for Rome, where Gino turned over the documents to her, then went on to Rocca della Caminate, where Mussolini had been staying since early October. Her father, seeing how agitated she had become, suggested she enter a clinic to rest and recuperate. Edda went back to Rome to get some clothes and to hide Ciano's documents. Edda told Buffarini Guidi, who had become Minister of the Interior in Mussolini's new government: "My husband was right to want to detach himself from those German pigs, while that weakling who is my father still believed he could go in agreement with them."[59] On October 10, she entered a clinic at Ramiola, near Parma, under the name of Emilia Santos. But her real name began to circulate when people came asking for her, among them Emilio Pucci. Edda had gone to his house in Florence to ask for his help, and found him recovering from jaundice.

Back in Germany, Ciano twice phoned Anfuso, Mussolini's ambassador in Berlin, and asked him to let Mussolini know he wanted to return to Italy. On October 17, Höttl suddenly appeared at Oberallmannshausen and told Ciano the Germans had decided to transfer him to Italy and hand him over to the Italian police. "Then does that mean they will put me in prison?" Ciano asked. Höttl nodded his head. Ciano lashed out at Höttl, accusing him of a clear violation of the agreement they had reached in Rome in August to transfer him and his family to Spain.[60] In fact, Höttl was powerless. Alessandro Pavolini, now secretary of the new Republican Fascist Party, had asked Hitler for Ciano's extradition, and the Führer granted it. Höttl, according to Beetz, was furious because he felt honor bound to keep his agreement with Ciano. Höttl went to the central office of security in Berlin to protest and had a bitter discussion with Kaltenbrunner, who cut him short by saying Ciano was being returned on the personal order of the Führer.

As for Pavolini, he was to prove the Judas Iscariot of the Ciano tragedy, for he had owed his career to the man he now wanted condemned to death. Born into a well-to-do Florentine family, he displayed a perennial nervous tension and seldom smiled. Mussolini once described him as "faithful, mediocre and courageous."[61] During the Ethiopian war, Pavolini had accompanied Ciano as his personal publicist. He had also enrolled as a soldier, but was ridiculed as a fighter and accused of making money by dubious means. Ciano defended him and said his attackers should be castrated. Later, when Mussolini doubted Pavolini's political loyalty, Ciano defended him again and helped him advance. He was responsible for Pavolini's appointment at the age of thirty-six as Minister of Popular Culture, and on the surface the men appeared to be friends. But Pavolini evidently bore a secret resentment against Ciano for having achieved high office through marriage and not through merit. Or, as Edda suggested, he realized the Fascist adventure would end badly and was determined to kill all those who had not chosen the same path as himself. Mario Mondello said, "Pavolini was the best friend of Ciano for years, in a certain sense his No. 2. What he did was like the revolt of an undergraduate."[62]

When Mussolini was arrested, Pavolini, then editor of the Rome newspaper *Il Messaggero*, was among the first to flee Rome because he feared arrest by Badoglio. In the resurrected Fascist republic, he organized Black Brigades that were charged with fighting the partisans, and he carried violence to such an extreme that SS Commander Wolff accused him of "terroristic excesses." When Mussolini tried to flee Italy in April 1945 in a German truck, and was caught and executed by partisans, Pavolini was aboard the truck dressed in German uniform. He came out firing wildly and, wounded, threw himself into a nearby lake. The partisans went after him in a boat, shot him in the legs and hit him on the head with an oar. Later they finished him off with a gunshot in the Piazzale Loreto in Milan, where they had hung the bodies of Mussolini and Clara Petacci. His last words were: "Viva l'Italia."

Ciano was allowed to pay a farewell visit to his children at the Mussolini residence. "*Ciao*, kids, we will not see each other for a while," he said. Fabrizio later wrote: "My sister and I remained mute. We had within us so many questions, but they remained in our throats." The family was seated in a salon, and Rachele poured tea. Ciano took a sip, then hurriedly got up, wanting to cut short a painful parting. "*Ciao*, Ciccino, always behave with honor," he told Fabrizio. To Raimonda he said, "Don't forget ever that we are Italians." He drew the children to him, and gave a big kiss to little Marzio. He knew there was little chance he would see them again.[63]

Chapter Seventeen

Treason

Ciano was put aboard a German military plane at Munich-Riem Airport and flown to Verona on October 19. Wearing a light gray flannel suit and tan raincoat, he was accompanied by ten SS men in battle dress and by Frau Beetz but, enveloped in bitterness and depression, he talked to no one during the flight. On arrival, he found uniformed members of the Italian Social Republic militia waiting for him in a dark blue car parked on the tarmac. "Galeazzo Ciano, you are under arrest," one of them called. "I am aware of that," he replied.[1] The arrest meant he would face treason charges, with conviction virtually a foregone conclusion. Ciano's only hope of escaping a death sentence lay in whatever authority Mussolini continued to exercise over the extreme Fascists, led by Pavolini, who wanted to put Ciano to death.

He was taken to the Scalzi, a sixteenth-century Carmelite monastery which had been converted into a prison in 1900. It was destroyed by American bombing later in the war. Fascist officials had prepared nineteen special cells on an upper floor for Ciano and the other members of the Grand Council who had voted against Mussolini. He was subjected to a minute body search, and relieved of his money and other personal possessions, but was allowed to keep a small icon of the Madonna and photographs of his wife and children. The icon had been given to Mussolini by a Russian princess, and the Duce had offered it to Edda as a wedding present. Ciano was enrolled in a special prison register and given the number 11902. "Even in a prison, I prefer to be here, an Italian among Italians, to being in a German royal palace among Germans," he said.[2]

Anfuso, in Berlin, said Mussolini had thought it better to get Ciano away from "the German indignation rather than that of the Italians." But if Ciano had remained in Germany, he said, it would have been difficult for the Germans to execute him because they would have feared to offend Mussolini.[3] The Duce retained a certain amount of sympathy for his son-in-law. On October 20, talking to his secretary Giovanni Dolfin, he expressed indignation over Italian newspaper reports about Ciano's supposed riches. "An apartment has become an entire palace," he said.[4]

At Ciano's request, Frau Beetz went to Ramiola to inform Edda of his arrest. Edda, furious, rushed to see her father at the Villa Feltrinelli, beyond Gargnano on Lake Garda, on October 21. Mussolini agreed to her request to see her husband, and assured her: "There will undoubtedly be a trial, but don't worry. I shall make the necessary provisions for the outcome."[5] After she departed, the German security police captain at Gargnano was called to Verona and given a severe reprimand for not having prevented her from seeing her father.[6] Dolfin reported this to Mussolini who, after reflection, asked him to advise Edda to make her visits less frequent so as to avoid "truly unpleasant complications." Dolfin found this assignment distasteful, and told Mussolini he should get a member of his family to deliver the message.

In Verona Edda went to the chief of the province, Piero Cosmin, and told him she had her father's permission to see her husband. Cosmin did not attempt to hide his hostility, but he had to bow to Mussolini's order. He was then in the last stages of tuberculosis, and would die after the war in the same clinic in which Ciano's mother Carolina stayed. When Edda saw Ciano in the presence of Cosmin and the prison director Sergio Olas on October 22, she managed to murmur to him, as she kissed him goodbye, that she had retrieved his papers. The Italian and German authorities in Verona were then determined to make sure she never saw Ciano again. Mussolini entrusted Vittorio Mussolini with the task of contacting Edda and asking her to visit Gargnano less frequently. Vittorio wrote to Edda on the subject, mentioned that he was going to Germany and said he hoped to bring back her children. He urged her to remain calm and not move from Ramiola. Staying put, he said, could produce excellent results, but any contrary behavior could provoke coercive measures. Edda characteristically ignored the advice, returning several times to Gargnano and Verona.

Vittorio drove to Berlin and met an under-secretary of foreign affairs in a bunker under the Hotel Adlon, while hundreds of British planes bombed the city. He requested permission to take the Ciano children to Italy but was turned down. Vittorio returned to Ramiola and informed Edda, warning her that excessive pressure would only stiffen German resistance. But Edda reacted angrily. "You promised me my children, and you must bring them to me," she said.[7] Vittorio left again for Germany. This time he met a high official of the foreign ministry in Munich and told him Mussolini wanted his entire family with him. The official agreed to give an exit permit for the children and arranged a supply of gasoline for the return trip. Vittorio set off with the children and traveled without incident until they reached the outskirts of Bolzano. He had to stop the car while a massive American bombardment was under way, but he and the children arrived in Ramiola that evening. Edda was overjoyed, but simply said, "Thanks, Vittorio."[8] She told Ciano's mother Carolina, who was also in Ramiola, "Don't have many illusions, Mamma. A not very benevolent wind is blowing for Galeazzo. I'm doing everything I can to help him, while I still have the strength."[9]

On October 27, Mussolini's new Cabinet created an extraordinary special tribunal to try Ciano and five other members of the Grand Council. Mussolini told Dolfin, "Ciano is judged very severely by the Italians. He is neither better nor worse than the others. All the hatred is aimed at him in order to strike at me. It is an old game that has been repeated for years."[10]

After her arrival in Italy, Beetz met with Wilhelm Harster, national commander of the Sicherheitsdienst (SD), the security service of the SS, and showed him credentials authorizing her to re-establish contact with Ciano for the purpose of getting hold of his diary. Harster gave her a permit that allowed her to visit the prison any time she wished, and Beetz availed herself of that privilege often, bringing Ciano food, playing cards and chess with him and reading him books. Within a short time an extraordinary friendship, if not something more, developed between them.

As the weeks passed, Edda realized she could not count on the help of her father, especially since everything she told him was immediately known to the Germans. During one early conversation she said to Mussolini, "What is all this about there being difficulties in getting Galeazzo out? With just several determined men, I myself could see to it that he escaped from Scalzi, and with very little trouble."[11] After that Ciano was placed under the permanent watch of two SS marshals named Krutsch and Guck. When they first appeared, he said, "Oh oh, already the smell of death."[12] He was put in solitary confinement, and denied the daily exercise outside that was permitted to other prisoners. But he was allowed to use the money he had brought with him to buy his meals from the best restaurant in Verona. Ciano often spoke to his jailer Pellegrinotti about Mussolini. "Mussolini has made Italy a servant to the Germans," he said. "He is a presumptuous absolutist, has never accepted advice from anyone, has always held himself to be infallible . . .Such an idiot!" Another time he said, "Look at the deep abyss into which he has thrown Italy. Now the Duce has set out to be the new Lucius Junius Brutus*, with the only difference that he sacrifices his son-in-law instead of his children."[13]

---

* Brutus founded the Roman Republic in the sixth century BC. He condemned his sons to death when they joined in a conspiracy to restore the old order.

On November 4, other members of the Grand Council who were to be tried with Ciano were transferred to the Scalzi from various jails: Giovanni Marinelli, former administrative secretary of the Fascist Party; Tullio Cianetti, former Minister of Corporations; Luciano Gottardi, president of the Confederation of Industrial Workers, and Carlo Pareschi, former Minister of Agriculture and Forests. None had tried to flee Italy or gone into hiding after July 25. It was clear that Ciano was the real target and they were arrested primarily to give consistency to the idea that anyone who voted for the Grandi resolution was guilty of treason. The Fascist press was unremittingly hostile to the prisoners, and especially Ciano. Goebbels wrote in his diary on November 9: "It's true that Mussolini had his son-in-law, Ciano, arrested, but those in the know are certain he will not let him be condemned to death."[14] But by now Mussolini was resigned to the fact that Ciano's fate was sealed and he could do nothing to save him. "The Germans hate him because they know he was never their friend," he told Dolfin. "They watch him. They don't trust even me. If Ciano is condemned to death, the Italians will say I was the executioner. You are my witness that I am the least convinced of all of the usefulness of this trial, which will not resolve anything. But there will be no shortage of those who will say we have carried out a crime."[15] Mussolini, in short, was no longer in control of the extreme Fascists serving his dying regime, nor of the Germans who were the true rulers of Italy.

Ciano and Edda began to exchange letters. On November 13, he reported that the cold in his cell had caused a violent recurrence of asthma and the chronic problem with his ears. "I beg you, my Edda . . . to send me some warm clothing: an overcoat, a cap or a fur coat and sweaters. It is what I feel I need most. The food is fairly good and abundant. Life is sad. But I read, read, read . . . I think of you a lot. With hope and sadness, according to the moment, but always with infinite longing. Kiss our three darlings, if they are with you, and take the most tender kiss of your Gallo."[16] One day Ciano unburdened himself to Dr. Bottoli, the prison doctor. "They say I am a traitor. If I were such, I would have been worried, above all else, to save myself . . . and I assure you that it would not have been difficult for me," he said.[17]

At a Fascist Party conference in Verona on November 14, delegates were in agreement on just one thing: death for Ciano. One suggested he be drawn and quartered. Pavolini led the clamor and assured delegates that death was the only punishment for traitors. "Death to Ciano! Death to Ciano!" the crowd chanted. Edda wrote to Ciano on November 23. She held out hope he would be found innocent, and would then retire from the "dirty, ungrateful craft" of politics.[18] But the Fascists were just beginning to build their case. *Corriere della Sera* published an article saying the Neapolitan shipowner Achille Lauro, arrested by the Americans, had been "associated with Ciano." Ciano wrote to the newspaper saying: "No relationship of interests, never and for any reason, has taken place between me and any industrialist, businessman, financier or financial group, Italian or foreign." Once again, he lied. In fact, Ciano had supported negotiations by Lauro in 1941 to buy a part interest in the newspapers *Il Mattino*, *Corriere della Sera* and *Roma*. Mussolini refused to allow Lauro to buy more than 50 percent. On November 25, Ciano sent his letter of denial to Mussolini and asked him to see that it was published. Although Mussolini knew the denial was a lie, he gave it to *Corriere* publisher Ermanno Amicucci and ordered him to publish it, but the German military censors refused to allow it.[19]

On November 30 Zenone Benini was imprisoned at the Scalzi. He had been an industrialist and mathematician, and was a gourmet who had published a book of Tuscan recipes. He became Minister of Public Works under Mussolini, but was not on the Grand Council. His "crime" was to have contacted Cianetti at Ciano's request, before the Grand Council meeting, to ask if he would vote for the Grandi resolution. Soon after he arrived at the Scalzi, he had an unexpected visitor. "One afternoon I was dozing, stretched out on my bed, when I heard the lock turn in my cell door," he said. "The door opened and a pretty, smiling young woman—Frau Beetz—entered. Behind her a guard was carrying a cup of tea and a box of cookies on a tray. She spoke with a light German accent, but her Italian was perfect. 'Count Ciano has told me that you are a close friend of his, and he was sorry to learn you were arrested. He told me to tell you that you should not worry; he has not mentioned your name to a soul.'" Benini described Beetz as "rather small but well proportioned and slim. She had black hair arranged in two bands that joined on her neck. Brown eyes veiled with quiet melancholy. Thin but not displeasing lips. Hands small and well modeled. She dressed with simple elegance. There was in her person and her attire a perfect harmony of good taste. Her hair and her hands well cared for, her teeth quite splendid. She wore little makeup, like almost all German women." A few minutes after she left his cell, Pellegrinotti appeared. "Your Excellency, come to the bathroom," he said. "But I have no such need at the moment," Benini replied. "Never mind, come along," the jailer said, staring at him in a strange manner. Benini walked to a storeroom at the end of the corridor and Pellegrinotti pushed him inside, saying, "Be quick about it." Standing before him was Ciano, smiling and with his arms spread wide. "By now there is no escape for me," Ciano told him. "I was dead on July 25. But

I don't really care. The Germans have lost the war, and that is all that matters to me . . . Trust in the most absolute manner in Pellegrinotti and that woman; they are two sound people." "But who is that woman?" Benini asked. "She is a spy, but she's mine. Trust her as you would yourself. Don't be afraid," Ciano replied.[20]

Pellegrinotti by now had become extremely sympathetic to Ciano. "Before I met him, I cordially detested Galeazzo Ciano," he told Benini. "But when I saw him I discovered an entirely different man from the one I had imagined him to be. He was courteous and patient . . . " Later he wrote: "He spoke with sweetness and love of his children, with great admiration for his wife. He never complained about his situation, neither the food nor the other innumerable discomforts of prison. He never had an unpleasant word for us. He . . . didn't ask me for anything that I couldn't give him."[21] One evening Ciano told his jailer: "Someone has insinuated that if I come out of the Scalzi alive I could succeed Mussolini. These are foolish remarks. In reality I will come out of here one morning, but to go and take twelve bullets in the back."[22]

Edda managed to visit Ciano again on November 27, through the intervention of SS Lt. Robert Hutting, an aide to the general command of the SD at Verona. Afterward she wrote to her father: "Duce, for two months my husband has been in a cell and is forbidden the comfort of two hours of air assured to every detainee, even the worst criminals, by the prison regulations. I have had a talk with him, but in the presence of a representative of the Reich, of a member of the Fascist Party and of the commander of the prison; a discussion at three meters distance that has not allowed any continuity in the conversation. Here is a wife, Duce, who demands that the rights sacred for any prisoner be safeguarded for her husband."[23] Edda tried to get permission for another meeting, but was rebuffed. She wrote to Ciano to tell him, and in his reply he said his situation was not bad materially, but "boredom is truly the invincible enemy, always lying in wait." He expressed great longing to see his children, and said he tried not to think of them or even look at their photographs. "But my heart is always there and within days Dindina will have her birthday, then Marzio his and then Christmas and, for the first time, I will not be with you," he wrote. "My Edda, I don't want to give up the hope of re-embracing you soon and in this hope I live every hour."[24]

Mussolini told journalist Carlo Silvestri on December 10 that Edda failed to understand his position: "I can do nothing for Galeazzo . . . I have not been involved, I am not involved and I will not get involved in the proceeding . . . Justice must follow its regular course . . . Many of those who are asking for Ciano's head have nothing against him; they ask it instead because they want to see me in a decisive test, to see if I will have the courage to let him be condemned to death. So, to these people I would like to say that I will accept the sentence, whatever it is."[25] Mussolini later told Dolfin: "For me, Ciano is already dead . . . He could not now go about in Italy, be seen, have a name . . . Whoever voted for the Grandi resolution will be condemned."[26]

Edda met the Duce on December 13. The next day she wrote to Ciano: "I have seen my father . . . I have . . . told him of the restrictions they impose on us and he was amazed because he had been assured that you took a walk in the courtyard every day and the same rules applied for the other detainees as for us, that is, of not being able to be visited by their own relatives. I denied all that and he promised to involve himself." She added that Carolina had had a mild heart attack but was recovering well. "The children are very well and you must think of them with much serenity," she said. "You should see how Mowgli (Marzio) plays chess with the old deaf countess. It is extraordinary."[27] In fact, the children were no longer in Italy. Edda and Pucci had concluded there was little chance of saving Ciano, and their first task would be to smuggle the children into Switzerland. Fabrizio was then twelve years old, Raimonda nine and Marzio six. Just in case there were listening devices planted in the Ramiola clinic, Edda told the children they were going to Varese to join Carolina. But on the evening of December 9 she whispered to them their true destination.

Two friends, Tanino Pessina and Gerardo Gerardi, had agreed to help get the children out of the country. Pessina's father owned a large industrial cleaning establishment in Como, near the Swiss border. He and Gerardi, whom Edda had identified to the children as Uncle Piero, were in contact with an Italian who helped smuggle people across the frontier. "I had no money, only jewels, and finally most of them were given to this man," Edda said.[28] Among the jewels she gave away was a diamond brooch the king and queen had given her as a wedding present, as well as a ruby bracelet and a solitaire. Pucci took the children from Ramiola to Milan, where they stayed for a day in Gerardi's apartment. Then he and Pessina got them to the Swiss frontier. The children spent the night in an alpine shepherd's hut, with Raimonda sleeping in a cradle because nothing else was available. At the hut they were joined by another person dressed as a priest, who did not give his name.

On the night of December 12, a night of full moon, the children crossed the border, marked by a net reinforced with barbed wire. It was Raimonda's tenth birthday. Swiss police were waiting for them, having been advised they were members of the Aosta branch of the Savoy royal family. The police raised the net slightly, and signaled to the children, who crawled under without looking back. When they got to their feet, they saw the lights of a village, and a policeman handed each of them a piece of – what else? – Swiss chocolate. Marzio had never seen chocolate, and the other two children had last tasted it in 1940. They slept that night at the residence of the Bishop of Lugano, then were taken to what appeared to Fabrizio to be an elementary school connected to a convent. It was in the village of Neggio. A police officer arrived and told them: "You must now forget your family name. You are a Spanish family named Santos." Fabrizio was Jorge, Raimonda was Margarita and Marzio was Pedro. Edda would be Elsa. From the border, Pucci drove back to Ramiola to tell her he had gotten her children safely out of the country.[29]

Chapter Eighteen

The End of Hope

Vincenzo Cersosimo, the examining magistrate charged with preparing the case against Ciano and his associates, met with him in prison on December 14 to begin his interrogation. Cersosimo told him he was charged with treason and aiding the enemy by helping to undermine the resistance of the country. Cersosimo wrote afterward: "Slowly as I proceeded with the reading, I observed him: I saw in his eyes and in the expression of his face wonder, surprise, anger and terror, while his jaws contracted and a convulsive tremble shook his body." When Cersosimo finished, Ciano stood up, took a few steps in the restricted space of his cell, and erupted:

> "The stuff of madmen! That I should be accused of treason and helping the enemy! I was perhaps the only one in the Grand Council who argued for continuing the war until the end and I exhorted Mussolini very strongly to demand from the Germans much greater help than they seemed to give us . . . And now the tremendous accusation of treason is made against me . . . Let them shoot me immediately, like this, on two feet, without even listening to my voice, but not call me a traitor!"

He told Cersosimo he had faced death many times in combat, and did not fear it. "It is not life that I defend, it is honor, it is the name of my father who honored Italy, it is the name of my children who cannot, must not, be branded the children of a traitor of the country." He admitted he had made errors, which was not the same as treason. He spoke in a broken voice and his eyes were veiled with tears. He told Cersosimo he knew what the Fascists wanted, his diary, and they would never get it. The interrogation ended with Ciano making a formal declaration in which he rejected the charges against him. "It is absolutely absurd to imagine that I and the other members of the Grand Council might have wanted to provoke the fall of the Duce and the collapse of fascism, remaining thus ourselves buried in such ruins," he said.

He turned to Cersosimo and said, "Now that the official part is finished, clear up for me, please, a curiosity: who is that woman they have put at my side?" Cersosimo replied that she was the interpreter through whom he obtained German permission to interrogate him.

"Ah yes, something other than an interpreter," Ciano replied.

"Why, Count, and what other function could she have? What does she do?"

"I don't know . . . She stays continually with me. She prepares my coffee in the morning, she puts my cell in order, she stops to talk for a long time. She returns in the afternoon, she prepares my tea, she stops to play chess or checkers. In short, I don't manage to free myself from her. She is like my shadow."

"I think in any case that doesn't displease you," Cersosimo said. "The company of that woman must not be . . . unwelcome."

Ciano looked at him, then replied in a firm voice: "No, I don't think of certain things in the condition in which I find myself. I would only like to know what purpose she has in staying always close to me. They have glued me just like a stamp."[1]

That conversation can only have been intended by Ciano to allay any suspicions the Fascists may have developed about his relationship with Beetz. For in fact Beetz, while officially working for the Germans, was now determined to do all she could to help Ciano. The Italian press, and various Italian authors, have never been in any doubt that she fell in love with him. Edda believed Beetz had a "weakness" for Ciano and may have loved him. "Frau Beetz was what she was, but she never betrayed me," she said.[2] Pellegrinotti spoke of the "unequivocal behavior in which I casually surprised them once."[3] Benini had no doubt that Beetz was in love with his friend. But years later Beetz said "It is not true that I fell in love with him." At that time, she said, she was very much in love with her husband, Luftwaffe Captain Gerhard Beetz. "It is true, however, that I felt for Galeazzo Ciano something more intense than simply sympathy, something that arose from the depths of my heart. It was for this, then, that I risked my life to try to save him. For this, but also for another important reason: Galeazzo Ciano was betrayed by the Germans. I was then a little naive; I felt an obligation to repair this wrong."[4] But Beetz took enormous risks on behalf of Ciano, and it is difficult to believe she did so simply out of a feeling of friendship, or to right a wrong. She was quoted in one Italian magazine in 1996 as saying, "I loved him, certainly, but it is not true that I made love to him."[5]

After Cersosimo completed his interview with Ciano, he was called back to receive a five-page defense statement. In the document, Ciano tried to minimize the importance of his contacts with generals and said he hadn't seen Badoglio in three years. He said he had spent most of the summer, when the plotting against Mussolini was under way, in Livorno. He had supported the Grandi resolution, but never imagined it would lead to the collapse of the regime. The document went on to respond in some detail to the accusations that Ciano had grown wealthy in office. He listed his holdings and said they were not the "dishonored booty of a profiteer, rather the just fruits of an entirely working life." He noted that his father had not come into politics poor, but had headed the Il Mare shipping company for a number of years, and therefore had left him a substantial inheritance. "In these pages is enclosed the most scrupulous truth," he wrote. "One cannot lie when one is, like me, on the threshold of eternity. I intend to declare yet again that the vote of July 25 was an error, never betrayal; and politicians pay for their errors . . . even with their lives." After reading over the statement, Cersosimo observed that he had not found in it "even a vague and distant sign of worry for the fate of Mussolini. And yet—politics aside—he was and is your father-in-law, the grandfather of your children." Ciano remained thoughtful for a moment. "I was profoundly saddened by the arrest of Mussolini," he said. "But I thought it perfectly useless to express such an intimate sentiment in a defense memorandum. For another thing, in those tragic moments I could do nothing for him."[6]

Edda wrote to Ciano on December 17, saying she would request a further meeting with him. "But I fear that, having other and very ugly cats to skin, they may not have time to bother with us," she wrote. "What a happy life you have given me for years when I could think like a child that money grew on rose bushes. Fairy tales! I have nothing to tell you about me. I carry on a normal life because I don't want them to see on my face if I suffer or not . . ."[7] She saw her father the next day at Gargnano, their last and most tumultuous meeting. He warned her it was no longer in his power to separate the fate of Ciano from that of the other defendants. "You are all mad, you are all mad!" Edda stormed. "The war is lost, and it is useless to harbor illusions. The Germans will resist for a few months but not more. You know how much I wished they would win, but now there is nothing more to be done. Do you understand? And in these conditions they condemn Galeazzo?" Edda wept, and there were tears in her father's eyes as well. Then she returned to the attack. "Between us it is finished, finished forever, and if you knelt before me dying of thirst, and asked me for a glass of water, I would throw it on the ground before your eyes." Afterward Mussolini phoned the president of the tribunal and told him to render justice "without favor to anyone." He renewed the order to keep Ciano segregated from other prisoners, and ordered Edda watched.[8]

Ciano wrote to Edda on December 18, noting that it was Marzio's birthday. "I think of him a lot and I miss his fidgety gestures and his blond hair," he wrote. "For exactly two months I have not seen him. I approach Christmas feeling very sad, without them, without you. They have begun to interrogate me. Let's hope this is a good sign and this trial will be conducted rather quickly. The waiting from day to day is more oppressive and . . . I no longer find ways of passing the hours . . . My dear Edda, I think of you often and, as happens, I have hours of sadness and hours of confidence. Like the red and black at roulette. All wait to see where the ball will stop. By now I believe in only one thing: fate. And I accept it."[9]

Edda wrote on December 23 to say she had asked permission to spend Christmas day with him, but feared this would be denied. "Truly I have moments in which I seem to be going mad," she wrote. "But there is nothing to do but wait. The children are well. It will be the first Christmas we have not all been together since the day we married. I am sad and I love you so much and I am more than ever near you."[10] By then Ciano had abandoned all hope, and from his cell he penned three testamentary documents: letters to King Victor Emanuel and to Churchill, and an introduction to his diary. All were smuggled out of prison by Beetz and turned over to Edda. In his letter to the monarch, Ciano credited the king with having tried to spare the country the "crime" of going to war on the German side. "One man—just one man—Mussolini, for disturbed personal ambitions, 'for the thirst of military glory,' using his authentic words, has in a premeditated way led the country into the abyss," he wrote. "Your Majesty, I prepare myself for the supreme judgment with a serene spirit and pure conscience: I know I have served with loyalty and honor and without personal interest. The rest was only lies owed, in great part, to those who today drag me to my death."[11]

Churchill reproduced his letter from Ciano in Volume II of his war memoirs:

Signor Churchill.

You will not be surprised that as I approach the hour of my death I should turn to you whom I profoundly admire as the champion of a crusade, though you did at one time make an unjust statement against me.

I was never Mussolini's accomplice in that crime against our country and humanity, that of fighting side by side with the Germans. Indeed the opposite is the truth, and if last August I vanished from Rome it was because the Germans had convinced me that my children were in imminent danger. After they had pledged themselves to take me to Spain, they deported me and my family, against my will, to Bavaria. Now, I have been nearly three months in the prisons of Verona, abandoned to the barbarous treatment of the SS. My end is near, and I have been told that in a few days my death will be decided, which to me will be no more nor less [than] a release from this daily martyrdom. And I prefer death to witnessing the shame and irreparable damage of an Italy which has been under Hun domination.

The crime which I am now about to expiate is that of having witnessed and been disgusted by the cold, cruel and cynical preparation for this war by Hitler and the Germans. I was the only foreigner to see at close quarters this loathsome clique of bandits preparing to plunge the world into a bloody war. Now, in accordance with gangster rule, they are planning to suppress a dangerous witness. But they have miscalculated, for already a long time ago I put a diary of mine and various documents in a safe place, which will prove, more than I myself could, the crimes committed by those people with whom later that tragic and vile puppet Mussolini associated himself through his vanity and disregard of moral values.

I have made arrangements that as soon as possible after my death these documents, of the existence of which Sir Percy Loraine was aware at the time of his Mission in Rome, should be put at the disposal of the Allied Press.

Perhaps what I am offering you to-day is but little, but that and my life are all I can offer to the cause of liberty and justice, in the triumph of which I fanatically believe.

This testimony of mine should be brought to light so that the world may know, may hate and may remember, and that those who will have to judge the future should not be ignorant of the fact that the misfortune of Italy was not the fault of her people, but due to the shameful behavior of one man.

Yours sincerely,

G. Ciano[12]

The introduction to the diary was, like the letter to Churchill, intended to place all responsibility for the war on Mussolini and absolve himself. Here are excerpts:

If Providence had granted me a serene old age, what excellent material for writing my memoirs! . . . But perhaps in this skeleton form and in the absolute lack of the superfluous are to be found the real merits of my diary.

The Italian tragedy, in my opinion, had its beginnings in August 1939 when, having gone to Salzburg on my own initiative, I suddenly found myself face to face with the cold, cynical German determination to unleash the conflict. The Alliance had been signed in May. I had always been opposed to it, and for a long time I had so contrived that the persistent German offers were not followed up. There was no reason, in my opinion, for us to be bound in life and death to the fate of Nazi Germany. Instead, I was in favor of a policy of collaboration, for in our geographical situation we can and must detest the eighty million Germans, brutally set in the heart of Europe, but we cannot ignore them. The decision to conclude the Alliance was taken by Mussolini, suddenly, while I was in Milan with von Ribbentrop. Some American newspapers* had reported that the Lombard metropolis had received the German Minister with hostility, and that this proved the diminished personal prestige of Mussolini.

Inde ira [hence his wrath]. I received by telephone the most peremptory orders to accede to the German demands for an alliance, which for more than a year I had left in suspense . . . So "The Pact of Steel" was born. And a decision that has had such a sinister influence upon the entire life and future of the Italian people is due entirely to the spiteful reaction of a dictator to the irresponsible and valueless prose of some foreign journalists . . .

From Salzburg on . . . the policy of Berlin toward us was nothing but a network of lies, intrigue and deceit. We were always treated, not as partners, but as servants . . . Only the base cowardice of Mussolini could tolerate this without protest, and pretend not to see it . . .

Within a few days a sham tribunal will make public a sentence which has already been decided by Mussolini under the influence of that circle of prostitutes and pimps which for some years has plagued Italian political life and brought our country to the brink of the abyss. I accept with serenity what is to be my iniquitous destiny. I take some comfort in the thought that I may be considered a soldier who has fallen in combat for a cause in which he believed. The treatment inflicted upon me during these months of imprisonment has been shameful and inhuman. I am not allowed to communicate with anyone. All contacts with persons dear to me have been forbidden. And yet I feel that this cell, this gloomy Veronese cell in which I pass the last days of my earthly life, is full of those whom I have loved and who love me. Neither walls nor men can prevent it. It is hard to think, for no fault of my own, I shall not be able to gaze into the eyes of my three children or to press my mother to my heart, or my wife, who in my hours of sorrow has revealed herself a strong, sure and faithful

---

* Actually, French newspapers.

companion. But I must bow to the will of God, and a great calm is descending upon my soul. I am preparing myself for the Supreme Judgment.

In this state of mind which excludes any falsehood I declare that not a single word of what I have written in my diary is false or exaggerated or dictated by selfish resentment. Everything is just as I saw and heard. And if, when making ready to take leave of life, I consider allowing the publication of my notes, it is not because I hope for posthumous revaluation or vindication, but because I believe that an honest testimonial of the truth in this sad world may still be useful in bringing relief to the innocent and striking at those who are responsible.

After signing the document, he wrote: "December 23, 1943, Cell 27 of the Verona Jail."[13]

One of the worst indignities Ciano suffered in prison occurred on Christmas Eve. Three drunken German officers, accompanied by three equally inebriated prostitutes, arrived at the gates, demanded they be opened and shouted in broken Italian "*vedere Ciano*" [see Ciano]. At the door to his cell, shouting and brandishing pistols, the officers derided and insulted him and showed him off to the prostitutes. When the German Command learned of the incident the next day, the officers were reduced in rank and sent to the front. Ciano's only comment was: "They are savages."[14]

The next day, the prison authorities refused to allow Edda even to have a Christmas visit with her husband. Olas was courteous and understanding, but told her he could do no more than summon Beetz and ask her to deliver the presents Edda had brought. Edda got a severe shock when she spoke with Beetz and was told that Mussolini had ordered the trial to take place at 10 a.m. on December 28, specifying that all the defendants were to be shot two hours later. Beetz said Mussolini not only had done nothing to enable Edda to visit Ciano, but had confirmed the orders barring Ciano from walking in the prison courtyard with the other prisoners. Edda handed over her presents: a bottle of cologne, a bouquet of flowers and a box of sweets. She penned a quick note: "My dear Gallo, although I cannot see you, I have arrived at your prison to be nearer to you even across the wall. For that matter, neither walls nor men can prevent my being always near you . . . I embrace you with infinite affection together with the children. Excuse this mixture of gifts. I wanted to get you a set of golf clubs or something of that nature, but they are not to be found. Kisses. Your Edda."[15] Ciano cried when Beetz delivered the gifts. "His heart was filled with bitterness," Pellegrinotti said. "I remained with him until it seemed to me he had become calm again. He lay down on his bed, telling me he wanted to rest. But I am convinced that that night he did not sleep."[16]

The authorities did relent to the extent of permitting Ciano and his fellow prisoners to attend Christmas Mass, at the insistence of Don Giuseppe Chiot, the prison chaplain. The German commander stipulated that the prisoners must not leave their cells. Chiot put a table at the head of the corridor and, assisted only by a nun, celebrated Mass while the prisoners participated through half-open doors. Afterward Chiot visited each prisoner in his cell except Ciano. That had been expressly forbidden.

Later in the day Ciano learned from Beetz that Clara Petacci, whom Beetz had contacted in an attempt to save him, had written a letter on his behalf to Mussolini. Petacci, living on the shore of Lake Garda, said in her undated letter: "My Ben, I have had a long, terrible night. Nightmares, anxieties, blood and ruins. Among the figures, known and unknown, appearing in a red cloud, was that of Ciano. Ben, save that man! Show the Italians you still control your own will. Fate, perhaps, will be kinder to us . . ."[17] Mussolini, in an undated note for Petacci, wrote: "It's well that Ciano knows that, despite everything, I haven't abandoned him. I will know how to make the case, and convince myself first of all, that he was the victim of circumstances and not a voluntary accomplice of the planned intrigue."[18] Ciano gave Beetz a note for Petacci: "Signora, Frau Beetz has told me, and I am moved by your Christmas thought. But that cannot be all. The accusation, the arrest and worse are nothing if they do not deny me the chance to prove that I have not failed in honor or my duty. You are the only person who can determine a decision. May the trial come soon. The sentence is already decided, but I will make the truth known to everyone, and especially to him."[19]

On December 27, Edda returned to Verona but again was denied permission to visit her husband. She wrote to say she had sent him a dressing gown, adding: "I spent a very sad Christmas without seeing you. But I hope that before the end of the year they will give me the permit, who knows. However, be calm and don't let yourself be overcome by discomfort and boredom. Knowing how to bear boredom is an art."[20] Ciano replied on December 29, acknowledging receipt of all her gifts. "To know you were a few meters away and I could not embrace you is truly a very sad thing," he wrote. "Patience. Now I have recovered my serenity and I wait for decisions in my case to be taken . . . Meanwhile the days pass slowly and monotonously. I read, read everything I can find, from novels to the philosophy of Plato. Books are the only company permitted to me, other than that of my thoughts which, for the moment, one cannot say are very happy . . . The children? The new photographs gave me great joy.

They are very beautiful . . . What weighs on me is the lack of air and of your visits . . . Dear Deda, I think of you often and I send all my affectionate kisses for the four of you. Your Gallo."[21] Edda wrote again on December 30 to say she was waiting impatiently for the trial, and had been told by her father it would occur in early January. "I have only one wish for the New Year: that you are free and no one hears us spoken of ever again," she wrote.[22] But time was growing short, and freedom for Ciano no longer seemed within the realm of possibility. In the heart of one person, however, hope remained alive, and she had a plan to save his life.

Chapter Nineteen

A Flight to Freedom

After Christmas, Edda and Pucci laid plans for her escape to Switzerland to take place on December 27. They left for Como that morning, but decided to stop in Verona for a last meeting with Beetz. To their surprise, Beetz urged them to delay the escape, for she had a plan to save Ciano's life. The following day she went to General Harster, looking extremely worried, and told him there was now no hope for Ciano; his trial was imminent, the verdict beyond question. "If he is shot, as is by now certain, his diary and other German documents that he possesses will be published immediately in America and England," she warned. "Imagine, general, the damage to the Reich that would result." She said that must be prevented at all costs, and there was only one way to do it: barter Ciano's material for his life.[1]

Beetz was playing a game highly dangerous for herself. Earlier, Kaltenbrunner had asked her what progress she was making in finding where Ciano had hidden his diary, and she had lied. She told him the diary was secreted in Switzerland. Höttl, her immediate boss, thought the diary was in the Vatican. Beetz told him it might be in the hands of the Spanish Foreign Minister Ramon Serrano Suñer. She now insisted to Harster that he contact his superiors and relay her proposal. Harster sent a coded message to Kaltenbrunner, and got a reply the same day from Himmler and Kaltenbrunner, accepting the proposal in principle and saying that precise instructions would follow. Harster said later he learned that the two men, both hostile to Ribbentrop, hoped to find in the diary material that would drive him from office. Kaltenbrunner telephoned Harster to make it clear that neither he nor Himmler had informed Hitler of the proposed exchange because they were sure he would have prohibited it. They were thus putting Harster at risk, along with themselves, but he agreed to keep the Führer in the dark about what Kaltenbrunner now called "Operation Conte." Himmler phoned Harster with the promised instructions. Two SS men, specialists in such operations, would arrive in

Verona and present themselves to Harster. Disguised as Italian Fascists, the newly arrived operatives would arrange with Krutsch and Guck to overpower them and kidnap their prisoner. Thus, even Hitler would be led to believe that Fascists had rescued Ciano. He would be taken by plane to Hungary, where a friend of his, a Count Festetic, had agreed to receive him. From there he would be smuggled through the Balkans into Turkey. As soon as he arrived, and confirmed that in a phone call to Edda, she would hand over to the Germans the diary and other documents. Before anything could proceed, however, Himmler said Ciano himself would have to approve the plan. Harster relayed this information to Beetz, who then obtained Ciano's consent. She found him almost indifferent. "It is useless, nothing will come of it," he told her. "However, the game is amusing. Let's go on with it."[2]

Kaltenbrunner, a stickler for details, decided the plan needed to be formalized in a regular contract. Harster arranged a meeting on New Year's Day in Innsbruck, and when he arrived Kaltenbrunner greeted him with the news that the plan had changed. He and Himmler must have a proof of Ciano's goodwill; therefore, some of his documents must be handed over immediately. As Harster and Beetz watched, Kaltenbrunner wrote out a contract containing this clause, signed it and instructed Harster to get Ciano's signature. Ciano signed on January 2 and told Beetz: "I begin to hope that we will do it."[3] Harster dispatched the contract to Kaltenbrunner in Berlin by special courier plane, and the SS men charged with "kidnapping" Ciano arrived. They were two tall, well-built Dutchmen. It was established that the operation would take place on the evening of January 7. Ciano's trial had been delayed and was now scheduled to start the following morning.[4]

While all this was happening, Edda was waiting in Ramiola, growing frantic and beginning to despair. But on January 3, Beetz arrived from Verona, bringing two letters from Ciano. The first was written for the benefit of the German authorities. It informed Edda of the escape plan and instructed her to go to Rome to get his documents from their hiding place and turn them over to the Gestapo. He said he would meet her at 9 p.m. on January 7 at the Kilometer 10 mark beyond Brescia on the highway from Verona. The second, smuggled letter repeated these in-structions, but added that Edda should give the Germans only the five volumes headed "Conversations," bound in green leather, which contained his private minutes of talks with Italian and foreign officials while he was Foreign Minister. Another set of documents, headed "Germania," was to be handed over to Allied authorities. He did not mention the diary, which he knew had been hidden near Milan. Ciano asked her to bring a large amount of money to enable him to live abroad.

Beetz told Edda a Gestapo car would come for her at 4 a.m. the next day.[5] She was, however, too ill and weak to make the trip to Rome so Pucci agreed to go in her place with Beetz and the two Dutch agents. Beetz told Pucci one of the agents had a knack for killing a man with a blow to the face before he could utter a sound. He would handle the prison guards when the time came to free Ciano, killing them if any resisted. The drive to Rome, across snowbound mountain roads, took sixteen hours. Once there, Pucci left the Germans and went to the apartment of Ciano's Uncle Gino to get the documents. They were concealed behind a wall above a doorway. He separated the five volumes of "Conversations" from those dealing with Germany, then was faced with the dilemma of how he would keep the latter documents hidden during the long drive back to Verona. Finally he put the "Germania" documents under his long air force overcoat and went out to the car holding the other documents in front of him. As he got in the car, he was certain the Gestapo men had spotted the bulge under his coat, but they said nothing and Pucci relaxed. A few miles outside Rome, however, the car ran into a snowdrift and stalled. While the driver tried repeatedly to get it started, Pucci grew increasingly nervous and finally suggested he get out and look for another car. For the next eighteen hours he trudged through snow often up to his knees in a vain search for another car. The papers under his coat kept slipping and he had to stop to readjust them. Finally, he returned exhausted. After almost twenty-four hours, the Gestapo men got the car started again, but it kept breaking down and they finally reached Verona on the evening of January 6. Beetz gave Harster the documents Ciano had agreed to hand over, and Pucci left to join Edda in Ramiola.

Edda, left there with no news and an active imagination, suffered a nervous collapse, convinced Pucci had been arrested and the documents taken from him. But finally he arrived, and the next day they set out to keep the rendezvous with Ciano. They stopped near Milan to collect the seven small volumes of the diary, which they put into one suitcase, and put the German documents in another. At about 6 p.m. they set off for the rendezvous point, but halfway there both rear tires went flat. It was now 8 p.m. They decided Pucci would remain with the car, and both got out to flag down one for Edda. A car containing two Fascist government ministers stopped. Failing to recognize Edda, they said they were only going to Brescia but agreed to take her that far. In Brescia, Edda tried desperately to find another car but failed and began to run down the highway, stumbling over stones, twisting her ankle and falling on the icy road. Eventually a German military convoy gave her a ride. When they dropped her off, short of her destination, she stopped a bicyclist and told him she was desperately trying to reach the sick mother of her fiancé, an Italian soldier. The bicyclist took her several kilometers to the rendezvous point, but it was now 11 p.m., two hours late, and no one was there. Edda huddled in a ditch to protect herself from the icy cold. Each time a car passed, she looked up expectantly, then sank back, disappointed. She had to remain in the ditch until 5 a.m. because of a German-imposed curfew. Frozen, filthy and exhausted, she set out down the road again and came upon two very surprised men fixing a flat tire on their car. They agreed to take her to Verona.

Looking very strange indeed to the Germans at the Kommandantur, she introduced herself as Emilia Santos and asked to see Harster. She was told to wait, and only when it appeared she would not be allowed to see the general did she give her true identity. Harster saw her immediately. Unknown to Edda, her excruciating ordeal had been without purpose. Even if she had arrived on time, there would have been no Ciano at Kilometer 10. On the afternoon of January 6, Harster got a personal phone call from Hitler. The Führer had learned of Operation Conte and, speaking in a firm voice, ordered Harster to cancel it. He added that, if Ciano had escaped, Harster would have paid with his head. The general was completely taken aback. Later, he said, he discovered that Ribbentrop had somehow learned of the plan and rushed to Hitler with the news. Hitler called in Himmler and Kaltenbrunner and scolded them severely. They defended themselves by saying they had acted to save the Reich from the grave damage that publication of Ciano's diary would cause, and they had hoped he would sanction what they had done after the fact. Hitler, swayed by their arguments, was on the point of giving in, but Goebbels and Ribbentrop intervened and Hitler finally decided to stand by his original decision. Wilhelm Höttl, Harster's superior, gave a different account. He said Himmler and Kaltenbrunner got cold feet at the last moment, and decided they should obtain Hitler's permission for the operation, but he refused.

Harster relayed the bad news to Beetz, and she informed Ciano. He wrote a brief message to Edda, which he asked Beetz to deliver personally. "My Edda," he wrote, "while you live still in the blessed illusion that within a few hours I will be free and we will all be together again, the agony for me has begun. God bless our children. I ask you to raise them in respect of those principles of honor that I learned from my father and that I would have been able to inculcate in them if they had let me live."

He urged Edda to send threatening letters to Mussolini and Hitler, and to flee to Switzerland with the diary.[6]

The following morning, Edda had been in Harster's office only a few minutes when Beetz arrived. She stared at Edda, incredulous and panic-stricken. Taking her by the arm, Beetz rushed her out into the street, whispering: "You are crazy to have come here." She took Edda to her hotel room and, once inside, Edda began shouting: "You have deceived us in the most despicable manner and I would swear that you are ready to do it again. One can never trust you, not even when the life of a human being is in the bargain. But you will pay dearly for that, ah yes, you will pay for it." Then, holding her hands to her face, she collapsed on a chair, utterly drained. Beetz told her of the phone call from Hitler. She said she drove to the Brescia highway the previous evening to explain what had happened and to give Edda a message from Ciano, but it was very cold and after half an hour she left. Later, Edda said she never believed the story. But she apologized to Beetz for her outburst, took her hand, thanked her for everything and left.[7]

Pucci, having repaired his car, drove to Verona and found Edda there, but she was so pale and looked so ill that he hardly recognized her. He was unable to talk to her, for she was now surrounded by Gestapo agents. Escorted by fourteen agents in three cars, they were driven back to Ramiola, where Edda finally was able to read Ciano's last message that Beetz had slipped into her hand. She read it aloud to Pucci, and for the first time in his experience she broke down. Pucci told her they must escape at once.

That day in Verona, Ciano wrote his will. "Today 7 January 1944, healthy in body and mind, but on the eve of unjustly being condemned to death, I dispose thus of my property," he began. He gave everything to Edda and his three children, and asked that his Uncle Gino be made the guardian of the children. He listed his property holdings, and asked to be buried near his father in Livorno.[8]

That evening, Pavolini received an urgent summons to the German Embassy in Fasano. Counselor Von Reichert, substituting for Ambassador Rudolf Rahn who was in Berlin, asked Pavolini if it would be possible to postpone the trial, at least for a few days. Pavolini, surprised, said only Mussolini could make that decision, and he hurried to Gargnano to see the Duce. Mussolini was equally surprised and told him to inform the Germans that, considering the publicity given to the trial, it would be neither possible nor opportune to postpone it even by one day. Von Reichert informed Berlin that night of the decision. The Italians never learned why they had asked for the postponement, but Mussolini told Dolfin:

"The German request can be put in relation to a probable intervention by Spain and Hungary in favor of Ciano . . . unless it was a personal initiative of Hitler, who loves me and is basically a sentimental man . . . Maybe he tried to spare me a great pain."[9]

In Ramiola, Edda entrusted those documents that she could not carry with her to Switzerland to one of the Melocchi brothers, the owners of the clinic where she was staying. They included the twelve volumes of the *Conversations* that had not been given to the Germans, the *Germania* documents, two volumes of the diary covering the years 1937 and 1938, recordings of the voice of Bruno Mussolini, some jewelry and furs, and all her personal papers, including her diary as a nurse and notes written by Mussolini as a soldier at the front in 1916-17, which he had given to her. Pucci cut the leg from a pair of pajamas and sewed into it the five most important volumes of the diary, those dealing with the war years. He attached this to a belt which Edda fastened around her, under her coat.

Pucci's account of what followed contains a confusion of dates that cannot now be clarified with any certainty. But at some point, probably that same day, January 8, Edda slipped out of the clinic through the cellar door while fewer guards than usual were on duty. She walked across fields to join Pucci, who was waiting in his car. He had been given permission by the Gestapo to go to an air force hospital in Ferrara for a medical examination. Following back roads, they stopped in Como where they collected Tanino Pessina and another man who was to arrange her passage across the frontier. He was named Guardi and called himself Uncle Piero. They drove on to the frontier town of Viggiu and spent the night there. Edda then wrote three letters: to Harster, her father and Hitler. In all three, she said she had been repeatedly double-crossed by the Germans, demanded her husband be freed within three days and said if he were condemned she would disclose all the information she had to the Allies. Pucci helped her with the letters, which she dated January 10. The letter to Harster specified that Ciano must be delivered to her in front of Bern railway station, accompanied only by Frau Beetz, between ten o'clock in the morning and four o'clock in the afternoon of the third day. "If this is done in complete faith, we will retire to private life and you will no longer hear of us," she wrote. She said the diaries would be delivered the same day by Ciano to Beetz. Her letter to her father deplored his failure "to show me a minimum feeling of humanity and justice."[10]

At 7 a.m. on Sunday, January 9, SS Lt. Robert Hutting was called in urgently by Harster and shown a telegram from Kaltenbrunner. It read: "Watch closely the daughter of Mr. Mayer [a German code name for

Mussolini]. She can move and go where she wants, but she is not to put a foot in Switzerland. An eventual attempt by her to leave must be impeded even by force. The diaries of the son-in-law of Mr. Mayer are still to be found. Search for them."[11] Hutting and seven other SS men left Verona immediately for Ramiola. At the clinic, they were told she was still sleeping, and decided to wait. But hours passed and Hutting began to question the servants. From one he learned she had left the previous day for an unknown destination. He went to her room and found a card pinned to the door: "I am very tired and I don't feel well. Please do not disturb me for any reason." He knocked but there was no answer. He forced the lock but found the room deserted and in great disorder. Hutting made a search but found nothing. Orders were sent to SS units in Gargnano, Varese and Como to keep a lookout for Edda. But she was already in Switzerland.[12]

Uncle Piero had spent the previous night negotiating Edda's passage. At the last moment the guide he had engaged learned who she was and demanded a sack of rice in addition to the money to be paid to Swiss frontier guards. Piero somehow found the rice. Pucci accompanied her to the border late on the afternoon of January 9. At 5 p.m., with night closing in, she found herself with the guide still several hundred meters from the crossing point, with an open piece of land to cross. The guide pushed her to the ground just as a German patrol was passing. Then he said, "Go now!" "Instead of running, I crossed the moonlit field with tranquil steps, standing quite erect," Edda wrote later. "I don't know why, but at that point I didn't care what might happen to me. The Swiss customs inspector was expecting the Princess d'Aosta—that had been the name given him—and he was astonished and annoyed to hear me say that I was Edda Ciano." After a series of phone calls between the frontier post and Bern, Edda was obliged to spend the night there, but the next day was sent to Neggio, where her children were living.[13] Fabrizio recalled her appearance when she joined them: "Small, very thin, upset, in dire straits and wearing a navy blue short coat. She carried the diaries around her waist."[14]

Pucci, after waiting near the frontier for an hour or so to make sure Edda was safely across, returned to his hotel and left immediately for Verona. Ciano's trial there had begun the previous day. Pucci reached Verona at 1 a.m. and went immediately to Beetz's hotel room to hand over Edda's letters and to report that she had escaped with the diary. Beetz promised to deliver the letters at 8 a.m., to give him a chance to get across the frontier himself. As he was going out of the hotel, an SS agent asked him where he had been. Pucci told him the truth, and the man let him go, but immediately went to Beetz's room. Hearing his approaching footsteps, Beetz dropped the letters on the floor and pretended she had been asleep. But the agent saw the letters, and wanted to take them to Harster immediately. Beetz said she would do it herself, and dressed slowly to give Pucci more time to get away. When Beetz finally went to Harster, she informed him Edda was in Switzerland. "I guessed it!" he exclaimed. "However, she has done well; otherwise at this hour great troubles would have begun for her." Edda's letters to Hitler and Mussolini poured out all her bitterness. "Duce, I waited until the last," she wrote, "hoping that you might have a little honesty and a little humanity. But since I see that you do nothing, I will know also how to strike." If Ciano were not freed within three days, she wrote, she would publish the diary. To Hitler she said: "Twice you deceived me, giving me assurances that you didn't keep. Now enough! Think of the blood shed in common and have clemency and justice!" Harster sent the letter to Mussolini with a special courier, then telephoned the Reichsicherheitshauptamt in Berlin, dictating the letter to Hitler which was then transmitted by phone to Hitler's headquarters. "But unfortunately the text reached his hands too late," Mussolini said later.

Pucci headed for Sondrio, but he was ill and had hardly slept in eight days so he pulled over to the side of the road and fell asleep. Shortly before 4 a.m., he woke up and, finding that his car wouldn't start, went to a nearby peasant's house for help. Just then he heard a car coming and ran back to the road, waving his arms. The car stopped. To his dismay, four Germans got out and demanded his papers. When they discovered who he was, they began shouting furiously, "Where is the Countess?" Four machine-guns were thrust against his throat, and he was shoved against a wall.[15] The Germans continued to demand that he tell them where Edda was, but Pucci did not reply. The Germans gave him a minute to answer and one of them started counting the seconds. When the minute was up, Pucci was kicked around, then shoved into the car and taken to Gestapo headquarters in Verona. Frau Beetz saw him briefly there, and said she would try to get him cleared. From Verona he was taken that evening to Ramiola to be interrogated in the presence of a doctor, one of the Melocchi brothers from Edda's clinic. After questioning Pucci for a few hours, the Germans drove him to the Hotel Regina in Milan, where the proprietor of the Hotel Madonnina in Viggiu was brought in. He identified Pucci as the man who had taken Edda across the border.

"Soon afterward I was ushered into the 'torture chamber' before a strangely elegant Prussian colonel, a smiling Austrian major and their staff," Pucci recounted. "As I came in, I noticed the colonel's carefully parted hair, his beautifully pressed uniform, his clean-shaven face; but what struck me were his hands, small, well-manicured hands which seemed incapable of hurting a fly. The colonel smiled with delight at seeing his prey. At his left sat his aide-de-camp, another Prussian. In a corner a woman, an old, haggard thing, was seated at a typewriter. "The questioning started. They wanted to know everything about the escape of the Countess and her children, whether she had taken the diary or other documents with her, and if not where they were hidden. All kinds of questions were showered on me in broken English or in even more ungrammatical French. I had made up my mind not to answer, and calmly told the three officers I did not intend talking."

The colonel muttered something to the major on his right, and the old woman suddenly rose and ran from the room. The colonel got up, walked to a cupboard and selected three riding crops. He gave one to each of the other officers. Suddenly, the three officers began lashing Pucci. The first blows landed on his head, and blood poured down his face. "On and on they kept hitting me while calling me names of all kinds and shouting insults in savage fashion," Pucci said. "Finally the blows stopped and I found myself leaning heavily against the wall. I was completely groggy." The major approached him and began shouting. Again, Pucci refused to talk, so the beating resumed.

"I was now a mess of blood," he said. "I must have been a regular sight, for the colonel stopped the hitting and told me gruffly to wipe the blood off me. And at that moment, suddenly, out of nowhere, I got a notion that there was a funny side to the whole business. Here, before me, were three men accustomed to getting what they wanted in some way or other, and here was I, a problem they did not seem able to solve. So I took out my handkerchief and carefully wiped the blood from my face and neck. I found a small comb . . . and started combing my hair in a leisurely fashion. When I had finished I asked the colonel if it was all right. He looked at me with a bewildered expression, as if I had been an impertinent child with whom it was difficult to deal. I felt satisfied."

Then the colonel walked to the cupboard again and took out some strange steel objects. Pucci was placed in a chair, and these objects were fitted to his fingers and wrists and twisted. "I felt as if my bones were going to split and cold sweat ran down my back; then I fainted," he said. "When I came to, the major was striking me with his riding crop. In my mouth I had the sweet, warm taste of blood. At my sides the captain and the colonel were shouting questions in my ears. I managed again to be silent. I did not want to talk and I did not want to complain before these people. And so on and on, through the night, they went on hitting me

and twisting my wrists and fingers. But now I fainted every few minutes."
At ten o'clock there was a lull. The Germans were hungry. So, while one
went out to have a meal, the other two continued their work. As each
man departed to eat, his comrades jovially wished him *"guten Appetit."*
At midnight, the Germans left the room but came back carrying tommy
guns. Pucci was pushed against a wall and the guns placed under his
chin. The colonel told him: "You haf one minute to answer. Wen you
answer not we shoot." He took out a pocket watch and started counting
down. When he got to one second, Pucci fainted. The Germans took
him outside, and the cold night air revived him. He could not believe
for a moment he was still alive. They drove to a prison and he was thrown
into an icy cell. "As I lay trembling with cold on the floor I could see
the stars glittering in the velvety blue sky," he said. "I thought of the
clear nights in Africa, when I used to fly over the desert, and I tried to
imagine the wonderful feeling of being again free and a human being.
But the cold was so intense and the pain in my head and body so strong
I couldn't think, and gradually I slipped again into the unconsciousness
which had blessed me through that terrible night."

He was tortured again the next day. In the evening, he was taken back
to his cell and told he would be tortured day and night from now on
until he begged to talk. Pucci decided to kill himself. He had hidden a
razor blade in his shorts at Ramiola and, although he was handcuffed, he
managed to reach it with his mouth. He cut his lips and tongue but
finally managed to open the vein in his left wrist. Although some blood
dripped from his wrist, he soon realized he had not done the job properly
and tried again with no success. Then, taking the razor blade in his fingers,
he tried to slash a vein in his neck but again failed. Early the next morning
the guards took him to the torture chamber and started working on him
again. But suddenly their attitude changed. He was taken back to his cell
and the Germans put on a rough display of kindness which puzzled their
victim until Frau Beetz came into the cell. Pucci, half-conscious, thought
at first he was hallucinating. Then he heard her voice. She burst into
tears at the sight of him. She said she had persuaded the authorities to
release Pucci on the grounds he might persuade Edda not to do anything
against Germany. Pucci told Beetz he would not accept such a condition,
and she began to cry. She said she didn't care what he did, she only
wanted to get him out of prison and into Switzerland. She felt personally
responsible for his life, since she had handed in the letters too soon and
that had led to his arrest. Finally Pucci agreed to talk to a Gestapo general
who had accompanied her.

After a long discussion, he agreed to convey the message to Edda: she and the children would be killed if she did anything against the Germans. As soon as he was able to stand, Pucci was smuggled across the Swiss border by boat during the night, while Beetz entered Switzerland legally as a temporary replacement of a clerical secretary at the German consulate in Lugano. Pucci tried to interest the British in the Ciano diary through their vice-consul in Lugano, Lancelot de Garston, but failed. He stayed on his feet for three days, trying to find Edda, but finally collapsed and went to a hospital. The doctors found that his skull was fractured in several places.

Chapter Twenty

Trial and Execution

Ciano and his fellow defendants went on trial on the morning of January 8, 1944, in the music room of the Castelvecchio, a fortress on the banks of the Adige River in Verona that dates back to 1354. Ten days earlier, Mussolini had asked Justice Minister Piero Pisenti to examine the prosecution case against Ciano and make recommendations, but this clearly was done for form's sake. Pisenti reported back on December 31 that there was no basis for the charge of treason, but observed that the death sentence already was contained in the decree that set up the tribunal. After a moment's silence, Mussolini erupted. "You, Pisenti, you only see this trial under its judicial angle, while I, I must see it under its political angle," he said. "Po-lit-i-cal! Reasons of state must prevail over all other considerations. And now we must continue straight to the end." Pisenti suggested extenuating circumstances might be found to spare the lives of the defendants. "Then speak of it to President Vecchini," Mussolini replied. Aldo Vecchini, the tribunal president, had been removed as president of the Italian Bar Association by the Badoglio government. He spurned Pisenti's suggestion.[1]

The German chargé d'affaires Bock, in a message to Ribbentrop, said Mussolini had decided not to interfere in the trial because Ciano had tried to push onto the Duce the responsibility for his own conduct in foreign policy with the intention of absolving himself before the Fascist Party, the Führer and the Reich government. But Rahn, the German ambassador, wanted Ciano freed and, as the trial opened, he flew to Hitler's headquarters to propose that Ciano be allowed to escape to Switzerland. Rahn told Hitler that, in view of Italian feelings about family loyalties, it would undermine Mussolini's standing with his people if he allowed his son-in-law to be executed. Hitler reiterated his instruction that the trial was exclusively the affair of Mussolini and that the Germans must not interfere.[2]

Inside the Scalzi prison, Ciano was in an aggressive mood. He would tell the judges what he thought of them and their bosses, and would warn them that they would soon die as well. Cianetti threatened to punch him unless he stayed quiet. "Do you really have it in your head to put us all in danger?" he demanded. Ciano replied: "But you must understand this trial is nothing but a tragic clown show. Our fate already has been decided elsewhere and no one, I say no one of us, will succeed in saving himself. Is it possible that after so many years you haven't gotten to know that big coward Mussolini?"[3]

The trial opened under heavy security. The public was given access to the courtroom but ordinary Italians largely stayed away, and it was crowded with local Fascist officials and Germans, almost all in blackshirts. Behind the judges was an enormous black drape, imprinted with a red Fascist emblem and surmounted by a small crucifix. Just before the trial started, a Fascist official discovered that high leather chairs had been reserved for the defendants. He ordered the military to replace them with half-broken wooden chairs. Old Marinelli came in with a bewildered expression. The other defendants were calm. Ciano, striding in with a display of bravura, wore an elegant beige overcoat that he removed to reveal a dark brown sports jacket and gray trousers. He had appointed Luigi Perego, Verona's leading trial lawyer, as his attorney, but Perego excused himself, saying he was sick. Two other attorneys turned down the assignment, and the court nominated a lawyer named Paolo Tommasini.

Marshal Emilio De Bono, seventy-seven years old, was the first to be questioned. He was one of Mussolini's earliest comrades, one of the founders of fascism who had been at the Duce's side when he came to power in 1922. He had led the forces that invaded Ethiopia in 1938 but had been replaced by Badoglio within a few days when the Ethiopian resistance blunted his attack. De Bono had been transferred to the Scalzi from his home at Cassano d'Adda only on the eve of the trial. He told the court he signed the Grandi resolution not to eliminate Mussolini, but to unite Italians around the king in resistance to the enemy. He had no intention, he said, of betraying the Duce, fascism or the alliance with Germany. All other defendants took a similar line.

Ciano, still bristling with anger, was the last one called at the afternoon sitting. "I reject categorically and indignantly the accusations against me," he said. "They represent an offense to my entire past as a citizen, soldier and above all Fascist . . . If the Duce had asked me about the meeting of the Grand Council, I would have advised him against it because in that moment such a convocation was not prudent, due to the international repercussions it could have . . . With my vote I only intended to engage the Crown and make it intervene in the war because it had remained outside it during the entire conflict."

Ciano's testimony was punctuated by cries from the specators. "To death!" "Traitor!" "It's not true!"[4] Prosecutor Andrea Fortunato, a Sicilian who had lost part of his right arm in World War I, asked Ciano, "How is it you didn't bother, on your initiative, to speak to the Duce of the meeting of the Grand Council?"

"Being no longer the Minister of Foreign Affairs, I had no means of easily approaching the head of government," Ciano answered. "Beyond that I must add that I always treated the Duce as head of government and therefore maintained a certain distance."[5]

Judge Franz Pagliani asked, "What did you do for Mussolini when you came to know of his arrest? You, who owed him gratitude for having elevated you to high office while very young and above all knowing him to be the grandfather of your children and father of your wife?"

"Suspected, watched, even guarded on sight as I was," Ciano said, "I found it absolutely impossible to act in his favor. I remember, rather, that my telephone was cut off from the afternoon of July 25. I will say more: I feared I myself, from one moment to the other, would be arrested by Badoglio. That's not to mention the newspapers that were unleashed against me from July 26. In such conditions what could I do?"

Vecchini asked, "What do you say of the dilemma indicated by the Duce, and that is that if the Grand Council adopted the Grandi resolution he would have found himself in an unsustainable situation . . . because he, these are his words, was not one to remain in paradise against the wishes of the saints?"

Ciano replied, "I must say I didn't consider it a true and proper dilemma because the position of the Duce was for me beyond discussion." He admitted he had committed an error, but not a betrayal. "I have always been faithful to the Duce, I have always served him, I owe him everything, and if he had called me I would not have hesitated to tell him the whole truth," he said. Vecchini observed, "But you did not in fact think to save him. You should have done it, at least as a relative." Ciano lowered his head.

The prosecution case was weak. The state presented no witnesses who could furnish any precise evidence of a plot to remove Mussolini from power. The trial was adjourned for the day after Ciano had testified. He told Pellegrinotti that evening the judges wanted "red meat."[6]

The following morning, a Sunday, Judge Enrico Vezzalini put two questions to the defendants: How could they have thought of giving military powers to the monarchy, which they themselves thought had shown a culpable lack of interest in the war and which was suspected of betrayal by the General Staff? Did De Bono and Ciano, both holders of the Order of the Annunciation, ever intervene with the monarch on behalf of the Duce after his arrest? To the first question Ciano replied, "I supported the Grandi resolution because I wanted to involve the monarchy and make it come down out of the clouds, making the king assume the supreme command." To the second question he said, "I did nothing because I was the only holder of the Order of the Annunciation who had no contacts with the royal house. I spoke, however, with Senise . . . and Acquarone. Acquarone told me the Duce had been sent to Rocca delle Caminate, and they prohibited us from making contact with him. With Badoglio nothing could be done because the tribunal knows of the relations that existed between us. However, from a personal friend in the Royal Navy I knew of various movements of the Duce and informed a foreign personality of them."[7]

Fortunato summed up the state's case. He said the moral order had been shattered by the meeting of the Grand Council, and accused the defendants of seeking to save themselves by eliminating the Duce. He asked for the death sentence for all of them. The defense lawyers then rose. All were clearly embarrassed by the task that had been thrust upon them, and all insisted their clients had simply evaluated the Grandi resolution wrongly and had no intention of betraying the Duce. Later General Renzo Montagna, a judge who had been briefly imprisoned by Badoglio, said it had been "painful" to listen to Tommasini's defense of Ciano. "Lawyer Tommasini . . . did a poor job, and repeated several times the same words, constantly getting flustered. He said such stupid things that the spectators, and Ciano himself, laughed several times. That seemed to me in the worst taste." Ciano whispered to Pellegrinotti, "If they don't shoot me after a defense such as this, you will see that I don't have to die." Then he thanked Tommasini warmly for his presentation.[8]

Vecchini dwelt on juridical questions to such an extent that some thought he was looking for a way to help the defendants escape the supreme penalty. Ciano turned once to Cersosimo and said, "Until this morning I believed I would be shot; now no longer." But Montagna said Vecchini in fact was the most determined of the judges not to listen to anything that went in favor of the defendants. Before being taken back to prison at the end of the afternoon session, Ciano asked a police officer, "What do you think? Will they shoot us?" "I wouldn't know," the officer replied. Ciano continued, "I was very pessimistic until yesterday, but today . . ." Then he joked with a young trainee who escorted the prisoners, "You will shoot us tomorrow . . ." The trainee did not reply, but the guard commander said, "The task to which you refer doesn't belong to us. The execution squad is already formed and is here."[9]

The judges began their deliberations in the evening. Montagna was against the death penalty for some of the accused, and he found support from three other judges. They thought Cianetti, De Bono and Gottardi should be spared, but Vecchini and three other judges were adamant that all must die. The ninth judge, Giovanni Riggio, was undecided. At ten o'clock the next morning, after the last of the defense lawyers had been heard, the court retired to consider its verdict. The defense lawyers received a private warning to keep their heads down because, if the defendants were absolved, there were men in the room who would shoot the "traitors" immediately. Ciano was now downcast. He told Cersosimo, "If you remember well, lawyer, yesterday I gave way to some illusions. Now I no longer hope. I have felt in the audience a hostility, especially toward me, that, more than frightening me, pains me. Why so much hatred against me? Is it possible the Italians don't understand me and let themselves be influenced by the Germans? This time it is truly finished . . . If the tribunal doesn't condemn us to death, the more excited and fanatical Fascists will do it to us outside immediately."[10]

When the judges were alone, Montagna still wanted to spare some of the defendants, but Vezzalini was adamant. The court decided to judge each defendant individually, but Vezzalini objected: "The only distinction to be made is to know who ought to be shot in the back and who full face, and that is all." The judges, voting with black and white balls, decided to spare Cianetti and then De Bono as well by a margin of just five to four. Vezzalini suddenly rose and shouted, "You are in the process of betraying fascism! You too should end up in court being tried as traitors! I propose a second vote, but remember what I have just said!" Riggio, who had voted to spare De Bono, now changed his vote. De Bono, Marinelli, Gottardi and Pareschi were all condemned by the same five to four margin. The vote to condemn Ciano was unanimous. In the end, only Cianetti was spared. He was given thirty years.[11] The court reconvened at 1.30 p.m. and Vecchini read out the sentences in a very low voice. When he came to Ciano, he recalled Ciano's reaction upon learning from Ettore Muti of the arrest of Mussolini: "It is too bad; now they will handcuff us as well." That demonstrated, he said, that Ciano was more concerned about himself than about the fate of his chief, his benefactor and relative. From the beginning of the voting in the Grand Council, Vecchini added, Ciano knew the consequences "and wanted the removal of the Duce from power."[12] Ciano responded with an angry outburst, and the other defendants listened in silence. De Bono had not heard what Vecchini said and he turned to Ciano. Pointing at Cianetti, Ciano said, "Only he is saved; for us it is finished." Then he crossed himself. Marinelli, also bewildered, turned to Ciano and said, "And for me, what have they decided?" "Death, as for the rest of us," he replied. Marinelli fainted.[13]

Mussolini learned of the verdicts from Dolfin just before 3 p.m. "He seems very calm, but his face is contracted and his eyelids are redder than usual," Dolfin wrote in his diary. "I don't believe he has slept in these nights. Also his stomach cramps, which had almost disappeared, have come back. Mussolini is silent for a minute; he seems to reflect. Then, rising brusquely to his feet, almost as if to relieve himself of an oppression that torments him, he says to me: 'The dilemma I put to the Grand Council was clear. To vote for the Grandi resolution meant opening the crisis of the regime and my succession; to plunge it, in other words, into the abyss. Grandi, Bottai, Federzoni, Albini and the others knew all this and they knowingly provoked the catastrophe . . . Ciano himself was not ignorant of these ends, and he played the extreme game with them." Sitting down again, he concluded: "If I have conquered my own impulse with this extreme act, it is because I hope it is useful . . . to the country . . . I, I have never had a blood lust."[14] At 4 p.m. Mussolini telephoned Cosmin and asked, "Didn't Ciano say anything after the verdict?" Cosmin called back later and said, "Just after the sentence was read, Ciano turned to Cianetti and whispered to him: 'I am happy for you that you will be able one day to defend our memory."[15]

Back in prison, Benini fell into Ciano's arms, sobbing. "Ah, I come to see you so that you can give me courage," Ciano told him, "and you burst into tears! It is I who will be obliged to cheer you up."[16] Ciano wrote farewell letters to his wife and mother, which Beetz later delivered. In the first letter he wrote:

Adored Edda, adored children, the pain of detaching myself from you is too strong to enable me to find the words that I would want to say to you in these last hours. Know my love for you: now multiply it to infinity and, beyond my life on earth, it will remain with you to protect you and console you. I know I have never stained my honor, and I leave you a name that you will always be able to carry with head held high before everyone . . . Dear Edda, you are good, strong and generous. I entrust to you our three children and I am certain you will guide them on a life of virtue. It is in their name, for their future, that you must have courage and overcome these hours of anxiety. It is a hard trial that heaven has reserved to you, but have faith and think that if in life I have been far away from you at times, now I will be with you, beside you, always. And you, adored children, be good. Love your mother and your grandmother Ina . . . In tenacious affection among you, in study, in love of country, in faith in God you must seek the purposes and the foundations of your young lives, that your papa blesses with all his soul. Farewell dear Edda. Farewell Ciccino, Dindina, Marzio. I take you to my heart with infinite tenderness and pray God to give you every good thing. He kisses you with much love, your papa forever.[17]

Ciano's letter to his mother was similar in tone. In being reunited with his father, he said, he would have "nothing for which to reproach myself."[18]

He had a long talk that evening with Benini. "He was extraordinarily calm," his childhood friend recalled. "He spoke to me a long time of his children and his wife, who had tried and risked the impossible to save him. He told me that immediately after the reading of the sentence he was about to shout at the judges: 'Let's proceed to you next!' He had not done it so as not to depart from the posture of indifference he had imposed upon himself."[19] While the two men talked, the prison director, Olas, arrived and asked Ciano to sign a request for pardon, but Ciano refused. "Do you perhaps believe I am afraid of dying?" he asked indignantly. "I will not give this satisfaction to Hitler and Mussolini. It is absolutely useless." But Cianetti pointed out that the chances of the other condemned men could be harmed if Ciano refused to join them. Ciano reluctantly added his signature at seven o'clock.[20] From ten o'clock, Beetz remained with Ciano in his cell. Her superior, Wilhelm Höttl, later claimed Ciano spent the entire night reading Seneca with Beetz. Don Chiot, the chaplain, passed by and Ciano called to him. Chiot stopped on the threshhold, as he was barred from entering. Later he recalled, "He was pale, but his pupils shone as with a repressed anger. He said, 'Father, I want to die in the Apostolic Roman Catholic religion. I want to take communion and first confess.'" Ciano started to leave the cell, but his SS jailers, Krutsch and Guck, barred the way. Ciano began shouting in Italian and then German, "Rascals, sellouts, barbarians, rabble!" Beetz then telephoned the General Command of the SD and received authorization for the priest to perform his duties in Ciano's cell. She informed Krutsch and Guck their job was finished and they should return to the Command.[21] Ciano told Don Chiot, "I believe they will shoot us in the back to signify we are traitors."[22]

Cosmin came to the prison around midnight, exchanged some words with Ciano and wished him good night. Ciano replied, "This seems to me a bit much." With Olas' permission, Ciano then went into the corridor, took Benini aside and talked to him for a long time. "When you return among the people and this damned war is finished, and it will end soon, don't abandon my children and my wife," he said. "They are the only things which I hold dear. Edda . . . now is in flight and trying to reach Switzerland, where the children preceded her. She has with her my diary and other important documents, some of which I have written here." He spoke of his approaching death. "Don't think I don't prize life," he said. "I love it immensely, but I know that it is finished, that there is absolutely nothing more to be done. And I try to pass these last hours in the best way so my children may know one day who was their father and so my assassins will not have the satisfaction of seeing me vacillate. Whatever may be inside me, no one will be aware of anything; be very sure of that." Then he surprised Benini by telling him he would not be shot in the morning. "I will not give this joy to Hitler and to others," he said. "Also, I don't know how to resign myself to the ice of the bullet in the neck. I feel it, I feel it! And I don't want it, I can't bear it, I won't have it!" He would cheat the execution squad, he said, by swallowing potassium cyanide that Beetz had given him. Beetz had urged him not to do it, but he implored Benini not to try to dissuade him.

"Don't take away from me that little bit of courage that remains to me," he said. "I have left a note saying I brought the poison with me when I came to the prison, hidden in a way that not even the devil could have found it. So no one will have a problem. God will pardon me. I must die, and one can kill oneself when death is certain." He said Beetz had made him swear solemnly that he would not take the poison until there was an answer to the request for pardon.[23] Earlier, asking Beetz to obtain the poison, Ciano had told her, "I am not afraid of going, since I know I will not suffer. But if I think of the cold bullets those executioners will fire into my back and neck, I rebel. Those dogs in Berlin and on the Garda are capable of making a film of the execution. I see them already enjoying themselves in front of the screen, commenting and sneering. I don't want to give them this sadistic joy. And you must help me."[24] Half an hour after leaving Benini, Ciano was back with him. He said he had taken the draught, but nothing happened. "It was a false poison. Thus I must die two times," he said. Beetz reproached him for not keeping his promise to await the answer to the request for pardon. Ciano said he feared she would give the alarm to stop him from taking the poison so, as soon as she left, he lay down on his bed, said a brief prayer and swallowed the contents of the phial. "My heart started beating violently and I thought I was dying," he said. "But then I became aware: my heart was beating normally. This was dying? What, I was alive, very alive." Beetz later claimed she had asked a doctor for potassium cyanide but he had given her instead a harmless solution of chlorate of potassium.[25] Edda's version was that she had procured the "poison" for her husband and had given it to Beetz.

She said she never learned whether the doctor who provided it had deceived her, or whether Beetz had switched phials to prevent Ciano's suicide.[26]

Ciano told Don Chiot, "I have no illusions, I know the moral deafness of my father-in-law. When he is stubborn, he is worse than Machiavelli. And then, how can he not want what Hitler wants?" He got to his feet and shouted, "And meanwhile I am here with the rope at my neck. How stupid I was to tie my fate to theirs!"[27] As the evening wore on, Ciano stretched out on his bed, telling Beetz and Benini, "Now I would like to stay a little while alone with you who are my greatest friends. I am tired." Benini suggested he sleep, but Ciano said, "No, no, I have so much time to sleep! Now I want to enjoy your company. I need to reinvigorate myself a little after what has happened to me." Beetz cried softly, and Ciano took her hand and Benini's "almost so that we might draw him yet a little while above the waves before he disappeared forever," Benini wrote. Ciano spoke of his children and his eyes filled with tears. He said he only wished to know, before he died, that the children and Edda were safely in Switzerland. Beetz, of course, knew this already; why she failed to tell him is a mystery. Just before three o'clock, Benini went out of the cell to smoke a cigarette, and learned from Olas that Edda had succeeded in reaching Switzerland. He rushed to tell Ciano. "He lighted up with joy," Benini said. "He talked, talked without ever interrupting himself, of his children, of the work his wife would be able to carry out to inform public opinion of the truth of events, of his confidence in a better tomorrow for Italy . . . He was as happy as a boy who is preparing for a long-dreamed-of trip. Then he quieted down, as if exhausted." Eventually Benini, moved by a strong impulse, got up, embraced Ciano and pressed him to his heart. "Farewell! Farewell, Galeazzo!" he cried.[28]

The other condemned men gathered around Don Chiot in De Bono's cell, and Ciano joined them. At six o'clock, the sound of bells from a nearby monastery penetrated the cells. De Bono got to his feet and said, "Boys, let's give the last salute on this earth to the Madonna, whom we will see in paradise." They recited together the Angelus.[29] The early morning wore on, and then a rumor filled the void just after eight o'clock: the Cabinet was meeting at Gargnano. If it were true, the only possible reason was that Mussolini wanted to force the hand of his ministers in conceding a pardon. Benini, Ciano and Cianetti began to walk together in the corridor, suddenly euphoric. Benini even reproached Ciano for his rashness, pointing out that if the phial of liquid he had consumed had been poison he would be dead now and a pardon for him would be meaningless. Ciano smiled to show that Benini was right. The prisoners were now in an almost festive mood. At 8.45, some decided they would go to sleep at nine. But

De Bono shook his head and dismissed all thoughts of pardon. "It's an empty hope," he said. "We have Galeazzo with us."[30]

The law establishing the tribunal had not specified who was to receive requests for pardon. Through much of the night, Fascist officials, military men and magistrates met to try to resolve the question. Pavolini and Cosmin were resolutely opposed to referring the requests to Mussolini. The officials eventually decided to leave the decision to the highest military authority of the region, General Count Piatti del Pozzo, but he argued that political matters were outside his competence. Several Fascists then went to Brescia to consult Justice Minister Pisenti. Forewarned by telephone, he received them in his office at the Court of Appeal at eleven o'clock. He said he was ready to receive the requests and pass them on to Mussolini, but Pavolini objected that the Duce should not have to decide the fate of his son-in-law. As they drove away, Pavolini decided to take it upon himself to refuse pardons, but Fortunato and Cersosimo told him he didn't have that authority. The men then telephoned Interior Minister Buffarini, who suggested the decision should be made by the highest military authority in Verona, the consul Italo Vianini. Vianini pleaded illness, but he was summoned to the prefecture at five o'clock in the morning. He was reluctant to put his signature on such a document, but after a call to his commander, Renato Ricci, he finally sealed the fate of the condemned men at eight o'clock.[31]

Mussolini did not sleep that night, nor did Rachele. Several times she approached his bedroom door, saw a light under the door and heard him pacing, but she did not have the courage to enter. At one o'clock, Mussolini telephoned Dolfin to ask if he had any news, but got a negative reply.[32] At three o'clock Captain Hoppe, an official of the German General Staff, arrived with Edda's final bitter letter to her father. Upset after reading it, Mussolini placed a call to General Wolff, the head of the SS in Italy, who was in Fasano. Their conversation in German, recorded by the intelligence service, was as follows:

M: Excuse the late hour, but after the letter of my daughter I am perplexed.
W: The order of the Führer is to consider the Ciano case as a question of an exclusive and absolute internal Italian nature. The German authority in Italy must not interfere. As commandant of the SS in Italy I cannot give an opinion.
M: I know, I know. But I beg you to give me a personal and confidential opinion.
W: [after hesitation] Very well, Duce. I accept, but only as a comrade and a man, and according to the German point of view.

M: Then?

W: The enigma, in my opinion, is this: should you let yourself be blackmailed and, as a consequence, pardon your son-in-law?

M: How would you behave?

W: In your place, I would remain inflexible.

M: What does the Führer think?

W: The Führer doesn't believe that the sentence will be carried out.

M: A failure to execute could harm me in the consideration of the Führer?

W: Yes, and very much so.

M: And Himmler?

W: Himmler believes execution is probable.

M: I thank you, general. I will study the solution. I may telephone you again.

W: At your disposal, Duce.[33]

Mussolini telephoned Dolfin again at eight o'clock, expressing his worry that Edda would publish the diary. "It is my singular destiny to be betrayed by everyone, even my daughter," he said. "Probably she has fled to Switzerland. My daughter has a firm and violent character. She is capable therefore of any sort of madness."[34]

Shortly after 9 a.m., Benini heard a group of people approach, then stop at the first cell, Ciano's. After a few moments they went to the next cell, spoke to the prisoner and moved on. Benini soon became aware they were delivering "a funeral announcement." There was only silence from the prisoners until the officials got to Marinelli's cell. Benini heard from him "a terrible, very loud rending scream: Marinelli has shouted his terror and his desperation." Beetz watched from the end of the corridor, her face bathed in tears. She wore the gold watch Ciano had with him when he entered the Scalzi. He had given it to her as a memento. The condemned men were manacled, and Don Chiot led the procession toward the exit. He suddenly heard a commotion behind him on the stairs. It was Ciano, cursing Mussolini loudly. Don Chiot pleaded with Ciano to forgive him. "No!" he shouted. Then De Bono walked up, put his frail hand on the younger man's shoulder and looked him in the eye. "Galeazzo, I have pardoned him. Pardon him! We are about to appear before the tribunal of God and we all need to be pardoned. Pardon him!" Chiot took Ciano's hand and looked at him without speaking. Finally Ciano's anger subsided. "Yes, we have all erred; we are all swept away by the same gale. Tell my family that I die without rancor toward anyone."[35]

The five condemned men were put in a police van and driven through the silent, nearly deserted streets of the city to the firing range at Fort Procolo outside Porta Catena, one of the ancient city gates. The ground was covered in a heavy frost, and rickety wooden folding chairs were lined up near a wall. Twenty witnesses were on hand. De Bono got out first, wearing a dark suit and black hat and sporting a white goatee. His lips moved in silent prayer. Ciano came out behind him. Marinelli emerged trembling and had to be dragged to the place of execution. Ciano pointed to the right-hand chair and said to De Bono, "That is your seat by right, Marshal." De Bono replied, "On the journey we are about to take, I cannot believe that precedence is of any importance." Both men asked to face the rifles, but were refused. As Ciano threw himself onto his creaky chair, it tipped over and he fell to the ground. Then he got up and sat down again.[36] When the prisoners were tied to the backs of the chairs, facing away from the execution squad, Ciano exclaimed, "Who would have thought it!" But he remained calm and refused a blindfold. He thanked Don Chiot for his spiritual support and asked him to look after his children. He told Cosmin, "I wish to be buried near my father." As Marinelli was tied to his chair, he shouted, "Don't do it, don't do it! You are committing murder!" As he twisted and turned on his chair, one member of the execution squad said, "Calm down, old man! You will see, it will be nothing at all . . ."[37]

An officer read the sentence and, when he stopped, De Bono could be heard praying. The sky was overcast, and a German cameraman worried that his pictures might not come out very well. Nicola Furlotti commanded the execution squad of thirty federal policemen—six for each prisoner. They were dressed in black trousers, gray-green vests and black caps. Just before Furlotti gave the order to fire, Gottardi rose, gave the Fascist salute and shouted, "Long live the Duce, long live Italy!" Pareschi and De Bono also shouted, "Long live Italy!" Ciano remained silent but, at the command "Fire," he turned to face the firing squad. The first shots were fired at 9.20 a.m. A German SS officer described the execution:

> The firing squad took up their positions in two rows fifteen paces behind the prisoners, their small Italian rifles loaded and at the ready. At the word of command the men simultaneously opened fire on the five prisoners, the front row from a kneeling, the back row from a standing, position . . .
>
> After the first salvo four of the prisoners fell to the ground, taking their chairs with them, while one [Pareschi] remained sitting on his chair quite unaffected, to judge from his posture. From the distance at which I was standing I could not make out whether he had been kept erect by sheer equilibrium or whether he had not been hit at all. The men lying on the ground had been so inaccurately hit that they were writhing and screaming. After a short embarrassed pause a few more shots were fired from the

ranks of the firing squad at the man still on the chair and the others on the ground. Finally the ceasefire was given, and the men were finished off with pistols by the commander of the squad and a few other militiamen.[38] A German diplomat who was present said: "It was like the slaughtering of pigs."[39]

Ciano was hit five times in the back by the first round, but was not killed. He fell to the ground, his body contorted, and murmured, "Oh, help, help!" Furlotti rushed up and fired a shot into his temple, then another. Ciano lay dead, two months and seven days short of his forty-first birthday. Two German officials approached to witness that it was he, then Don Chiot covered the body. A prison doctor examined the bodies immediately after the shooting and said some still had a pulse. So Furlotti returned and shot them all again. Don Chiot, with a trembling hand, closed the eyes of the dead and made the sign of the cross. It was now 9.25 a.m.

Twenty-three years later, an Italian journalist found Furlotti, whom most people had thought was dead. Furlotti told him that, if Ciano had been sentenced to life imprisonment, he would have died during his transfer in the police van from the courtroom to the Scalzi prison.

"Died how?" the journalist, Gian Franco Vené, asked.

"Killed."

"By you?"

"It had been decided upon earlier."

"And weren't you afraid?"

"Afraid of whom?"

"Of Mussolini."

"Mussolini would never have interfered in that affair."[40]

A year earlier, Ciano had prophesied his end. Talking to a journalist, he said, "I will certainly be shot, by one side or the other. I don't know if it will be summer or winter. I would like it to be summer. It is less romantic."[41]

At nine o'clock Clara Petacci telephoned SS Captain Emil Göbel, liaison officer between Ambassador Rahn and Harster, for news from Verona. He said he had heard nothing, and she urged him to phone Harster immediately. The Duce, she said, had told her the execution had been delayed, apparently because the requests for pardon had not yet reached him. "He has waited all night, even if his hardness and intransigence have impeded him from informing himself directly about it," she said. "However, he is confident that they will be sent to him from one moment to the other."[42] Göbel telephoned the General Command of the SD in Verona and was told the sentences had been carried out. Dolfin informed Mussolini at ten o'clock. In his diary, he wrote that the Duce "raises his eyes toward me and slowly takes off his glasses, staring at me for some moments in silence. His face seems opaque, absent." Mussolini asked how Ciano had comported himself. "He died like a man, like the others, with a courage that commands respect," Dolfin replied. "He tried, turning at the last instant, to look death in the face." Mussolini replied: "It seems impossible: death causes fear only when it is far away." After a long pause, Mussolini asked for more details and Dolfin told him almost everything he knew, omitting only the fact that the firing squad had to shoot Ciano several times. "Mussolini listens to me in silence; his face is tense like his expression," Dolfin wrote. "His face is of an earthly pallor; his hands drum the table incessantly. His internal tension must be enormous." Mussolini then exclaimed, "Justice was required; and we, we will carry it out in depth so that it is equal for all." Later, talking to two Fascist officials, Mussolini said, "If I had not had Ciano shot, they would have said without doubt that I wanted to save my son-in-law. Today they will say I have had the father of my grandchildren shot. Now that we have begun to make heads turn, we will go forward, to the end."[43] That afternoon he learned the condemned men had signed requests for pardon that had been withheld from him. He telephoned Cosmin:

M: Is is true that Ciano and the others signed the requests for pardon?
C: [hesitates] Yes, Duce. However . . .
M: [interrupts] Why didn't you transmit them to me?
C: I will explain everything to you when I see you, Duce.
M: You have assumed a tremendous responsibility in not sending them to me.
C: But it was right that the traitors paid with their lives. You know . . .
M: [interrupts] I am the head of the Republic and the requests should have been sent to me. A very grave error has been committed.
C: Pavolini also was in agreement and Vianini decided. We didn't want to confront you with a tragic alternative. Now everything is finished, Duce.
M: You, Pavolini and Vianini will personally account to me. I await you tomorrow without fail.[44]

On the evening of the execution Mussolini listened to the radio, and the next day appeared to Dolfin to be "terribly upset" by the tone of the radio comments. He called them "obscene" and found it distasteful that the radio had played the Fascist theme *Giovanezza*. "Even the musical comment, as if it was a matter of a variety show," he complained. "The dead must always be respected . . . Only our propaganda, idiotic and mean as it often is, could give to this tragic event a festive character.

The Italians love to demonstrate on every occasion they are either ferocious or clowns."[45]

General Montagna asked for a meeting with Mussolini on the evening before the executions, but found they had already been carried out when he next called. "I then wrote a letter in which I manifested all my indignation for the crime that was carried out and my disgust at having been on such a tribunal," he said. Later, talking to Montagna, Mussolini reeled off the names of the members of the Grand Council who, he said, should have been condemned to capital punishment. "The men shot at Verona were all excluded, including Ciano," Montagna wrote afterward in his diary.[46] Don Chiot called on Mussolini, and the Duce was reassured to learn that Ciano's words of pardon were also for him. "In the horrible night before the execution, every time I turned on the light in my room I discovered the irresistible attraction of the revolver on my night table," he said.[47] In a conversation with the journalist Carlo Silvestri, Mussolini spoke with pride of the way Ciano had conducted himself, and showed him Ciano's will. "As you see, we are very far from the famous billionaire of whom the Fascist and anti-Fascist detractors have spoken," he said. "The will was written on the threshold of death, when one cannot lie." Some days later, Mussolini discussed with his wife the execution and said, "From that morning I have begun to die."[48]

Don Chiot arranged to have Ciano's body placed in a zinc-lined wooden coffin. He put a crucifix and rosary between the dead man's hands and surrounded the body with violets. Later that day, Beetz entered the mortuary chamber of the Verona cemetery, where the coffins were taken, and placed a bouquet of red roses beside that of Ciano. Her face covered with a veil, she knelt to pray, then went away slowly. During the preceding night, unknown hands had written on the walls of Verona, in charcoal and chalk: "Long live Ciano." As long as his tomb remained in Verona, it was covered in flowers—difficult to find there during the winter months of the war.[49] Carolina Ciano later claimed that Beetz brought Ciano's belongings to her. She said that at one point Beetz knelt beside her and said, in a voice broken by sobs, "I loved him, Countess. I love him still. He was the great love of my life." But Beetz insisted in later years that she never met Ciano's mother.[50]

Chapter Twenty-One

In Pursuit of the Ciano Diary

Galeazzo Ciano had the fatal flaw of complete political amorality coupled with vaulting ambition. Thus, while he was able to perceive the mediocrity and unprincipled cunning of the Nazis (when he had not lapsed into admiration for them), he did not grasp until too late the pure evil that the Hitler regime represented. He was not alone among Italians, of course, in being mesmerized by the hypnotic personality of Mussolini. But, in his wild oscillations between boyish hero-worship and unbridled hatred for his mentor and father-in-law, he displayed a crippling political and personal immaturity. He was a mass of contradictions, a man who could admire the great democracies, yet himself play a crucial role in launching wars against Albania and Greece that had no political or moral justification. Despite his protestations, he was no doubt corrupt financially, as his father had been. The great tragedy of his life was that he clung to high position rather than break openly with Mussolini and the Germans. Had he done so it probably would not have changed the course of history, but it undoubtedly would have been as great a blow to the regime as was, for example, the eccentric defection of Rudolf Hess, Hitler's deputy, from the Nazi government. Ciano could have planted a seed that would have emboldened other Fascist officials disturbed at the course of the war to act sooner than they did to bring the tragedy to an end. That cannot be known with any certainty, of course, but it is clear that Ciano could have redeemed his own soul and his place in history with an open break, and failed to do so. In part, this was due to his infinite capacity for self-delusion. "Galeazzo is a strange man," Curzio Malaparte once observed. "He deludes himself by thinking he is very popular in America and England." "That is nothing," replied Filippo Anfuso. "Just think that he believes himself to be very popular in Italy!"[1] Almost to the end, Ciano imagined that he could be Mussolini's successor and so remained a part of the regime, unaware that by doing so he could never be accepted as a successor. Ciano shared some of the deplorable qualities of the leaders he detested, and would have been appalled if forced to recognize that, but the comparisons are inescapable. He could find the Nazi invasion of helpless Poland morally indefensible, but saw nothing wrong in Italy's takeover of Albania or its unprovoked war of aggression against Greece. He was frequently pained at Nazi duplicity toward Italy, but he could treat the representatives of lesser powers with haughty disdain and an equal lack of honesty. And he did not hesitate to consider murder as a means of dealing with enemies. His personal life was just as flawed as his political one, and just as tinged with contradictions, yet beneath the swagger and pomposity there was a decent human being struggling to come out, and sometimes succeeding, as has been noted before. Although in his last days he falsified his record in office, and wrote in the face of all the evidence that he had nothing for which to reproach himself, he faced death with courage. In those last, terrible months of his life, he was at his best. He also rediscovered his love for Edda, and she responded with the fierce courage and devotion of a woman fighting for her husband and her family. Despite the disappointments of her marriage, she still loved Ciano. That came through clearly in her letters to him in prison, and seemed even to surprise him. There was an additional consideration whose causes will be discussed later (see p. 255): Edda apparently was motivated in part by guilt, arising from a feeling that she had failed Ciano as a wife.

Marcello del Drago was in Belgium when Ciano was executed. He later wrote: "Poor Galeazzo's death shocked us profoundly. I felt more than a little responsible for it. He had died for humanity and we were the first ones to talk to him about humanity, about the vital necessity to defend and stand up for outraged, blood-covered, downtrodden humanity."[2] Susanna Agnelli, then a university student in Lausanne, Switzerland, wrote: "I could not talk to my fellow students about being struck by Ciano's death. They all hated him; he was the symbol of fascism; they all said it served him right. I saw him as Galeazzo, a friend, weak and good, credulous and childishly vain. I imagined him disbelieving to the last, hoping in some magic charm that would save him."[3]

Bottai learned of Ciano's death on January 14 and penned this appreciation in his diary:

> Seldom in my life have I been near men of such contrasting qualities, joined in just one person: a very lively, quick and intuitive intelligence, and a grievous and idle intellectual laziness; a memory surprising in particulars, minutiae and frivolity and a not-less-surprising failure of memory of the essential, of ideas, of sentiments; a varied, prompt and curious culture and a total ignorance of the most current problems of social life; a very refined elegance of style, of relations and of behavior

and a vulgar carelessness of manners and accents . . . capricious in his admirations and in his affections, in his political tendencies and in his intellectual gestures. There was, in him, in a disturbing coexistence, something repulsive and something attractive. That ensured him very convinced detractors and admirers.

After a period of mutual diffidence, that assumed tones of open hostility on his part, I approached him in the summer of 1939 when the political crisis headed toward war. I saw him put himself in front of the unstoppable motor with a courage that gave rise to my admiration, and with a vision of the future that amazed me then and seems to me very exact afterward . . . In another, constitutional regime he would have kept Italy out of war . . . With another leader he would have been an upright person; with Mussolini he couldn't help but be corrupted . . . Now I think of that overgrown boy that he was, of his love of the easy and joyous life, of his taste for comforts and luxuries, of his maddened running in the flowered fields of pleasure and voluptuousness. All that must have made the passing of it painful for him.[4]

In his war memoirs, Winston Churchill wrote: "The end of Ciano was in keeping with all the elements of Renaissance tragedy. Mussolini's submission to Hitler's vengeful demands brought him only shame, and the miserable neo-Fascist republic dragged on by Lake Garda—a relic of the Broken Axis."[5]

Edda learned of her husband's death on January 14. On the previous three days, while staying in a convent outside Neggio, she had gone into the village with her children to look for a newspaper, but the Swiss police had ordered shopkeepers not to sell newspapers to her, nor to let her use a telephone. Finally, the Italian consul in Lugano, Natali, who had served as an aide in Ciano's Cabinet, arrived at the convent and broke the news to her in the refectory, seated at a table covered with a pink and white checked cloth. "Countess, I regret to inform you that your husband was condemned to death and that the execution has taken place," Natali said. Edda commented later: "It was a brusque shock, but my soul was by now predisposed to the eventuality." When Natali had left, Edda called to the children and, in a calm voice, said, "Come, let's go for a walk." Raimonda saw that she had been crying. The weather was cold, but the Swiss mountains were bathed in glorious sunshine as Edda led the children up a hill. She stopped at the peak near a large wooden cross and a field of flowers, sat down with the children and said, "Papa . . . papa is dead. They shot him. Papa . . . is no longer with us." The children, stunned, remained silent, but Fabrizio and Raimonda had tears in their eyes. "But he had nothing to do with it, he was innocent," Edda continued. "And so, my children, he was without fault." Little Marzio, six years old, pulled up blades of grass with seeming indifference, then asked, "Which papa?" He ran along the meadow, plucked a red flower and gave it to Edda, who turned it between her fingers. Then she looked up and said, "Let's go back down now."[6]

Hardly were they back in the convent before Raimonda ran to the bathroom and locked herself inside. Then she began breaking everything in sight. "And she shouted with an incredible force for a girl ten years old," Fabrizio recalled. "She shouted words that could not be understood, broken by sobs, and she beat her head against the wall." The nuns ran to the bathroom door, knocked and began calling to Raimonda with the false name she had been given when she crossed the border: "Margarita! Margarita, open the door!" The gardener came and forced open the door with his shoulders. It took hours to calm Raimonda.[7] That evening, Edda improvised a performance as an actress to divert her children. She made up stories about a girl at her first dance whom nobody invited to dance, a petulant and boring old woman and a wiseacre girl student. Several nights later Marzio, looking out the window with Edda, pointed toward a star and said, "Edda, do you believe that papa is up there?"[8]

Fabrizio, then thirteen, said the news of his father's death was for him "an earthquake, perhaps more in the heart than in the brain." His first thought was that Mussolini could have saved him. "From that consideration, an immediate and powerful instinct of hatred and revenge, that for her part Edda never encouraged," he wrote. "And then everything got mixed up, crossed together and fought together: hatred with affection, the obvious with the incomprehensible, great certainties with great doubts. Truly a psychologist could give his opinion, decipher certain behaviors of my later years, if he were able to draw out from the wounds of the soul that bitter block of the past. I cried at night, when no one saw me or heard me. I cried many nights following. As did Edda." When they later moved to the convent of the Sisters of the Holy Cross in Ingenbohl, Fabrizio shared a room with Edda. One night he awoke, became aware the bedside light was on and saw Edda holding *The Posthumous Papers of the Pickwick Club* by Dickens. "From her eyes ran a river of tears: it seemed never to finish," he said. "A continuous, silent crying, but without a sob. Only her shoulders trembled. Poor Edda: at that time she was really reduced to a rag, all skin and bones." Most of her hair fell out.[9]

A Swiss police inspector named Camponovo visited Edda on January 21 in the convent, and was scandalized by her appearance and behavior. She received him while still in bed, failed to restrain rudeness in Marzio and showed a "remarkable" indifference to the execution of her husband,

Camponovo said. "Even her twelve-year-old son [Fabrizio], self-possessed, very intelligent and audacious, had no word of regret," the inspector reported. "He shrugged his shoulders and simply said, 'So it goes, it is the destiny of men!'" Another police report on Edda's stay in Ingenbohl stated: "She smokes a lot of cigarettes, loves cognac and drinks a liter of wine every day. She doesn't get up before noon and leaves her three children without any maternal care." The police soon removed Raimonda and Marzio to the Theresianum College, several hundred meters away from the convent, and Fabrizio was enrolled in the cantonal college of Schwiz, eight kilometers away. Edda remained in the convent, and the four were allowed to meet only once a week. A week after arriving at his college, Fabrizio ate tobacco to make himself sick, was put in a clinic and, in the dead of night, sneaked out wearing only pajamas, house slippers and a raincoat. The ground was covered with snow and the temperature was −5°C, but Fabrizio followed the railroad tracks to Edda's convent. The police came for him the next day, but Edda objected and he was allowed to stay. Now the police rechristened the family Pini, the maiden name of their paternal grandmother. Fabrizio became Fabio, Raimonda got her name back and Marzio was Mario.[10]

Pucci was still confined at Bellinzona and in poor health; one of the fractures to his skull was slow in healing. While he waited to recover, he wrote to Edda a sorrowful, ten-page letter on February 9 which may never have reached her. It turned up in the Federal Archive in Bern in 1996. "Some day, when we see each other again, I will tell you everything that happened that evening of January 9 after I left you. It seemed to me, at the time, one of the most painful moments of my life, and now I think of it with emotion," he wrote. He went on to tell her of what he had learned from Beetz about Ciano's last hours. "Galeazzo faced death heroically, with an unparalleled serenity and calm," he wrote. Ciano's only worry had been the fate of his wife and children. Pucci ended by urging Edda to "repress your sorrow, your legitimate desire to have revenge and try to avoid the need to reveal the details of this tragedy that from 1938 until today has brought our country to ruin . . . Truly you should have been born a man. Today Italy would not be where it is if you had been able to act. Embrace with infinite tenderness the children. I am always, constantly, near you with my devoted and eternally faithful thought. Emilio."[11]

Shortly after Ciano's execution, Mussolini told Carlo Silvestri that the Germans were "very irritated" that Edda had escaped, but even more concerned that they had not managed to get hold of the diary. "Exasperated as she is, she could do something crazy," he said. "I will do everything possible to persuade her to reflect on what she is doing. The publication of Galeazzo's diary could provoke very serious consequences, perhaps irreparable."[12] On January 11, the day of Ciano's execution, Vittorio Mussolini set out at his father's behest to find Edda and try to persuade her to hand over the diary. He arrived at the Pessina residence in Como, learned that she had gone to Switzerland, and abandoned his mission. But Mussolini was determined to make contact with his daughter. On January 27 he met with Don Giusto Pancino, a childhood friend of Edda's who had been a military chaplain in Albania and later in Russia when Edda was serving there as a nurse. He assured Pancino that, if Edda came back to Italy, he would make sure she would not be put on trial. "Whoever touches my daughter touches my eyes," he said.[13] Pancino wanted to go to Switzerland immediately, but encountered difficulties in crossing the frontier and had to go to Rome to enlist Vatican assistance. He finally arrived at Bern on March 4. Soon afterward, German agents approached him and offered him 100 million lire if he would deliver the Ciano diary to them. According to Pucci, Mussolini had put the same price on his daughter's head. A Swiss police report of March 4 to a minister in Bern stated: "Marquis Pucci declared that Mussolini, when he knew his daughter could not be found and was about to flee to Bern, ordered her immediate arrest and offered a million lire to whoever had the luck to trace her alive or dead."[14]

Monsignor Bernadini, the apostolic nuncio, arranged for Pancino to meet with Edda in Ingenbohl on March 23. She was then running out of money, and at one point had told her children, "We have only a few francs left. What do you want to do? Put them aside, or spend them to buy a radio?" The children were all in agreement: "The radio, the radio!"[15] Pancino brought Edda 5 million lire that Mussolini had obtained from the sale of his newspaper, *Il Popolo d'Italia*. He found her implacably embittered toward her father, saying she didn't want to know anything more about him. "Tell him that his situation causes me pain; tell him that only two solutions could rehabilitate him in my eyes: to flee or kill himself." Pancino returned to Italy and reported these words to Mussolini on March 28. He showed no emotion.[16] The next day, Mussolini told Pancino, "I know Churchill has made a speech in which he said that I have presented myself again to the footlights of history after having stained my hands with the blood of Count Ciano. You know it isn't true, but how many others do? Not even my daughter believes me, and now this statement of Churchill's will ensure that I pass into history as the assassin of my son-in-law."[17] At dawn on April 4, the body of Galeazzo Ciano was transported from the Verona cemetery to Livorno, accompanied by his uncle Gino. Mussolini had arranged the reburial at Edda's request. The next day the body was buried in the Livorno Cemetery of Purification, next to the graves of his father and sister.

Having failed in their attempt to bribe Pancino to obtain the Ciano diary from Edda, the Gestapo decided to kidnap her. An Italian police report to Mussolini on April 29 said: "An informer who is very trusted, because he is a Fascist operating in Switzerland, has been approached by elements of the Gestapo . . . who have asked his help in arranging the exit from the Mentzingen convent of Countess Edda . . . For the Gestapo it would be sufficient to have the Countess go about 10 kilometers from the convent." The report added, either naively or disingenuously: "The intentions of the Gestapo are not known."[18]

On May 15, Mussolini gave Pancino a letter for Edda as he was leaving for Switzerland again. He urged her to listen to the priest's advice, brought her news of Romano, Anna and Vittorio and said he would be "truly happy" if she would write to him. This time Pancino found Edda buoyant in spirits and more serene toward her father. She gave him copies of the Ciano diary, and authorized him to have them published, with proceeds to go to the children, if she were to die. He placed the diary in a safety deposit box of the Credit Suisse in Bern under his name and that of Emilia Conti Marchi, a pseudonym chosen by Edda. She replied in writing to her father, thanking him for having arranged the reburial of her husband. She also noted that the Badoglio government had begun an inquiry into the "illegally accumulated riches" of various Fascists and wrote: "Fine! If the commission is composed of honest people, finally it will come out, as clear as the sun, that neither my father-in-law nor my husband was a thief and their fortune was neither immense nor wrongly acquired. But I don't have illusions about the result of the inquest. Too much courage would be required to tell the truth. I will be the wife of a traitor and a thief. And I will be extraordinarily proud of it. I carry the bloodied name of my husband with pride; it is an honor for me before you, your servants and your bosses."[19] Shortly afterward Edda was in a state of nervous collapse again and was transferred to a clinic in Monthey, which Fabrizio later described as "the provincial insane asylum." On July 13 Pancino was back, bearing another letter from Mussolini. "I understand your situation and hope that in a day not too distant you will understand about me personally and politically," the Duce wrote. Edda replied on July 24: "I don't know what to tell you. All is so black, but everyone must pay. For my part, the injustice and cowardice of men and of you have made me suffer so much that by now I cannot suffer more. I pray only that everything finishes soon."[20]

Frau Beetz in Switzerland learned from her superiors of Edda's meetings with Pancino. She suspected Pancino was working for the Germans as well as Mussolini, and she was afraid Edda would tell the priest how Beetz had helped her escape with the diary. If that happened, she knew she would be arrested and tortured. Susanna Agnelli came out of one of her university classes in Lausanne one today to find Beetz walking toward her "with a drawn, terrified face." Beetz introduced herself, sobbed and said, "Galeazzo told me about you. I was with him all the time he was in prison in Verona. I was supposed to make him talk; instead I became fond of him. I wanted to help him, to try to arrange his escape—at least to spare him the execution. I didn't even manage that." She told Agnelli about the episode with the fake potassium cyanide, and asked her to procure some real cyanide. "I have to go back to Italy," she said. "If the Germans discover me, if they kill me I don't care, but if they torture me—I know what it means—I know I will not be able to resist, I can't face it." Agnelli asked her why she did not seek Swiss asylum, but Beetz said she could not; her husband was fighting on the Russian front. Agnelli obtained the cyanide and, shortly afterward, Beetz returned to Italy where she enjoyed a couple of weeks vacation with her husband, whose military leave was arranged by Kaltenbrunner.[21] Afterward she was instructed to return to Switzerland to renew her attempts to contact Edda, but the Swiss refused to issue a new visa.

When Edda arrived in Switzerland, American intelligence authorities were ignorant of the existence of the Ciano diary. But on June 5, 1944, the day after the Allied armies entered Rome, the Communist Party newspaper *L'Unità* reported that "interested parties" were deliberately holding back publication of the diary. This put the Americans on the scent. In mid-August, American counterintelligence agents in Italy picked up Benini, now out of the Verona prison. He gave detailed information about the diary, which was incorporated in a fifteen-page memorandum drawn up by Lt.-Col. Henry H. Cuming, assistant chief of staff, G-2, Peninsular Base Section, and dated August 16. Benini quoted Ciano as telling him: "They have stripped me of my possessions. I am poor now. But there is one treasure they have not taken which is of more value to me than all the rest: my diary, now in the hands of my wife." In a telegram, Cuming added: "Benini is convinced that, as a life-long friend of Ciano and as financial manager of both Ciano and Edda, he can persuade the latter to make the document available to the Allied authorities. He is equally convinced that Edda Ciano, now reported in Switzerland, has not turned the diary over to the Germans, since she regards it as an instrument of eventual security for herself and children after the collapse of Germany and the Italian Republican Fascist government."[22]

Benini wrote to Edda on August 15, entrusting delivery of the letter to the Americans. He told her of his confinement in the Verona prison and his meetings with Ciano. "I am burning with the desire to bring you his last wishes, his last words and his advice," he wrote. "He praised all that you had done for him and upon you he placed the certainty that some day he will be truly understood as to his thoughts and actions in Italy and abroad. He has counted on you so that the world might have an irrefutable revelation of so many capital truths."[23] For the moment, the Americans had no address to which to deliver the letter.

In late summer, extracts from the diary were published in the Rome newspaper *Risorgimento*. An Italian journalist, who was one of the last people to speak to Ciano before his execution, had obtained authorization from Edda for the publication. These extracts were reprinted by the Spanish Catholic weekly *Mision* on August 26 and September 2. In a letter to her father, Edda said she had made seven copies of the diaries and had deposited them in seven different cities.[24] The American authorities apparently were unaware of the publication of the extracts, for the State Department informed the U.S. minister in Bern, Leland Harrison, on October 22 that it had reliable information the diary was in Edda's possession in Switzerland. Harrison was directed to get the diary or a microfilm copy, and it was suggested he might wish to use the help of the OSS.[25] Dulles, who had learned of Edda's arrival in Switzerland during the winter, then embarked on the search for her. He made inquiries with Count Magistrati, the Italian ambassador in Bern, but was given no indication whether Edda had the diary with her.

By now Pucci was out of hospital and confined in Estavayer-le-Lac under Swiss police guard. Then he moved to Fribourg and in the early autumn he met Frances de Chollet, an American married to the Swiss banker Louis de Chollet, and gained from her the impression that the Americans were very interested in finding Edda. At the end of October, he met Edda, talked to her at length about the diary and asked if he should contact the Americans. Edda agreed. On December 6 Pucci obtained police permission to return to Fribourg. He did not manage to see Madame de Chollet, but he talked to her on the phone and said he had something important to tell her. A few days later she arrived in Estavayer, accompanied by Paul Ghali, a man of mixed Egyptian and French parentage who was a correspondent of the *Chicago Daily News* in Bern. He had only recently been expelled from France for his "biased reporting" on Jews and Gaullism. Ghali had picked up the Swiss morning newspapers on December 7 and read a short, sensational story claiming that Edda was going to marry Pucci. He thought the story was nonsense but decided to investigate. A few days earlier, his friend Madame de Chollet had told him of her contacts with Pucci and said that if he needed information on Edda he could call on her. Ghali phoned de Chollet and was surprised to hear her say: "Pucci wishes to see you. He will come this afternoon. So hop on the train and be here at four." Ghali found Pucci businesslike. Pucci said Ciano had instructed Edda to deliver the diary either to Churchill or Roosevelt, and he asked Ghali to find out if Dulles would be interested in obtaining it. "I was startled by Pucci's offer," Ghali recounted later. "I had come for a trivial inquiry and here was the biggest scoop in my career." He informed Pucci he would act as intermediary with Dulles only if Edda agreed to sell newspaper publication rights to the *Chicago Daily News*. Pucci telephoned Edda that night to get her consent and the next morning informed Ghali he could proceed. A few days later Ghali and de Chollet took the train to Monthey to visit Edda and found her "full of pep and enthusiasm." She told them of her bad experiences with the Nazis, particularly Ribbentrop and Himmler, whom she hated. She said Himmler had betrayed her and her husband by taking them to Bavaria instead of Spain. Edda also gave them detailed accounts of life in Hitler's "Eagles Nest" at Berchtesgaden, and was the first person to reveal the existence of Eva Braun to the outside world. She described Eva as vulgar and uninteresting. Later, in a letter to Ghali, she said, "I'll be glad if I've done something to give the Boches what they deserve." But she said she did not hate Hitler; she found him "emotional and sensitive." Ghali had the impression that, despite her rupture with her father, she remained a Fascist and was proud of being the Duce's daughter. In a later conversation she said: "Some countries must have a dictator if they are to accomplish anything."[26]

Dulles, informed by Ghali of his initial contact with Edda, wrote to her on December 15, enclosing his letter in a book. He said he had to leave for Paris the next day but hoped to see her on his return on December 20. Dulles had made contact with Pucci with the help of Cordelia Dodson, a young OSS counterintelligence officer in Bern who had known Pucci since they had been students together at Reed College in Portland, Oregon. Now Cordelia Dodson Hood, and living in Maine, she said, "I saw Emilio quite often in Switzerland. He was having bad headaches. The Gestapo had put his head in a vise, and his head had been cracked."[27] On December 15, Dulles cabled the OSS in Washington about the Ghali–de Chollet contact with Edda and his own talks with Pucci. He wrote: "Edda is psychopathic case under influence Swiss psychoanalyst whose motives and connections dubious. She promises diaries as goodwill gesture one day and the next asks large monetary payment to protect interest children and also some letter of acknowledgment. Naturally matter requires most discreet handling from every viewpoint."[28]

Edda refused to part with the diary, even to allow it to be photographed, so Dulles decided the filming would have to take place at the Monthey clinic. He made out a certificate stating that Daniel Schachter, an OSS agent, was officially authorized "to make photographic reproductions of documents, records and reports desired to complete the official documentation of United States Government Offices. Any documents so photographed by him are for official uses only."[29] Schachter went to see Edda, but she said she would have to talk to Dulles directly before allowing him to photograph the diary. In a December 20 letter to de Chollet she wrote: "When your 'important friend' comes back—please ask him to come and see me as soon as possible. I should like to talk with him because, though I am willing with all my heart to carry through the deal, the whole thing is too important for me (and I am not thinking of money) to take wild chances blindfolded . . . Your important friend could come with his car and take me for a ride (not in the American sense of it I mean to say)."[30]

On January 7, 1945, Dulles drove to Monthey, accompanied by de Chollet and Ghali. Edda was smuggled out of the clinic, and met them for dinner at a small railway station restaurant on the line between Lausanne and St. Maurice. Over dinner, Edda regaled the party with tales of her meetings with Hitler and Ribbentrop and her description of Eva Braun. After dinner, she asked to be left alone with Dulles. They talked for an hour, and when they came out she looked grim. Ghali said Edda had wanted Dulles to use his influence with the Swiss to obtain asylum for her mother, brothers and sisters, but Dulles refused to commit himself, much to her disappointment.[31] Edda told Dulles she wanted to carry out Ciano's will and vindicate his political reputation, but she hated to give up her last assets. She wanted to bargain for the diary, yet wanted to give the impression of a generous act toward America. She said she was anxious to get out of Switzerland, beyond the reach of the German SD, and needed help in reaching Spain or Portugal. She also needed clear assurances she would retain rights for commercial publication of the diary. Dulles replied that the diary was losing value every day; this was her last real chance to make a generous act. He said the U.S. government was not interested in bargaining or paying money. He could assure her that her rights of commercial publication would not be infringed, but the government might wish to publish parts of the diary if it thought that would help in the war. At the end of the meeting, Edda agreed to hand over the diary. But at 5 a.m. the next day, she wrote to Dulles asking for these specific guarantees: (1) formal acknowledgement that she had donated the diary; (2) a written promise from the government that the material would only be used for political and military purposes, secretly, and nothing would be published without her consent; (3) the government would provide assistance in commercial publication as soon as it had gone over the material.

She had mentioned to Dulles at their meeting that additional material of Ciano's, the "chocolates" as she called them, was still hidden in Italy. In her letter of January 8, she wrote: "The complement to the diaries are still in Italy—if you take me out of here, I am willing to go and fetch them. Only Pucci and I know where they are. Pucci does not know that I know."[32] She told Dulles she was waiting with "great anxiety" for his answer, adding: "Don't make me wait too long or I shall have a second and fatal nervous breakdown."[33] In a cable to Washington on January 11, Dulles said he had not accepted the conditions she imposed, but would give her a personal letter of acknowledgment that her rights of commercial publication would not be infringed. Edda finally agreed to hand over the diary, and in another, one-sentence cable the same day Dulles advised Washington: "Edda is willing."[34]

Ghali accompanied Schachter and Captain Tracy Barnes to the Monthey clinic to photograph the diary secretly at night in Edda's room. Barnes, thirty-four years old and a product of Groton, Yale and Harvard Law School, was a handsome, athletic man who was later to become one of the glamour boys of the Central Intelligence Agency. With the OSS, he was parachuted behind enemy lines in France after D-Day and, years later with the CIA, he was a liaison officer with the State Department during the Bay of Pigs debacle. The operation in Monthey did not go well. The three men only succeeded in blowing the clinic's electrical fuses, greatly upsetting its psychiatric patients. The Americans then decided the only way to photograph the documents was to smuggle Edda out at night and take her to the home of de Chollet, eighty miles away in Fribourg. This was accomplished, and Edda climbed back into her room at 5 a.m. the next day, but Swiss newspapermen spotted her return and the Swiss press bristled with accounts of her misbehavior,[35] though none of the newspapermen had any idea what Edda was doing out of the clinic at night. Dulles dispatched the film to the OSS in Paris on January 20, and it was then taken to Washington.

Ciano had insisted that Edda should not accept payment from the U.S. government, but the Swiss government was keeping her on restricted funds and she needed money. Dulles gave her an advance of 3,500 Swiss francs against possible future royalties.[36] Dulles thought Washington should make immediate use of the diary, but the State Department wanted to withhold publication until it could be used after the war in the Nuremberg war crimes trials—as indeed it was. Part of the prosecution of Ribbentrop rested on Ciano's diary entries, particularly his references to the Salzburg meeting at which Ribbentrop told him, "We want war." In his defense Ribbentrop denied he ever said that. He said he merely told Ciano that the Führer was determined to resolve the Polish question "one way or the other," and he, Ribbentrop, continued to believe it could be solved by diplomatic means. While in prison in Nuremberg, Ribbentrop wrote a memoir in which he discussed Ciano and his diary at some length and repeated his preposterous defense of himself. "I know for certain that there are at least two diaries by Ciano, one of which I saw the Führer with as early as 1943," he wrote. That diary, he said, did not contain the famous phrase attributed to him, "We want war." "One of Ciano's diaries is certainly a forgery," Ribbentrop continued. "It was not possible to find out from which manuscript the photocopies were taken which were submitted in Nuremberg. It is not even certain whether the book from which the photocopies were taken was in fact written by Count Ciano . . . Presumably the whole diary was rewritten several times by Count Ciano in order to create a cast-iron 'peace alibi' for himself and to bring out as a contrast my own and the Führer's 'lust for war.' . . . Without a doubt Ciano maintained permanent contact with the enemy." He went on to denounce Ciano as "jealous and vain," "deceitful and unreliable" and a man of "reprehensible character." "The Duce told me later that no one had ever told him so many lies as Ciano—and this for years—and he was probably also to blame for the corruption and consequent splitting of the Fascist Party," he said.[37] Ribbentrop was hanged in Nuremberg on October 16, 1946.

The 1,200 pages of diary that Schachter photographed covered the period January 1, 1939, through February 8, 1943. Edda also included Ciano's note to her of December 23, 1943, from his prison cell. Dulles noticed that some pages were missing, particularly those between January 25 and April 24, 1941, apparently relating to the Greek war. The late Professor Gaetano Salvemini examined the photographs of the diary later, and noted that the entries for October 27 and 28, 1940, had been removed and substituted. Dulles suspected Edda might have excised passages she considered offensive to the Americans and British, but Edda denied this and said she had no explanation for the gaps in the diary. She repeated that denial in her memoirs. "I could easily have torn out a page or two that seemed embarrassing to him or to me, but I never did so, for that would have been contrary to my nature," she said.[38] One other thing about the diary puzzled Dulles. There was a series of initials in red pencil and capital letters at the top right-hand corner of many pages. Edda examined these pages and said she knew no reason for the initials. Dulles and his team later studied them again and realized they were the initials of some of Ciano's lady friends. They concluded he had made the notations to record the days on which assignations had occurred.[39]

Meantime, Ghali was involved in laborious negotiations with Edda for newspaper publication rights, complicated by the fact that other publications had learned of the diary and entered the bidding. The *Saturday Evening Post* offered $20,000 and indicated it was prepared to increase that if necessary. The Swiss publishing house Oprecht also expressed interest. Edda asked Ghali for $25,000. Then Curt Reiss of the Scripps-Howard Syndicate contacted Edda and began negotiations. Dulles, in a cable to Washington in March, quoted G-2 officers as saying Reiss' record was "rather questionable," but did not elaborate. "I should label him as astute and unscrupulous," Dulles wrote.[40] Finally, on April 9, Edda signed a contract with the *Chicago Daily News*, giving it exclusive newspaper and magazine publication rights for $25,000, a considerable sum of money at the time. The newspaper had initially offered only $3,500. Edda retained book rights, with de Chollet authorized to negotiate for a French edition to be published in France and Switzerland. The *Chicago Daily News* published the diaries over a thirty-day period, beginning in June 1945.

By then Dulles had turned his attention to obtaining the documents Edda left behind at Ramiola. These included the Ciano diary for 1937 and 1938, Edda's own Red Cross nurse's diary and Ciano's official memoranda on his conversations with various foreign diplomats. "From parts of diary I have read, three seem of substantial importance," Dulles cabled Washington. "Progress with Edda slow and view possibility German evacuation North Italy plus danger involved in clandestine passage of substantial bulk written material such as above, suggest desirability make plans to secure material immediately after evacuation. To accomplish this possibly necessary give Edda something more substantial than henceforth. What she probably wants most is facility to leave Switzerland for USA or South America or possibly Spain. Do you consider that prospective value of material warrants any such action, of course against delivery of documentation?"[41] Edda was at first coy with Dulles, telling him the documents were secreted just north of Bologna in an area probably occupied by German troops, but later she admitted they were hidden near Parma. On March 12, she wrote to Dulles telling him she had learned the documents had been stolen by the Gestapo, which in fact was true. But Dulles cabled

Washington on May 2, well after the German surrender in Italy, suggesting he go to Italy to ascertain the truth for himself. "As Edda letter of authorization is to me personally, delegation this task impossible," he cabled.[42] Dulles went to the Melocchi brothers' clinic at Ramiola on May 22 and interviewed the doctors. He discovered that, several days after Edda fled to Switzerland, SS officers had appeared at the clinic and threatened the doctors, then left, apparently expecting they would learn what they wanted from Pucci, who was undergoing torture. Six months later, the Gestapo sent an Italian emissary to the clinic, posing as a friend of Edda's. He asked for the documents Edda had left behind. Caught off guard, the doctors asked for a written order from Edda, which she had agreed to send if she wanted the papers delivered. The Germans now had confirmation the papers were there.

Several days later the agent returned with an obviously forged letter from Edda. To gain time the doctors said the papers had been taken away and hidden elsewhere. Then the Gestapo arrived in force, took one of the doctors to Parma and threatened him with imprisonment. He revealed all. The documents were hidden in the basement of the clinic, near its electrical installations and behind a door marked with a skull and crossbones to indicate danger. The documents and a box containing Edda's jewels were taken away by the Germans. The material was turned over to Beetz, who was asked to make a summary of the information they contained, then ordered to return to her home in Weimar to make a full translation. In April 1945, shortly before his death, Hitler ordered the documents and Beetz's translations to be destroyed, but Beetz had preserved Ciano's diary for the period August 22, 1937 to December 31, 1938. An earlier segment, from June 10, 1936, to July 31, 1937, was among the material destroyed in Berlin. Ciano's other papers were also destroyed, but Beetz had secretly made a carbon copy of her translations of these papers and buried the copy in her rose garden as the Russian army was closing in. The U.S. Army Special Counterintelligence detachment in Germany picked up Beetz in the summer of 1945, and she mentioned having part of Ciano's papers. The intelligence officers turned the material over to the Documents Center of 12th Army Group Headquarters, and the diary was restored to Edda prior to its publication in 1948. Almost a year after the missing material was found, ambassador to Germany Robert Murphy relayed word of the find to the State Department. Aside from the diary, he described the material as "complete copies of Ciano's records of conferences of Hitler, Mussolini and Ribbentrop, and all telegraphic and letter correspondence between Hitler and Mussolini." The papers consisted of a couple of bundles of loose sheets of carbon copies in German translation, with some of the Italian originals scattered among them. These documents were later published as *Ciano's Diplomatic Papers*.[43]

During her stay in Monthey, Edda was a patient at the Malevoz clinic of André Repond, one of the pioneers of Swiss psychiatry. It was he to whom Dulles ascribed dubious motives and connections. In the spring of 1996, researchers found in the Federal Archives in Bern a report that Repond had prepared on his treatment of Edda. Repond wrote:

> It is certain that, from the psychiatric point of view, the Mussolini family suffered from hereditary weakness. Mussolini himself was always a nervous, impulsive, voluble, emotive, very suggestible person and, at the same time, a great persuader. For almost all his life he suffered from hypochondria, in particular from a nervous condition in his stomach and intestines . . . His wife Donna Rachele, according to what the daughter says, was not the anonymous, patient and submissive woman whom legend has portrayed . . . In the family, she ridiculed her husband constantly, injured him, treated him as an imbecile, as an idiot, as a coward in front of the children and the servants. Her hands on her hips, she shouted at him at the top of her voice. Once Signora Ciano came to find her father ill with influenza, and her mother began to scream from the stairs: "You should see him, this poor old man, how beautiful he is in pajamas and how he chases any skirt whatsoever."

Repond went on to say that Edda was a delicate child, her health a constant worry to her parents. He described her as being subject to neuropathic disturbances, hypochondria and physiological ills owing to a poor state of health. She often suffered from insomnia and blamed that on her father, tracing it back to the nights when he played his violin beside her crib, hoping to lull her to sleep, and the nights when he took her with him to his newspaper while she was still very young.

"Edda seems to have taken from her father also a good number of digestive disturbances," Repond wrote. "She has a capricious, irregular appetite, alternating periods of not eating with bulimic phases . . . headaches, migraines, feelings of fatigue and exhaustion. But it is above all on the psychological plane that Edda shows the most marked anomalies: unstable, impulsive, alternating periods of depression and of euphoria, flights from reality. She subordinates reasoning and judgment to her emotional phases . . . In substance, despite a fine, cultivated, lucid and acute intelligence: a great neuropathy."

Edda told Repond she had been a difficult child who rebelled against her mother. Rachele, she said, responded by slapping her and hitting her with a broom. Later, she asked to be sent to school in Florence to get away from the tempestuous family atmosphere. Her parents, she said, had the habit of making her the witness and arbiter of their marital disputes. Then Repond delved into Edda's sexuality, and found a previously unknown key to her marital difficulties. As a young woman, she confessed to him, she experienced "an absolutely profound disgust for all sexual matters, reinforced by the exhibition of the marital miseries between her parents."

"The union with Galeazzo Ciano was quite a long way from being happy. Edda was absolutely frigid," he wrote. He recounted the story of how she had resisted Ciano on the first night of their marriage, adding:

> And she did not calm down afterward, but violently resisted all the marital advances of her husband, as she did also later those of other men. The coldness of this lady, her inability to love normally, to give herself, was the ruin of her existence and the principal cause of her bad reputation. In effect, not letting herself go with men beyond simple flirts, she did not think it in the least necessary to worry about appearances when these did not hide anything serious or effective. But people didn't think in the same way and the fact that she put herself on show without discretion, with great intimacy, together with numerous men earned her the fame of having had all of them as lovers. So much so that Edda had a particular inclination, a kind of taste, for types who were anything but austere, the Don Giovanni sort. She knew she was protected by her coldness against all their offers.

Repond said that, when Edda arrived at his clinic, she fell into a serious physical and moral depression. "She blamed herself for not having been the woman Ciano would have wanted, the one he would have needed," Repond wrote. "And she asked herself if she had made him unhappy, if she should not have behaved differently, had more patience and understanding."[44]

Edda happened to turn on her radio on April 28, and heard the news that her father had been killed and his body displayed in the Piazzale Loreto in Milan. Ten days earlier, he had left Lake Garda for Milan, against the wishes of his German guards. From there, undecided what to do, he made his way up the west side of Lake Como, apparently hoping to get into Switzerland. But Italian frontier guards deserted to the partisans and blocked that route. He finally joined a passing group of German soldiers who hoped the partisans would allow them to cross into Austria. Mussolini disguised himself in a Luftwaffe greatcoat and helmet, but partisans stopped the column at Dongo near the head of the lake. Mussolini's presence was discovered, and the partisans summarily shot him, along with Clara Petacci. Their bodies, and those of Pavolini, Buffarini, Farinacci and Starace, were thrown into a truck and taken to Milan, where they were strung up by the heels near a gas station. When Edda heard the news, she turned to Fabrizio and embraced him. Neither spoke. Many years later she said of her father: "I hated him, I really hated him. I believe you can really hate only a person you have loved. And when I saw him, my father and all the others hanging in that barbarous way at the gas station in the Piazzale Loreto in Milan, I said to myself: 'It was the final act of love of the Italians for him.'"[45] Repond's report said Edda swore to him she would never forgive her father for having let her husband be shot. But he said, "In reality Edda remained profoundly attached to her father. Even if she maintains that his tragic end has struck her less than that of her husband, she remained totally upset by it." The psychiatrist added this pompous coda: "One can perhaps hope that the influence of this catastrophe on her character will be lasting and will lead her, in a certain measure, to improve her character and attitudes."

Edda's continuing presence in Switzerland was a source of concern to the Swiss government. Leland Harrison had informed the State Department in a cable shortly after her arrival that the decision to admit her had been "generally viewed by Swiss public as a matter of regret and [her] tolerance on Swiss territory as a necessary evil."[46] Over the succeeding months, the publicity she attracted fed public discontent to the point that the Swiss had told her she must leave. "Why is a mystery," she wrote in a letter to Dulles in June 1945. "My government has not asked for me. I have never in my life done anything against the Swiss. Anyway, if they send me back to Italy I'll know the meaning of death soon enough."[47] The Swiss waited until passions had cooled somewhat, then served her with an expulsion order on August 27, 1945, telling her she must leave within forty-eight hours. Her children were permitted to stay, and Edda left them in the charge of a Frau Schwarz, a Swiss nanny who had worked for the family in Rome. She gave her wristwatch to Raimonda, embraced the children and departed with an American colonel, who put her in an armored car and drove her to Milan. The Italians brought four charges against Edda, only three of which she could later remember: Actions in favor of fascism; persecution of Jews; contributing to the unleashing of the war. For such crimes, she was treated more leniently than might have been expected. She was sentenced to two years' confinement on the fourteen-square-mile island of Lipari off the northern coast of Sicily, the same island her father had used to exile his political opponents. Edda had come home not to the death she anticipated but to the true aftermath of her tragedy, the beginning of a long, solitary remembering.

Epilogue

On the sunny spring morning of April 11, 1995, several hundred people filled the modern Roman church of the Sacred Immaculate Heart of Mary in the exclusive Parioli quarter, to pay their respects to Edda Mussolini Ciano. She had died two days earlier, aged eighty-five, in a Rome clinic of a kidney blockage. She had suffered a long illness, moving only between her bed and an armchair, attended by two servants. At the funeral there were the usual family members sitting in the front rows. Government officials, politicians, the few surviving friends of her youth and journalists occupied the remainder of the seats. Susanna Agnelli came later, after the crowd had departed. For a half century after the fall of fascism, Edda had been the most prominent link with its history, even if she herself had shown no interest in politics after World War II. To the old Fascists who had come to mourn her, it mattered not. They had always called her *Eccellenza*, an honorific normally reserved for government ministers, ambassadors and bishops. When the service was over, they filed out of the church, stood on the steps and proudly, in contravention of the law, gave the Fascist salute. It was not so much a salute to Edda as to Il Duce. She might have broken with him, reviled and cursed him, but she was still a Mussolini and that was all that mattered. They loved Edda or, more to the point, what she had once stood for, and a few of them shed a tear for her and their own youthful past. Her niece Alessandra Mussolini, by then a politician with the neo-Fascist Italian Social Movement, paid tribute to Edda after her death. "She was strong like a man," Alessandra said. "And like a man she faced the tragedies of her life." She said Edda's life had been like a fable, "but instead it was history, lived in the first person by a woman outside the machinations of her time. I learned dignity and courage from her." Politically, she said, Edda did not really belong to the right wing, "in the sense that she was beyond definitions. Her characteristic was pride."[1]

Except for the stray cats and dogs that became one of the passions of her later years, Edda lived alone in the half century that remained to her after the execution of her husband. For a long time she had a lover, a colorful Neapolitan jeweler named Pietro Capuano, who was better known by his nickname of Chanteclair. A few years older than Edda, and a lifelong bachelor, he had first met her when she stayed on Capri before the war and they had then become lovers. When she returned to Capri after the war and renewed her relationship with him, they used to swim at noon every day in the waters of the Green Grotto. Chanteclair also arranged parties and banquets to keep Edda entertained, and Noel Coward was a frequent guest.[2]

Shortly after her arrival on Lipari, she gave interviews on September 20 and 21, 1945, to two Italian and three American journalists. She mentioned that she had been reading Pucci's account of Ciano's last days and her escape to Switzerland, in which he had disguised Beetz as "Signor X." Edda kept up the deception: "Signor X is a German who is now in an Allied concentration camp and the Allies know his name," she said. "He is perhaps the one German who is human." In the interviews she referred often to Ciano and expressed her love and admiration for him. Jader Jacobelli, a correspondent for *Il Giornale del Mattino* in Rome, wrote: "We all asked ourselves why this woman, who for so many years openly showed extraordinary indifference to the conjugal bonds, should now instead be so bound up by his memory. Was this a true sentiment or only pretence?"[3] Although she had been sentenced to two years' confinement, she was released on July 2, 1946, after spending less than a year there. She kept up a correspondence with Pucci throughout her stay on Lipari, and rumors that they would marry persisted until 1947. Pucci himself had returned to Italy, after some difficulty caused by the fact he was AWOL from the Italian air force. The Italian air attaché in Bern told him members of the Italian Legation were quite pessimistic about his chances of escaping arrest if he returned to Italy. The attaché, Major Elbano Ghiglia, thought there were only two possibilities: a statement by some Allied authority that Pucci had been working for them, or an Allied declaration that his return to Italy would be useful to them. Pucci appealed to his former classmate Cornelia Dodson for help, and she enlisted the aid of Dulles, who intervened with Italian authorities to enable Pucci to go home. He embarked soon afterward on the career as a fashion designer that was to make him world famous, but the going initially was rough. Count Bartolommeo Attolico, son of the former ambassador to Germany, remembers Pucci trying to sell him a bathing suit on Capri. "Pucci hadn't a penny to his name," he said.[4] Later, after he had become famous, Pucci entered politics and was for a time a Liberal Party Member of Parliament.

Within days of Edda's release, her children were driven to the Italian border and handed over to Ciano's mother, who took them to her home at Ponte a Moriano where Edda was waiting. According to Fabrizio, the family's finances were initially precarious, since the Badoglio government had sequestrated much of Ciano's property, including his interest in *Il Telegrafo* of Livorno, his houses in Livorno and Ponte a Moriano and the two apartments on Via Angelo Secchi in Rome. Edda was left with her villa on Capri. She also owned ninety-five apartments in Rome which Ciano had not listed among his holdings when he tried to counter the charges that he had enriched himself. The family lived from the produce of five hundred acres of farmland that Ciano's mother owned. Edda made occasional trips to Rome to try to obtain the return of some of the family property, and was given hospitality by two old friends, Princess Lola Giovinelli and Marchioness Delia Di Bagno. Most of her other friends had deserted her. The Rev. Jean Charles-Roux, a Catholic priest and son of the wartime French ambassador to the Holy See, saw Edda walking up the Via Sistina in Rome one day, and noticed that a couple who knew her well crossed the street so as not to have to shake hands with her. "I did the opposite," he said.[5]

The relationship between Carolina Ciano and Edda, never very good, did not improve while they lived together. Fabrizio recalled one evening when Carolina said to Edda: "And stop looking at me with those Mussolini eyes." A chill went through the room. Then Edda got up, said, "Please excuse me," and left the room. Carolina died in 1959 at the age of eighty-four. Eventually Edda was given back the apartments in Rome, which were now in bad condition. She restored them and gave a cocktail party for five hundred people to celebrate. "Everyone came, including those who until then had not sought our company or had absolutely snubbed us," Fabrizio said.[6]

Rachele Mussolini and her other children were interned on the island of Ischia after the war. "It was like being confined in paradise," said Romano.[7] The Cianos saw them for the first time in 1947 when they were allowed to go to Ischia for a visit. Edda and her mother embraced, but their differences remained. The journalist Anita Pensotti was present at one meeting that went on until 3 a.m., each of the women defending her own man. "Mamma, Galeazzo was in good faith," Edda pleaded. "Otherwise he wouldn't have returned home to sleep. He could have escaped . . ." But Rachele, head down and arms crossed on the table, remained obdurate, repeating often: "Yes, yes, but he wanted to make him [Mussolini] lose his post . . ." Rachele died in 1980.[8]

Edda later sold the two apartments in Rome and rented a more modest, two-bedroom apartment, also in Parioli. She lived there with two servants, one an Italian woman who served her for forty years. She also had two Siamese cats and a Yorkshire terrier. She was no longer rich, but she was able to live in reasonable comfort. She drank heavily—gin was her preferred tipple—and had a circle of women friends from the old days with whom she liked to play backgammon and canasta. "She had a sort of court," said Romano Mussolini. "I went to her when I wanted a good meal because she always ate well. She had a lot of friends, many of them in the nobility. And she had a mania for stray cats and dogs."[9] Her friend Countess Marozia Borromeo d'Adda said, "She had very little money. I don't say she lived in poverty, but near it. We used to play gin rummy, and we always tried not to let her lose." She said Edda's neighbors were often furious over her attention to stray animals. "Cats from all over the neighborhood were going to eat at Edda's," she said.[10]

In fact Edda was not as hard up as the countess supposed. She traveled widely, making several trips to Kenya and at least one to Argentina. She had a state pension of only about $2,000 a month, but she had income from her property holdings. Father Charles-Roux said Edda, who had prided herself on her dress sense when she was young, never dressed well or appeared elegant after the war. "She was an intelligent woman and well read," he said. "She didn't like cheap behavior, not because of moral principles but because she thought that if you do a thing, you must do it with style. She was certainly attached to Galeazzo, and they were a team. Their separate romances never broke the link between them."[11] Whether she was happy in her later years is debatable. The neurosis that Repond had diagnosed in Switzerland was something she never overcame. "She had a great sense of humor, and sometimes she was very nice," said one woman who knew her. "The next day, she would act as if she didn't know who you were." She was certainly lonely, sometimes keeping a relative on the phone for as long as eight hours as she rambled on about mundane matters. But Marozia Borromeo, who had found her "a bit sharp" in her younger years, said she became much milder after the war.[12] The film producer Dino De Laurentiis offered Edda money for a movie about her life and that of her husband, but she refused it with indignation. De Laurentiis went ahead and made the film, with Silvana Mangano playing Edda, and Edda paid a famous lawyer a large amount of money in an unsuccessful attempt to prevent it being shown. She said the film contained a series of historical errors and arbitrary interpretations of some episodes of her private life.

A few years before her death, Edda attended a memorial Mass for her father, and she kept prominently displayed in her apartment three large bronze plaques bearing his image in bas-relief. She also treasured a photo of him on which he had written "To Edda, with love, Papa–1930." In her memoirs, she partially absolved him of responsibility for the death of her husband. She said he was not directly involved at the beginning in the decision to try Ciano, but followed a policy of noninterference, either because of a lack of courage or a fatalistic attitude. She maintained he would have intervened to spare the men at Verona if he could have, but said the Fascists undoubtedly would have killed them even if Mussolini had pardoned them. "At a certain moment, because of a mysterious conjunction of circumstances, my husband's doom became inescapable, and I believe that he would have died whatever my father's attitude had been," she wrote.[13] She made a visit once each year to Mussolini's tomb at Predappio, and she once told her parish priest: "I feel no resentment toward my father Benito. Rather, I owe him my gratitude."[14] Souvenirs of Ciano were less in evidence in her apartment than those of Mussolini. The most noticeable was a framed photograph of him as a young man in naval uniform. At her death Edda left a diary which might have been of considerable historical value, but it was destroyed by a member of her family.

The Ciano children bore, in later years, the effects of the terrible trauma they had suffered in early life. Their personal lives were chaotic and often unhappy, and remain so for the two who survive. Politically, all three gave their allegiance to the Italian Social Movement, the successor to Mussolini's Fascist Party, despite the fact it was Fascists who killed their father. One person who knows them claims all three eventually came to the conclusion that the verdict of the Verona tribunal was correct. This cannot be confirmed with the principals, for they declined to cooperate in the research for this book.

Raimonda was married in October 1952 to Sandro Giunta, the son of Francesco Giunta who had been secretary of the National Fascist Party under Mussolini. When Edda entered the church the crowd applauded, drawing a rebuke from the officiating priest who said only the Pope should be applauded in church. Raimonda and her husband went to live in Brazil, where the Giunta family owned land, but the marriage lasted only seven years and produced no children. After their divorce, she returned to Rome where, in 1999, she was living alone in poor health.

By his own account, Fabrizio became a feckless young man. He studied law, but did not like university, preferring nightclubs, travel and sports. Finally, in a moment of rebellion, he threw his law books into the sea at Capri and announced that he was finished with university. Edda insisted he resume his studies and sent him to a university in Switzerland, but he spent more time with girls, at nightclubs and on sail boats, than in classes.

When he came back to Italy, Edda resorted to a measure that parents everywhere use to try to make a man of a difficult child: she made Fabrizio enlist in the army. He served his term of enlistment, but didn't like it, and afterward worked for a shoe polish manufacturer in Milan. In Italy's 1958 national election, Fabrizio decided to become a candidate of the neo-Fascist Movimento Sociale Italiano in Livorno, which had not elected a right-wing candidate since 1922. Almost all the top MSI officials tried to dissuade him, and the party would give him no funding for what was regarded as a hopeless candidacy. But Fabrizio spent a lot of his own money on what proved a more difficult campaign than he expected. Often rocks were thrown at him as he made speeches, and sometimes he had to flee hostile crowds. Despite that, he came within a few votes of being elected. The first tally showed him to be the winner, but in a recount he lost. "I realized bitterly that politics was more complicated and less honest than one could imagine," he wrote. "And from that time I never voted again."[15] But he did not give up politics immediately. The MSI sent him on a mission to Spain to get money from Franco, and later on a similar mission to Morocco. In 1960 he was present when the MSI tried to hold a national convention in Genoa, a stronghold of anti-fascism. Clashes broke out, and eventually the party was forced to cancel the convention. Fabrizio, now nearly thirty years old, abandoned politics and started looking for a job. He admitted he only enjoyed having a good time. "It is possible, rather I am fairly certain of it," he wrote, "that that constant search for pleasure, stimulated by a disquieting sense of dissatisfaction, had its roots in the traumas that had scarred and conditioned my early years."[16] He fell in love with a girl whom he identified in his memoirs only as Patrizia, and a wedding was planned for October. But as the great day approached, Fabrizio panicked. He decided not merely to abandon his fiancée but to flee Italy. He obtained a large sum of money from the family administrator, took a train to Geneva, flew from there to New York and continued to Caracas, where he had a number of friends. Italian newspapers speculated he had been kidnaped or committed suicide. A month later he was recognized, newspapers reported his whereabouts and photographers descended on Caracas. Fabrizio fled to Panama, Guatemala, Hawaii and then Tahiti. There he remained for a year, and acquired four native "wives."[17] At the end of the year, he returned to Caracas, where he invested in a factory making zippers. When the business failed, he went to work in a bank and recouped his fortunes. At that point, Fabrizio's story became entwined in a bizarre way with that of his brother.

Marzio was the most tragic figure among the Ciano children, an intelligent man who never worked, frittered his life away and died of alcoholism at age thirty-seven in 1974. He was regarded by many acquaintances as the brightest of the three children, and certainly the most spirited. That was apparent from an early age. When he was five years old, he accompanied his parents and his siblings to the Vatican for Ciano's presentation of credentials to Pope Pius. While the Pope was speaking, Marzio was attracted by the gold phone on the Pope's desk and made a grab for it. The Pope broke off speaking and tried to take it away from him. For a few seconds, the child and the Roman pontiff waged a tug of war for the telephone that ended with Edda's energetic intervention and with Ciano directing thunderous looks at Marzio. When Marzio was twenty-three years old he went with a group of friends into a bar in a Communist area of Pesaro, a city on the Adriatic coast where he studied for a time to be an agronomist. The bar was full of truck drivers, some of them reading *L'Unità*, the Communist newspaper. In a loud voice, he announced he was buying beer for the house "in honor of my grandfather." The truck drivers appreciatively raised their glasses: "Here's to your grandfather." By the third round one of them asked who his grandfather was. Marzio and his friends moved to the door and as he went out he called: "My grandfather was Mussolini. Thanks and so long, everyone."[18] Earlier, when the Cianos moved back into their apartment in the Via Angelo Secchi, Marzio had discovered a telephone that had a direct line to his father's old office in the Palazzo Chigi. No one had thought to remove it. The palazzo was now the office of the prime minister, who at that time was Amintore Fanfani. Marzio delighted in picking up the receiver and saying: "Hello. Am I speaking with His Excellency Ciano?" This went on until technicians arrived one day to take out the line.[19] Marzio married a beautiful Sicilian woman, Gloria Lucchesi, in 1964. They had two sons, Pier Francesco and Lorenzo, but Marzio's steady consumption of vodka and his idleness took their toll on the marriage. It was during one particularly rocky patch in 1969 that Fabrizio returned to Italy, met his sister-in-law for the first time and proceeded to seduce her. She later told a friend, with a bitter laugh: "If I could go back in time, I would kill him."[20] But at the time, Gloria was swept off her feet. Fabrizio persuaded her to return to Venezuela with him, and they lived together for three years. It was an increasingly difficult relationship, and finally Gloria returned to Rome and her husband in 1972. Marzio's life was ebbing away, however, and he died of cirrhosis of the liver in 1974. His sons were then nine and twelve years old. They are the only grandchildren of Galeazzo Ciano and Edda.

Not surprisingly, Fabrizio made no mention in his memoirs of his affair with Gloria. He continued living in Venezuela, and in 1977 he suffered a heart attack but survived. In that year, Edda visited the Dominican Republic and met with President Balaguer to request a residence permit, which she received within twenty-four hours. Edda told Fabrizio the political situation in Italy had grown precarious and she faced threats of sequestration. But she did not remain long in Santo Domingo. On October 16, 1981, at the age of fifty, Fabrizio finally married. He and his bride, Beatriz Uzcategui, moved to Costa Rica and he opened a factory that produced insect repellents. His memoirs, entitled *Quando Il Nonno Fece Fucilare Papa*, (When Grandfather Had Papa Shot) was published in Italy in 1993. Edda considered the title, chosen by the publisher Mondadori, in the worst possible taste, but she made her last public appearance at a book launch party out of solidarity with Fabrizio. She confined herself to saying she had rediscovered, with the passage of years, her love for her father. In his book, Fabrizio put primary responsibility for the death of his father on Pavolini, but answered in the affirmative his own question of whether Mussolini shared responsibility. "Even if the requests [for pardon] had arrived, he would have rejected them," Fabrizio wrote. "Therefore the one who permitted, rather wanted, the Verona trial and the consequent executions, was the head of the Italian Social Republic, my grandfather Benito Mussolini." He added that Mussolini, to recover credibility in the eyes of republican Fascists, allowed five persons, including his son-in-law, to die in the name of "reasons of state." But, like Edda, he had forgiven the crime, if crime he considered it. "Today I don't hate anyone," he said. "This, for what concerns my grandfather." But he said he would not be pleased to run into Nino Furlotti, who not only fired the coup de grâce into his father's right temple but boasted of it years later "as of a heroic, glorious gesture."[21] Hildegard Beetz, born Burkhardt at Obernissa near Weimar in 1919, lost her husband when he was killed on the Russian front in the closing months of the war. Later she married an American lieutenant, a counterespionage officer named Harry Dax, but that marriage ended in divorce. In 1951 she became the wife of a German, Dr Karl Heinz Purwin, but was later widowed. One of Ciano's biographers, Duilio Susmel, traced her to Bonn in the 1960s and she agreed, after strong initial resistance, to talk about her experiences with Ciano. Nothing more was heard of her until early 1996 when two reporters from the Italian magazine *Gente* traced her to "a European town," which they agreed not to name, and found her living under a false name, Hilde Neimann. "She lives in a decorous two-story villa, surrounded by a small garden," they reported. "She leads an anonymous existence as a quiet pensioner. She is alone and sick."[22] All her memories of Ciano that were reported in *Gente* are contained in earlier chapters of this book.

In Verona, memories of Ciano have faded. A plaque marks the site of the Scalzi Prison where he was held, a site now largely occupied by a modern bank. Across the street, there is a statue of Don Chiot, the prison chaplain who witnessed his execution. Unsurprisingly, there is no mention of Galeazzo Ciano.

Notes

Chapter One : Galeazzo and Edda

1. Edda Ciano, My Truth, pp. 60–3.
2. Edvige Mussolini, Mio fratello Benito, pp. 124–5.
3. Dino Biondi, La fabbrica del Duce, p. 212.
4. Renzo De Felice, Mussolini Il Duce, pp. 534–96.
5. Captured Italian archives in the U.S. National Archives, T586, Roll 456, Nos. 029681 and 029682.
6. Edvige Mussolini, op. cit, pp. 121–2.
7. Edda Ciano, op. cit., pp. 58–9.
8. Edvige Mussolini, op. cit., p.123.
9. Giordano Bruno Guerri, Galeazzo Ciano, p. 45.
10. Edda Ciano, op. cit., p. 51.
11. Ibid.
12. Guerri, op. cit., p. 15.
13. Edda Ciano, op. cit., p. 51.
14. Guerri, op. cit., p. 28.
15. Ibid., p. 13.
16. Interview with the author.
17. Guerri, op. cit., p. 43.
18. Ibid., p. 44.
19. Guerri, op. cit., p. 58, and Edda Ciano, op. cit., pp. 54–5.
20. Edda Ciano, op. cit., p. 68.
21. Duilio Susmel, Vita sbagliata di Galeazzo Ciano, p. 33.
22. Edvige Mussolini, op. cit., pp. 124–5.
23. Gaetano Afeltra, La spia che amo' Ciano, p. 137.
24. Anita Pensotti, Rachele, p. 53.
25. Interview with the author.
26. Eugen Dollmann, The Interpreter, p. 182.
27. Antonio Spinosa, Edda: una tragedia italiana, pp. 15–16.
28. Edda Ciano, op. cit., pp. 68–9.
29. Ibid., pp. 61–3.
30. Ibid., pp. 68–9.
31. Interview with the author.
32. Edda Ciano, op. cit., pp. 65–7.
33. Afeltra, op. cit., p. 142.
34. Edda Ciano, op. cit., pp. 65–7.

Chapter Two : Diplomat to Bomber Pilot

1. Susmel, op. cit., p. 32.
2. Guerri, op. cit., p. 60.
3. Roberto Ducci, La bella gioventu', pp. 143–4.
4. Edda Ciano, op. cit., p. 119.
5. Ibid., p. 50.
6. Ibid., pp. 75–6.
7. Pensotti, op. cit., p. 69.
8. Edda Ciano, op. cit., p. 72.
9. Orio Vergani, Ciano, una lunga confessione, p. 36.
10. Susmel, op. cit., pp. 49–51.
11. Vittorio Mussolini, Voli sulle ambe, p. 48.
12. Guerri, op. cit., p. 112.
13. Alessandro Lessona, Memorie, pp. 239–40.
14. Susmel, op. cit., pp. 52.
15. Captured Italian archives in the U.S. National Archives, T586, Job No. 104, Bag 29, Roll 453, No. 028387.

16. Ibid., No. 028388.
17. Ibid., No. 028392.
18. Guerri, op. cit., p. 132.
19. Vergani, op. cit., p. 44.
20. Susmel, op. cit., pp. 53–4.

Chapter Three : Europe's Youngest Foreign Minister

1. Unpublished memoirs of Marcello del Drago, made available by his widow, Cyprienne Charles-Roux del Drago. These memoirs were written in English and are a rich source of observations about Ciano.
2. Guerri, op. cit., p. 61.
3. Dino Grandi, Il mio paese, pp. 410–13.
4. Vergani, op. cit., pp. 43–4.
5. Susmel, op. cit., p.120.
6. Galeazzo Ciano, Ciano's Diary 1939–43. Welles, wrote the introduction to the English edition of the diary, pp. ix–x.
7. Malcolm Muggeridge, Ciano's Diary 1939–43. Muggeridge wrote the preface to the diary, pp. xvii–xviii.
8. Galeazzo Ciano, Diario 1937–1938, pp. 79–80.
9. Dino Alfieri, Due dittatori di fronte, p. 269.
10. Vergani, op. cit., p. 118.
11. Galeazzo Ciano, Diario 1937–1938, pp. 20–1.
12. Ibid., pp. 70, 102, 136–7, 172.
13. Ibid., pp. 206, 70, 156, 253, 282, 37–59–61, 97, 101, 8.
14. Ibid., pp. 7, 121, 133 and 207. And from the 1939–43 diary, p. 46.
15. Guerri, op. cit., pp. 178–80, and Susmel, op. cit., pp. 77–9.
16. Galeazzo Ciano, Ciano's Diary 1939–43, from Welles's introduction, p. ix.
17. William Phillips, Ventures in Diplomacy, p. 225.
18. Alfieri, op. cit., pp. 259–61.
19. Roberto Cantalupo, Fu la Spagna, p. 56.
20. Guerri, op. cit., 239.
21. Edda Ciano, op. cit., p. 119.
22. Ibid., pp. 121–2.
23. Susmel, op. cit., p. 57.
24. Spinosa, op. cit., p. 185.
25. Susmel, op. cit., p. 58.
26. Ibid., p. 64.

27. Ibid., pp. 65–6.
28. Ibid., p. 64.
29. Ibid., pp. 65–6.
30. Filippo Anfuso, Da Palazzo Venezia al Lago di Garda, p. 30.
31. Susmel, op. cit., p. 67.
32. Elisabetta Cerruti, Ambassador's Wife, p. 230.
33. Phillips, op. cit., p. 218.
34. Ibid., p. 198.
35. Del Drago, unpublished memoirs.
36. Giuseppe Bastianini, Uomini, cose, fatti, pp. 237–8.
37. Cerruti, op. cit., p. 229.
38. Cantalupo, op. cit., pp. 52–3.
39. Mario Donosti (pseudonym of the diplomat Mario Luciolli), Mussolini e l'-Europa, pp. 86–7.
40. Galeazzo Ciano, Diario 1939–1943, pp. 40–41.
41. Guido Leto, OVRA fascismo-antifascismo, pp. 176–8.
42. Ibid., p. 178.
43. Renzo De Felice, Mussolini il duce, Vol. 2, p. 270.
44. Ibid., p. 289.
45. Galeazzo Ciano, Ciano's Diary 1939–43, from Welles's introduction, p. xii.
46. Charles F. Delzell, Mussolini's Enemies, and Ernesto Rossi, No al fascismo. Rossi's book contains a lengthy chapter by Professor Gaetano Salvemini on the Rosselli case.
47. Guerri, op. cit., p. 251.
48. Rossi, op. cit., p. 281.
49. Giacomo Carboni, Memorie segrete, pp. 62, 144–5.

Chapter Four : Ciano and the Germans

1. Cantalupo, op. cit., pp. 63 and 261.
2. Galeazzo Ciano, Diario 1937–1938, p. 23; Diario 1939–1943, p. 138, Vol. 2.
3. Edda Ciano, op. cit., pp. 151–4.
4. Interview with the author.
5. Susmel, op. cit., p. 73.
6. Giuseppe Bottai, Diario 1935–1944, p. 112.
7. Anfuso, op. cit., p. 36.
8. Yvon De Begnac, Palazzo Venezia, p. 592.

9. Bottai, op. cit., p. 120.
10. Ibid., p. 120.
11. Galeazzo Ciano, *Diario 1937–1938*, pp. 45–6.
12. Ibid., pp. 69–70.
13. Ibid., p. 11.
14. Interview with the author.
15. Fey von Hassell, *A Mother's War*, p. 44.
16. Interview with the author.
17. Galeazzo Ciano, *Diario 1937-1938*, pp. 120–21.
18. Ibid., p. 106.
19. Ibid., p. 30, Vol. 2.
20. Guerri, op. cit., p. 331.
21. Interview with the author.
22. Michael Bloch, *Ribbentrop*, pp. 140–41.
23. Lord Vansittart, *The Mist Procession*, p. 524.
24. Guerri, op. cit., p. 334.
25. Galeazzo Ciano, *Diario 1939–1943*, p. 152.
26. Guerri, op. cit., p. 284.
27. Spinosa, op. cit., p. 312.
28. Galeazzo Ciano, *Diario 1937–1938*, p. 117.
29. Sumner Welles, *The Time for Decision*, p. 81.
30. Paul Schmidt, *Hitler's Interpreter*, pp. 83–4.
31. Galeazzo Ciano, *Ciano's Diary 1937–1938*, p. 168.
32. Ibid., p. 169.
33. Ibid., p. 171.
34. Ibid., p. 190–91.
35. Susmel, op. cit., pp. 100–101.
36. Bottai, op. cit., pp. 121–2.
37. Susmel, op. cit., p. 105.
38. Ibid., p. 104.
39. Galeazzo Ciano, *Ciano's Diary 1937–1938*, p. 247.
40. Phillips, op. cit., p. 220.
41. Donosti, op. cit., p. 120.
42. Galeazzo Ciano, *Ciano's Diary 1937–1938*, p. 251.
43. Ibid., p. 253.
44. Ibid., p. 254.
45. Ibid., p. 279.
46. Susmel, op. cit., p. 112.
47. Ibid.
48. Ibid., p. 113.
49. Donosti, op. cit., p. 136.
50. Denis Mack Smith, *Mussolini*, pp. 256–8.

51. Glauco Buffarini Guidi, *La vera verita'*, p. 29.
52. Mack Smith, op. cit., p. 363.
53. Galeazzo Ciano, *Diario 1937–1938*, p. 54.
54. Meir Michaelis, *Mussolini and the Jews*, p. 136.
55. Phillips, op. cit., p. 223.
56. Galeazzo Ciano, *Diario 1937–1938*, p. 13.
57. Ibid., pp. 61–2.
58. Ibid., p. 107.
59. Letter to the author.
60. Michele Sarfatti, *Mussolini contro gli ebrei*, pp. 17–18.
61. Michaelis, op. cit., p. 131.
62. Phillips, op. cit., p. 223.
63. Galeazzo Ciano, *Diario 1937–1938*, p. 235.
64. Ibid.
65. Ibid., p. 290–91.
66. Edda Ciano, op. cit., p. 70.

Chapter Five : War in Albania

1. Galeazzo Ciano, *Diario 1939–1943*, p. 58.
2. Ibid., p. 52.
3. Ibid., p. 56.
4. Ibid., p. 60.
5. Ibid.
6. Ibid., pp. 61–2.
7. Ibid., pp. 62–3.
8. Guerri, op. cit., p. 369.
9. Ibid., op. cit., p. 363.
10. Ibid., p. 365.
11. Donosti, op.cit., pp. 157–8.
12. Mack Smith, *Mussolini's Roman Empire*, p. 150.
13. Galeazzo Ciano, *Diario 1937–1938*, p. 278.
14. Susmel, op. cit., pp. 116–17.
15. This was an entry of Dec. 1, 1938, in Ciano's diary that was omitted from the Italian and English editions published after the war. The Italian magazine *Epoca* reported the missing sentence on August 9, 1953.
16. Galeazzo Ciano, *Diario 1939–1943*, p. 305.
17. Ibid., pp. 66–7.
18. Ibid., pp. 66–7.

19. Ibid., pp. 44–5.
20. Donosti, op. cit., p. 159.
21. Susmel, op. cit., p. 135.
22. Guerri, op. cit., p. 382.
23. Ibid., p. 398.
24. Galeazzo Ciano, *Diario 1939–1943*, p. 78. Unless otherwise marked, all subsequent references are to the 1939–43 diary in two volumes. Vol. 2 references are so indicated.
25. Donosti, op. cit., p. 167.
26. Guerri, op. cit., pp. 387–8.
27. Susmel, op. cit., pp. 139.
28. Ibid., p. 140.
29. Leto, op. cit., p. 178.
30. Ibid., p. 197.
31. Emanuele Grazzi, *Il principio della fine*, p. 184.
32. Galeazzo Ciano, op. cit., p. 98.
33. Guerri, op. cit., p. 370.
34. Galeazzo Ciano, op. cit., pp. 202–3.

Chapter Six : An Open Marriage

1. Edda Ciano, op. cit., pp. 81–2.
2. Ducci, op. cit., pp. 144–5.
3. Cerruti, op. cit., p. 230.
4. Guerri, op. cit., p. 69.
5. Edda Ciano, op. cit., pp. 86–7.
6. Lord Vansittart, op. cit., p. 503.
7. Guerri, op. cit., p. 123.
8. Del Drago, op. cit., unpublished memoirs.
9. Agnelli, op. cit., pp. 70–71.
10. Dollmann, op. cit., pp. 104–5.
11. Ibid., p. 173.
12. Galeazzo Ciano, op. cit., Vol. 2, p. 83.
13. Curzio Malaparte, *Kaputt*, p. 444. This appears only in the Italian edition of the book.
14. Michael Sheridan, *Romans—Their Lives and Times*, Foreign Office dispatch cited on p. 103.
15. Edda Ciano, op. cit., p. 87.
16. Spinosa, op. cit., p. 187.
17. Malaparte, op. cit., pp. 453–4.
18. Vergani, op. cit., p. 57.
19. Malaparte, op. cit., p. 328.
20. Ibid., p. 331.
21. Cerruti, op. cit., pp. 232–3.
22. Edda Ciano, op. cit., p. 80.
23. Interview with the author.
24. Ducci, op. cit., p. 135.
25. Cerruti, op. cit., p. 231.
26. Edda Ciano, op. cit., p. 93.
27. Giorgio Nelson Page, *L'americano di Roma*, p. 475.

Chapter Seven : The Pact of Steel

1. Galeazzo Ciano, op. cit., p. 87.
2. Ibid., p. 90.
3. Susmel, op. cit., p. 127.
4. Ibid., p. 128.
5. Vergani, op. cit., pp. 76–7.
6. Susmel, op. cit., p. 146.
7. Donosti, op. cit., p. 202.
8. Susmel, op. cit., p. 147.
9. Donosti, op. cit., p. 183.
10. Cerruti, op. cit., p. 235.
11. Susmel, op. cit., p. 148.
12. Galeazzo Ciano, op. cit., pp. 103–4.
13. Ibid., p. 104.
14. Ibid.
15. Susmel, op. cit., p. 150.
16. Ibid.
17. Bastianini, op. cit., p. 253.
18. Galeazzo Ciano, op. cit., pp. 104–5.
19. Ibid.
20. Susmel, op. cit., pp. 156–7.
21. Sheridan, op. cit., p. 91.
22. *Newsweek*, March 6, 1939.
23. *Time*, July 24, 1939.
24. Captured Italian archives in the U.S. National Archives, T586, Roll 406, No. 865.002.
25. Susmel, op. cit., p. 158.
26. Galeazzo Ciano, op. cit., p. 132.
27. Ibid.
28. Ibid., p. 129.
29. Ibid., pp. 132–3.
30. Leonardo Losito, *Bernardo Attolico*, p. 123.
31. Bartolomeo Attolico, interview with the author.
32. Galeazzo Ciano, op. cit., pp. 135–6.
33. Ibid., pp. 136–7.
34. Ibid., p. 137.
35. Ibid.
36. Sheridan, op. cit., p. 91.
37. Susmel, op. cit., pp. 170–71.
38. Galeazzo Ciano, op. cit., pp. 137–8.
39. Ibid., p. 139.

Chapter Eight : The Invasion of Poland

1. Del Drago, unpublished memoirs.
2. Galeazzo Ciano, op. cit., p. 139.
3. Susmel, op. cit., pp. 164–5.
4. Del Drago, unpublished memoirs.
5. Susmel, op. cit., pp. 164–5.
6. Ibid., p. 165.
7. Schmidt, op. cit., p. 131.
8. Interview with the author. The source asked to remain anonymous.
9. Susmel, op. cit., pp. 165–6.
10. Galeazzo Ciano, op. cit., p.140.
11. Del Drago, unpublished memoirs.
12. Enrico Caviglia, *Diario*, p. 225.
13. William L. Shirer, *The Rise and Fall of the Third Reich*, p. 510.
14. Galeazzo Ciano, *Ciano's Diplomatic Papers*, pp. 296–304.
15. Dollmann, op. cit., pp. 166–7.
16. Del Drago, unpublished memoirs.
17. Nerin E. Gun, *Eva Braun: Hitler's Mistress*, pp. 158–9.
18. Galeazzo Ciano, *Diario 1939–1943*, pp. 140–41.
19. Melton Davis, *Who Defends Rome?*, p. 19
20. Del Drago, unpublished memoirs.
21. Schmidt, op. cit., pp. 132–3.
22. Dollmann, op. cit., p. 168.
23. Susmel, op. cit., pp. 168–9.
24. Galeazzo Ciano, op. cit., p. 141.
25. Del Drago, unpublished memoirs.
26. Susmel, op. cit., p. 170.
27. André François-Poncet, *Au Palais Farnese*, p. 127.
28. Vergani, op. cit., p. 80.
29. Galeazzo Ciano, op. cit., p. 146.
30. Donosti, op. cit., p. 209.
31. Galeazzo Ciano, op. cit., p. 146.
32. Ibid., pp. 146–7.
33. Donosti, op. cit., pp. 210, 212–13.
34. Galeazzo Ciano, op. cit., pp. 147–8.
35. Ibid., pp. 149–50.
36. Ibid., pp. 150–51.
37. Ibid., p. 152.
38. Bottai, op. cit., pp. 154–6.
39. François-Poncet, op. cit., p. 130.
40. Bottai, op. cit., pp. 154–6.
41. Del Drago, unpublished memoirs.
42. Ibid.
43. Susmel, op. cit., p. 176.
44. François-Poncet, op. cit., p. 130.
45. Bottai, op. cit., pp. 156–7.
46. Dino Grandi, *Il mio paese*, p. 545.
47. François-Poncet, op. cit., pp. 131–4.

Chapter Nine : The Break with Mussolini

1. Galeazzo Ciano, op. cit., pp. 202–3.
2. Bottai, op. cit., p. 161.
3. Susmel, op. cit., pp. 180–81.
4. Edda Ciano, op. cit., p. 157.
5. Galeazzo Ciano, op. cit., pp. 174–5.
6. Schmidt, op. cit., p. 165.
7. Susmel, op. cit., p. 182.
8. Galeazzo Ciano, op. cit., pp. 176–7.
9. Bottai, op. cit., p. 167.
10. Galeazzo Ciano, op. cit., p. 178.
11. Ibid., pp. 186, 189.
12. Ibid., p. 185.
13. Joseph Goebbels, *Goebbels' Diaries 1939–41*, p. 54.
14. Galeazzo Ciano, op. cit., pp. 193–4.
15. Susmel, op. cit., pp. 187–8.
16. Guerri, op. cit., p. 445.
17. Galeazzo Ciano, op. cit., pp. 198–9.
18. Phillips, op. cit., p. 249.
19. Goebbels, op. cit., p. 68.
20. Captured Italian archives in the U.S. National Archives, T586, Roll 405, Nos. 000443–000453.
21. Galeazzo Ciano, op. cit., p. 205.
22. John Colville, *The Fringes of Power*, p. 61.
23. Galeazzo Ciano, op. cit., p. 214.
24. Ibid., p. 219.
25. Ibid., p. 221.
26. Ibid.
27. Ibid., p. 224.
28. Ibid., p. 225.
29. Susmel, op. cit., p. 195.
30. Galeazzo Ciano, op. cit., pp. 227–8.
31. Welles, *The Time for Decision*, p. 282.
32. Galeazzo Ciano, *Ciano's Diary 1939–43*, from Welles's introduction, p. viii.
33. Galeazzo Ciano, op. cit., p. 229.
34. Ennio Di Nolfo, *Vaticano e Stati Uniti 1939–1952*, p. 105. This book is based on the diaries of Myron G. Taylor.
35. Galeazzo Ciano, op. cit., pp. 230–31.
36. Ibid., p. 232.
37. Ibid., p. 233.
38. Susmel, op. cit., p. 198.

39. Galeazzo Ciano, op. cit., p. 236.
40. Ibid., p. 237.
41. Ibid., pp. 237–8.
42. Welles, op. cit., pp. 135–6.
43. Galeazzo Ciano, op. cit., p. 239.
44. Welles, op. cit., pp. 143–4.
45. François-Poncet, op. cit., pp. 162, 166.
46. Galeazzo Ciano, op. cit., pp. 242–3.
47. Guerri, op. cit., p. 456.
48. Galeazzo Ciano, Diario 1939–1943, p. 245.
49. Ibid., p. 249.
50. Ibid., p. 250.
51. Ibid., pp. 250–51.
52. Ibid., p. 251.
53. Susmel, op. cit., pp. 205–6.
54. Ibid., p. 202.
55. Leto, op. cit., pp. 198–9.
56. Galeazzo Ciano, op. cit., pp. 252–3, 256.
57. Ibid., p. 259.
58. Ibid., pp. 253–4 and 256, and p. 109, Vol. 2.
59. Ibid., pp. 261–2.
60. François-Poncet, op. cit., pp. 170–71.
61. Anthony Cave Brown, Bodyguard of Lies, p. 198.
62. Galeazzo Ciano, op. cit., pp. 263–4.
63. Phillips, op. cit., p. 271.
64. Cordell Hull, Memoirs, Vol. 1, p. 780.
65. Galeazzo Ciano, op. cit., p. 264.
66. Ibid., p. 269.
67. Phillips, op. cit., pp. 276–7.
68. Pietro Badoglio, Italy in the Second World War, p. 15.
69. Sheridan, op. cit., p. 106.
70. Alexander Cadogan, The Diaries of Sir Alexander Cadogan 1938–1945, p. 292.
71. Galeazzo Ciano, op. cit., p. 273.
72. Susmel, op. cit., pp. 212–13.
73. Ibid., pp. 211–12.
74. Phillips, op. cit., p. 278.
75. François-Poncet, op. cit., pp. 16–17, 120.
76. Galeazzo Ciano, op. cit., p. 277.

Chapter Ten : Italy Enters the War

1. Marco Innocenti, L'Italia del 1940, pp. 13–34.
2. Galeazzo Ciano, op. cit., p. 272.
3. Susmel, op. cit., p. 214.

4. Galeazzo Ciano, op. cit., p. 278, and François-Poncet, op. cit., pp. 178–9.
5. Innocenti, op. cit., pp. 39–40.
6. Galeazzo Ciano, op. cit., p. 278.
7. Winston Churchill, War Speeches, Vol. 2.
8. Del Drago, unpublished memoirs.
9. Grandi, op. cit., p. 588.
10. Susmel, op. cit., pp. 215–16.
11. Galeazzo Ciano, op. cit., p. 279.
12. Ibid., p. 280.
13. Ibid.
14. Ibid., p. 281.
15. Innocenti, op. cit., pp. 54–55.
16. Ibid.
17. Galeazzo Ciano, op. cit., pp. 282–3.
18 Ibid., p. 289.
19. Bastianini, op. cit., pp. 149–50, 257.
20. Leonardo Simoni, Berlino ambasciata d'-Italia 1939–1943, pp. 141–2. Leonardo Simoni was the pseudonym of the diplomat Michele Lanza.
21. Galeazzo Ciano, op. cit., p. 291.
22. Susmel, op. cit., pp. 221–2.
23. F.W. Deakin, The Brutal Friendship, p. 11.
24. Simoni, op. cit., p. 146.
25. Marie Vassiltchikov, Berlin Diaries 1940–1945, p. 22.
26. Bottai, op. cit., p. 210.
27. Ibid., pp. 213–15.
28. Susmel, op. cit., p. 223.
29. Phillips, op. cit., p. 288.
30. William L. Shirer, The Nightmare Years, pp. 556–7, and Berlin Diary, p. 456.
31. Galeazzo Ciano, op. cit., pp. 297, 300.
32. Ibid., p. 294.
33. Bottai, op. cit., p. 216.
34. Susmel, op. cit., p. 227.
35. Galeazzo Ciano, op. cit., pp. 297, 299–300.

Chapter Eleven : Ciano's War: the Attack on Greece

1. Sheridan, op. cit., p. 90.
2. Galeazzo Ciano, op. cit., pp. 98–9.
3. Grazzi, op. cit., p. 100.
4. Grandi, op. cit.., p. 601.
5. Susmel, op. cit., pp. 209–11.
6. Innocenti, op. cit., p. 57.
7. Grazzi, op. cit., pp. 149–55, 173.
8. Anfuso, op. cit., p. 242.
9. Galeazzo Ciano, op. cit., pp. 303–4.

10. Ibid., pp. 308–9.
11. Simoni, op. cit., p. 170.
12. Susmel, op. cit., p. 231.
13. Bottai, op. cit., p. 221.
14. Raffaele Guariglia, *Ricordi*, p. 477.
15. Susmel, op. cit., p. 232.
16. Reynolds & Eleanor Packard, *Balcony Empire*, p. 115.
17. Galeazzo Ciano, op. cit., p. 314.
18. Badoglio, op. cit., p. 25.
19. Captured Italian archives in the U.S. National Archives, T586, Roll 406, Nos. 10004–18.
20. Galeazzo Ciano, op. cit., Vol. 2, p. 17.
21. Galeazzo Ciano, op. cit., pp. 315–16.
22. Ibid., p. 317.
23. Bastianini, op. cit., pp. 257–8.
24. Bottai, op. cit., p. 228.
25. Galeazzo Ciano, op. cit., p. 319.
26. Del Drago, unpublished memoirs.
27. Bottai, op. cit., pp. 229–30.
28. Grazzi, op. cit., pp. 256–7.
29. Goebbels, *Goebbels' Diaries 1939-41*, p. 173.
30. Galeazzo Ciano, op. cit., pp. 323–4.
31. Guerri, op. cit., p. 499.
32. Captured Italian archives in the U.S. National Archives, T586, Roll 453, Nos. 028395–6.
33. Del Drago, unpublished memoirs.
34. Grazzi, op. cit., p. 185.
35. Innocenti, op. cit., p. 157.
36. Galeazzo Ciano, op. cit., pp. 324–5.
37. Captured Italian archives in the U.S. National Archives, T586, Roll 406, No. 000997.
38. Galeazzo Ciano, op. cit., p. 330.
39. Goebbels, op. cit., p. 196.
40. Galeazzo Ciano, op. cit., pp. 330–31.
41. Ibid., p. 332.
42. Ibid., pp. 335.
43. Goebbels, op. cit., pp. 198, 208.
44. Galeazzo Ciano, op. cit., p. 339.
45. Ibid., p. 340.
46. Ibid., Vol. 2, p. 13.
47. Ibid., p. 15.
48. Mapalarte, op. cit., p. 360.
49. Guerri, op. cit., pp. 502–3.
50. Bottai, op. cit., p. 247.
51. Goebbels, op. cit., pp. 231–3.
52. Guerri, op. cit., p. 503.
53. Susmel, op. cit., p. 237.
54. Anfuso, op. cit., p. 153.
55. Alfieri, op. cit., pp. 261–4.
56. Susanna Agnelli, op. cit., p. 88.
57. Afeltra, op. cit., p. 150.
58. *La Voce*, Milan, April 12, 1995.
59. Goebbels, op. cit., pp. 281, 290.
60. Ibid., p. 252.
61. Mario Cervi, *The Hollow Legions*, p. 308.
62. Ibid., pp. 303–6.
63. Ibid., p. 303.
64. Ibid., pp. 305–6.
65. Bastianini, op. cit., p. 260.

Chapter Twelve : The Most Hated Man in Italy

1. Page, op. cit.. The account of Evans' mission to Rome is covered in pp. 626–30.
2. Galeazzo Ciano, op. cit., Vol. 2, p.6.
3. Captured Italian archives, T816, Roll 7.
4. Galeazzo Ciano, op.cit., Vol. 2, p. 43.
5. Paolo Monelli, *Roma 1943*, p. 58.
6. Galeazzo Ciano, op. cit., Vol. 2, pp. 50–51.
7. Bottai, op. cit., p. 274.
8. Susmel, op. cit., pp. 243–4.
9. Galeazzo Ciano, op. cit., Vol. 2, p. 56.
10. Ibid. pp. 57–8.
11. Susmel, op. cit., p. 245.
12. Galeazzo Ciano, op.cit., Vol. 2, pp. 58, 62–3.
13. Ibid., p. 60.
14. Ibid., p. 372.
15. Bottai, op. cit., p. 279.
16. Guerri, op. cit., p. 59.
17. Spinosa, op. cit., p. 250.
18. Galeazzo Ciano, op. cit., Vol. 2, pp. 31–2, 40–41.
19. Susmel, op. cit., p. 246.
20. Galeazzo Ciano, op. cit., Vol. 2, p. 62.
21. Bottai, op. cit., p. 283.
22. Galeazzo Ciano, op. cit., Vol. 2, p. 64.
23. Ibid., pp. 64, 65.
24. Ibid., pp. 64–5.
25. Ibid., pp. 65–6.
26. Ibid., p. 67.
27. Vergani, op. cit., p. 126.
28. Interview by author of a Ciano friend who wished to remain anonymous.
29. Spinosa, op. cit., pp. 266–7.
30. Galeazzo Ciano, op.cit., Vol. 2, p. 70.
31. Ibid., p. 72.

32. Ibid., p. 73.
33. Ibid., pp. 74–5.
34. Ibid., p. 76.
35. Ibid., p. 77.
36. Susmel, op. cit., p. 248.
37. Galeazzo Ciano, op. cit., Vol. 2, pp. 78–9.
38. Ibid., p. 79.
39. Ibid., p. 80.
40. Ibid., pp. 80–81.
41. Carmine Senise, *Quando ero il capo della polizia*, p. 68.
42. Galeazzo Ciano, op.cit., Vol. 2, pp. 81-2.
43. Ibid., p. 84.
44. Ibid., p. 85.
45. Edda Ciano, op. cit., p. 157.
46. Galeazzo Ciano, op.cit., Vol. 2, p. 90.
47. Ibid., pp. 90–91.
48. Guerri, op. cit., p. 525.
49. Galeazzo Ciano, op. cit., Vol. 2, p. 95.
50. Ibid., pp. 96–7.
51. Reynolds and Eleanor Packard, op. cit., p. 320.
52. Galeazzo Ciano, op. cit., Vol. 2, p. 36.
53. Ibid., p. 95.
54. Ibid., p. 102.
55. Ibid., p. 103.
56. Vergani, op. cit., p. 172.

Chapter Thirteen : Plotting Against the Duce

1. Bottai, op. cit., pp. 322–3.
2. Susmel, op. cit., pp. 252–3.
3. Ibid., p. 253.
4. Galeazzo Ciano, op. cit., Vol. 2, pp. 114–15.
5. Ibid., p. 116.
6. Ibid., p. 197.
7. Ibid., p. 118.
8. Ibid., p. 121.
9. Ibid., p. 129.
10. Ibid., p. 131.
11. Ibid., p. 136.
12. Susmel, op. cit., p. 254.
13. Goebbels, op. cit., p. 135.
14. Edda Ciano, op. cit., pp. 124–6.
15. Susmel, op. cit., p. 255.
16. Edda Ciano, op. cit., p. 143.
17. Goebbels, op. cit., pp. 151–2.
18. Edda Ciano, op. cit., pp. 146–7.
19. Galeazzo Ciano, op. cit., Vol. 2, pp. 153–5.
20. Ibid., pp. 154–5.
21. Ibid., p. 162.
22. Ibid., p. 146.
23. Ibid., p. 147.
24. Susmel, op. cit., p. 257.
25. Carboni, op. cit., p. 144.
26. Susmel, op. cit., pp. 258–9.
27. Galeazzo Ciano, op. cit., pp. 174–5.
28. Ibid., p. 175.
29. Ibid., p. 143.
30. Ibid., pp. 148–9.
31. Ibid., p. 152.
32. Ibid., pp. 187–8.
33. Edda Ciano, op.cit., pp. 183–4.
34. Galeazzo Ciano, op. cit., Vol. 2, p. 233.
35. Ibid., pp. 238–9.
36. Ibid., p. 186.
37. Spinosa, op. cit., p. 270.
38. Bottai, op. cit., pp. 325–6.
39. Di Nolfo, op. cit., p. 198.
40. Guerri, op. cit., pp. 532–3.
41. Galeazzo Ciano, op. cit., Vol. 2, p. 197.
42. Ibid., p. 200.
43. Susmel, op. cit., pp. 261–2.
44. Galeazzo Ciano, op. cit., Vol. 2, pp. 213–14.
45. Vergani, op. cit., p. 142.
46. Ibid., p. 192.
47. Galeazzo Ciano, op. cit., Vol. 2, p. 215.
48. Vergani, op. cit., pp. 213–16.
49. Simoni, op. cit., p.286.
50. Galeazzo Ciano, op. cit., Vol. 2, pp. 216, 231.
51. Mario Toscano, *Dal 25 Iuglio all'8 settembre*, pp. 144–6, 157–8.
52. Galeazzo Ciano, op. cit., pp. 228–9.
53. Vergani, op. cit., pp. 228–9.
54. Galeazzo Ciano, op. cit., Vol. 2, pp. 230.
55. Alfieri, op. cit., p. 282.
56. Galeazzo Ciano, op. cit., Vol. 2, pp. 230–31.
57. Simoni, op. cit., p. 300.
58. Ibid.
59. Malaparte, op. cit., pp. 447–8.
60. John Bierman, *The Italian Refuge*, p. 219.
61. Renzo De Felice, *Storia degli ebrei italiani sotto il fascismo*, p. 400.
62. Jonathan Steinberg, *All or Nothing*, pp. 52–3, 58.
63. Letter to the author.

Chapter Fourteen : Into the Cage of the Beasts

1. Peter Grose, *Gentleman Spy*, pp.176–8; Leonard Mosley, *Dulles*, p. 139, and Allen W. Dulles, *Germany's Underground*, p. 130.
2. Grose, op. cit., p. 178.
3. Galeazzo Ciano, op. cit., Vol. 2, p. 249.
4. Vergani, op. cit., p. 239.
5. Dulles, op. cit., p. 130.
6. British Public Records Office, Foreign Office telegram, FO 371, 37547–February 24, 1943.
7. Interview with the author.
8. Del Drago, unpublished memoirs.
9. Ibid.
10. Susmel, pp. 269–70.
11. Michaelis, op. cit., pp. 323–4.
12. Susmel, op. cit., pp. 270–71.
13. Bastianini, op. cit., p. 259.
14. Guerri, op. cit., p. 536.
15. Vergani, op. cit., p. 249.
16. Ibid., pp. 541–2.
17. Edda Ciano, op. cit., pp. 183–4.
18. Ibid., pp. 183–7.
19. Pensotti, op. cit., pp. 83–4.
20. Goebbels, op. cit., pp. 218, 341.
21. Captured Italian archives, T586, Job No. 104, Bag 29, Roll 453, No. 028408.
22. Del Drago, unpublished memoirs.
23. Galeazzo Ciano, op.cit., Vol. 2, p. 124.
24. Ibid., p. 250.
25. Susmel, op. cit., pp. 273–4.
26. Vergani, op. cit., pp. 238, 240–41.
27. Ibid., p. 244.
28. Ibid., p. 252.
29. Galeazzo Ciano, op. cit., Vol. 2, pp. 250–51.
30. Davis, op.cit., p. 23.
31. De Begnac, op. cit., p. 666.
32. Agnelli, op. cit., p. 99.
33. Interview with the author.
34. Susmel, op. cit., p. 274.
35. Ibid.
36. Bottai, op. cit., p. 365.
37. Anfuso, op. cit., p. 278.
38. Bottai, op. cit., p. 373.
39. Guerri, op. cit., p. 325.
40. Interview with the author.
41. Interview with the author.
42. Davis, op. cit., p. 52.
43. Susmel, op. cit., pp. 275–6.
44. Bastianini, op. cit., pp. 241–2.
45. Captured Italian archives, T586, Job No. 104, Bag 29, Roll 453, No. 028409.
46. Guerri, op. cit., p. 551.
47. Susmel, op. cit., p. 277.
48. Ivanoe Bonomi, *Memorie*, p. xxix.
49. Susmel, op. cit., p. 277.
50. Captured Italian archives, T586, Job No. 104, Bag 29, Roll 453, Nos. 028404–6.
51. Susmel, op. cit., pp. 278–9.
52. Davis, op. cit., pp. 39–40.
53. Captured Italian archives, T586, Job No. 104, Bag 29, Roll 453, No. 028410.
54. Dollmann, op. cit., p. 220.
55. Guerri, op. cit., p. 564.
56. Interview with author
57. *Corriere della Sera*, Sept. 22, 1996.
58. Carlo Falconi, *The Silence of Pius XII*, p. 364.
59. Davis, op. cit., pp. 24–5.

Chapter Fifteen : Collapse of Mussolini's Regime

1. Susmel, op. cit., pp. 280–81.
2. Edda Ciano, op. cit., p. 187.
3. Guerri, op. cit., p. 576.
4. Susmel, op. cit., p. 281.
5. Guerri, op. cit., p. 578.
6. Susmel, op. cit., pp. 281–2.
7. Ibid., p. 282.
8. Davis, op. cit., p. 85.
9. Guerri, op. cit., p. 562.
10. Susmel, op. cit., pp. 283–4.
11. Alfieri, op. cit., p. 324.
12. Davis, op. cit., p. 85.
13. Guerri, op. cit., p. 587.
14. Monelli, op. cit., p. 163.
15. Susmel, op. cit., pp. 284–5.
16. Guerri, op. cit., pp. 589–90.
17. Susmel, op. cit., p. 285.
18. Davis, op. cit., p. 117.
19. Susmel, op. cit., p. 286.
20. Guerri, op. cit., p. 591.
21. Bastianini, op. cit., p. 128.
22. Guerri, op. cit., pp. 590-91.
23. Monelli, op. cit., p. 156.
24. Guerri, op. cit., p. 593.
25. Ibid.
26. Monelli, op. cit., p. 183.
27. Davis, op. cit., p. 127.

28. Susmel, op. cit., p. 287.
29. Dollmann, op. cit., p. 233.
30. Guerri, op. cit., p. 596.
31. Anfuso, op. cit., p. 296.

Chapter Sixteen : Escape to Germany

1. Edda Ciano, op. cit., pp. 190–91.
2. Andrea Niccoletti, *Colliers* April 20, 1946. Allen Dulles is almost certainly the author of two articles in *Colliers* that appeared under the byline of Andrea Niccoletti. Emilio Pucci reported that Dulles wrote about Edda's flight to Switzerland for *Colliers* under a pseudonym.
3. Guerri, op. cit., p. 597.
4. Edda Ciano, op. cit., pp. 190–91.
5. Ibid., pp. 191–3.
6. Fabrizio Ciano, *Quando il nonno fece fucilare papa'*, pp. 69–70.
7. Interview with the author.
8. Susmel, op. cit., p. 291.
9. Alfieri, op. cit., pp. 352–3.
10. Guerri, op. cit., p. 603.
11. Susmel, op. cit., pp. 289–90.
12. Ibid., p. 290.
13. Ibid., pp. 291–2.
14. Guerri, op. cit., p. 609.
15. Edda Ciano, op. cit., p. 195.
16. Dollmann, op. cit., pp. 291–2.
17. Ibid.
18. Interview with the author.
19. Agnelli, op. cit., p. 109.
20. U.S. Archives, RG226, OSS E134, Folder 16827.
21. Spinosa, op. cit., pp. 263–4.
22. Interview with the author.
23. Edda Ciano, op. cit., p. 196.
24. Senise, op. cit., p. 227.
25. Höttl, *The Secret Front*, pp. 271–3.
26. Fabrizio Ciano, op. cit., pp. 72–4.
27. Senise, op. cit., p. 228.
28. Höttl, op. cit., p. 274.
29. Edda Ciano, op. cit., pp. 196–7.
30. Susmel, op. cit., p. 295.
31. Edda Ciano, op. cit., pp. 196–7.
32. Winston Churchill, *War Speeches*, Vol. 2, p. 509.
33. Höttl, op. cit., pp. 274–81.
34. Ibid., pp. 277–8.

35. *Gente*, Nos. 4–5, 1996.
36. Edda Ciano, op. cit., pp. 122–3.
37. Ibid., pp. 124–5.
38. Goebbels, op. cit., pp. 380–81.
39. Höttl, op. cit., pp. 280–81.
40. Edda Ciano, op. cit., pp. 199–200.
41. Fabrizio Ciano, op. cit., pp. 75–76.
42. Ibid., pp. 78–9.
43. *Gente*, Nos. 4–5, 1996.
44. Guerri, op. cit., pp. 618–19.
45. Glenn B. Infield, *Eva and Adolf*, p. 213.
46. Carlo Silvestri, *Mussolini, Graziani e l'antifascismo*, p. 32.
47. Ibid., p. 34.
48. Pensotti, op. cit., pp. 100–101.
49. Anfuso, op. cit., p. 333.
50. Goebbels, op. cit., pp. 378–9.
51. Pensotti, op. cit., pp. 100–101.
52. Guerri, op. cit., p. 621.
53. Interview with the author.
54. Goebbels, op. cit., pp. 380–81.
55. Guerri, op. cit., p. 621.
56. Vittorio Mussolini, *Vita con mio padre*, pp. 14–23.
57. Goebbels, op. cit., pp. 388–90.
58. Ibid., pp. 389–90.
59. Susmel, op. cit., pp. 302–3.
60. *Gente*, Nos. 4–5, 1996.
61. Innocenti, op. cit., p. 82.
62. Interview with the author.
63. Fabrizio Ciano, op. cit., pp. 84–5.

Chapter Seventeen : Treason

1. Edda Ciano, op. cit., p. 210.
2. Susmel, op. cit., p. 304.
3. Anfuso, op. cit., pp. 409–10.
4. Giovanni Dolfin, *Con Mussolini nella tragedia*, p. 42.
5. Edda Ciano, op. cit., p. 211.
6. Dolfin, op. cit., p. 61, and captured Italian archives, T586, Roll 456, No. 029699/A.
7. Afeltra, op. cit., p. 64.
8. Ibid., p. 64.
9. Susmel, op. cit., p. 307.
10. Dolfin, op. cit., p. 32.
11. Edda, op. cit., p. 223.
12. Guerri, op. cit., p. 629.
13. Ibid., p. 639.
14. Goebbels, *Tagebucher 1942–3*, p. 474.
15. Dolfin, op. cit., pp. 59–60.

16. Afeltra, op. cit., pp. 179–80.
17. Ibid., pp. 313–14.
18. Ibid., pp. 180–81.
19. Ibid., pp. 314–15.
20. Ibid., pp. 9–12.
21. Edda Ciano, op. cit., p. 219.
22. Susmel, op. cit., p. 315.
23. Ibid., p. 316.
24. Afeltra, op. cit., pp. 182–3.
25. Susmel, op. cit., p. 319.
26. Dolfin, op. cit., p. 189.
27. Susmel, op. cit., pp. 319–20.
28. Edda Ciano, op. cit., p. 215.
29. Fabrizio Ciano, op. cit., pp. 89–94.

Chapter Eighteen : The End of Hope

1. Vincenzo Cersosimo, *Dall'istruttoria alla fucilazione*, pp. 43–70.
2. Edda Ciano, op. cit., pp. 225–6.
3. Guerri, op. cit., p. 632.
4. *Gente*, Nos. 4–5, 1996.
5. Ibid.
6. Cersosimo, op. cit., pp. 62–81.
7. Susmel, op. cit., pp. 320–21.
8. Ibid.
9. Afeltra, op. cit., pp. 186–7.
10. Ibid., pp. 187–8.
11. Ibid., pp. 195–6.
12. Winston Churchill, *Their Finest Hour*, pp. 115–16.
13. Galeazzo Ciano, op. cit., Vol. 1. pp. 3–7. Presented at the end of the English edition of the diary , it forms an introduction in the Italian edition.
14. Guerri, op. cit., p. 646.
15. Enrico Manucci, *Il marchese rampante*, p. 110.
16. Susmel, op. cit., p. 327.
17. Ibid.
18. Afeltra, op. cit., pp. 198–9.
19. Susmel, op. cit., pp. 325–6.
20. Afeltra, op. cit., p. 199.
21. Ibid., p. 189.
22. Ibid., pp. 189–90.
23. Ibid., pp. 190–1.

Chapter Nineteen: A Flight to Freedom

1. Susmel, op. cit., pp. 328–9.
2. Guerri, op. cit., p. 651.
3. Ibid., p. 651.
4. Susmel, op. cit., pp. 329–30.
5. Howard McGaw Smyth, *Secrets of the Fascist Era*, pp. 36–8, and Andrea Niccoletti, *The Decline and Fall of Edda Ciano, Colliers*, April 27, 1946.
6. Domenico Mayer, *La verita' sul processo di Verona*, p. 122.
7. Afeltra, op. cit., p. 82.
8. Ibid., p. 192.
9. Dolfin, op. cit., p. 189.
10. Afeltra, op. cit., pp. 200–201.
11. Susmel, op. cit., p. 335–7.
12. Ibid.
13. Edda Ciano, op. cit., pp. 227–33.
14. Fabrizio Ciano, op. cit., pp. 89–94.
15. Smyth, op. cit., p. 52, and Niccoletti.

Chapter Twenty: Trial and Execution

1. Edda Ciano, op. cit., p. 236, and Piero Pisenti, *Una repubblica necessaria*, p. 93.
2. Deakin, op. cit., p. 637.
3. Guerri, op. cit., p. 665.
4. Ibid., pp. 666–8.
5. Mayer, op. cit., p. 30.
6. Susmel, op. cit., p. 340.
7. Mayer, op. cit., pp. 61, 100.
8. Guerri, op. cit., pp. 671–2.
9. Susmel, op. cit., pp. 341–2.
10. Cersosimo, op. cit., p. 236.
11. Susmel, op. cit., p. 343.
12. Mayer, op. cit., p. 158.
13. Deakin, op. cit., p. 640.
14. Dolfin, op. cit., pp. 196–7.
15. Edda Ciano, op. cit., p. 244.
16. Susmel, op. cit., pp. 344–5.
17. Afletra, op. cit., p. 193.
18. Ibid., p. 194.
19. Susmel, op. cit., p. 345.
20. Ibid., p. 346.
21. Ibid., p. 347.

22. Gian Franco Vene', *Il processo di Verona*, pp. 212–14.
23. Susmel, op. cit., pp. 344–7.
24. Afeltra, op. cit., p. 90.
25. Susmel, op. cit., pp. 349–50.
26. Fabrizio Ciano, op. cit., p. 96.
27. Guerri, op. cit., p. 687.
28. Ibid., p. 688.
29. Susmel, op. cit., p. 350.
30. Christopher Hibbert, *Benito Mussolini*, p. 301.
31. Susmel, op. cit., p. 352.
32. Dolfin, op. cit., p. 199.
33. Susmel, op. cit., pp. 352–3.
34. Dolfin, op. cit., pp. 200–201.
35. Guerri, op. cit., pp. 689–90.
36. Vene', op. cit., p. 220.
37. Edda Ciano, op. cit., pp. 246–7.
38. Deakin, op. cit., p. 645.
39. Elizabeth Wiskemann, *The Rome-Berlin Axis*, p. 321.
40. Edda Ciano, op. cit., p. 242.
41. Mayer, op. cit., p. 125.
42. Susmel, op. cit., p. 355.
43. Dolfin, op. cit., pp. 201–2.
44. Susmel, op. cit., pp. 356–7.
45. Dolfin, op. cit., p. 205.
46. Cersosimo, op. cit., p. 258.
47. Vene', op. cit., p. 225.
48. Pensotti, op. cit., pp. 103–4.
49. Guerri, op. cit., pp. 689–90.
50. Susmel, op. cit., pp. 364–5.

Chapter Twenty-one: In Pursuit of the Ciano Diary

1. Malaparte, op. cit., p. 433.
2. Del Drago, unpublished memoirs.
3. Agnelli, op. cit., p. 125.
4. Bottai, op. cit., pp. 486–7.
5. Churchill, *Closing the Ring*, p. 439.
6. Fabrizio Ciano, op. cit., pp. 96–8.
7. Ibid., pp. 96–9.
8. Edda Ciano, op. cit., pp. 360–61.
9. Fabrizio Ciano, op. cit., pp. 99–101.
10. Manucci, op. cit., pp. 124, 155.
11. Fabrizio Ciano, op. cit., pp. 99–102.
12. *Corriere della Sera*, September 22, 1996.
13. Susmel, op. cit., p. 363.
14. Ibid., p. 365.
15. Manucci, op. cit., p. 125.
16. Fabrizio Ciano, op. cit., p. 103.

17. Susmel, op. cit., pp. 367–8.
18. Ibid., pp. 367–9.
19. Ibid., p. 371.
20. Captured Italian archives, T586, Roll 456, No. 029701/A.
21. Susmel, op. cit., p. 372.
22. Agnelli, op. cit., pp. 126–8.
23. Smyth, op. cit., p. 57.
24. Ibid, p. 59.
25. Captured Italian archives, T586, Roll 456, Nos. 029688/A and 029692A–029698.
26. Paul Ghali, *Cincinnati Enquirer*, February 22, 1949.
27. Interview with the author.
28. U.S. National Archives, RG226, OSS E134, Folder 1345.
29. Smyth, op. cit., p. 62.
30. Ibid., p. 63.
31. Ghali, op. cit., February 22, 1949.
32. Smyth, op. cit., pp. 64–5.
33. Andrea Niccoletti, *Colliers*, April 27, 1946.
34. U.S. National Archives RG226, OSS E134, Folder 1345.
35. Ghali, op. cit., February 22, 1949.
36. Smyth, op. cit., p. 66.
37. Joachim von Ribbentrop, *The Ribbentrop Memoirs*, p. 188.
38. Edda Ciano, op. cit., p. 28.
39. Grose, op. cit., p. 220.
40. U.S. National Archives RG 226, OSS E134, Folder 1345.
41. Ibid.
42. Ibid.
43. Smyth, op. cit., p. 73.
44. *Corriere della Sera*, Milan, April 19, 1996.
45. Edda Ciano, *Il testamento del mio padre Benito*, p. 32.
46. U.S. National Archives, DOS740.0011/32871.
47. Andrea Niccoletti, *Colliers*, April 20 and 27, 1946.

Epilogue

1. *Corriere della Sera*, Milan, April 10, 1995.
2. Spinosa, op. cit., pp. 190–91.
3. Smyth, op. cit., p. 72.
4. Interview with the author.

5. Interview with the author.

6. Fabrizio Ciano, op. cit., pp.126, pp. 133–4.

7. Interview with the author.

8. Pensotti, op. cit., p. 104.

9. Interview with the author.

10. Interview with the author.

11. Interview with the author.

12. Interview with the author.

13. Edda Ciano, op. cit., pp. 18–20.

14. *La Voce*, Milan, April 12, 1995.

15. Fabrizio Ciano, op. cit., p. 149.

16. Ibid., pp. 150–5.

17. Ibid., pp. 145–55.

18. Ibid., p. 158.

19. Ibid., pp. 157–8, 44–5, 70.

20. Interview with the author.

21. Fabrizio Ciano, op. cit., pp. 21–3.

22. *Gente*, Nos. 4–5, 1996.

Bibliography

Afeltra, Gaetano, *La spia che amo' Ciano*, Rizzoli, Milan, 1993

Agnelli, Susanna, *We All Wore Sailor Suits*, Weidenfeld & Nicolson, London, 1976

Alfieri, Dino, *Due dittatori di fronte*, Rizzoli, Milan, 1948

Amè, Cesare, *Guerra segreta in Italia, 1940-43*, Gherardo Casini, Rome, 1954

Amicucci, Ermanno, *I 600 giorni di Mussolini*, Faro, Rome, 1948

Anfuso, Filippo, *Da Palazzo Venezia al Lago di Garda*, Cappelli, Bologna, 1957

Badoglio, Pietro, *Italy in the Second World War*, Greenwood Press, Westport, Conn., 1976

Bastianini, Giuseppe, *Uomini, cose, fatti*, Vitagliano, Milan, 1959

Bierman, John, article in *The Italian Refuge*, edited by Ivo Herzer, Catholic University of America Press, Washington D.C., 1989

Biondi, Dino, *La fabbrica del Duce*, Valsecchi, Florence, 1973

Bloch, Michael, *Ribbentrop*, Bantam Press, New York, 1992

Bonomi, Ivanoe, *Diario di un anno*, Garzanti, Milan, 1947

Bottai, Giuseppe, *Diario 1935-1944*, Rizzoli, Milan, 1983

Buffarini Guidi, Glauco, *La vera verita'*, Sugar, Milan, 1970

Cadogan, Alexander, *The Diaries of Sir Alexander Cadogan 1938-1945*, Cassell, London, 1971

Cantalupo, Roberto, *Fu la Spagna*, Mondadori, Milan, 1948

Carboni, Giacomo, *Memorie segrete 1935-1948*, Parenti, Florence, 1956

Casey, William, *The Secret War against Hitler*, Regnery Gateway, Washington, D.C., 1988

Cave Brown, Anthony, *Bodyguard of Lies*, W.H. Allen, London, 1976

Caviglia, Enrico, *Diario*, Gherardo Casini, Rome, 1952

Cerruti, Elisabetta, *Ambassador's Wife*, George Allen & Unwin, London, 1952

Cersosimo, Vincenzo, *Dall'istruttoria alla fucilazione*, Garzanti, Milan, 1961

Cervi, Mario, *The Hollow Legions*, Chatto & Windus, London, 1972

Chicago Daily News, June 16, 1945. Article announcing its publication of the Ciano diaries

Churchill, Winston, *History of the Second World War, Vol. 2 Their Finest Hour*, Cassell, London, 1949

Churchill, Winston, *History of the Second World War, Vol. 5, Closing the Ring*, Cassell, London, 1949

Churchill, Winston, *War Speeches 1939-45*, Vol. 2, Cassell, London, 1952

Ciano, Edda, *My Truth*, Weidenfeld & Nicolson, London, 1977

Ciano, Edda, *Il testamento del mio padre Benito*, Dino, 1990

Ciano, Fabrizio, *Quando il nonno fece fucilare papa'*, Mondadori, Milan, 1993

Ciano, Galeazzo, *Ciano's Diary 1939-43*, William Heinemann, London, 1947

Ciano, Galeazzo, *Diario 1937-1938*, Cappelli, Bologna, 1948

Ciano, Galeazzo, *Diario 1939-1943*, Vols. 1 and 2, Rizzoli, Milan, 1950

Ciano, Galeazzo, *Ciano's Diplomatic Papers*, Odhams Press, London, 1948

Cincinnati Enquirer, "Dulles Got Secrets from Il Duce's Daughter," February 23, 1969. Article by Paul Ghali

Colville, John, *The Fringes of Power*, Hodder & Stoughton, London, 1985

Corriere della Sera, Milan, April 10, 1995. Article on death of Edda Ciano

Corriere della Sera, Milan, *I fantasmi ed Edda, anatomia di un delirio.* April 19, 1996. Article on Edda Ciano's treatment by a Swiss psychiatrist

Corriere della Sera, Milan, September 22, 1996. Article on Emilio Pucci's role in saving Edda Ciano

Corriere della Sera, Milan, October 8, 1996. Article on Ciano's hidden wealth, p. 13

Dalton, Hugh, *Fateful Years: Memoirs 1931-45*, Frederick Muller, London, 1957

Davis, Melton, *Who Defends Rome?*, Dial Press, New York 1972

Deakin, F. W., *The Brutal Friendship*, Weidenfeld & Nicolson, London, 1962

De Begnac, Yvon, *Palazzo Venezia*, La Rocca, Rome, 1951

De Felice, Renzo, *Mussolini il duce*, Vol. 1, Giulio Einaudi, Turin, 1974

De Felice, Renzo, *Mussolini il duce*, Vol. II, Giulio Einaudi, Turin, 1981

De Felice, Renzo, *Storia degli ebrei italiani sotto il fascismo*, Giulio Einaudi, Turin, 1961

Delzell, Charles F., *Mussolini's Enemies*, Princeton University Press, Princeton, N.J., 1961

Di Nolfo, Ennio, *Vaticano e Stati Uniti 1939-1952*, Franco Angeli, Milan, 1978

Dolfin, Giovanni, *Con Mussolini nella tragedia*, Garzanti, Milan, 1949

Dollmann, Eugen, *The Interpreter*, Hutchinson, London, 1967

Dombrowski, Roman, *Mussolini: Twilight and Fall*, William Heinemann, London, 1956

Donosti, Mario, *Mussolini e l'Europa*, Edizione Leonardo, Rome, 1945

Ducci, Roberto, *La bella gioventu'*, Il Mulino, Bologna, 1996

Dulles, Allen, *Germany's Underground*, Macmillan, New York, 1947

Falconi, Carlo, *The Silence of Pius XII*, Little, Brown, Boston, 1970

Françis-Poncet, André, *Au Palais Farnese*, Artheme Fayard, Paris, 1961

Garlinski, Jozef, *The Swiss Corridor*, J.M. Dent & Sons, London, 1981

Gente, Milan, Nos. 4, 5, 6 & 7, January and February 1996. Articles on Frau Hildegard Beetz

Goebbels, Joseph, *Goebbels' Diaries*, Hamish Hamilton, London, 1948

Goebbels, Joseph, *Goebbels' Diaries 1939-41,* Hamish Hamilton, London, 1982

Goebbels, Joseph, *Tagebücher 1942-3*, Atlantic, Zurich, 1948

Grandi, Dino, *Il mio paese*, Il Mulino, Bologna, 1985

Grazzi, Emanuele, *Il principio della fine*, Faro, Rome, 1945

Grose, Peter, *Gentleman Spy*, Andre Deutsch, London, 1995

Guariglia, Raffaele, *Ricordi*, Edizione Scientifiche, Naples, 1950

Guerri, Giordano Bruno, *Galeazzo Ciano*, Bompiani, Milan, 1979

Gun, Nerin E., *Eva Braun: Hitler's Mistress*, Leslie Frewin, London, 1968

Il Giorno, Milan, April 10, 1995. Article by Giordano Bruno Guerri on the death of Edda Ciano

Harrison, Leland, National Archives, Washington. 740.0011/32871. Cablegram of January 26, 1944, on Edda Ciano's arrival in Switzerland

Hibbert, Christopher, *Benito Mussolini*, Richard Clay, London, 1963

Higham, Charles, *Wallis*, Pan Books, London, 1988

Höttl, Wilhelm, *The Secret Front*, Weidenfeld & Nicolson, London, 1953

Hull, Cordell, *Memoirs*, Hodder & Stoughton, London, 1948

Infield, Glenn B., *Eva and Adolf*, New English Library, London, 1975

Innocenti, Marco, *L'Italia del 1940*, Mursia, Milan, 1996

International Military Tribunal, *Trial of the Major War Criminals*, Vol. 10, Nuremberg, 1947

Lamb, Richard,*War in Italy*, John Murray, London, 1993

Lessona, Alessandro, *Memorie*, Sansoni, Florence, 1958

Leto, Guido, *OVRA fascismo-antifascismo*, Cappelli, Bologna, 1951

Losito, Leonardo, *Bernardo Attolico*, Schena, Bari, 1994

MacGregor-Hastie, Roy, *The Day of the Lion*, MacDonald, London, 1963

Mack Smith, Denis, *Mussolini's Roman Empire*, Penguin, London, 1976

Mack Smith, Denis, *Mussolini*, Paladin, London, 1981

Magistrati, Massimo, *L'Italia a Berlino*, Mondadori, Milan, 1956

Malaparte, Curzio, *Kaputt*, Daria Guarnati, Milan, 1948

Manucci, Enrico, *Il marchese rampante*, Baldini & Castoldi, Milan, 1998

Mayer, Domenico, *La verita' sul processso di Verona*, Mondadori, Milan, 1945

Michaelis, Meir, *Mussolini and the Jews*, Clarendon Press, Oxford, 1978

Monelli, Paolo, *Roma 1943*, Migliaresi, Rome, 1946

Mosley, Leonard, *Dulles*, Dial Press, New York, 1978

Mussolini, Edvige, *Mio fratello Benito*, La Fenice, Florence, 1957

Mussolini, Vittorio, *Vita con mio padre*, Mondadori, Milan, 1957

Mussolini, Vittorio, *Voli sulle ambe*, G.C. Sansoni, Florence, 1937

National Archives, Washington, D. C., No. 16827. Cablegram from U.S. Embassy, Buenos Aires, on Galeazzo Ciano's secret Argentine bank account. OSS Files Nos. 1345 and 1346. Various cables referring to Dulles' attempts to obtain the Ciano diaries. Microfilm records T586 (rolls 405, 406, 453 and 456) and T816 (roll 1), the captured Italian archives covering Mussolini's files.

Newsweek March 6, 1939. Cover story on Galeazzo Ciano

Niccoletti, Andrea, *The Decline and Fall of Edda Ciano*, Colliers New York, April 20 and 27, 1946

Packard, Reynolds and Eleanor, *Balcony Empire*, Chatto & Windus, New York, 1943

Page, Giorgio Nelson, *L'americano di Roma*, Longanesi, Milan, 1950

Pensotti, Anita, *Rachele*, Bompiani, Milan, 1983

Phillips, William, *Ventures in Diplomacy*, John Murray, London, 1955

Pisenti, Piero, *Una repubblica necessaria*, Giovanni Volpe, Milan, 1977

Public Records Office, London, FO371,37547. Cablegrams referring to plotting against Mussolini

Ranelagh, John, *The Agency*, Simon & Schuster, New York, 1986

Ribbentrop, Joachim von, *The Ribbentrop Memoirs*, Weidenfeld & Nicolson, London, 1954

Rossi, Ernesto, *No al fascismo*, Giulio Einaudi, Turin, 1957

Sarfatti, Michele, *Mussolini contro gli ebrei*, Silvio Zamorani , Millan, 1994

Schmidt, Paul, *Hitler's Interpreter*, William Heinemann, London, 1951

Senise, Carmine, *Quando ero Il capo della polizia*, 1940-43, Ruffolo, Rome, 1946

Sheridan, Michael, *Romans – Their Lives and Times*, Phoenix, London, 1995.

Shirer, William L., *Berlin Diary*, Book of the Month Club, New York, 1987

Shirer, William L., *The Nightmare Years*, Little Brown, Boston, 1984

Shirer, William L., *The Rise and Fall of the Third Reich*, Simon & Schuster, New York, 1959

Silvestri, Carlo, *Mussolini, Graziani e l'antifascismo*, Longanesi, Milan, 1949

Simoni, Leonardo, *Berlino ambasciata d'Italia 1939-1943*, Migliaresi, Rome, 1946

Smyth, Howard McGaw, *Secrets of the Fascist Era*, Southern Illinois University Press, Carbondale, 1975

Spinosa, Antonio, *Edda: una tragedia italiana*, Arnoldo Mondadori, Milan, 1993

Steinberg, Jonathan, *All or Nothing*, Routledge, London and New York, 1990

Susmel, Duilio, *Vita sbagliata di Galeazzo Ciano*, Aldo Palazzi, Milan, 1962

Thomas, Evan, *The Very Best Men*, Simon & Schuster, New York, 1995

Time, November 23, 1936. Article on Edda Ciano

Time, July 24, 1939. Cover story on Edda Ciano

Time, September 4, 1939. Article about Galeazzo Ciano

Toscano, Mario, *Dal 25 luglio all 8 settembre*, Felice le Monnier, Florence, 1966

Trial of the Major War Criminals, vol. 10, International Military Tribunal, Nuremberg 1947

Vansittart, Lord, *The Mist Procession*, Hutchinson, London, 1958

Vassiltchikov, Marie, *Berlin Diaries 1940-1945*, Alfred Knopf, New York, 1987

Vene', Gian Franco, *Il processo di Verona*, Mondadori, Milan, 1963

Vergani, Orio, *Ciano, una lunga confessione*, Longanesi, Milan, 1974

Von Hassell, Fey, *A Mother's War*, John Murray, London, 1990

Von Hassell, Ulrich, *Von Hassell Diaries*, Hamish Hamilton, London, 1948

Welles, Sumner, *The Time for Decision*, Harper, New York, 1944

Wiskemann, Elizabeth, *The Rome-Berlin Axis*, Oxford University Press, Oxford, 1949

Index